国家精品课程系列教材

新媒体英语阅读

Selective Readings from New Media of English

主　编　张　卓

编　者　（按拼音顺序）

丁咪咪　李金柯

钱正福　王　琪

夏　天　周轶亚

左步雷

苏州大学出版社

图书在版编目(CIP)数据

新媒体英语阅读 = Selective Readings from New Media of English / 张卓主编. —苏州：苏州大学出版社，2020.1(2024.7重印)
国家精品课程系列教材
ISBN 978-7-5672-3098-9

Ⅰ.①新… Ⅱ.①张… Ⅲ.①新闻—英语—阅读教学—高等学校—教材 Ⅳ.①G210

中国版本图书馆CIP数据核字(2020)第006921号

书　　名：	新媒体英语阅读
	Selective Readings from New Media of English
主　　编：	张　卓
责任编辑：	金莉莉
封面设计：	刘　俊
出版发行：	苏州大学出版社(Soochow University Press)
地　　址：	苏州市十梓街1号　邮编：215006
印　　装：	广东虎彩云印刷有限公司
网　　址：	http://www.sudapress.com
邮　　箱：	sdcbs@suda.edu.cn
邮购热线：	0512-67480030
销售热线：	0512-67481020
开　　本：	787 mm×1 092 mm　1/16　印张：27.75　字数：710千
版　　次：	2020年1月第1版
印　　次：	2024年7月第5次印刷
书　　号：	ISBN 978-7-5672-3098-9
定　　价：	85.00元

凡购本社图书发现印装错误，请与本社联系调换。服务热线：0512-67481020

前言

相对于其他语言资料,英语报刊内容贴近现实,语言贴近时代,题材广泛,体裁丰富多样,具有独特的语言教学价值。通过阅读英语报刊,我们可以了解英语国家乃至世界各国的价值观念、思维方式、审美情趣、宗教信仰、民族心理、道德情操、行为方式、人际礼仪以及生活时尚。英语报刊所提供的这些丰富的社会文化知识以及所反映的不同的价值取向、文化观念和意识形态使英语报刊教学具有综合教育价值。

中国高校外语教育的改革与发展清楚地表明,在文化多元化、经济全球化的今天,外语教学不仅仅是提高学生的语言技能,它还承担着培养学生的思辨能力和跨文化交际能力、让学生了解世界文化并提高人文素质的重任。中国外语教育理念与发展方向的变化使得英语报刊作为教学材料的重要价值越来越受到中国外语教学界的肯定与重视。

新媒体是新的技术支撑体系下出现的媒体形态,如数字杂志、数字报纸、数字广播、移动电视、网络、数字电视、数字电影、手机网络等。随着新媒体技术和运营的发展,英语报刊阅读将跨越纸质文本阅读的时代,具有悠久历史和刚刚成长的新闻媒体通过纸质媒体和多种形式的网络媒体传播世界各国的思想与文化,各具特色的新媒体和多种形式文本(纸质文本、音频和视频文本)的"阅读"成了人们了解和认识世界、进行跨文化交流的畅通渠道。

本书取材于中国、英国、美国、加拿大等国家著名的英语报纸、杂志和媒体,主要包括:中国的中国日报(*China Daily*)、中国环球电视网(CGTN:China Global Television Network);英国的《卫报》(*The Guardian*)、《经济学家》(*The Economist*)、英国广播公司(BBC:British Broadcasting Corporation);美国的《纽约时报》(*The New York Times*)、《华盛顿邮报》(*The Washington Post*)、《华尔街日报》(*The Wall Street Journal*)、《基督教科学箴言报》(*The Christian Science Monitor*)、《美国新闻与世界报道》(*U. S. News & World Report*)、美国之音(VOA:Voice of America);加拿大的《环球邮报》(*The Globe and Mail*);等等。

本书由报刊英语的文体特色、媒体文章阅读、附录组成。报刊英语的文体特色简要介绍了新闻的定义、新闻的价值、新闻的分类、新闻的体裁与结构以及报刊英语的标题特色、用词策略和语法特征。媒体文章阅读由十个单元组成,内容涉及中国、英语国家及世界其了国家的政治、经济、文化、教育、科技、环境、体育、健康、艺术等方面。每个单元包括4个板块、9个部分:(1) Learning Before Class:Listening, Watching and Thinking, Reading and

Discussing. (2) Learning in Class: Warm Up, Text A, Text B, Academic Reading. (3) Learning After Class: Additional Reading 1, Additional Reading 2, Additional Reading 3. (4) Topical Vocabulary. 附录部分包括英语报刊常用缩略语、英美著名媒体简介、美国行政州及其简称、课后练习答案、音频或视频文本全文。

基于国内现有的同类教材,本书着力体现以下特色:

1. 选材重视中国观点和中国视角,重视用英语表述中国的意义和价值。构建人类命运共同体的世界发展观使我们的世界正发生着前所未有的变革,世界各国正在开展更加广泛的跨文化交流与合作,用英语表述中国的历史和文化、中国的发展观和价值观具有重要的意义和价值。本书从中国观点和中国视角甄选了一些文章,让学生广泛深入领悟中国的价值观和发展观,有理有据地用英语展开与中国相关话题的讨论,坚定中国观点和中国立场。

2. 甄选具有时代精神的经典文章作为理解和阐释文本的基础。本书关注新闻的时效性和新闻的价值,关注对社会产生重要影响的国内外新闻事件和热点讨论,让学生了解中国、英语国家及世界其他国家的价值观念、思维方式、审美情趣、民族心理、道德情操、行为方式、人际礼仪及生活时尚,把握正确的价值取向、文化观念,客观评价社会文化生活发生的变化。

3. 着力提供优质的学习资源,利用网络资源和纸质媒体,以阅读材料为主,编写音频、视频与阅读文章相结合的立体化教材。通过文字文本和音频、视频文本的学习,学生接触进而掌握多模态文本的学习内容和学习方法,学会通过多种形式的文本深度认知中国、了解世界。

4. 提供个性化、多样化的学习内容,重视课前自主学习、课堂教学、课后拓展学习有机结合的深度学习模式,把深度学习作为信息化教学的主要目标。课前自主学习设计了音频、视频和阅读学习材料,让学生在课前初步了解并思考相关话题。课堂教学内容甄选的2篇文章在语言和观点上凝练、客观,有助于语言学习和观点讨论。课堂学习内容还包含学术阅读(Academic Reading)的理论指导与实践,提供让学生进行深度阅读的方法和理论指导。课后拓展学习提供3篇同类话题、多种视角、多个媒体的拓展阅读文章,在不同观点纷呈的阅读文本中提高阅读理解和媒介素养。

5. 本书设计大量形式多样的阅读练习,练习的设计既重视快速搜索重要信息的能力,更着力培养学生分析问题和解决问题的能力,增强学生的问题意识和研究意识,提高学生的思辨能力、分析能力和媒介素养,有意推动学生进行任务型、项目型、合作型等多种模式的深度学习。

6. 本书在第一部分"报刊英语的文体特色"部分提供新闻的定义、新闻价值、新闻体裁、新闻文本独具的语言和文化特色等简明扼要的新闻理论知识,期望有助于提高学生的新闻意识和媒介素养,形成正确的价值观念,客观评论新闻。

7. 本书选材广泛,包括中国、英语国家及世界其他国家的政治、经济、文化、教育、科技、环境等10个方面的内容，信息量大，覆盖面广。本书可让学生接触到世界各地时事新闻，获得丰富的文化信息，体会世界各国文化和思维方式的差异，提升跨文化交际意识和跨文化交际能力。

8. 保证教材的可教性与可学性，所选文章难度适中、可读性强。强调选材的趣味性、知识性、可思性，从而激发学生的学习兴趣。此外，本书重视提供常识性和知识性信息，扩展教材内容，对文章中涉及的重要人物、重要事件和重要专有名词提供详尽的英语解释。

本书是苏州大学大学外语部国家精品课程教材建设的一部分，获得苏州大学教材培育项目（5831501618）、江苏高校"青蓝工程"优秀教学团队（SR10400117）、"苏州大学本科课程教学团队：大学英语教学团队"及江苏省社科应用研究精品工程外语类课题"面向线上线下混合式'金课'的课程资源优化与构建（19SWB-018）"的资助。在此，我们衷心感谢苏州大学各级领导的支持和信任，尤其是外国语学院孙倚娜教授，她从教材最初的框架设计、题型设计、选材原则到最后的修改完善都给我们提供了许多宝贵的建议和真诚的帮助，并在编写过程中一直给予我们鼓励和支持；衷心感谢苏州大学出版社相关领导和各位编辑精细专业的审核。

本书所有编写人员都具有赴英语国家进行学习交流或从事语言教学的经历，具有多年外语教学经验，对外语教学尤其报刊英语教学充满热情和热爱。在本书编写过程中，所有编写人员通力合作，反复推敲，仔细斟酌，精心完善。但是由于受到学识水平和学术视野的限制，书中难免会存在一些缺憾，恳请广大读者提出宝贵意见，使本书可以得到不断的修改与完善。

编　者

2019年9月

报刊英语的文体特色		1
Unit 1　Education		33
Part 1　Learning Before Class		33
Listening	College Success: Making Use of Academic Supports	33
Watching and Thinking	What Are the Most Educated Countries in the World?	33
Reading and Discussing	Why China Can Give Every Child Equal Access to Education	34
Part 2　Learning in Class		35
Warm Up	Why You Should Read Books: 15 Benefits of Reading More	35
Text A	University Experts Address Common Challenges	36
Text B	You Are What You Watch? The Social Effects of TV	42
Academic Reading	Understanding Vocabulary (1)	50
Part 3　Learning After Class		54
Additional Reading 1	China's Education Reform: Study Hard, for What	54
Additional Reading 2	Online Preschool Is Winning More Support, But Is That a Good Thing?	58
Additional Reading 3	Alternative to Gaokao: Behind the Tide of Studying Abroad	63
Part 4　Topical Vocabulary		66
Unit 2　Culture and Society		69
Part 1　Learning Before Class		69
Listening	Asians Celebrate the Lunar New Year Around the World	69
Watching and Thinking	Couples Enjoy Romantic Evening at Beijing's Capital Museum on the Qixi Festival	69
Reading and Discussing	Cultural Differences Start Early	70
Part 2　Learning in Class		72
Warm Up	Why China Can Be Culturally Confident?	72
Text A	No Way to Turn the Cultural Clock Back	73
Text B	Different Cultures, Different Temperaments for Kids	80
Academic Reading	Understanding Vocabulary (2)	85

Part 3	Learning After Class	89
Additional Reading 1	Intl Mother Language Day 2019: Revitalizing Languages, Cultures	89
Additional Reading 2	A Holiday of Dread for China's Single Women	93
Additional Reading 3	The Biggest Lie We Tell on the Internet Is Ourselves	97
Part 4	Topical Vocabulary	101
Unit 3	**Politics**	**103**
Part 1	Learning Before Class	103
Listening	British Lawmakers Deal Another Blow to Johnson's EU Plan	103
Watching and Thinking	Tariffs on China: Economics Out, Politics In	103
Reading and Discussing	Why China Can Lift Hundreds of Millions of People Out of Poverty?	104
Part 2	Learning in Class	105
Warm Up	The Politics of Human Rights	105
Text A	How to Restore the Damaged US Credibility	106
Text B	The Biggest Threat to America Is Us	112
Academic Reading	Understanding What You Read (1)	118
Part 3	Learning After Class	122
Additional Reading 1	British Prime Minister, Theresa May Resigns	122
Additional Reading 2	China Is Not the Source of Our Economic Problems—Corporate Greed Is	125
Additional Reading 3	EU Elections: Will Young People Turn Up?	129
Part 4	Topical Vocabulary	133
Unit 4	**Economy**	**134**
Part 1	Learning Before Class	134
Listening	China Launches Tech Hub Megalopolis to Rival Silicon Valley	134
Watching and Thinking	Global Firms Welcome China's First Foreign Investment Law	134
Reading and Discussing	World Economy Facing Delicate Moment, IMF Says	135
Part 2	Learning in Class	137
Warm Up	US-China Tariff Dispute Threatens to Cause Economic Damage on All Sides	137
Text A	Forget China—It's America's Own Economic System That's Broken	137
Text B	Tariffs Will Ultimately Harm US Economy	143
Academic Reading	Understanding What You Read (2)	149
Part 3	Learning After Class	155
Additional Reading 1	Whoever Runs the World Bank Needs a Plan for Emerging Markets	155
Additional Reading 2	Xi Jinping's Second Belt and Road Forum: The Key Takeaways	159
Additional Reading 3	Global Economy Emerges from Gloom into a Bright Spring	162

Part 4 Topical Vocabulary		166
Unit 5 Science and Technology		167
Part 1 Learning Before Class		167
Listening	High School Cheaters Nabbed by Neural Network	167
Watching and Thinking	AI Is Monitoring Your Right Now and Here's How They're Using Your Data	167
Reading and Discussing	How Best to Use AI for Human Development	168
Part 2 Learning in Class		170
Warm Up	How a Driverless Car Sees the Road	170
Text A	As Cars Become Computers on Wheels, Drivers Need to Lock More than Just the Doors	170
Text B	The Internet Knows You Better than Your Spouse Does	177
Academic Reading	Critical Thinking (1)	182
Part 3 Learning After Class		184
Additional Reading 1	It's Complicated: Facebook Users' Fraught Relationship with Social Giant	184
Additional Reading 2	China, US Still Have Room to Cooperate in Science and Technology	188
Additional Reading 3	CES 2019: The 4 Biggest Trends, Demystified	192
Part 4 Topical Vocabulary		197
Unit 6 Environment		199
Part 1 Learning Before Class		199
Listening	Air Pollution Contributes to Childhood Asthma	199
Watching and Thinking	Global Warming—Is It Real?	199
Reading and Discussing	It's Not Entirely Up to School Students to Save the World	200
Part 2 Learning in Class		202
Warm Up	China and India Making Earth Greener, NASA Study Shows	202
Text A	The False Choice Between Economic Growth and Combating Climate Change	204
Text B	Crude Awakening: ExxonMobil and the Oil Industry Are Making a Bet That Could End Up Wrecking the Climate	212
Academic Reading	Critical Thinking (2)	218
Part 3 Learning After Class		225
Additional Reading 1	These Bacteria Eat Plastic	225
Additional Reading 2	Australia's Biodiversity at Breaking Point	229
Additional Reading 3	Inspired Life: In a World Drowning in Trash, These Cities Have Slashed Waste by 80%	235
Part 4 Topical Vocabulary		240

Unit 7 Social Security and Crime Prevention		242
Part 1 Learning Before Class		242
Listening	Who Listens to Google Assistant Recordings?	242
Watching and Thinking	Saving Them, Saving Us	242
Reading and Discussing	Zhang Yingying Murder Case: Jury Deliberations Begin After Lengthy Closing Arguments	243
Part 2 Learning in Class		244
Warm Up	To This Day	244
Text A	This Viral Schwarzenegger Deepfake Isn't Just Entertaining. It's a Warning.	244
Text B	Why China Can Guarantee Food Safety	251
Academic Reading	Using Inference	257
Part 3 Learning After Class		261
Additional Reading 1	Hong Kong: A Story of Self-harm	261
Additional Reading 2	Missing 9-year-old girl, Whose Disappearance Gripped China, Found Dead	265
Additional Reading 3	Driver Protection to Improve After Fatal Bus Plunge	268
Part 4 Topical Vocabulary		272
Unit 8 Health		274
Part 1 Learning Before Class		274
Listening	What's So Bad About Processed Foods?	274
Watching and Thinking	How Stress Affects Your Body	274
Reading and Discussing	Why China Can Provide 1.4 Billion People with Healthcare Coverage?	275
Part 2 Learning in Class		277
Warm Up	Why Is It So Hard to Cure ALS?	277
Text A	What Mental Health Statistics Can Tell Us	277
Text B	The Global Efforts to Boost Childhood Cancer Care	285
Academic Reading	Distinguishing Between Facts and Opinions	292
Part 3 Learning After Class		296
Additional Reading 1	Healing Hands	296
Additional Reading 2	How Job Stress Can Age Us	299
Additional Reading 3	Food Insecurity in America Tied to Prices, Poverty	303
Part 4 Topical Vocabulary		307
Unit 9 Arts and Youth		309
Part 1 Learning Before Class		309
Listening	Summer Camp Uses Dance to Teach Students Life Skills	309

Watching and Thinking	Art Explores African Americans' Past and Present	309
Reading and Discussing	An Old New World	310
Part 2　Learning in Class		311
Warm Up	Architect I. M. Pei Dies at 102	311
Text A	Exploring Unknown: What's So Fascinating About Sci-fi Films?	312
Text B	Arts for Youth Development	317
Academic Reading	Recognizing Purpose and Tone (1)	322
Part 3　Learning After Class		327
Additional Reading 1	Chinese Film Industry Joins "Space Race"	327
Additional Reading 2	Veteran Author Still Young at Art	331
Additional Reading 3	My Life as a Work of Art	334
Part 4　Topical Vocabulary		337
Unit 10　Sports		339
Part 1　Learning Before Class		339
Listening	Copenhagen Turns Mountain of Waste into Sport	339
Watching and Thinking	The Woman Leading the Global Promotion of F1	339
Reading and Discussing	"A Huge Step Forward": British Breakers Hail Olympic Proposal	340
Part 2　Learning in Class		341
Warm Up	The Surprising Reason Our Muscles Get Tired	341
Text A	Fixing College Sports Is Vital to Increasing Public Support for Colleges	342
Text B	Sport and Safety: Knocking heads together	347
Academic Reading	Recognizing Purpose and Tone (2)	352
Part 3　Learning After Class		356
Additional Reading 1	Shanghai Pressing All the Right Buttons	356
Additional Reading 2	The NBA three-point Contest Has Grown Stale. Here's How to Make It Fun.	359
Additional Reading 3	Going It Alone: What Drives Solo Endurance Athletes?	362
Part 4　Topical Vocabulary		366
Appendix 1　英语报刊常用缩略语		368
Appendix 2　英美著名媒体简介		379
Appendix 3　美国行政州及其简称		382
Appendix 4　Keys		384
Appendix 5　Scripts		399

报刊英语的文体特色

新闻传播的媒介包括图书、报刊、广播、电视、广告、网络等。在信息全球化的今天,阅读新闻仍然是人们了解世界发展动态、进行跨文化交流的重要方式之一。报刊作为一种极其重要的大众传媒,具有鲜明的语言形式和独特的文体特点。

第一节 新闻属性

1. 新闻的定义

英语新闻界的许多专家和学者都对"新闻"(news)下过定义。虽然至今仍然没有一个简单而又被公认的定义,但以下列举的颇具代表性的定义仍然可以使我们对于到底什么是新闻有一定的了解和认识:

- News is a fresh report of events, facts, or opinions that people did not know before they read your story.
- News is anything timely that interests a number of persons, and the best news is that which has the greatest interest of the greatest number.
- News is any event, idea or opinion that is timely, that interests or affects a large number of people in a community and that is capable of being understood by them.
- News is the reporting of anything timely which has importance, use, or interest to a considerable number of persons in a publication audience.
- News is full and current information made available to an audience.
- News is the report of a recent event, marked by fairness, currency, accuracy, conciseness and objectivity.
- When a dog bites a man that is not news, but when a man bites a dog, that is (big) news.

以上定义都强调了新闻的3个主要特征:第一,新闻的本源是客观事实,新闻是对事实的报道。新闻是客观事物经过人的思维活动分析、综合、加工创作而成的。事实本身并未构成新闻,经过人们报道和传播才成为新闻。第二,新闻讲究时效,是对新近(包括刚刚、正在或将要)发生的事实的最及时的报道。第三,新闻注重新奇性和重要性,所反映的是有意义的事实、重要的事实、公众普遍关心的事实。

2. 新闻价值

新闻价值(news value)是新闻工作者用以衡量客观事实是否能够构成新闻的标准。在英语新闻报道中,构成新闻价值的要素主要包括:时效性、重要性、显著性、接近性、奇异性、趣味性等。

- 时效性(timeliness)又称"时新性"(freshness),指新闻事件的新近发生和及时传播,包含时间近、内容新两个含义。新闻事件发生和公开报道之间的时间差越短,新闻价值越大;内容越新鲜,新闻价值也越大。

- 重要性(importance, consequence, impact, significance)是由新闻报道的事件、现象对社会产生的影响所决定的。新闻内容涉及的社会领域、社会成员越广泛,影响的程度越深刻,新闻价值越大。

- 显著性(prominence)指新闻中的人物、地点或事件越显著、突出,就越能吸引读者,新闻价值就越大。西方流行一时的新闻数学公式可以形象地描述新闻的"显著性":

  ordinary person(s) + usual occurrence(s) ≠ news
  ordinary person(s) + unusual occurrence(s) = news
  extraordinary person(s) + usual occurrence(s) = news
  extraordinary person(s) + unusual occurrence(s) = big/good news

- 接近性(nearness, proximity, locality)指新闻与读者地理上或心理上的接近。导致心理接近的因素很多,比如,新闻中的人物、地点、事件等与读者或是有较密切的关系,或是读者所熟悉的、向往的,或是新闻中的人物与读者具有相同、相似之处(如年龄、性别、职业、民族等)。概括而言,事件发生的地点距离读者越近,读者越关心,新闻价值就越大;事件涉及读者的切身利益和思想感情越密切,读者越重视,新闻价值就越大。

- 奇异性(unusualness, bizarreness, oddity, novelty)指新闻事件或新闻人物具有的不同寻常的方面或特性。

- 趣味性(interest)指受众对新闻感兴趣的程度,受众兴趣越大,新闻价值就越大。趣味性事实指的是能够引起人们情感共鸣、富有人情味(human interest)和生活情趣的事实,即通常所讲的奇闻趣事。新闻中的趣味性一般要反映人间的真善美,在传递信息的同时传递一种价值取向,这样才能真正打动读者。

3. 新闻的分类

新闻的种类繁多,分类的标准各异。目前比较通行的分类方法如下:

- 按照传播工具进行分类,新闻可以分为:报纸新闻(newspaper coverages)、杂志新闻(magazine coverages)、图片新闻(picture news)、广播新闻(radio news)、电视新闻(TV news)、有线电视新闻(cable news)、通讯社新闻(dispatches)和网络新闻(Internet news)。
- 按照新闻事实发生的地域和范围,新闻可以分为:国际新闻(world news)、国内新闻(national news)和地方新闻(local news)。
- 按照报道内容进行分类,新闻可以分为:政治新闻(political news)、经济新闻(economic news)、科技新闻(technological news)、文娱新闻(cultural and entertainment news)、军事新闻(military news)、体育新闻(sports news)、法律新闻(legal news)、暴力与犯罪新闻(violence and crime news)、灾难新闻(disaster news)和天气新闻(weather news)。
- 按照事件的性质,新闻又可以分为:"硬新闻"(hard news)和"软新闻"(soft news)。硬新闻亦称"纯消息报道"(spot news or straight news),指题材较为严肃、具有一定时新性的客观事实报道,不加解释分析,不以文采和材料的有趣取胜,所以纪实性(factualness)最强。软新闻是指人情味较浓、写法轻松活泼的社会新闻。其题材可能会显得陈旧或无关紧要,但绝非枯燥乏味。软新闻纪实性较弱,娱乐性较强,注重趣味性,和人们的切身利益关系不大,旨在向受众提供娱乐,使受众开阔眼界、增长知识、陶冶情操。
- 按照事发状态进行分类,新闻可以分为:持续性新闻(follow-up news)、突发性新闻(breaking news)、一般性新闻(general news)和综合性新闻(round-up news)。
- 按照新闻体裁进行分类,新闻可以分为:消息报道(news reporting)、特写文章(feature articles)、新闻言论(editorials, commentaries and columns)、解释性报道(interpretive reporting)、调查性报道(investigative reporting)、"新新闻"报道(new journalism,亦称"文学新闻")。

4. 新闻体裁与新闻结构

尽管新闻的种类繁多,分类的标准各异,但都必须通过新闻工作者按不同的报道形式,即新闻体裁(type of news reporting),予以采写。如前所述,新闻体裁可以大体上分为消息报道(news reporting)、新闻言论(editorials, commentaries and columns)、特写文章(feature articles)、解释性报道(interpretive reporting)、调查性报道(investigative reporting)、"新新闻"报道(new journalism)等几大类。

由于新闻活动的范围是一个广阔多姿、变化无穷的世界,其间的客观事物也呈多样性,报道的内容丰富多彩,所以新闻体裁也在不断更新。同时,各种新闻体裁之间尽管有所区别,却并非界限分明,因此不能对新闻体裁进行绝对的划分。

(1) 消息报道

消息是以简要的文字迅速报道新闻事实的一种体裁,是广泛且经常采用的新闻体裁。消息通常由三个部分构成,即标题(headline)、导语(lead)和正文(body)。消息的写作结构主要有"倒金字塔结构"(inverted pyramid form)和"金字塔结构"(pyramid form)。

① 导语与消息报道

消息报道中的导语一般是全文的第一自然段,有时也由两个自然段组成。导语作为一则新闻的开篇,是新闻好坏的决定性因素。导语以凝练的语言把消息的要旨或轮廓首先揭示出来告诉读者,从而吸引读者继续阅读,这是消息报道这种新闻体裁区别于其他新闻体裁的一个重要特征。

美国新闻学家威廉·梅茨在其新闻学著作《新闻写作:从导语到结尾》(*News Writing: From Lead to "30"*)中指出:"导语是新闻报道中最重要的部分。抓住或者失去读者,取决于新闻稿的第一段、第一句,甚至第一行。导语是记者展示其杰作的橱窗。"可见,导语既可以使新闻紧紧抓住读者,也可能使读者罢读;导语的设计颇能体现记者的才华和功力。此外,导语还可以为整篇新闻定下基调,在很大程度上决定着一篇新闻如何顺利展开,甚至决定着新闻主体等部分的格调和行文风格。导语是一篇新闻的最核心、最精彩的部分,既要能够驾驭全篇、提纲挈领,又不允许在下文重复。

英语报刊消息报道常见的导语主要有概括性导语、要点式导语、描写性导语、直呼式导语、引语式导语、悬念式导语、延缓性导语、对比式导语、提问式导语、轶事式导语、复合式导语、标签式导语12种。通常由"5个W+1个H"组成的"概括性导语"(summary lead),又称"综合性导语"(round-up lead)或"硬导语"(hard lead),是导语写作中最早使用的一种形式。5个W和1个H分别指What(何事)、Who(何人)、Where(何地)、When(何时)、Why(为何)和How(如何)6个要素。西方新闻学鼻祖之一的戴纳认为,新闻导语必须回答5个W和1个H。这个观点曾经在相当长的时间里被认为是导语写作的金科玉律(周学艺,2010:17)。这类导语的长处是:为读者提供全篇消息梗概,信息传递简洁明了。其短处是:内容多,主次不清,重点不突出并容易重复,缺乏悬念感,也不适用于软新闻体裁。

"概括性导语"的写作方式自20世纪初起就面临激烈的挑战,一些新闻工作者对导语的写作进行了改革。通过改革,许多消息导语里只突出一两个新闻要素,其余新闻要素放在后面的主体或结尾,以便突出重点。这种主要出现在20世纪50年代至70年代的新闻导语,被称为第二代导语,其形式主要包括叙述式、设问式、描写式、对比式、评论式、结论式等。一个世纪以来,新闻导语写作风格上发生了许多变化,但到目前为止,概括性导语仍然在当今英语报纸上占据统领地位。

② 消息报道的基本结构

▲ 倒金字塔结构

消息报道一般采用"倒金字塔结构"(inverted pyramid form)。这种结构是按新闻事实的重要性递减的顺序进行布局,把最重要的新闻事实安排在文章的开头(即新闻导语),较为次要的内容紧接导语之后(一般是导语中的主要新闻要素的说明和扩展),最为次要的内容放在末尾。这样组合的文章便形成顶部大、底部小的倒三角形状,西方新闻学称此为"倒金字塔结构"。"倒金字塔结构"适合报道"硬新闻"。

"倒金字塔结构"起源于美国南北战争和电报的运用。在战争期间,电报业务刚开始投入使用,记者的稿件通过电报传送,但由于电报技术上的不成熟和军事临时征用的原因,稿件有时不能完全传送,时常中断。后来,记者们想出一种新的发稿方法:把战况的结果写在最前面,然后按事实的重要性依次写下去,最重要的写在最前面,这种应急措施产生了新的文体结构——"倒金字塔结构"。

对于报纸来说,"倒金字塔结构"的新闻有自己的优势:方便读者(读者可以从导语获得主要信息)、方便写作(记者按此模式写作十分便捷)、方便编辑(编辑排版根据篇幅、自上而下删减不会漏掉文章重要内容)。由于"倒金字塔结构"具有这些优点,新闻撰写人员比较喜欢采用这种结构。然而,也有不少新闻学者反对这一结构,认为它"头重脚轻",批评这种结构浪费篇幅,重要新闻事实重复3次(标题、导语、正文)。也有人指出,这种结构已经不合时宜,面临电子新闻媒介的挑战,时新性不再是报纸的长处,因为导语中的新闻事实读者已从广播电视中获悉。正因为如此,不少新的新闻写作结构已经出现。

为了帮助读者了解这种"倒金字塔结构",请见西方新闻学著作中的图表说明。

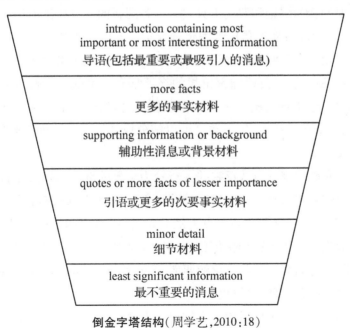

倒金字塔结构(周学艺,2010:18)

▲ 金字塔结构

与"倒金字塔结构"恰好相反,"金字塔结构"(pyramid form)将报道的事实按时间顺序排列,逐渐进入高潮,这种写法又称"编年史结构"(chronological style)。这种结构可以保持消息的完整性,便于把情节步步推进,直至高潮,从而增强读者的阅读兴趣,特别适合报道故事性强、以情节取胜的事件。但由于展开情节的节奏较慢,这种结构不适宜于报道"硬新闻"。"金字塔结构"通常由"开头"(beginning)、"正文"(body)、"结尾"(ending)三部分组成。

采用"金字塔结构"写消息,绝不意味着事无巨细,记流水账。这种结构要求记者有一定的概括能力,能用较为简练的语言叙述事件发展的几个阶段,然后抓住从一个阶段过渡到另一个阶段的转折点来写。

(2) 新闻言论

新闻言论是结合新近发生的重要新闻的主要事实,针对当前人们普遍关注和存在的实际问题和思想问题,通过新闻媒介发表的一种具有政治倾向、以广大读者为对象的论说性文体。如果说新闻报道是英语报刊的主体,以叙事为主,那么新闻言论则是英语报刊的灵魂,以议论见长,据事说理,兼具新闻性和政论性的特点。新闻言论是英语报刊的重要组成部分,新闻界在评价一家报纸或杂志的特色的时候,除了对它的报道选题、报道深度进行分析外,最重要的就是看这家媒体言论文章的深度和力度。

① 新闻言论的样式

当代英语报刊中,新闻言论的样式很多,大体上可以分为社论(editorials)、新闻述评(reviews or commentaries)、专栏言论(columns)等。新闻言论是上述各种评论文体的总称。

社论是最重要的新闻评论和舆论工具之一。各国新闻界对社论的定义表述不一,但有一点大家的看法是一致的:社论是报纸编辑部就重大问题发表的权威性评论,代表报社的意见。美国著名报业大王普利策把社论喻为"报纸的心脏",它是各种言论中最重要的一类。社论版最早出现在美国,英语国家正规的报纸都有社论版。一般而言,英语报纸的言论版首先刊登本报评论员撰写的社论。社论依据论述的内容可以分为当地事务、地区事务、国内事务及国际事务的社论,每一类又可以细分成政治、经济、外交政策、社会福利、教育文化等多个门类。

新闻述评是以夹叙夹议的方式反映并评析较为重要的事件、形势或问题的一种新闻领域的边缘体裁,又称"新闻分析"或"记者述评"。新闻述评篇幅较短,常配合新闻报道,借题发挥,着重从问题的某一侧面或某一点上展开论述,给人以深一层的思想启发。其基本特点是融新闻与政论于一体:既及时报道新闻事实,反映现实生活的发展变化,又注重直接揭示其本质、意义和趋向,集新闻与评论的职能于一身。述中有评,评中有述,由述而评,以评驭述,较之新闻综述有更多的议论色彩。

专栏言论是指那些在固定栏目中发表的由个人署名(有时甚至还配有其照片)的颇具独立见解的言论。专栏作家在选题、评论观点、写作内容等方面的自由度更大,专栏的影响力也因其覆盖面广而超过报纸的社论。目前,几乎所有报纸的言论版都开设一种至几种专栏,专栏言论已经成为言论版具有举足轻重意义的组成部分。现代英语报刊常常聘请资历深、声望高的记者担任专栏作家,在言论版上辟一个专栏,每天或定期刊登他们的署名评论性文章。这些专栏作家不但具有丰富的新闻工作经验、渊博的知识和相当的专业修养,而且还具备敏锐的分析能力和精湛的驾驭文字的功底。因此,他们笔下的言论往往具有巨大的吸引力。

② 新闻言论的基本结构

新闻言论以发表议论、阐明事理为主,主要运用逻辑思维去说服读者。新闻学家认为,新闻言论的写法像新闻写作一样,应当多样化,一般没有任何公式可言。就篇章结构而言,新闻言论不同于消息报道和特写文章,却与一般的议论文颇为相似,即通常由引论(theme)、论证(demonstration)和结论(conclusion, clincher)3个部分组成。

英语新闻评论的引论一般以"开门见山"居多,即不兜圈子而尽快进入正题,使读者刚读几句就看出一点眉目,产生阅读兴趣,进而迫切地想把全文看完。开门见山的方法很多,有的先从"新闻由头"(news peg)说开去,有的先把问题摆出来,有的先把结论摆出来,还有的从经典著作中引出一段话说开去。其中以"新闻由头"开头的形式最为常见。

论证指用论据证明论点的过程,即通过摆事实、讲道理来说明、证明引论的观点。有力的论证能使观点无懈可击,使读者心悦诚服。出色的英文新闻评论,其论证部分往往语言精练、逻辑严密、层次分明。新闻评论的结尾不是言论的陪衬和点缀,而是起到突出论点、呼应主题和引人深思的作用。一篇写得清晰明了的英文新闻评论,其结论多以一个独立的句子或段落置于全文末尾。

③ 新闻言论的写作笔调

准确、简明,富有概括性、哲理性,是新闻言论典型的语言特色。新闻言论的语言比较正式,语气较为严肃,文中语法结构烦琐的长句、难句比消息和特写中的多。撰稿人有时还要考虑句子的典雅等因素。为了给人一种客观公正的感觉,英文新闻言论往往力求以第三者,即"非个人的"(impersonal)言论调子来说理。有时为了缩短与读者的距离,或显示撰稿人与读者之间的融洽关系,新闻言论还使用把读者也包括在内的"复数第一人称言论口吻"(the editorial "we")的写作笔调,使言论好像在与读者交谈一样,避免给人一种严肃、呆板的感觉,从而达到更好的言论目的。

(3) 特写文章

特写文章、解释性报道和调查性报道是最常见的深度报道(in-depth reporting)形式。深度报道是一种系统而深入地反映重大新闻事件和社会问题,阐明事件因果关系,揭示实质,追踪和探索事件发展趋势的报道方式。

① 特写的定义

特写文章(feature articles),简称"特写"(features),又称"特稿"或"新闻特写",是再现新闻事件、人物和场景的形象化的报道形式。特写通常为软新闻。"特写"一词源于电影中的近镜头(特写镜头)的表现手法,即生动形象地描绘人物或事件的富有特征的片段、镜头、瞬间,给读者留下强烈而深刻的印象。对特写的定义有很多不同意见。有人认为特写是从消息中派生出来的一种报道形式,也有人认为任何对一个或几个新闻要素所做的详细描述都是特写。美国新闻学家丹尼尔·威廉森教授认为特写是一种带有创作性的,有时也带有主观性的文章;特写的目的是使读者对某件事、某种情况或对生活中的某个侧面有所了解。

特写贵在"特"字,具有形式多样、题材不限、篇幅随意等特点,但形式上的多样性并不等于没有质的规定性。西方新闻界对特写有一些具体的要求。美国新闻学家布鲁斯·盖里森在其专著《专业特写写作》(*Professional Feature Writing*)一书中指出,一篇好的特写文章应该具有以下几个要素:吸引人,有事实,有个性,有好的角度,有行动,既具有独特性又具有普遍性、重要性和活力。(张健,2007:85)

② 特写与消息报道的主要区别

与消息报道不同,特写的信息并不立即呈现在读者面前,而是慢慢展开,记者一层层地把事实剖现在读者面前,激发读者的阅读兴趣。新闻特写是消息报道的继续,也是一种更新,它常常跟随在消息报道之后,给记者相对充裕的时间去挖掘素材,进行综合、思辨和分析。经过记者的提炼,新闻特写往往更深入、更详实。特写文章与消息报道之间的种种差异可以简要概括如下(张健,2007:95)。

	消息报道	特写文章
报道范围	注重报道的全面性(inclusiveness)与整体性(integrity);呈现在读者面前的新闻内容是一幅全景画面(panorama)	侧重现实生活中某个典型而精彩的片段(episode);呈现在读者面前的新闻内容是一组组"放大了的近影"(enlarged close-ups)
报道目的	为读者提供事实	激起读者的好奇心,惊奇、猜疑或幽默感
报道题材	比较严肃,具有一定时新性的客观事实	不受限制,可"新"可"旧",可远可近
写作结构	多采用"倒金字塔结构"	形式多样,具有灵活性和随意性
写作文笔	用词简洁,叙事手法直截了当;具有"求全不求细"的典型特征	措辞传神达意,精彩纷呈;为读者提供"消息背后的消息"(news behind the news)
导语形式	程式化(如概括性导语等)	灵活多样,引人入胜
引语选用	因其内容重要或有力而被逐字逐句引用;富含新闻价值	稍有甚至没有重要的信息,目的在于使读者一直保持高度的阅读兴趣
结尾手法	可有可无	全篇之高潮或点睛式的归纳
文章篇幅	通常简短或适中	长短随意,短则几百字,长则数千甚至上万字,视题材而定
时效特征	属"易碎品",强调时效,有很强的时效性	受时效性的影响较小,具有耐压性;如同冰冻食品一样,可以被"冰封"数周或数月,甚至更长的时间

③ 特写的常见种类

特写的种类繁多,没有统一、固定的分类标准。从特写体现的新闻价值而言,英文特写可以分为新闻性特写(news-oriented features)和趣味性特写(interest-oriented features)。新闻性特写常是某一重大新闻的点缀或衬托,或与相关纯消息报道同处一个版面,或作为某新闻事件的补充报道。这类特写包括新闻分析、反映潮流趋势的报道、解释事件并预测其结果的文章等。新闻特写当前占据主流,但趣味性特写也不过时。趣味性特写不强调时效性,不以时间取胜,而是通过选择合适的角度,借助富有创造力的语言,提升文章的趣味性和故事性,旨在吸引并打动读者,满足读者的好奇心,缩短读者与记者间的距离。英文特写按采写的题材进行分类,又可以分为人物特写、事件特写、经历特写、风光特写等。

就时效性而言,英语报刊上的特写文章远不如广播和电视报道,但文字性的东西可以反复阅读,提供鲜为人知的细节,同时还留给读者思考和想象的空间。特写文章使报刊不再是生硬刻板的一堆干瘪文字,而是增添了一种生动特别的新形象:以哀婉动人、幽默诙谐的笔调,倾注浓郁的人情味,展示了充满思想深度的精神世界。可见,特写是以提供更多细节给读者带来精神享受的新闻题材,是当今报刊生存与发展的强劲推动力。

(4) 解释性报道

解释性报道(interpretive reporting)又称"分析性报道",是深度报道的一种主要表现形式,是运用背景材料来分析一个新闻事件发生的原因、意义、影响以及预示其发展趋势的一种新闻报道体裁。

解释性报道最早出现于20世纪二三十年代的美国,发展于20世纪中叶,是一种有别于传统的纯消息报道的文体形式。解释性报道是当今媒体,尤其是印刷媒体(print media)的主流。美国的《纽约时报》《新闻周刊》《华盛顿邮报》《洛杉矶时报》等著名的大报刊中,解释性报道占了70%以上的版面。其他国家,如英国、法国、日本,解释性报道一般都占据50%左右的报纸版面。需要指出的是,尽管解释性报道目前在新闻界占有举足轻重的作用,但它始终不能完全取代以"倒金字塔"为代表的新闻写作方式。

"一战"之前,西方报刊是纯新闻报道一统天下的局面。报界严格奉行所谓的客观主义原则,只提供新闻事实,不发表个人看法。这种报道原则的弊端后来充分暴露。第一次世界大战的爆发使美国民众感到惊愕和困惑,他们无法从报刊中了解战争爆发的根本原因。1929年经济大萧条(the Great Depression)突然降临:股市崩盘、银行倒闭、公司破产、工人失业,广大读者难以从报刊中寻得答案。1923年亨利·卢斯(Henry Luce)创办了《时代》周刊,一改传统新闻报道的做法,而是采用对一周消息重新加工、提供新闻背景的方式,《时代》周刊获得巨大成功。这种被卢斯称为"新闻注释家"的风格不仅被其他新闻周刊所仿效,而且对许多报纸也产生了强烈影响。20世纪50年代麦卡锡主义肆虐美国,不加分析的纯新闻报道起了推波助澜的作用。麦卡锡的身败名裂也使人们认清了传声筒式的"客观报道"的致命弱点。从此以后,解释性报道在报坛上的地位得以牢固确立。当今国际形势扑朔迷离,社会问题错综复杂,新的情况不断产生,人们期望报刊能解决自己的困惑,因此解释性报道越来越受青睐。

纯新闻报道是以直接的方式提供新闻事实,强调客观性,作者不陈述看法,不表露感情,因此纯新闻报道只起到"信息功能",常被称作"无个性的报道"(impersonal reporting),这类报道一般不署名。解释性报道是对新闻事件进行分析和解释的报道,其主要功能是提供相关背景,分析前因后果,讲清来龙去脉,阐明事件意义,推测发展趋势,等等。因此,解释性报道除信息功能外,还有劝说功能。它是有深度、有分析、有观点、有个性的写作,一般都署名。

解释性报道又不同于新闻评论。新闻评论的作者往往采取逻辑分析的方法,对某个新闻事件进行分析,评判该事件的利弊、得失、荣辱、好恶,作者的立场明确、观点鲜明。而解释性报道对某个事件的分析,采取的是对大量背景材料进行分析的方法,作者也有自己的立场、观点,但并不明确地表达出来。高明的解释性报道致力于提供背景事实,将意见寓于背景的叙述中,让读者在阅读了大量背景材料之后自己得出结论。

(5) 调查性报道

调查性报道(investigative reporting)出现于19世纪末20世纪初,是英语报刊上的一种特殊报道形式,是从美国的揭丑报道(muckraking reporting),即专门揭露政府和公共机构中的腐化行为和丑闻的新闻报道发展而来的,是一种以系统深入地揭露问题为主旨的新闻报道形式。

在美国的新闻发展史上,调查性报道强调揭露被隐藏、被掩盖的信息,题材广泛,涉及人类活动的各个方面,包括调查腐化的政治家、政治组织、公司企业、慈善机构、外交机构及经济领域中的欺骗活动。调查性报道有别于大多数一般性报道,是一种更为详尽、更带有分析性、更花费时间的报道。一般性报道只报道孤立的、公开的突发事件的结果,而调查性报道则注重挖掘已发生的新闻事件的内在的、隐蔽的关系,并向公众分析这些内在联系的重大意义。这些隐蔽的关系潜藏在公众日常谈论的新闻事件之下,如果不是那些敏锐而又具有强烈的社会责任感的新闻记者付出比日常报道多出数十倍的努力将其揭示给受众,这些被隐藏、被掩盖的信息将永远不会被公布于世。

调查性报道与解释性报道也有所不同。虽然两者都重视 how and why,但前者更强调揭露,显示记者公正的立场;后者则注重提供背景材料,是新闻背后的新闻,记者较少直接显露自己的观点。调查性报道也不同于新闻评论,虽然两者都表达了记者的观点,但表达的方式不同。新闻评论注重议论长处、短处、荣誉、丑恶、热爱、憎恨等,并在字里行间透露事件的原因、意义、影响、发展趋势等,作者对自己的观点也有一番评论。在调查性报道中,作者的观点是在揭露事实的过程中自然流露的,没有自我议论,更注重事实因果。

美国普利策新闻奖在1985年设立了调查性报道奖。在西方读者的心目中,调查性报道的地位是其他任何报道所不能取代的,许多优秀的记者也都把写调查性报道看作自己的天职。一篇成功的调查性报道往往能引起公众的广泛关注,同时为其所属媒介赢得巨大的声誉。美国前总统尼克松政府的"水门事件"(the Watergate Scandal)和里根政府的"伊朗门事件"(the Irangate Scandal)都是调查性报道的杰作。调查性报道也有不足之处:耗时耗财,有时过多涉及隐私,证人压力过大,记者风险过多,等等。

第二节　报刊英语的标题特色

　　从新闻学角度来看,报刊标题的功能是推销文章、概述内容、美化版面。这些功能要求报刊标题不仅要以高度浓缩的语言提示文章最主要或最值得注意的内容,而且要以醒目的形式抓住读者还在游移浏览的目光,为时间繁忙、匆匆浏览报刊的读者起"向导"作用。
　　初次接触报刊英语的读者常常对报刊标题不理解,这是因为标题英语与我们接触的日常英语不同,有其自身的特点,新闻英语学者称其为"标题语言"(headlines)。英语报刊标题的特点主要表现在语法、词汇、修辞、标点符号四个方面。

1. 英语报刊标题的语法特点

英语报刊标题的语法特点主要指:(1)省略;(2)标题的时态;(3)标题的语态。
(1) 省　略
英语报刊标题语法的最大特点就是省略。为了高度凝练语言,达到言简意赅、突出主要内容的效果,标题中常常会省略某些语法成分或词语,尤其省略无实义的虚词。在不发生歧义的情况下,报刊标题中常常省略冠词、连词、代词、系动词、助动词等。

　　① 省略冠词
　　Bankers Silent as Dollars Falls = The Bankers Silent as the Dollar Falls
　　Bush's Approval Rating Plunges to New Low = Bush's Approval Rating Plunges to a New Low
　　② 省略连词
　　连词省略以省略 and 为主。省略了 and 之后,通常用逗号代替。
　　Poverty, Pregnancy Linked = Poverty and Pregnancy Linked
　　The US, Vietnam Resume Talks = The US and Vietnam Resume Talks
　　③ 省略代词
　　在英语报刊标题中,人称代词通常被省略。
　　Mother, Daughter Share Fulbright Year = A Mother and Her Daughter Share a Fulbright Year
　　China Launches First Manned Spacecraft = China Launches Its First Manned Spacecraft
　　④ 省略系动词
　　Gates Still World's Richest = Gates Is Still the World's Richest

The Key to America's Growth: International Sales = The Key to America's Growth <u>Is</u> International Sales

⑤ 省略助动词

构成被动语态和进行时的助动词 be,其各种时态形式在报刊标题中常常被省略。
Financier Killed by Burglars = A Financier <u>Is</u> Killed by Burglars
India Mending Fences = India <u>Is</u> Mending Fences

(2) 英语报刊标题的时态

新闻是对新近发生的事实的报道,它所叙述的事实一般都是已经发生或刚刚发生的事实。若按照日常英语语法的动词时态规则,应该用一般过去时或现在完成时,但是英语报刊标题一般不用过去时态,而采用现在时态。其主要目的是为了突出新闻事件的现实感(reality)、新鲜感(freshness)和直接感(immediacy),使读者读报时如同置身于这条新闻事件中,增强读者的阅读兴趣。因此,英文报刊在报道过去发生的事实时,在标题中广泛使用一般现在时。

例如:Clinton Clinches His Second Term

　　　Bomb Injures 26 on Paris Train

　　　Greece Wins Euro Championship

英语报刊标题中常用的动词时态还包括一般将来时和现在进行时。标题中动词的将来时表达形式可以用"will + 动词原形",如:Machines Will Be Smarter than We Are。但标题中更多的还是采用"be + 动词不定式"结构,其中 be 通常省略。因此,动词不定式在英语报刊标题中可直接表示未来行为。

例如:Russian Defense Minister to Visit China

　　　India, Pakistan to Resume Border Talk

　　　Florida Freeze to Increase Area Produce Prices

对于正在发生的事件或动作,标题通常采用现在进行时"be + 现在分词"的形式,其中 be 通常省略。因此,现在分词在英文报刊标题中就可以直接表示正在进行的动作或正在变化的事件。

例如:IT Sector Growing Fast

　　　BBC Considering Starting Global Television Service

　　　Deposits, Loans Rising in Hong Kong

(3) 英语报刊标题的语态

在英语报刊标题中,被动语态结构"be + 过去分词"形式中的 be 通常省略,剩下的过去分词在标题里可直接表示被动意义,而 by 和它引出的动作的执行者也经常省略。读者切忌将其误解为该动词的过去式。

例如:Skilled Hands Needed

　　　Journalist Fired in Spy Debate

New Oxford Chancellor Elected

事实上,英语新闻标题使用主动语态的频率远远超过被动语态。从修辞角度而言,主动语态比被动语态更加丰富多彩且富有感染力,所表达的意义更为直接或更具说服力。英语新闻标题只有在事件或动作的接受者比执行者更重要时才使用被动语态。

2. 英语报刊标题的词汇特点

英语报刊标题用词也具有自己的特色。有的语言学家称报刊标题所用词语为"特别词语"(special vocabulary)。报刊标题用词之所以特别是为了取得节约篇幅、吸引读者的效果。为此,报刊标题的用词力求简短明了、准确达意。主要采用以下几种方法。

(1) 普遍使用短词

英语报刊标题普遍选用字形短小、音节不多而意义又比较广泛的词。这类小词在标题中频繁出现,一是由于报纸篇幅有限,用小词既可以节省空间又可以免于移行;二是由于小词的词义范畴不仅宽广,而且生动形象。下面例句中的画线词是报刊标题中常用的一些小词:

1. US Refuses to Back Environment Fund (back=support) 美国拒付环保基金
2. Governor to Axe Aide (axe=dismiss) 州长将解雇随从
3. Border Feud Leads to War (feud=dispute) 边界争端引发战争
4. World Eyes Mid-East Peace Talks (eyes=watches) 世界关注中东和平会谈
5. Peace Pact Not Yet in Sight (pact=agreement) 和平协议遥遥无期

上述这些短词简洁、形象,令读者耳目一新。为便于读者更好地理解英语报刊标题,现再列举一些常见诸英文报刊标题中的这类短词:

aid=help; assist 帮助,援助
alter=change; modify 改变
assail=denounce 谴责
back=support 支持
ban=prohibit; forbid 禁止
bare=expose; reveal; disclose 揭露;透露
block=obstruct 阻碍
bid=attempt 努力
blast=criticize 批评,指责
boost=increase 增加,提高
check=examine 检查
cite=mention 提及
claim=cause the death of 夺去……的生命
cut=reduce 削减;减少

air=publicize; express 公开;表达
ask=inquire 询问
axe=dismiss; reduce 解雇;减少
balk=impede 阻碍
bar=prevent 防止,阻止
blast=explode 爆炸
begin=commence 开始
bilk=cheat 欺骗
bolt=desert; abandon 放弃;抛弃
buy=purchase 购买
chide=rebuke 指责
clash=disagree strongly 发生分歧
curb=control; restrict 控制;限制
dip=decline; decrease 下降;减少

drive = campaign 运动
due = schedule 安排;预订
end = terminate 结束,中止
flout = insult 侮辱
grip = seize 抓住;控制
gut = destroy 摧毁
hold = arrest 逮捕
laud = praise 赞扬
map = work out 制订
moot = discuss 讨论
nab = arrest 逮捕
net = capture 捕获
nix = deny;disapprove 否决;拒绝
oust = expel 驱逐
pledge = determine 发誓
plunge = plummet 价格等暴跌
probe = investigate 调查
rap = criticize 批评
rout = defeat completely 击溃;打垮
slay = murder 谋杀
soar = skyrocket 急剧上升
spark = cause;trigger 引发;引起
stem = prevent;check 阻止;制止
sway = influence 影响
thwart = obstruct 阻碍
vow = determine 决心;发誓
wed = marry 结婚

draw = attract 吸引
ease = lessen;alleviate 减轻;缓和
flay = criticize 批评
foil = prevent from 阻止;防止
grill = investigate 调查
head = direct 率领;主管
ink = sign 签署
lop = diminish 下降;减少
mark = celebrate 庆祝
mull = consider 考虑
name = appoint;nominate 命名;提名
nip = defeat 击败
opt = choose 选择
peril = endanger 危害,危及
plot = conspire 预谋;密谋策划
poise = ready for action 做好准备
raid = attack 进攻
rock = shock;surprise 震惊;使惊讶
rule = judge 裁定;判定
snub = ignore 忽视
spur = encourage 激励;鞭策
stall = stagnate 停滞不前
swap = exchange 交流;交换
trim = reduce 削减
vie = compete 竞争
weigh = consider 考虑
woo = seek to win 争取;追求

除了以上所列及的简短动词外,标题中还常常使用简短的名词,例如:

accord = agreement 协议
aid = assistance 帮助
arms = weapons 武器
body = committee;commission 委员会
crash = collision 碰撞;坠毁
deal = agreement;transaction 协议;交易
fake = counterfeit 赝品;骗局

aide = assistant 助手
aim = purpose 目的
blast = explosion 爆炸
clash = dispute;controversy 分歧;争议
danger = precariousness 危险
envoy = ambassador 大使
fear = apprehension 畏惧,恐惧

fete = celebration 庆祝

fire = conflagration 火灾

foe = opponent；enemy 对手；敌人

kid = child 孩子

nod = approval 许可；批准

probe = investigation 调查

rally = mass assembly 集会

strife = conflict 冲突；矛盾

talk = negotiation 会谈

poll = election；public opinion poll 投票选举；民意测验

feud = strong dispute 严重分歧

flop = failure 失败

gems = jewels 珠宝；首饰

link = connection 联系

pact = treaty；contract；agreement 协议

pullout = withdrawal 撤退，撤离

rise = increase 增加；增长

ties =（diplomatic）relations（外交）关系

（2）大量使用缩写词

英语缩写词包括首字母缩略词（initialism）和首字母拼音词（acronym），是通过组合几个词的首字母构成的新词或专有名词。英语新闻标题中经常出现的缩写词主要分为三类。

① 组织机构的名称

EU = European Union 欧洲联盟

NPC = National People's Congress 全国人民代表大会

UNESCO = United Nations Educational, Scientific and Cultural Organization 联合国教科文组织

IMF = International Monetary Fund 国际货币基金组织

ASEAN = Association of Southeast Asian Nations 东南亚国家联盟

GATT = General Agreement on Tariffs and Trade 关贸总协定

WTO = World Trade Organization 世界贸易组织

OPEC = Organization of Petroleum Exporting Countries 石油输出国组织

PLO = Palestine Liberation Organization 巴勒斯坦解放组织

IOC = International Olympic Committee 国际奥林匹克委员会

WHO = World Health Organization 世界卫生组织

OAU = Organization of African Unity 非洲统一组织

② 常见事物的名称

AIDS = Acquired Immune Deficiency Syndrome 获得性免疫缺陷综合征；艾滋病

UFO = Unidentified Flying Object 不明飞行物；"飞碟"

DJI = Dow-Jones Index 道琼斯指数

GMT = Greenwich Mean Time 格林尼治标准时间

IT = information technology 信息技术

PC = personal computer 个人电脑

ABM = anti-ballistic missile 反弹道导弹

PR = Public Relations 公共关系
SALT = Strategic Arms Limitation Talks 限制战略武器会谈
SDI = Strategic Defense Initiative 战略防御措施
SARS = severe acute respiratory syndromes 严重急性呼吸综合征；非典型肺炎
DVD = digital video disc 数码影碟

③ 职业或职务的名称

MP = member of parliament 议员
CEO = chief executive officer 首席执行官；执行总裁
PM = Prime Minister 总理；首相
GM = general manager 总经理
VIP = very important person 贵宾；要人
TP = traffic policeman 交通警察
PA = personal assistant 私人助理

(3) 大量使用节缩词

报刊标题除了使用缩写词外，还经常使用节缩词，通过"截头去尾"（clipping or shortening）的方法将一些常用的名词、形容词等截短或缩短，其宗旨同样是为了节省报刊版面，如：hospital→hosp；billion→bn；cigarette→cig；high technology→hi-tech；business→biz；gasoline→gas；automobile suicide→autocide；international→intl；等等。节缩词在英文报刊标题中十分活跃，并且数量不断增加。这类节缩词不仅在标题中广泛使用，而且还时常出现在新闻报道的行文中。常见于英语报刊的节缩词主要可分为以下几类：

• 留头去尾

ad = advertisement 广告
bach = bachelor 学士；单身汉
champ = champion 冠军
divi = dividend 红利
doc = doctor 医生
exam = examination 检查；考试
frat = fraternity 友爱；博爱
homo = homosexual 同性恋
Japs = Japanese 日本人
lav = lavatory 厕所；盥洗室
mag = magazine 杂志
mod = modern 现代的
pix = pictures 电影；照片
rail = railway 铁路

auto = automobile 汽车
celeb = celebrity 名人；名流
deli = delicatessen 熟食（店）
disco = discotheque 迪斯科舞曲
dorm = dormitory 宿舍
expo = exposition 博览会
gym = gymnasium 体育馆；健身房
info = information 信息
lab = laboratory 实验室
lib = liberation 解放
memo = memorandum 备忘录
pic = picture 图片；照片；电影
pro = professional 专业的；职业的
rep = representative 代表

Russ = Russia 俄罗斯
sub = subway; submarine 地铁; 潜水艇
van = vanguard 先锋
sec = secretary 秘书
uni = university 大学
vet = veteran 有经验的, 资深的

- 截头留尾

cello = violoncello 大提琴
coper = helicopter 直升机
quake = earthquake 地震
chute = parachute 降落伞
dozer = bulldozer 推土机
wig = periwig 假发

- 截去首尾, 保留中间

flu = influenza 流感
tec = detective 侦探
fridge = refrigerator 冰箱
vic = convict 罪犯

- 截去中间, 保留首尾

c'tee = committee 委员会
com'l = commercial 商业的; 电视广告
heliport = helicopter airport 直升机机场
motel = motor hotel 汽车旅馆
maglev train = magnetic levitation train 磁悬浮列车
C'wealth = Commonwealth 英联邦
cric = critic 评论家; 批评性的
infoport = information airport 信息港
nat'l = national 全国的

- 不规则裁剪词

Aussie = Australian 澳大利亚人
hanky = handkerchief 手帕
telly = television 电视
bookie = bookmaker 编者
pram = perambulator 婴儿车; 童车

(4) 灵活使用"生造词"

在新闻标题中有时会出现一种由两个或两个以上的词临时组合而成的新词, 新闻学者称之为"新闻生造词"(journalistic coinage)。这些临时生造词中, 有的由于形象生动、构词别致, 很快地流传下来, 成为日常词汇的一部分, 有的则很快被人遗忘。生造词的构词方法是将两个或两个以上的旧词组合在一起, 省去其中的若干音节。例如:

comsat = communication satellite 通信卫星
Euromart = European Common Market 欧洲共同市场
stagflation = stagnation and inflation 经济滞胀
lunacast = lunar telecast 登月电视广播
newscast = news broadcast 新闻广播
blacketeer = black marketeer 黑市商人
cinemanufacturer = cinema manufacturer 电影制片商
slanguage = slang language 俚语
fruice = fruit juice 果汁
temps = temporary staff 临时工

medicare = medical care 医疗保险
sitcom = situation comedy 情景喜剧
politburo = political bureau 政治局

(5) 酌情采用外来语

英语新闻标题中经常会出现外来词(loanwords),即从非英语的语言中借用的一些词或词组。它们在报刊标题中经常出现,有些已被长期使用。这些外来语可以使新闻标题标新立异、不落俗套,增强读者的好奇心和阅读兴趣。例如:

encore(French): a demand by an audience for an additional performance 再演唱的要求

blitz(German): a sudden heavy attack; a period of great activity for some special purpose 闪电战;大规模的行动

incognito(Italian): hiding one's identity, esp. by taking another name when one's own name is well-known 隐姓埋名的(人);隐瞒真实身份的(人)

quid pro quo(Latin): something given or received in exchange for something else 交换物;交换条件

rendezvous(French): a meeting planned at a certain time and place 会面

status quo(French): the existing state of affairs 现状

rapport(French): a relationship of mutual understanding or trust and agreement between people 融洽(关系);和谐

laissez faire(French): the doctrine that government should not interfere in commercial affairs 不干涉政策;自由贸易

3. 英语报刊标题的修辞特点

理想的标题不仅要语言简洁精练,而且要能激发读者的兴趣。英语报刊标题中常采用修辞手段来增强语言的简练性、形象性和趣味性。比喻、借代、双关、夸张、仿拟、对仗、典故、押韵等是英语报刊标题中常用的修辞手法。

(1) 比喻

比喻包括明喻(simile)和暗喻(metaphor)。英文报刊中常用比喻来使语言生动活泼,使新闻人物或新闻事件更加鲜明突出,吸引并加深读者印象。例如:

Wall Street Takes a Dive (takes a dive 比喻股票价格大幅度急剧下降)
Russian Reform Old Wine in New Bottle (以 old wine 比喻旧政,new bottle 形容改革)
Children Under Parents' Wing (用 wing 来喻指父母的保护)

(2) 借代

借代(metonymy)是用此物之名指彼物之实。这种艺术上的换名使英语报刊标题更为新鲜活泼、生动传神。例如:

Suing Uncle Sam（Uncle Sam 指代美国政府）

Britain Deputy PM Visits "Bird's Nest" in Beijing（Bird Nest 指代具有鸟巢外形的奥运会主体育场）

Wall Street Shocked by New Inside Arrests（以 Wall Street 指代美国金融界）

（3）双关

双关（pun）是一个词或词组，以文字游戏的形式出其不意地把互不关联的双重含义同时结合起来。双关是对同形异义词（homonym）或同音异义词（homophone）的巧妙使用，包括词义双关和谐音双关。例如：

Microsoft Opens a New Window 微软又开"新窗"（Window 是双关语，既有本意，又指微软新品 Window XP）

"Silent" Office Workers Demand to Be Heard "不闻不问"的办公室员工，今后将不再不闻不问（silent 一语双关，既指安静工作的办公人员，又指这些人没有牢骚满腹）

Couple Say "Eye Do" 饱览美景，喜结连理（在西式婚礼上，双方表示自愿结合时会说"I do"，标题中的"Eye Do"既与"I do"同音，又指饱览美景，形成谐音双关）

（4）夸张

夸张（hyperbole）是一种故意言过其实，或夸大或缩小事物的形象，借以突出事物的某种特征或品格，鲜明地表达思想情感的修辞方式。将夸张用于英文报刊标题，可以强化情感，也可以起到幽默和嘲弄的效果。例如：

Graying Armies to Defend Social Security（graying army 指老年人，这里运用夸张的手法描述了捍卫社会保障的老年人的人数之多）

Vow to Zip His Lips 誓将守口如瓶（zip 指如同拉链一样密不透风）

（5）仿拟

仿拟（parody）是一种巧妙、机智、有趣的修辞格，它有意仿照人们熟知的现成的语言材料，根据表达的需要临时创造出新的语、句、篇来，以使语言生动活泼、幽默诙谐。例如：

A Tale of Two Capitals（模仿英国作家狄更斯的名著 A Tale of Two Cities）

Hashimoto's Dilemma：To Reform or Not to Reform（模仿莎士比亚《哈姆雷特》中的名句"To be or not to be"）

（6）对仗

对仗（antithesis）是用两个字数相等、结构相似的语句表现相关或相反的意思。对仗可以加强语言表达力，还可以产生幽默或讽刺效果，在英语报刊标题中也很常用。例如：

Rich Man, Poor Fan 富球星，穷观众（这是一篇有关球星高额薪金，赛票价格昂贵，观众承受不起的报道）

Many Questions, Few Answers 问题多多，答案少少（文章讲述了英国疯牛病引发的一系列悬而未决的问题）

Capital Rich, Revenue Poor 资本雄厚，收益可怜（文章报道了一家金融公司因经营

不善而导致收入锐减的情况)

(7) 典故

典故(allusion)多源于历史、寓言、神话、传说和事件,多见于历史记载、文学作品和报刊。英语报刊标题中的典故有助于利用有限的报刊空间,蕴含丰富的文化内涵和寓意,使标题具有较强的认知意义。值得注意的是,标题在用典时常常改字或加字,不仅取得新意,而且产生幽默和趣味。例如:

The Old Man and the Economic Sea(典出美国作家海明威的名著 *The Old Man and the Sea*)

Farewell to Wall Street(典出海明威的代表作 *A Farewell to Arms*)

(8) 押韵

押韵(rhyme)的主要作用是增强语言的节奏感和音律美,从而增强语言表达的感染力。常见的押韵形式包括头韵(alliteration)、半谐音(assonance,又称准押韵或部分押韵)、辅音押韵(consonance)、拟声(onomatopoetia)等,它们彼此相近,但各不相同。例如:

Pressure in Work, Pleasure in Life

Hopes to Host Games in Future

Young Wheelers, Big Dealers

Gloom, Boom and Doom

Needy or Greedy?

Pei's Pyramids Puzzle Paris

4. 英语报刊标题的标点符号特点

英文报刊栏目狭窄、篇幅有限,要求标题结构简洁精练、内容言简意赅,在有限的篇幅里尽量浓缩较多的新闻内容,因此形成了报刊标题的特点:尽量少用长句,化长为短,以符代词。常用的标点符号有逗号、冒号、分号、破折号、问号、引号、感叹号。

(1) 逗号

逗号除了表示标题中并列成分之间的停顿外,还常常被用来代替连词 and,以节省标题字数。例如:

Iron, Steel Industries Told to Cut Costs = Iron <u>and</u> Steel Industries Told to Cut Costs

(2) 冒号

冒号的功能在于提示下文,既可以表示讲话的内容,替代"说"意动词,又经常用来代替系动词,甚至其他动词(如 have, show, prove 等)。例如:

Putin: Muslim Nations Call for End to Tension in Bosnia-Hergezervena = Putin <u>Says</u> That Muslim Nations Call for End to Tension in Bosnia-Hergezervena

Defense: The Real Debate = Defense <u>Is</u> the Real Debate

Israelis: A Compelling Need to Peace Process = Israelis <u>Have</u> a Compelling Need to

Peace Process

(3) 分号

分号将标题一分为二,表示两个独立的意思。例如:

India Goes Nuclear;US Concerned 印度发展核武器;美国表示关注

Clashes Follow Hebron Killing;Mayor Removed 希布伦屠杀引发冲突;市长遭解职

(4) 破折号

破折号用在没有引号的引语后面引出说话人或表示解释。例如:

Labor Councils Face Bankruptcy—Officials = Officials Say that Labor Councils Face Bankruptcy(引出说话人)

Take Care—It's a Jungle Out There 当心——那里可是弱肉强食的地方(表示解释)

(5) 问号

大多数带有问号的标题并不是真正的问句,它们只是带有问号的陈述句。一般情况下,问号用于以下两种情况:

① 标题报道的事情有可能在将来发生。例如:

Oil Price to Rise?

New Cabinet Today?

② 对所报道事件的真实性和准确性表示怀疑。例如:

Jones Planned to Kill Carter?

Police Allowed Jailbreak?

(6) 引号

英语中引号有单引号和双引号。引号除了用来表示直接引用别人的话外,有时还用来指引号内的词或句子所表达的意思并非其本意。单引号显得简练,因而在报刊标题中较为常见。例如:

Norse "Invasion"

"Violence Is Always a Real Possibility"

(7) 感叹号

感叹号用于轰动性新闻的标题。例如:

Fireballs!Twisters!Upside-Down F-18s!

第三节　报刊英语的用词策略

新闻写作一般遵循 ABC 原则,即力求报道内容的精确性(accuracy)、语言文字的简洁度(brevity)和文章结构条理上的清晰感(clarity)。为了达到这三方面的统一,英语报刊在长期的办报实践中逐渐形成了自己的语法和词汇特点,即区别于普通英语的所谓"报刊英语"。

报刊英语主要受到大众性、节俭性、趣味性、时新性、客观性五个因素的制约。首先,报刊是一种大众传媒,这就要求报刊要适合大众的文化水平和阅读习惯,因此报刊语言必须通俗易懂。其次,报业十分珍惜版面,要求新闻写作人员在有限的篇幅内提供尽可能多的信息,这就形成了报刊语言简洁的风格。此外,西方新闻界十分注重趣味性,这要求报刊语言生动有趣。再次,新闻报道要遵循客观性原则,没有客观性报道就会失去信任,失去读者,这要求新闻报道文字准确具体。最后,新闻报道注重时新性,新闻报道在提供最新消息的同时也传播了相关的新词;不少新闻写作人员为了增加文章的吸引力,在语言上求新,因此新闻英语也具有新颖活泼的语言特色。这使报刊不仅成为报道新闻的媒介,而且成了使用新词的庞大机器和杜撰新词的巨大工厂。

报刊英语语言简洁、生动有趣、准确具体、新颖活泼,主要表现为:(1)使用简洁具体的词;(2)大量使用节缩词;(3)灵活使用生造词;(4)巧用词性变化;(5)不断推出新词。英语报刊的标题鲜明地体现了报刊英语的一些用词特点。本节主要探讨报刊英语用词简洁具体、巧用词性变化、不断推出新词等用词特点。此外,本节还探讨报刊英语中的"说"意动词。这些"说"意动词的恰当使用体现了报刊语言简洁、准确、生动的特色。

1. 用词简洁具体

报刊英语提倡多用简洁明了的常用词,少用"高雅的"(elegant)或冗长的(long)词,多用确切具体的词,少用抽象深奥的词,尽可能少用形容词和副词,达到既可以吸引广大读者,又准确无误地报道事实的目的。因此,在新闻写作中,很少有人会用 blithe 来表达 joyful 的含义,很少会用 final outcome, controversial issue 这样的表达,而是直接采用 outcome 和 issue。更多的实例,请见下表:

Simple words	Elegant or long words
about	approximately; concerning the matter of
agreement	concordance
although	despite the fact that
as a rule	as a general rule
consensus	consensus of opinion
crisis	serious crisis
danger	precariousness
expect	anticipate
fear	apprehension
meeting	rendezvous
murder	brutal murder

(续表)

Simple words	Elegant or long words
nearness	contiguity
proposal	proposition
show	demonstrate
destroyed	totally destroyed
begin	commence
use	utilize

2. 巧用词性变化

词性转化(conversion)可以节约篇幅,并可以使语言生动有力,因而在报刊英语中经常使用。报刊中常见的词性转化类型有:

(1) 名词转化为动词

He <u>mouthed</u> fine words about friendship. 他满口是友谊。

The White House press secretary is once more <u>backgrounding</u> newsmen for the president. 白宫新闻秘书再次代表总统给新闻记者提供背景资料。

(2) 动词或动词词组转化为名词

Like today's <u>haves</u> and <u>havenots</u>, we will have a society of the <u>knows</u> and <u>knowsnots</u>. 就像今天社会上有富人和穷人一样,将来社会上会出现有知识的人和无知识的人。

(Computer Gap …) These aging <u>choose-nots</u> become a more serious issue when they are teachers in schools. 这些日益变老又不愿意学电脑的人如果在学校当教师的话,那么问题就更为严重了。

(3) 形容词转化为名词

在英语报刊中,常常见到舍去名词而将其形容词修饰语用作名词的做法。例如:

undesirables 不受欢迎的人或物   valuables 值钱的东西
unreachables 不可接近的人   variables 易变的东西
gays 同性恋者   never-marrieds 从未结婚的人
unwanteds 不想要的人或物   unemployables 不能被雇用的人
perishables 易腐败的东西   pin-ups 钉在墙上的美女照
unreadables 无法读懂的东西   retireds 退了休的人
undecides 未下决心的人   the young marrieds 新婚的年轻人

3. 不断推出新词

英语是一门开放的语言,它比世界上其他许多语言更具开放性和容纳性,它随时随地接纳着新的事物和新的变化。新事物、新变化催生新词语,这些层出不穷的新词语往往最先出现在英语报刊中。新词的生命力各不相同,有的新词可能昙花一现,有的新词可能在语言中活跃一段时间,也有的新词可能成为语言中的基本词汇。这些新词有的是新造的单词和短语,有的是旧词衍生出的新义。这些词反映了现代西方社会生活的各个方面。下面举典型实例加以说明。

(1) 政治

西方国家新首脑上台后各自执行的特色政策给英语带来了一些新词。民主党人克林顿(Bill Clinton)在1993年到1997年间担任美国总统,他的名字自然跟美国的政治词汇联系在一起,如:Clintonism(克林顿的政策),Clintonian(克林顿的;克林顿式的),Clintonomics(克林顿的经济政策),Clintonite(克林顿的支持者),Clintonize(使克林顿化;使适合克林顿的政策)。同样,梅杰(John Major)在1990年到1997年间担任英国首相,英语里出现了Majorism(梅杰的政策)和Majorite(梅杰的支持者)。

其他的政治新词还有:Whitewatergate(克林顿的白水门事件),Commonwealth of Independent States(CIS)(独联体),European Union(EU)(欧洲联盟,简称欧盟),Euroland(欧元区),G7/G-7/G7nations(7个重要工业化国家,包括加拿大、法国、德国、意大利、日本、英国、美国),new world order(世界新秩序)。

(2) 商业

随着全球经济的发展,涌现了不少商业和经济方面的新词,如:WTO(World Trade Organization,世界贸易组织),NAFTA(North American Free Trade Agreement,北美自由贸易协议),SME(small- or medium-sized enterprises,中小企业),for-profit(盈利的),not-for-profit(非盈利的),level paying field(公平竞争的领域),power breakfast(商业早餐),marketeer(营销人员),kick-start(重新振兴),short-termism(短期效益),human resources(人事部门),dehiring(裁员,解雇),plastic(信用卡),loyalty card(购物卡;优惠卡)。

(3) 科学技术

科学技术的迅猛发展给英语带来了大量的新词,如:chaotic system(混沌系统),chaos theory/chaology(混沌理论),digital audio broadcasting(数字广播),digital compression(数字压缩),GPS(Global Positioning System,全球定位系统),knowbot(knowledge + robot,智能机器人),microwave(微波),superconductor(超导体),picturephone(可视电话),transceiver(transmitter + receiver,无线电收发器),nanolaser(nanometre + laser,纳米激光器),comsat(communication + satellite,通信卫星),lunacast(lunar + telecast,登月电视广播)。

(4) 计算机和网络

计算机科学和网络技术的飞速发展使英语增加了许多新词,如:multimedia(多媒体),information superhighway(信息高速公路),mouse(鼠标),home page(主页),cut and paste(剪贴),download(下载),data warehouse(数据库),e-mail(电子邮件),e-currency(电子货币),e-commerce(电子商务),e-paper(电子报),sleep mode(电脑的睡眠模式),escape key(退出

键),techie(计算机的技术人员),netizen(网民),Internet(因特网),netfile(网络文件),web page(网页),website(网站),web surf(网上浏览),webmaster(网络管理员),webcasting(网络播放),hyperlink(超链接),hypertext(超文本),cyberculture(电脑文化),cyberspeak(网络用语),cybernaut(网络用户),warez(盗版软件),virtual reality(虚拟现实),virtual environment(虚拟环境),virtual space(虚拟空间),virtual classroom(虚拟教室)。

(5) 人与社会

现代文明改变了人们的生活方式,同时也带来了各种新的社会问题和社会现象,这一切都在英语词汇中留下了痕迹,如:harassment(sexual harassment,性骚扰),carjacking(劫持汽车),cardboard city(无家可归人的聚居区),skell(无家可归者),serial killer(连续作案杀人者),granny dumping(遗弃老人),prenup(婚前协议),mule(drug mule,贩运毒品的人),drug abuse(滥用毒品),stuffer(把毒品藏在身体的器官里偷运毒品的人),swallower(把毒品吞食腹内偷运毒品的人),slacker(无所追求的人,逃避工作的人),post-feminism(后女权运动),physically challenged(身体有残疾的),visually challenged(视力有障碍的),mentally challenged(精神不正常的)。

(6) 环境

环境保护问题是当代世界的热点问题之一。英语中很多新词反映了全球的环境问题、全球对环境问题的关注以及采取的相关措施,如:carbon tax(排放二氧化碳税),carbon footprint(碳排放量),energy audit(能源监控),blue box(蓝色垃圾箱),alternative fuel(代用燃料),biodiesel(生物柴油),sustainable development(可持续发展),eco-efficiency(生态效率),eco-friendly vehicle(环保型汽车;绿色汽车),eco-farming(生态农业),ecotecture(生态建筑),eco-tourism(生态旅游)。

(7) 医疗保健

现代医疗技术的发展反映了人们对健康问题的关注,英语中随之产生了很多相关词汇,如:Aids(艾滋病),HIV(human immunodeficiency virus,艾滋病病毒),person with Aids(艾滋病患者),buddy(帮助艾滋病患者的志愿者),Aids vaccine(艾滋病疫苗),chemotherapy(化学疗法),chemoprevention(化学预防),mad cow disease(疯牛病),SBS(sick building syndrome,空调大楼综合征),RSI(repetitive strain injury,重复性劳损),ADD(attention deficit disorder,注意力缺乏症),SAD(seasonal affective depression,季节情感性抑郁症),PTSD(post-traumatic stress disorder,创伤后精神紧张症),recovered memory syndrome(恢复记忆综合征),recovery movement(康复运动),kinesiology(运动治疗术),keyhole surgery(微孔手术,亦作 mainimally invasive surgery),magnetic resonance imaging(核磁共振),genetic engineering(基因工程),emergicenter(应急医疗中心),community care(社区保健),skimmed(脱脂牛奶),aerobics(有氧运动),multigym(多功能健身器材)。

4. "说"意动词

新闻报道经常转述、援引新闻相关人物的谈话,因而频频出现"说"意动词。报刊上所出现的"说"意动词数量很多。这些词如果使用妥帖,会使语言更加准确、简洁、鲜明、生动。

(1) 准确

"We're not making any progress," concludes Dallas officer Nabors.

"I need my creative space behind closed doors," she explains.

(2) 简洁

"And mine, too!" hastened Little Lucas. (hasten:say in a hurry)

Addressing foreign journalists here, he emphasized the ANC would not revert to violence … (emphasize:say in an emphatic manner)

(3) (态度)鲜明

"We're tennis fanatics:We love it," cheers Christie Ann's aunt …

"One of the finest speeches I've ever heard," praised Ford speaking of the brief, touching text drafted by Reagan.

(4) 生动

"The next guy who hollers 'Headache!', I'm gonna kick his ass," sputters a winded James. (sputter:因激动、愤怒而唾沫飞溅地说)

Shrugged a Defense Department official:"The Soviets are the ones who walked out of the arms limitation talks." (shrug:耸了耸肩不满地说)

英语报刊中常见的"说"意动词主要有:

acknowledge 承认	add 补充说	admit 承认
affirm 肯定	agree 同意	allege 断言
announce 宣布	argue 争辩	assert 宣称
ask 询问	boast 夸口说	challenge 提出异议
complain 抱怨	contend 争辩	claim 声称
conclude 推断;下结论	declare 宣称	elaborate 详述
explain 解释	emphasize 强调	enquire/inquire 询问
imply 暗示	insist 坚持说;主张	maintain 主张;断言
note 表明;强调	object 反对	observe 评述
pledge 保证	promise 许愿	refute 反驳
remark 评论;议论	reply 回答	reveal 透露
retort 反诘	state 声称	stress 强调
suggest 建议	warn 警告说;告诫	urge 敦促;力劝

相对而言,纯新闻报道由于强调客观公正,含有情感意思的"说"意动词一般少用或不

用;而解释性报道、特写和"新新闻"(new journalism)类的新闻写作中较多地使用这类"说"意动词。

第四节 报刊英语的语法特征

英文报刊记者除了遵循新闻写作的 ABC 原则外,还必须尽可能地赶在截稿时间之前,借助各种行之有效的语法手段,在有限的版面内为读者展现清晰的新闻内容。因此,在长期的实践中,报刊英语形成了一些有别于普通英语的语法特征。

1. 省略句式

新闻报道为了节约篇幅,常常使用省略手段,即将句子中可以省略的语言成分略去。除了标题中的省略现象外,报刊英语行文过程中经常省略的语法成分包括以下五个方面。

(1) 省略可以省去的冠词

They were run over by trucks and killed under (the) order of the commander.

(2) 省略前置词

In the broader marker, the Nasdaq composite index fell (by) 27.49 points to 1773.25.

(3) 省略宾语从句的连接词

Butros-Ghali said (that) the rich nations were to blame for the rising of the Earth's temperature—the greenhouse effect, while the poor nations were to blame for destruction of the planet's resources.

(4) 省略介词 on

按照传统语法规则,星期、日期之前使用介词 on,但在英语报刊中却常常将其省略,这种现象(尤其是美国报刊)已经越来越普遍。

NABLUS, Israel-occupied West Bank—Backers of the Palestine Liberation Organization defeated Islamic fundamentalists (on) Friday in an election here.

(5) 使用省略句

He said (that) he intended to keep fighting if (he is) elected.

2. 嵌入结构

新闻报道为了在有限的篇幅内尽可能多地传递信息,采用多种手段浓缩精练句式,大量使用嵌入结构是其中的一种主要方式。插入语是嵌入结构中最为常见的形式。插入语的两侧既可用逗号,亦可用破折号标明。插入语可以代替一个句子,起到简化句子结构的作用。从文体效果来看,使用破折号标出的插入成分更具独立性,更明确地表明这个插入成分是独立于句子主线结构之外的,以此使整个句子主次分明、重点突出,更容易抓住读者的注意力。使用逗号标出的插入成分交代人物的身份、职业、年龄,组织机构的地点、性质,以及城市的位置、特点,是相对于主句的次要信息,一般在句子中作同位语。例如:

(1) Washington Hotel, part of Washington's exclusive and notorious Watergate Complex, has been sold to the investment bank Blackstone Group.

(2) The group of five Senators, led by Frank Church, Democrat of Idaho, the committee chairman, is on a six-day visit to China.

(3) Although children have been gambling for years, the fundamental principle of gambling—buying a chance to win more money—is indeed more prevalent in the lives of young people than it has ever been.

(4) New federal rules for truck drivers—the first major change since 1939—will require truckers to increase their rest time to 10 hours from eight in a 24-hour period.

3. 前置定语

在现代英语中,前置定语使用频率日趋增加。前置定语可以浓缩结构、节约篇幅,是精练句式的十分有效的手段,深得新闻写作人员的青睐。《美国新闻与世界报道》专栏作家约翰·利奥(John Leo)认为,前置定语是新闻语言的基本成分。前置定语具有多种构成形式,主要构成如下:

(1) 名词 + 名词

arms-reduction talks 裁军谈判　　supply-demand imbalance 供需失衡
labor-management conflict 劳资冲突　　north-south dialog 南北对话
hunger-strike sitdown 绝食静坐　　year-end report 年终报告

(2) 名词 + 形容词

water-proof materials 防水材料　　interest-free loan 无息贷款
inflation-proof deposit 保值储蓄　　earthquake-prone area 地震多发地区
war-weary soldiers 厌战的士兵　　capital-intensive country 资本密集型国家
vehicle-free promenade 步行街　　baby-friendly hospital 爱婴医院
hand-free phone 免提电话　　oil-poor country 贫油国

(3) 名词 + 现在分词或过去分词

peace-keeping force 维和部队　　ice-melting trip 融冰之旅
quality-oriented education 素质教育　　disaster-hit area 灾区
cancer-causing drug 致癌药物　　oil-producing country 产油国
policy-making body 决策机构　　energy-saving device 节能装置
export-oriented economy 外向型经济　　poverty-stricken area 贫困地区
state-owned enterprise 国有企业　　knowledge-based economy 知识经济

(4) 形容词 + 现在分词或过去分词

high-paying job 高薪工作　　　　　far-reaching significance 深远意义
high-ranking official 高级官员　　　long-standing issue 由来已久的问题
quick-frozen food 速冻食品　　　　foreign-owned enterprise 外资企业
deep-rooted social problems 根深蒂固的社会问题

(5) 形容词 + 名词

fair-trade agreement 互惠贸易协定　　top-level talk 最高级会谈
low-interest loan 低息贷款　　　　　long-range nuclear missile 远程核导弹
red-carpet welcome 隆重欢迎

(6) 数词 + 名词

100-metre dash 百米赛跑　　　　　one-way traffic 单向交通
two-day summit 为期两天的首脑会议　one-man government 独裁政府
21-gun salute 21 响礼炮

(7) 副词 + 过去分词

well-educated people 受过良好教育的人　richly-paid job 薪水丰厚的工作
well-informed source 消息灵通人士　　　newly-found coal mine 新发现的煤矿
dimly-lit room 光线昏暗的房间　　　　　sparsely-populated area 人口稀少的地区
hard-won result 来之不易的成果
highly-sophisticated technology 高尖端技术

(8) 介词短语作前置定语

on-the-job problem 工作时出的问题　　on-the-spot interview 现场采访
on-site service 现场服务　　　　　　under-the-counter dealing 台下交易

(9) 由 to 或 and 连接的前置定语

face-to-face talk 会晤；面谈　　　　　dusk-to-dawn curfew 彻夜宵禁
waste-to-energy power plant 垃圾发电厂　ground-to-air missile 地对空导弹
a down-to-earth guy 一个脚踏实地的人　hand-to-mouth pay 糊口工资
belly-to-back bus 拥挤不堪的公共汽车　off-and-on war 断断续续的战争
hit-and-run driver 肇事后逃跑的司机　　wait-and-see policy 坐守观望的政策
up-and-down relation 时好时坏的关系　　good-to-excellent care 无微不至的关怀
touch-and-go affairs 一触即发的局势
rags-to-riches businessman 白手起家的商人

4. "说"意句式

新闻报道为了提高所述内容的客观性，常常转述或援引提供消息或发表意见人士所说的话，因而表示"说"的句子往往多次出现。为了避免句式单调刻板，用笔娴熟的新闻写作人员总是注意变化句式,从而使语言生动活泼。英语报刊上所出现的"说"意句式可以归纳为以下六种。

(1) SVO(主语+谓语+宾语)

The court added, "If it is the will of the people in this country to amend the United States Constitution to protect our nation's symbol, it must be done through our normal political channels."

(2) VSO(谓语动词+主语+宾语)

Said the officer:"Saddam Hussien doesn't want to do much damage for fear of alienating Washington and other foreign powers."

(3) OVS(宾语+谓语动词+主语)

"Today marks the day when TV Guide is no longer just a magazine," says News America Publishing Group CEO Anthea Disney.

(4) OSV(宾语+主语+谓语动词)

"We think we are doing very well repairing and rebuilding our economy," he said.

(5) O1SVO2(宾语$_1$+主语+谓语动词+宾语$_2$)

"We were all concerned … about the breakdown of the family," Tipper Gore says. "We thought 'What can we do to be part of the solution? What can we do to start strengthening families?'"

(6) O1VSO2(宾语$_1$+谓语动词+主语+宾语$_2$)

"Our focus," says Guard Steve Kerr, one of the best three-point shooters in the NBA, "is to play it out and see what happens. That's what we can do."

5. 消息来源

英语新闻报道习惯于标明消息出处,不仅注明新闻事实的来源,而且对有关的言论、观点、意见等也都注明来历。以此说明记者没有掺进个人的观点或态度,所报道的内容是真实、客观、可信的。英语报道的新闻来源主要有三种。

(1) 具体确切的消息来源

这类消息来源常有名有姓地交代有关的机构、组织和个人。具体确切的消息来源,特别是某些重要人士、权威部门的话或观点,不仅可以提高新闻报道的可信度和权威性,而且可以引起读者的注意。例如:

The Organization of Islamic Conference (OIC) summit unanimously adopted a number of resolutions on the Palestine issue, <u>the Palestine Liberation Organization leader Yasser Arafat said on Tuesday evening.</u>

(2) 含蓄不露的消息来源

有时记者不直接透露消息的来源,而是含蓄地透露一点,即匿名或隐名消息来源。这样做的原因有两个:第一,保护不愿透露姓名或单位名称的新闻提供者;第二,消息提供者并非十分重要的人士,而他们所代表的机构或所披露的消息比他们的姓名更重要。间接暗示消息来源的词或词语主要有:

analyst 分析家
authority 权威人士
diplomatic sources 外交人士
document released by 由……发布的文件
expert 专家
Foreign Ministry spokesman 外交部发言人
highly-placed sources 高层消息灵通人士
judicial circles 司法界
neutral sources 中立人士
official sources 官方人士
reliable sources 消息可靠人士
spokesman 发言人
unconfirmed report 未经证实的消息
well-informed sources 消息灵通人士
witnesses 证人;目击者

authoritative sources 权威人士
commercial quarters 商界方面
government statement 政府的声明
educational circles 教育界
financial quarters 金融界方面
government official 政府官员
in-circle sources 圈内人士
military sources 军方人士
observer 观察家
police sources 警方人士
sources close to 接近……来源的人士
the quarters concerned 有关方面
unimpeachable sources 消息可靠人士
well-wired sources 重要消息灵通人士

(3) 似真非真的消息来源

记者有时出于严谨的报道态度,或由于消息来源本身尚不十分清楚等原因,撰稿时经常使用某些惯用短语来含糊、委婉地交代一下消息来源。这种写作手法一方面可以表示报道是公正、客观的;另一方面,万一消息不符合事实,记者可以以此搪塞或推卸责任。常见的这类短语主要有:

Foreign radios announced ... 据外电报道
According to an anonymous source ... 据一位不愿透露姓名的消息灵通人士说
According to a source who asked not to be identified ... 据一位不愿透露姓名的消息灵通人士说
Foreign wire services were quoted/cited as saying ... 援引外国通讯社的消息说
Foreign radios announced ... 据外电报道
It cannot be denied that ... 不可否认
It has been calculated that ... 据估计
It has been found that ... 已经发现
It has been proved ... 经证实
It is demonstrated that ... 据证实,经证实
It is alleged that ... 据称

It is announced that ... 据称

It is asserted that ... 有人主张

It is assumed that ... 有人假设

It is authoritatively learned that ... 自权威方面获悉

It is reported that ... 据报道

It is estimated that ... 据估计

It is expected that ... 人们希望，人们期待

It is declared that ... 据称

It is established that ... 可以认定

It is found that ... 人们认为

It is held that ... 有人认为

It is learned that ... 据悉

It is maintained that ... 有人主张

It is pointed out that ... 人们指出

It is proposed that ... 有人提出

It is understood that ... 据了解，大家知道

It is supposed that ... 人们猜测

It is usually considered that ... 人们通常认为

It may be argued that 也许有人会主张

It is believed that ... 人们相信

It is undeniable that ... 事实不容否认

It is well-known that ... 众所周知

Reports say that ... 据报道

本章参考文献

1. Mencher, Melvin. *News Reporting and Writing*. Beijing：Tsinghua University Press，2003.

2. Metz, William. *NewsWriting: From Lead to "30"*. New Jersey：Prentice-Hall, 1985.

3. Wynford, Hicks. *English for Journalists*. London：Routledge, 1998.

4. 张健. 报刊英语研究. 上海：上海外语教育出版社，2007.

5. 陈明瑶，卢彩虹. 新闻英语语体与翻译研究. 北京：国防工业出版社，2006.

Unit 1

Education

Part 1 Learning Before Class

- **Listening**

College Success: Making Use of Academic Supports

Directions: Listen to the news and answer the questions.

1. What is the difficulty that many students may not expect when they arrive at a college or university?
2. What do student assistants gain by helping others in areas where they might have experience?
3. What do college professors expect students to be able to write?
4. What is the first step for any struggling college student according to Lozada?

- **Watching and Thinking**

What Are the Most Educated Countries in the World?

Directions: Watch the video and discuss the questions with your partner.

1. Which countries are the most educated in the world today?
2. What has contributed to many psychological tolls on young people in South Korea (ROK)?
3. What made Israelis on average the oldest undergraduate graduates in the world?

4. What is the troubling trend that a growing number of young Canadians have to face?

• Reading and Discussing

Why China Can Give Every Child Equal Access to Education

June 1, 2019

CGTN[①]

Confucius, China's most renowned philosopher, believed that everyone should have equal access to education. One out of every five Chinese people in the world's most populous nation is a student. Since knowledge fuels a powerful nation, it is imperative to prioritize education.

To achieve this and cater to all educational needs, China, the largest developing country in the world, has set its sights on modernizing education and becoming a strong educational power by 2035.

The country's policy of compulsory education has produced a more knowledgeable populace, sustaining economic development in the past two decades.

It might be hard to believe that back in 1949, China's illiteracy rate stood at 80 percent. Even in the 1980s, this rate was higher than those of most countries. Today, this figure is lower than the global average thanks to the central government's emphasis on education.

The country has especially dedicated resources to expanding basic education in less-developed regions, while spending in the sector in those regions has grown each year. Now, the rate of those partaking in nine-year compulsory education in certain poor regions, such as Chuxiong Yi Autonomous Prefecture in Yunnan Province, has reached 96.38 percent.

Technology education was once the Achilles' heel of China's basic education system. Now, it is one of the most popular fields, with the country possessing the greatest number of science and engineering students. The country is also upgrading its teaching facilities as

---

① CGTN (China Global Television Network) is an international media organization launched by CCTV on December 31, 2016. It is now part of China's predominant radio and television broadcaster, China Media Group, which has incorporated CCTV, CNR and CRI since March, 2018.

As a multi-language and multi-platform media organization, CGTN operates in television and online. It also incorporates a video news agency CCTV +. Headquartered in Beijing, CGTN has an international team of professionals based around the world with production centers located in Nairobi, Washington D.C. and London.

CGTN's six TV channels—English, Spanish, French, Arabic, Russian and Documentary—are available in more than 170 countries and regions worldwide.

well as IT equipment for basic education.

Technology has become integral to schools lacking sufficient resources, narrowing the education gap between rural and urban areas as well as improving students' holistic performances.

As such, Chinese teachers and parents no longer solely look at a student's academic outcome. According to a survey organized by the Chinese Ministry of Education in 2019, nearly 87 percent of students received art education in primary and high schools, while 65 percent of students had participated in art clubs or other groups of interest.

The country has pivoted toward fostering the students' innovative thinking and practical abilities while boosting their holistic development in ethics, intelligence and sports.

In 2019, the Chinese government launched the "Modernization of China's Education: 2035" and set the goal of becoming an educational power by that year. Cultivating a large number of innovative talents is a major challenge facing the entire world. And China's basic education, too, has a long way to go.

Directions: *Read the passage and discuss the questions with your partner.*

1. What are China's educational goals by 2035?
2. What is the role of China's policy of compulsory education?
3. What has China done to narrow the education gap between rural and urban areas?
4. What has China's education focused on?

Part 2 Learning in Class

Warm Up

Why You Should Read Books: 15 Benefits of Reading More

Directions: *Watch the video and discuss the questions with your partner.*

1. What is the most obvious and important benefit of reading?
2. What is the third benefit that reading books can bring us?
3. Who tends to get promotions more quickly and more often?
4. Why reading can help us increase our lifespan?

Text A

University Experts Address Common Challenges

March 30, 2019
CGTN

Heavyweights from universities in the East and West addressed common missions and challenges for global higher education and shared experiences in making their colleges prestigious and even world-class on the sidelines of the just-concluded Boao Forum for Asia (BFA) annual conference in Boao in the southern Chinese province of Hainan.

While employment remains one of the major concerns among universities across the world, the development of students' cultural identities as well as value orientations are also a task not to be underestimated, according to the attending experts at the session "A Conversation with University Presidents: When East Meets West" held on Thursday.

A. What makes a world-class university?

A world-class university thinks in the long term, makes social contributions and has a global impact, Yang Bin, vice president and provost of Tsinghua University, said when asked to name three attributes of a world-leading university. Tsinghua University, one of China's most highly-regarded institutions, became the first university from the Chinese mainland to make it into the world top 20 colleges in 2018, as per the latest QS World University Rankings released in June last year.

Making contributions to the world as a whole is also among the many characters expected from a prestigious university, said Kim Yong-hak, president of Yonsei University in South Korea①, and Winston Soboyejo, provost of Worcester Polytechnic Institute, who called on top colleges to be actively engaged in offering solutions to global issues and inspiring innovation in various areas.

To become well recognized in the world, universities "have to produce knowledge that has social impact, produce social elites who can change the world, and get involved in social and global problems to solve them", Kim Yong-hak said.

Li Jiange, chancellor of Guangdong-Technion Israel Institute of Technology, also stressed the importance of having outstanding professors and advanced facilities to make a university world-class. "Established professors help set up first-class academic disciplines,"

---

① South Korea 规范名称是 Republic of Korea,尊重原文,下文不再作说明。

according to Li.

B. What are the differences between universities in the East and West?

The atmosphere in class, as well as learning approaches, differ at universities in the East and West, the guests pointed out at the session.

While Asian students are rather **taciturn** in class in line with their long-developed practice to learn through meditation and exercises, and respect professors as part of the campus discipline, those in Western universities are encouraged to interact and challenge their professors to develop critical and creative thinking, the education experts said.

The fundamental nature of universities is all about providing students with a "safe place to be silly", to express and challenge ideas, said Pilsbury, pointing at higher education in the UK. Universities are "communities where people learn to think by themselves", he added.

To have students participate more in the classroom, Kim Yong-hak suggested "dispatching the classroom into the community" to solve real-life problems so that students and professors could work collectively through communication while enhancing the community welfare.

Besides approaches to acquire knowledge, the difference between students from universities in the East and West also lies in their planning for life, according to Yang Bin. While students in Asia may prefer to pursue their degrees one after another at a stretch under cultural influence and peer pressure, their Western counterparts would take more time like a gap year to think what they truly long for before pursuing further studies.

C. What are the missions and challenges for today's higher education?

Despite the differences between Eastern and Western universities, higher education around the globe has faced shared challenges with employment of students after graduation remaining a major concern for the presidents.

According to Kim Yong-hak, booming artificial intelligence (AI) has put a large number of occupations at risk of being replaced and thus added to the uncertainties for graduates in the labor market.

A recent study by the UK government has warned that 1.5 million jobs in England are in danger of being automated based on an analysis of 20 million people in the region in 2017. Young people, along with women and part-time staff, are more likely to work in roles at higher risk of automation, the Office of National Statistics (ONS) report concluded. It is thus of great significance to make adjustments to the curricula so that students can meet the changing demands of job markets, vice chancellor of the University of Colombo Lakshman Dissanayak said, adding that the cultivation of entrepreneurship on campuses is also expected to help students become competitive in the workplace.

However, Peter Tufano, professorial fellow at Balliol College, University of Oxford, believes higher education is much more than just preparing students for jobs. "I worry a lot about humanity and social sciences," Tufano said. "We are not only teaching them as workers, but also voters, sisters, mothers and fathers."

Tufano, along with Eric Labaye, president of École Polytechnique, a major French institution of higher education and research in sciences and engineering, also sees promoting sustainable development and cross-school collaboration as an important mission for universities. Through introducing the concept of sustainable development into subjects and forging ahead in interdisciplinary cooperation, Labaye hopes universities could be able to provide sustainable solutions to global challenges.

The cultivation of students' local cultural identities is another tough task faced by universities around the world, especially in the era of globalization, Yang Bin reckoned. "There is still a lot of work for universities to do in fostering cultural identity of their students," he said.

 Words and Expressions

heavyweight	['hevɪweɪt]	n.	a person of exceptional importance and reputation 极具影响力的人
prestigious	[pre'stɪdʒəs]	a.	having a prominent reputation; respected 有声望的;受尊敬的
on the sideline			作为旁观者;不参与
cultural identity			the identity of a group or culture, or of an individual as far as one is influenced by one's belonging to a group or culture 文化身份;文化认同
orientation	[ˌɔːriən'teɪʃn]	n.	an integrated set of attitudes and beliefs 态度,取向
provost	['prɒvəst]	n.	a high-ranking university administrator 教务长;学院院长
attribute	[ə'trɪbjuːt]	n.	a construct whereby objects or individuals can be distinguished (人或物的)特征,特性
innovation	[ˌɪnə'veɪʃn]	n.	a creation (a new device or process) resulting from study and experimentation 创新;革新

elite	[eɪˈliːt]	n.	a group or class of persons enjoying superior intellectual or social or economic status 精英
chancellor	[ˈtʃɑːnsələ]	n.	the (honorary) head of a university 大学校长；大学名誉校长
established	[ɪˈstæblɪʃt]	a.	accepted in a particular state or position 资深的；获得认可的
discipline	[ˈdɪsɪplɪn]	n.	a branch of knowledge 学科
taciturn	[ˈtæsɪtɜːn]	a.	habitually reserved and uncommunicative 沉默寡言的
meditation	[ˌmedɪˈteɪʃn]	n.	continuous and profound contemplation 沉思，深思
interact	[ˌɪntərˈækt]	v.	have an effect on each other or something else by being or working close together 相互影响；相互配合
dispatch	[dɪˈspætʃ]	v.	send to a place or for a particular purpose 派遣；调遣
enhance	[ɪnˈhɑːns]	v.	increase; make better or more attractive 提高；增强
peer pressure			同辈压力；来自同龄人的压力
counterpart	[ˈkaʊntəpɑːt]	n.	a person or thing having the same function or characteristics as another 对应的人或物
gap year			a period of time in which people disengage from curricular education and undertake activities such as traveling, volunteering or working abroad 空档年，间隔年
automated	[ˈɔːtəˌmeɪtɪd]	a.	machine-controlled, machine-driven 自动化的；机械化的
curriculum	[kəˈrɪkjələm]	n.	an integrated course of academic studies 课程（复数形式 curricula）
cultivation	[ˌkʌltɪˈveɪʃn]	n.	socialization through training and education 培养
entrepreneurship	[ˌɒntrəprəˈnɜːʃɪp]	n.	企业家；企业家精神
humanity	[hjuːˈmænəti]	n.	a state of being human 人性；人道；人情
sustainable	[səˈsteɪnəb(ə)l]	a.	capable of being sustained 可持续的
collaboration	[kəˌlæbəˈreɪʃn]	n.	act of working jointly 合作；协同
forge ahead			继续进行；取得进展

interdisciplinary	[ˌɪntəˈdɪsɪplɪnəri]	a.	involving more than one academic subject 跨学科的
reckon	[ˈrekən]	v.	expect, believe, or suppose 料想；认为；估计
foster	[ˈfɒstə]	v.	promote the growth of 促进；鼓励

- **Multiple Choice**

Select the most appropriate answer for each of the following questions.

1. According to the attending experts at the session "A Conversation with University Presidents, all of the following should be the concerns of universities for the students EXCEPT _____."
   A) value orientations B) cultural identities
   C) shared experience   D) employment

2. Kim Yong-hak, president of Yonsei University in South Korea, holds that prestigious universities have to _____.
   A) make great contributions to their countries
   B) get involved in social and global problems to solve them
   C) inspire innovation in various areas
   D) be actively engaged in global issues

3. The underlined word "taciturn" in Section B is closest in meaning to "_____".
   A) reserved   B) communicative
   C) lonely   D) introverted

4. According to the passage, students in Western universities are encouraged to _____.
   A) solve all real-life problems by themselves
   B) learn through meditation and exercises
   C) respect professors as part of the campus discipline
   D) interact and challenge their professors to develop critical thinking

5. Asian students may prefer to pursue their degrees one after another owing to _____.
   A) their planning for life   B) cultural influence and peer pressure
   C) their missions and challenges D) their approaches to acquire knowledge

6. All of the following are the missions and challenges for today's higher education EXCEPT _____.

A) employment of students after graduation

B) students' qualities of humanity and social sciences

C) the cultivation of students' local cultural identities

D) reaching sustainable solutions to global issues

- **Matching**

Match the following opinions as referring to

A. Yang Bin (vice president and provost of Tsinghua University)

B. Kim Yong-hak (president of Yonsei University in South Korea)

C. Winston Soboyejo (provost of Worcester Polytechnic Institute)

D. Peter Tufano (professorial fellow at Balliol College, University of Oxford)

1. Top colleges should be actively engaged in offering solutions to global issues and inspiring innovation.

2. Universities have to produce knowledge that has social impact, and produce social elites who can change the world.

3. A world-leading university thinks in the long term, makes social contributions and has a global impact.

4. Booming artificial intelligence added to the uncertainties for graduates in the labor market.

5. Humanity and social sciences are also the concerns of higher education.

6. The difference between students from universities in the East and West also lies in their planning for life.

7. Promoting sustainable development and cross-school collaboration is also an important mission for universities.

8. The cultivation of students' local cultural identities is another tough task faced by universities.

- **Sentence Completion**

Complete the sentences below with words taken from Text A. Use NO MORE THAN THREE WORDS for each answer.

1. The development of students' cultural identities as well as _____ is also a task not to be underestimated.

2. Kim Yong-hak holds the view that making contributions to the world as a whole is also among the many characters expected from _____ .

3. Li Jiange also stressed the importance of having outstanding professors and _____ _____ to make a university world-class.

4. Asian students are rather taciturn in class in line with their long-developed practice to

learn through _____, and respect professors as part of the campus discipline.

5. According to the Office of National Statistics report, young people, along with women and part-time staff, are more likely to work in roles at higher _____.

6. Lakshman Dissanayak added that the _____ on campuses is also expected to help students become competitive in the workplace.

- **Writing**

University experts in the East and West addressed common missions and challenges for global higher education at the Boao Forum for Asia annual conference 2019. What are the common missions and challenges for global university students? Write a composition of no less than 300 words to state your opinions.

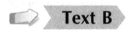 Text B

You Are What You Watch? The Social Effects of TV

By Jonathan Rothwell ①

July 25, 2019

The New York Times ②

A. Other than sleeping and working, Americans are more likely to watch television than engage in any other activity. A wave of new social science research shows that the quality of shows can influence us in important ways, shaping our thinking and political preferences, even affecting our cognitive ability.

B. In this so-called golden age of television, some critics have pointed out that the best of the form is equivalent to the most enriching novels. And high-quality programming for children can be educational. But the latest evidence also suggests there can be negative consequences to our abundant watching, particularly when the shows are mostly entertainment. The harm seems to come not so much from the content itself but from the fact that it replaces more enlightening ways of spending time.

---

① Jonathan Rothwell is the principal economist at Gallup, a nonresident senior fellow at the Brookings Institution and a visiting scholar at the George Washington University Institute of Public Policy. He is the author of a book, *A Republic of Equals: A Manifesto for a Just Society*, to be published by Princeton University Press in the fall, on the causes of income inequality.

② *The New York Times* is an American daily newspaper founded and continuously published in New York City since 1851. *The New York Times* has won 106 Pulitzer Prizes, the most of any news organization. Although the print version of the paper remains both the largest local metropolitan newspaper in the United States, as well the third largest newspaper overall, behind *The Wall Street Journal* and *USA Today*, its weekday circulation has fallen since 1990 to fewer than one million copies daily.

"*Sesame Street*"① as a social experiment

C. Cognitive ability is a complex characteristic that emerges from interactions between biological dispositions, nutrition and health, parenting behaviors, formal and informal educational opportunities, and culture. Studying the connection between intelligence and television consumption is far from straightforward, but researchers have developed compelling ways to isolate the effects of television.

D. Some of the best research has been done on the television program *Sesame Street*. The show, which began in 1969, was meant to develop early literacy, numeracy and emotional skills for children of preschool age. A detailed analysis of the show's content in its first and second years reveals that 80 percent of the program was dedicated to those goals, with the rest meant to entertain.

E. Researchers randomly assigned groups of low-income children aged 3 to 5 into an experimental group and a control group. In the experimental group, parents were given access to the show if they lacked it and encouraged in person once a month to have their children watch the show. Almost all (93 percent) parents of children in the experimental group reported that their children subsequently watched the show, compared with roughly one-third (35 percent) of children in the control group. Among watchers, those in the experimental group also watched more frequently.

F. Over six months, from November 1970 to May 1971, the experimental group gained 5.4 IQ points—a large effect—relative to the control group and showed stronger evidence of learning along several other dimensions. Gains in cognitive performance were especially large for those who viewed the show frequently relative to those who did so rarely or never. A more recent meta-analysis of published research in 15 countries shows that *Sesame Street* has similar effects around the world.

G. In newly published research, the economists Melissa Kearney and Phillip Levine examined longer-term effects of *Sesame Street* by comparing the educational outcomes of children and young adults in counties more or less likely to have access to the program during its early years. They found that children living in counties with better *Sesame Street*

---

① *Sesame Street* is an educational television program designed for preschoolers, recognized as a pioneer of the contemporary standard which combines education and entertainment in children's television. It is one of the longest-running shows in television history, and in 2019, the series celebrated its 50th anniversary. The series has now produced over 4,500 episodes. In its long history, *Sesame Street* has captured the esteem and affections of millions of viewers worldwide.

Sesame Street uses a combination of puppets, animation, and live actors to teach young children the fundamentals of reading and arithmetic, as well as geometric forms, cognitive processes, and classification. There is also a subtle sense of humor on the show that has appealed to older viewers, and was devised as a means to encourage parents and older siblings to watch the series with younger children, and thus become more involved in the learning process rather than letting *Sesame Street* act as a babysitter.

coverage were less likely to be held behind a grade level.

H. Other experimental research is consistent with the original *Sesame Street* findings. Low-income prekindergarten children scored higher on a social competence index six months after being randomly assigned to an experimental group, in which their parents were encouraged to replace age-inappropriate television with educational television.

Less reading and more watching

I. In Norway, and a handful of other developed countries, average IQ scores have declined slightly in recent years, after rising for many decades. This is known as the negative Flynn effect, a variation of the more famous Flynn effect, which is named after the psychologist who first published comprehensive evidence of IQ gains over time. Among native Norwegian men taking an exam at age 18 for military conscription, those born in 1974 scored two IQ points higher than those born in 1987.

J. In an academic article published this year, the Norwegian economist Oystein Hernaes and his co-authors attributed some of this decline in IQ scores to access to cable television, which also coincided with a sharp decline in reading. After the introduction of cable in 1981, Norwegian teenagers and young adults drastically cut back on daily time spent reading from 1980 to 2000, and increased their time watching TV. Moreover, relative to public television, cable television had far less educational content and was focused on entertainment and advertisements.

K. To estimate the effect of cable television on IQ scores, the Norwegian scholars analyzed data on the introduction of cable network infrastructure by municipality. They calculated years of exposure to cable by considering the age of eventual test takers when cable became available in their municipality. They controlled for any potential geographic bias by comparing siblings with greater or less exposure to cable television based on their age when cable infrastructure was put in. They estimate that 10 years of exposure to cable television lowered IQ scores by 1.8 points. In related research, Mr. Hernaes finds that exposure to cable television reduced voter turnout in local elections.

Berlusconi television

L. A similar study was conducted by the Italian economist Ruben Durante and his co-authors and released in this month's issue of the American Economic Review. They examined the introduction of Silvio Berlusconi's television network, Mediaset, which specialized in light entertainment such as game shows featuring scantily clad women.

M. The economists document that Mediaset devoted almost no programming to educational content and did not offer news in early years, whereas its main competitor— the state-owned channel—devoted the majority of its airtime to news or educational material.

N. To study the effects of Mediaset, Mr. Durante and his co-authors obtained data on the location of Mediaset transmitters in 1985 and calculated the strength of the broadcasting signal in every Italian municipality based on the position of the transmitters and other technical features of the municipality. They found that children raised in areas with greater access to Mediaset (a standard deviation in signal strength) had lower cognitive scores as adults by the equivalent of 3 to 4 IQ points. People more exposed to Mediaset as children were also less likely to be civically engaged adults and more likely to vote for parties with populist tendencies like Forza Italia and the Five Star Movement.

O. A handful of American studies along these lines have focused on the political consequences that news media coverage can have, showing that exposure to Fox News could increase Republican Party vote shares significantly, and that exposure to MSNBC increased Democratic Party voting share (but with a much weaker effect).

Art and public health

P. We know that education increases cognitive ability, so it stands to reason that educational television would also have a positive effect.

Q. Concerns about culture are hardly novel: Plato made a case for regulating the quality of artistic productions to avoid the corruption of youth and weakening of their character. Twenty-three centuries later, it is easier than ever to placate children as well as lose yourself in entertainment options—in the ocean of online videos, podcasts, cable, and streaming shows and movies.

R. These options are most likely harmless. Some provide relaxation, and others may modestly reshape cultural attitudes for the better; one study found that the introduction of cable TV empowered women in India. High-quality shows and films can be inspiring, even edifying.

S. Still, media providers and advertisers compete aggressively for our attention. Most lack the altruistic motivations that guided the producers of the original *Sesame Street*. The evidence from social science suggests that biased or sensationalist news programs may misinform citizens or discourage civic engagement, and that we should also be cautious about what we give up for the sake of entertainment.

Words and Expressions

cognitive	[ˈkɒgnətɪv]	a.	relating to the mental process involved in knowing, learning, and understanding things 认知的
consequence	[ˈkɒnsɪkwəns]	n.	the outcome of an event especially as relative to an individual 结果；后果；影响
enlightening	[ɪnˈlaɪtnɪŋ]	a.	tending to give someone more knowledge and greater understanding about something 使人领悟的；有启发作用的
disposition	[ˌdɪspəˈzɪʃn]	n.	temperament; inclination 性情；习性
compelling	[kəmˈpelɪŋ]	a.	tending to persuade by forcefulness of argument 令人信服的
literacy	[ˈlɪtərəsi]	n.	the ability to read and write 读写能力
numeracy	[ˈnjuːmərəsi]	n.	the ability to do arithmetic 计算能力
dedicated to			be committed to 专心致志于；致力于
randomly	[ˈrændəmli]	adv.	in a random manner 任意地；随机地
subsequently	[ˈsʌbsɪkwəntli]	adv.	afterwards 随后；后来
roughly	[ˈrʌfli]	adv.	(of quantities) imprecisely but fairly close to correct 粗略地；大概地
meta-analysis		n.	methods focused on contrasting and combining results from different studies, in the hope of identifying patterns among study results, sources of disagreement among those results, or other interesting relationships that may come to light in the context of multiple studies 元分析
index	[ˈɪndeks]	n.	a system by which changes in the value of something and the rate at which it changes can be recorded, measured, or interpreted 指标；指数
conscription	[kənˈskrɪpʃn]	n.	compulsory military service 征兵；征召入伍
attribute (to)	[əˈtrɪbjuːt]	v.	把……归因于
drastically	[ˈdræstɪkəli]	adv.	in a drastic manner 大幅度地；彻底地

Unit 1 Education

infrastructure	[ˈɪnfrəstrʌktʃə]	n.	the stock of basic facilities and capital equipment needed for the functioning of a country or area 基础设施
municipality	[mjuːˌnɪsɪˈpæləti]	n.	an urban district having corporate status and powers of self-government 市政当局
exposure	[ɪkˈspəʊʒə]	n.	the state of being in a place or situation where there is no protection from sth. harmful or unpleasant 面临, 遭受(危险或不快)
bias	[ˈbaɪəs]	n.	an opinion or feeling that strongly favors one side in an argument or one item in a group or series 偏见, 偏袒
turnout	[ˈtɜːnaʊt]	n.	the number of people who actually vote at an election 投票人数
feature	[ˈfiːtʃə]	v.	be a feature of; make sb./sth. a feature 以……为特色; 突出
		n.	special component 特殊部件; 附加部件
scantily clad			inadequately clothed 衣着暴露的
document	[ˈdɒkjumənt]	v.	record; prove with document 记载; (用文件等)证明
transmitter	[trænsˈmɪtə(r)]	n.	a set used to broadcast radio or television signals 发射机; 发射台
civic	[ˈsɪvɪk]	a.	of a city or its citizens 城市的; 市民的; 公民的
civically	[ˈsɪvɪkli]	adv.	从城市的角度; 从市民的角度; 从公民的角度
populist	[ˈpɒpjəlɪst]	a.	claiming to care about the interests and opinions of ordinary people rather than those of a small group 平民化的; 平民主义的; 民粹主义的
coverage	[ˈkʌvərɪdʒ]	n.	the news as presented by reporters for newspapers or radio or television 新闻报道
corruption	[kəˈrʌpʃn]	n.	impairment of virtue and moral principles 堕落
placate	[pləˈkeɪt]	v.	cause to stop feeling angry; appease 抚慰; 安抚
podcast	[pɒdˈkʌst]	n.	an audio file similar to a radio broadcast, which can be downloaded and listened to on a computer or iPod 播客

streaming	[ˈstriːmɪŋ]	n.	a method of transmitting data from the Internet directly to a user's computer screen without the need to download it 流播
empower	[ɪmˈpaʊə]	v.	make strong 使强大；使有掌控力
edifying	[ˈedɪfaɪɪŋ]	a.	enlightening or uplifting so as to encourage intellectual or moral improvement 启迪心智的；起教化作用的
aggressively	[əˈgresɪvli]	adv.	forcefully 积极地；有干劲地
altruistic	[ˌæltruˈɪstɪk]	a.	showing unselfish concern for the welfare of others 利他的；无私心的

- **True/False/Not Given**

Do the following statements agree with the information given in Text B?

In Blanks 1-10 write

True   if the statement is true

False   if the statement is false

Not Given   if the information is not given in Text B

_____ 1. New evidence indicates that the quality of shows can entirely change our thinking, political preferences, and our cognitive ability.

_____ 2. High-quality programming for children can be instructive.

_____ 3. The content of entertainment programmes definitively results in the negative consequences to our cognitive ability.

_____ 4. *Sesame Street* was meant to develop early literacy, numeracy and emotional skills for preschool children without any entertainment included in.

_____ 5. Researchers selectively assigned groups of low-income children aged 3 to 5 into an experimental group and a control group.

_____ 6. Melissa Kearney and Phillip Levine found that children living in counties with better *Sesame Street* coverage were less probably to be held behind a grade level.

_____ 7. Average IQ scores have declined slightly in recent years in Norway and a number of other developed countries.

_____ 8. Compared with public television, cable television had far less educational content and was focused on entertainment and advertisements.

_____ 9. Mediaset specialized in light entertainment and devoted almost no programming to educational content.

_____ 10. People more exposed to Mediaset as children were less likely to vote for parties with populist tendencies like Forza Italia and the Five Star Movement.

- **Matching**

Which paragraph contains the following information?

1. The latest evidence suggests there can be negative consequences to our abundant watching, particularly when the shows are mostly entertainment.
2. Studying the connection between intelligence and television consumption is far from straightforward.
3. Gains in cognitive performance were especially large for those who viewed the show frequently relative to those who did so rarely or never.
4. Flynn effect is named after the psychologist who first published comprehensive evidence of IQ gains over time.
5. Norwegian teenagers and young adults drastically cut back on daily time spent reading from 1980 to 2000.
6. Mr. Hernaes finds that exposure to cable television reduced voter turnout in local elections.
7. Entertainment options are most likely harmless, but high-quality shows and films can be inspiring, even edifying.
8. The evidence from social science suggests that biased or sensationalist news programs may misinform citizens or discourage civic engagement.

- **Short Answer Questions**

1. What can the quality of shows influence us according to the new social research?
2. How does cognitive ability emerge?
3. What does the recent meta-analysis of published research in 15 countries show?
4. What did Oystein Hernaes and his co-authors attribute some of the decline in IQ scores to? V
5. How did the Norwegian scholars control for any potential geographic bias?

- **Writing**

Producers of television programmes should realize that they have a responsibility to educate the public, not just entertain it. Write a composition of no less than 300 words commenting on this opinion.

Academic Reading

Understanding Vocabulary (1)

Learning Objective

In the section, you will learn to use context clues to uncover word meanings.

A large vocabulary is an asset to you as a student and an employee and for your personal life. The more words you know, the more you will understand what you read and hear and then can apply to your speaking and writing. Thus, a greater range of topics will be of interest to you, and you can also project a more interesting background.

In addition to using dictionary, this section explores different ways of finding the meanings of unfamiliar words.

Using Context Clues

The context refers to the surrounding words in a sentence that give a word its specific meaning. Many words have multiple meanings, and you can determine which meaning applies by the way those words are used in a sentence. Thus, you can often use the context to help you figure out the meanings of unfamiliar words without consulting a dictionary.

Various aspects of the context can be used individually or in combination to reveal word meanings, including punctuation, synonyms, antonyms, examples, and general sentence clues.

(1) Punctuation

After introducing a word or term, writers sometimes provide its meaning and set it off through the use of punctuation marks, making the definition easy for readers to recognize. For example, a definition can be introduced with a colon:

> Pedro's general condition deteriorated after the physician discovered that he was suffering from **edema**: the accumulation of fluid in various organs of the body.

edema = the accumulation of fluid in various organs of the body

The meaning of a word can be set off between commas (or by just one comma if the definition falls at the end of a sentence):

> Lovelock's theory is intricately tied to **cybernetics**, the study and analysis of how information flows in electronic, mechanical, and biological systems.

cybernetics = the study and analysis of how information flows in electronic, mechanical, and biological systems

For greater emphasis, dashes can be used instead of commas:

> Regulation increased substantially during the 1970s. By the end of that decade, numerous proposals for **deregulation**—the removal of old regulations—had been made.

deregulation = the removal of old regulations

Definitions can also be enclosed in parentheses:

> Music consists of three basic elements: **pitch** (melody); **rhythm** (sounds grouped according to a prescribed system); and **timbre** (the qualities of a tone that make a C-sharp sound different, say, on a tuba than on a guitar). From these building blocks, human beings have created rock and roll, rap, sonatas, blues, folk songs, chants, symphonies, jazz, opera ... the variations are endless. Where there are human beings, there is music.

pitch = melody

rhythm = sounds grouped according to a prescribed system

timbre = the qualities of a tone that make a C-sharp sound different, say, on a tuba than on a guitar

The definition of a term in a foreign language is usually placed in quotation marks:

> The **Ceteris Paribus** Assumption: *All Other Things Being Equal*. Everything in the world seems to relate in some way to everything else in the world. It would be impossible to isolate the effects of changes in one variable on another variable if we always had to worry about many other variables that might also enter the analysis. As in other sciences, economics uses the ceteris paribus assumption. **Ceteris paribus** means "other things constant" or "other things equal".

ceteris paribus = "other things constant" or "other things equal"

(2) **Synonyms**

Writers sometimes use synonyms, or words that mean the same or almost the same, to provide you with the meanings of unfamiliar words, as in the following sentence:

> First, **psychotropic** or **mood-altering** drugs became increasingly popular among health practitioners, made patients easier to handle and increased their chances of being released.

Psychotropic and **mood-altering** are synonyms. Therefore, psychotropic drugs are drugs that alter or change our mood.

(3) **Antonyms**

Writers may use antonyms, or words that mean the opposite, to help you figure out the meanings of unfamiliar words, as in the following sentence:

> **Whereas** Princess Diana was rather **tall**, Mother Teresa was **diminutive**.

Whereas indicates that a contrast is being drawn between Princess Diana and Mother Teresa. **Tall** and **diminutive** must be antonyms; therefore, diminutive means "short" or "small".

(4) Examples

Sometimes writers use familiar examples that may be helpful in determining word meanings, as in the following sentence:

> The United States, Canada, Britain, and France are all examples of **autonomous** nations, because they are not controlled by any other governments.

If you have knowledge about some or all of these countries and are aware of what they have in common, perhaps you can figure out that **autonomous** means "independent" or "self-governing".

(5) **General Sentence Clues**

You may be able to figure out the meaning of an unfamiliar word by studying the general sense of the sentence and focusing on the key words used in it, as in the following example:

> The **driver's eyes** were **bloodshot** and his **speech** was **slurred**; the police officer quickly concluded that he was **inebriated**.

The sense of the sentence—with the use of the key words **driver**, **bloodshot** with reference to **eyes**, **slurred** with reference to **speech**, and **the police officer**—is that this is a scene involving a drunken driver and hence that **inebriated** must mean "intoxicated" or "drunk".

Directions: *Using the context, try to determine the meanings of the words that appear under the sentences.*

1. Judy does not talk very much at the staff meetings, but James is quite **loquacious**.
   loquacious: _____

2. For years, cigarette manufacturers denied that cigarette smoke was **carcinogenic** even though millions of smokers were dying from lung cancer.
   carcinogenic: _____

3. Although the movie character James Bond is always involved in "**clandestine**" or "secret" activities, some intelligence work today is actually accomplished out in the

Unit 1 Education

   open.

   clandestine: _____

4. With podcasting, consumers can download audio files (**podcasts**) or video files (**vodcasts**) via the Internet to an iPod or other handheld device and then listen to or view them whenever and wherever they wish.

   podcasts: _____

   vodcasts: _____

5. The electoral system affects policy-making because legislators worried about winning reelection focus their energy on **pork barrel spending**, which are expenditures to fund local projects that are not critically important from a national perspective.

   pork barrel spending: _____

6. Within every culture, there is an overall sense of what is beautiful and what is not beautiful, what represents good taste as opposed to tastelessness or even obscenity, and so on. Such considerations are matters of **aesthetics.**

   aesthetics: _____

7. You'll need to know **fallacies**—errors in argument—as both a reader (to spot them) and a writer (to avoid them). The many common fallacies fall into two groups. Some evade the issue of the argument. Others treat the argument as if it were much simpler than it is.

   fallacies: _____

8. Both the baby boomers and Gen Xers will one day be passing the reins to the **Millennials** (also called Generation Y or echo boomers). Born between 1977 and 2000, these children of the baby boomers number 83 million, dwarfing the Gen Xers and larger even than the baby boomer segment.

   Millennials: _____

Part 3　Learning After Class

Additional Reading 1

China's Education Reform: Study Hard, for What

By Dean Yang
March 16, 2018
CGTN

Chinese school students are among the most under pressure in the world, toiling for hours every day to develop their talents.

On average, Chinese children spent 8.1 hours at primary school on weekdays and 11 hours a day in high school, according to a 2015 study by China Youth and Children Research Center (CYCRC). Schoolwork also bites into their home time. A 2017 survey by Afanti, an education firm, found that homework took up nearly three hours a day for Chinese school students, 3.7 times more than for their Japanese counterparts and 4.8 times that of South Korean kids. In addition to weekday work, extra curricular activities on weekends took up another 2.1 hours of supposed leisure time, the CYCRC study reported. All these rates are among the highest in the world.

On the back of the mounting pressure is the toll on young people's health. From 2002 to 2012, the obesity rate among Chinese aged 6 to 17 increased by 4.7 percentage points, according to a report by China's public health authority. Half of all students aged 7 to 15 were near-sighted in 2014.

The system, and those within it, from students to parents, educators to officials, is crying out for reform to ease the burden. During this year's two sessions, China's ongoing top legislative event, the issue of reducing workload for school children has been raised yet again, but a comprehensive solution probably remains out of sight.

In the context of China's economic success, the education system should have served the country well. It has always had a clear objective to fill in relation to the national development, from the early days of the founding of the People's Republic of China (PRC) to the market open-up in the 1980s. This has painted Chinese education in a somewhat "utilitarian" light. As the country shifts the focus of growth from accumulation of state wealth to improved individual well-being, it seems only natural that education of the old pragmatic philosophy is struggling to keep up.

Why study hard?

At the dawn of the PRC, the country's economy was in ruins after years of devastating war. The then Soviet Union's education system provided a template that featured mobilization of national resources to increase manpower in the economic sectors key to growth. In this manner, the Chinese government started to reshape its education infrastructure, giving universities and schools an assisting role during the young republic's laborious reconstruction.

The relationship between education and the country's development has been stressed in the following decades. But the purposes that education needed to serve have been adjusted in line with different developmental stages.

For the decades after China began opening-up, the thought that technology was crucial to development began to resonate increasingly on the one hand, the influence of an ever-freer market started growing on the other. Together with the impact of the still dominant state-owned players in the economy, the concepts, though not necessarily in conflict with each other, created different interpretations of the "meaning" of education among the general public.

Following years of economic deprivation before the reform, desires for consumer goods exploded. Businesses burgeoned as the market liberalized. With profit-driven salaries they soon became a magnet for people who feared falling back into poverty. Yet labor-intensity and low added value remained a hallmark for manufacturers, private- and state-owned alike, for many years to come. Commercial ambition was prioritized over a college degree. A belief in getting rich fast appealed to many. Four years in university seemed an unnecessary luxury cost, despite the government's effort to enhance the status of education. "Reading is useless" became a battle cry for the new money as China's economic boom accelerated, cementing education's utilitarian role by negating its non-commercial benefits.

Meanwhile, the sway of state-owned enterprises was felt in the market as well as in ordinary people's lives. Graduating from high school to become a trained worker in a state-owned factory remained a popular choice for many. A state-backed company appeared to offer security—people believed they would never be laid off, but the tuition fee for a college degree might not pay off.

Entering the 1990s, the danger of inflation loomed ever larger as a result of years of double-digit growth, incurring government interference to cool down the overheating economy that had a toll on employment. At the same time, the deepening state-owned enterprise reforms saw millions lose their jobs. Still along the utilitarian line though, the importance of education in relation to job security began to sink in. This was when a timely policy to increase university enrolment was introduced in 1999 that served a purpose, among others, of restructuring the country's labor market.

The next year saw 2.2 million candidates succeed in securing higher education positions. The number had grown more than threefold in 2016 to 7.7 million. The number of higher education institutions more than doubled between 2000 and 2016, from 1,041 to 2,596, according to China's National Bureau of Statistics.

Many have benefited from the expanded investment in education; however, the utilitarian view has changed little. Panic has arisen again for parents and students who view going to university as nothing more than a path to a secure career of financial stability, particularly those from deprived backgrounds that would bet the family fortune on such a future for their children. More aggressive competitions have scaled up for better resources out of the following logic: a seat at a top university requires quality education in a top-rated high school, which in turn is contingent on better teachers and working environment of an elite junior high, if not on a reputable primary school.

The pressure has prompted parents to push children to the limit to add even one more point to the final grading in the entrance examinations of any level. This eagerness has contributed to the national boom in extracurricular businesses that promise to enhance students' performances at exams, or to train them in an art or sport. Rather than discovering young talents and encouraging them to develop, these firms merely offer embellished applications. These activities increase not only the workloads for young students, but also financial pressure on the parents.

The market for off-school curriculums was valued at 300 billion *yuan* (around 47 billion US dollars at today's rate) in 2005. Ten years later, the total valuation had reached 800 billion *yuan*, according to official calculations. Research by Peking University estimated that nearly 48 percent of all Chinese school students had taken part in such courses in 2017.

Many experts and education practitioners have already pointed at the assessment system to be the fundamental cause of the problem: if students go to school for nothing but increasing their grades in the entrance exams, that will alone determine their future.

"To study hard so that you can get a good job and make more money has become what many Chinese parents expect of their children, and this has caused the students' backpacks to be heavier and heavier," said You Lizeng, a high school teacher who is also a lawmaker of China's National People's Congress.

Hu Wei, a member of the Chinese People's Political Consultative Conference, the country's top political advisory body, suggested that more efforts should be put into making the assessment more inclusive, so that the students can be confident about finding their own ways of succeeding.

China's central government has pledged to continue reducing burdens for school students in 2018, according to the government work report that was released on March 5. More important still is the report's wording of the passage on the task of reforming China's education system, promising a holistic approach in the future: "We need to ensure that every individual has an equal opportunity to change their life and realize their dreams through education."

Words and Expressions

toll	[təʊl]	n.	the cost in health or life of an illness, an accident, etc. 损失, 代价
legislative	[ˈledʒɪslətɪv]	a.	involving or relating to the process of making and passing laws 立法的; 有立法权的
utilitarian	[ˌjuːtɪlɪˈteərɪən]	a.	made to be useful rather than decorative; believing in utilitarianism 实用的, 功利的, 实用主义的, 功利主义的
pragmatic	[præɡˈmætɪk]	a.	concerned with practical matters 实际的; 实用主义的
template	[ˈtempleɪt]	n.	a model or standard for making comparisons 模板, 样板
mobilization	[ˌməʊbəlaɪˈzeɪʃn]	n.	an act of assembling and putting into readiness for war or other emergency 动员; 调动
resonate	[ˈrezəneɪt]	v.	be received or understood 产生共鸣
deprivation	[ˌdeprɪˈveɪʃn]	n.	a state of extreme poverty 贫困
burgeon	[ˈbɜːdʒən]	v.	grow or develop rapidly 迅速增长; 迅速发展
hallmark	[ˈhɔːlmɑːk]	n.	a distinctive characteristic 标志; 特征
prioritize	[praɪˈɒrətaɪz]	v.	assign a priority to 优先考虑
cement	[sɪˈment]	v.	strengthen; unite firmly 巩固; 加强

loom	[luːm]	v.	come into sight without a clear form, especially so as to seem very large and threatening 隐约出现；迫近
contingent (on)	[kən'tɪndʒənt]	a.	dependent on something uncertain or in the future 因情况而变的；视条件而定的
embellished	[ɪm'belɪʃt]	a.	excessively elaborate or showily expressed 装饰的；美化的

 Discussion Questions

1. Extracurricular firms do not focus on discovering young talents and encouraging them to develop. However, research by Peking University estimated that nearly 48 percent of all Chinese school students had taken part in off-school courses in 2017. What factors have caused the national boom in extracurricular business?

2. For quite a long time in China, studying hard to get a good job and make more money has become the only expectation of many parents and students. However, flexible and adaptable minds, rigorous critical thinking, transferable skills, development of character, citizenship and culture are also important. What are the aims and ends of education besides its utilitarian function?

 Additional Reading 2

Online Preschool Is Winning More Support, But Is That a Good Thing?

By Sarah Lindenfeld Hall
July 9, 2019
Mashable ①

At the Shaw University's child development center in Raleigh, N.C., a four-year-old boy sat with his preschool teacher one morning, looking at laminated cards featuring pictures of basketball hoops with numbers written on them.

"This is what number?" asked the teacher. "Eleven," said the young boy, who got a quick cheer from his teacher before he counted out and arranged 11 orange pom-poms

---

① Mashable is a global, multi-platform media and entertainment company. Powered by its own proprietary technology, Mashable is the go-to source for tech, digital culture and entertainment content for its dedicated and influential audience around the globe.

just below the hoop.

For the Ebanks family in Utah, preschool looks a little different. At 11 a.m. on weekdays, the boys, a preschooler and a rising kindergartner, log into the computer in their playroom to run through 15 minutes of reading, math and science skills via Upstart, a state-funded academic program. They'll also spend an hour with their dad, who stays at home, to work on other skills.

"What we saw in that first week is that Upstart really helped us create a structure around my kids' learning," said mom Najwa Ebanks, who gave up her older son's preschool spot a week after using Upstart.

It's a study in contrasts, but with a similar goal—to prepare kids for kindergarten. It's Utah-based nonprofit Waterford.org and its Upstart program that, in particular, are drawing criticism from early childhood development advocates and others as it secures government funding and high-profile philanthropic support.

Just as the World Health Organization recommends limited screen time for kids under 5, some experts say that these virtual programs are the last thing young kids need. Instead, they say, the focus should be on ensuring that all kids have access to a quality, play-based education at brick-and-mortar preschools. Online programs also can't replace preschools' roles as childcare facilities, enabling parents to work while their kids are in a safe and enriching environment.

Andy Myers, Waterford.org's chief operating officer, doesn't disagree that kids need access to topnotch preschools. But, he said, he's focused on serving today's four-year-olds right now, and there isn't the funding to ensure every child has a seat.

Preschool in America: "Uneven and very poor"

Studies consistently show the benefits of preschool for all young children, but especially those from low-income families as they enter kindergarten and move along in their academic studies and lives.

The HighScope Perry Preschool Project, for example, found that preschool students who were at risk for doing poorly in school were more likely to graduate from high school, and were more likely to have a job with higher earnings than their peers who didn't attend preschool.

But many of those children don't have access to affordable preschool. The National Institute for Early Education Research's State of Preschool 2018 annual report found that one-third of four-year-olds and 5.5% of three-year-olds are enrolled in public preschool programs. And funding, it said, is not keeping up with demand.

"Availability is very uneven and very poor overall in the United States," said Nancy

Carlsson-Paige, an early childhood expert, co-founder of Defending the Early Years and professor emerita at Lesley University.

Not just about the computer screen

The lack of affordable preschool was the problem Utah leaders challenged Waterford.org to solve after a report identified Utah as one of a handful of states without state-funded preschool. Waterford.org, which already was providing academic software and teacher training at schools across the country, developed Upstart.

Launched in Utah in 2009, Upstart is now expanding across the country thanks to private donations and a growing amount of local, state and federal funding, including a $14.2 million, five-year infusion from the US Department of Education in 2018 to start pilot programs in Wyoming, North Dakota, South Dakota, Idaho and Montana. North Carolina is among the latest states to consider funding for Upstart.

In 2019, TED also added Upstart to its Audacious Project, a philanthropic effort that could funnel another $20 million to the program over the next five years and help the nonprofit work toward its goal of launching pilot projects in all 50 states. By next fall, Waterford expects to have 19,500 children in Utah signed up for the free program. It also has received state funding in Indiana and South Carolina and launched Upstart pilot programs in more than a dozen other states.

The term "online preschool", says Kim Fischer, Waterford.org's public relations manager, conjures up visions of kids sitting in front of a computer for hours with no engagement. "That is just not us," she said.

As part of the program, parents are regularly sent information about their child's strengths and tips to help them shore up any weaknesses. They also have access to printable activity sheets and, soon, a workbook.

To help low-income families, Waterford.org supplies computers and Internet access to families without. Right now, it provides nearly 58 percent of its users in Mississippi with Internet access.

Myers said Waterford.org wants to complement, not compete, with traditional preschools. It particularly focuses on rural and low-income urban areas where there can be little access to affordable preschools or the transportation necessary to get to them. The goal, he said, is to provide academic enrichment for children who spend their days at home or in a childcare setting where caregivers or teachers aren't equipped to prepare them for kindergarten.

And, Myers points out, that the program has delivered results. According to a Utah analysis, the program had a "strong impact on children's emerging literacy skills", and that students who used the program as recommended had better reading outcomes than peers who did not.

Traditional preschools can't compete

But for early childhood advocates, the growth in programs like Upstart is startling.

In April, the Campaign for a Commercial-Free Childhood, along with Defending the Early Years, called on the Audacious Project to postpone its plans to include Upstart in its 2019 funding program. The groups warned that expanding funding for the much cheaper online preschool programs could thwart efforts to pay for universal preschool and only widen the gap between kids whose parents can afford quality preschool and those who can't.

At the same time, Carlsson-Paige said growth of these online programs only perpetuates a fundamental misunderstanding of how kids need to learn. To understand what the number four means, she said, they can't just memorize what the numeral looks like on a computer screen. To truly grasp the concept of four, kids must spend time playing with four blocks or four beads or four balls.

"These programs are teaching kids conventional spelling from the get-go and they're teaching them conventional math from the get-go, so the developmental process of understanding the print system or the numeracy system is lost," Carlsson-Paige said.

What's more, online-only programs without the benefit of face-to-face time with trained teachers could isolate young children who might need extra support for learning, speech or motor skills delays.

"That's an important piece of being in settings where they know children and they can help children and they can give whatever help is needed, which is really important because the early years is the time to intervene," Carlsson-Paige said.

More than just academics

That's the kind of education and intervention that's happening at Shaw's child development center, which some kids attend with government assistance. There, the social-emotional growth of the students is just as important as their reading and math capabilities, director Freida Dixon said.

In the entryways to some classrooms, children sign in by writing their names, but also by moving a clothespin with their picture on a board to indicate whether they're feeling "sad", "happy" or "frustrated" that day.

If an online program was all that was available to a child, Dixon said it might be better than nothing. But reading and math achievement isn't what kindergarten teachers tell her they want when kids enter the classroom. "If they can follow directions, sit still—

those are the focus of the kindergarten teacher," she said.

Parent involvement also will be critical for children using these online programs, she said. "You have parents that participate with their children and parents who don't."

At the Ebanks home in Utah, the parents are involved. Najwa Ebanks said the boys always sit with her or her husband when they do Upstart. Today, their rising kindergartner is reading well, and their preschooler can identify letters and numbers. Ebanks has no regrets about pulling her son from preschool. In fact, they'll continue to homeschool in the fall.

Words and Expressions

laminated	[ˈlæmɪneɪtɪd]	a.	consisting of several thin sheets or layers that are stuck together 薄板状的；由薄片叠成的
pom-pom		n.	a ball of threads or paper strips that are used to decorate things such as hats or furniture 装饰绒球；塑料丝球
philanthropic	[ˌfɪlənˈθrɒpɪk]	a.	kind and helpful to those who are poor or in trouble 博爱的；仁慈的
topnotch	[ˈtɒpnɒtʃ]	a.	of the highest quality 一流的；极好的
uneven	[ʌnˈiːvn]	a.	unfairly arranged or organized 不均匀的；不均衡的
emerita	[ɪˈmerɪtə]	n.	荣誉退休的女性
pilot project			试验项目；试点项目
conjure up			create a mental picture of; call to mind 使人想起；使浮现于脑海
shore up			strengthen 支持；加固
thwart	[θwɔːt]	v.	hinder or prevent (the efforts, plans, or desires) of 阻碍；挫败
perpetuate	[pəˈpetʃueɪt]	v.	cause to continue or prevail, esp. something bad 使持续，使永久化（尤指不好的事物）
clothespin	[ˈkləʊzpɪn]	n.	wood or plastic fastener for holding clothes on a clothesline 晒衣夹

Unit 1 Education

Discussion Questions

1. Do you think online preschools are the complement or the competitor with traditional preschools? Why?
2. Utah-based nonprofit Waterford. org and its Upstart program are drawing criticism from early childhood development advocates and others. Do you support Waterford. org and its Upstart program? Why or why not?
3. What are the strengths and weaknesses of online preschools?

Additional Reading 3

Alternative to Gaokao: Behind the Tide of Studying Abroad

June 8, 2019
CGTN

Monnie Yang never thought she would receive her undergraduate education at the University of San Francisco. Yang, who works in Beijing now, told CGTN, "It was an accident because I didn't get a satisfactory result in Gaokao."

Every year in early June, millions of students in China take a vital and competitive exam called Gaokao, the annual national college entrance examination. It is widely considered the most important exam for Chinese students, which can make or break their futures. According to China's Ministry of Education, about 10 million students this year participated in the exam, reaching a record high.

However, compared with their parents, students nowadays have more choices other than taking Gaokao. Official statistics show that the number of Chinese outbound students has kept increasing in the past 10 years. Besides postgraduate education, studying abroad at a younger age has become more common. "Other than undergraduate education, more students choose to go to countries like the US, the UK, and Australia for high school education," Yin Jiang, director of the overseas testing department at New Oriental Education Corporation, told CGTN.

Reasons behind the increase

"Parents of those who are at a proper age to go to universities were mainly born between 1975 and 1977," Yin explained. "Most of them has a bachelor's degree and are more open-minded compared with the last generation."

He added that the overseas experience of other family members can also make parents and their children more confident. "One of my relatives is studying abroad, so I also want to have a try," said Deng Yiyi, a 17-year-old girl who will go to the University of Minnesota Twin Cities this autumn.

Family income also plays an important role. Yin said there are more and more middle-class families thanks to the reform and opening-up, which makes it easier to support overseas studies. Xu Chenshu, now a rising sophomore in a US college, told CGTN that the cost of studying abroad including tuition fees, living expenses, and flight tickets are really high. "I am so grateful to my parents."

When talking about his choice of studying abroad, Xu said he yearns for the all-round education in the US universities and he is really interested in Western cultures, such as stand-up comedy.

In addition, Yin said the development of the international education industry in China provides sufficient information for parents and students, and the number of top universities in China is limited, which means Gaokao is really competitive.

Pressure behind two different choices

Traditionally, people hold the view that "studying abroad" is an easier choice compared with Gaokao, but the fact is more complicated.

"Everyone wants to be enrolled in the top universities in China, which contributes to the fierce competition," Guo Xiaolin, an English teacher from an international program in southwest China's Guizhou Province, told CGTN. She added that Gaokao only takes two or three days but will have a great influence on one's future. She agrees the competition for applying overseas universities is fierce but relatively better than Gaokao.

Yin argued that the intensity of study between the two choices is almost equal. For instance, if they want to apply to US universities, they need to prepare for a language test like TOEFL, the US counterpart to Gaokao such as the SAT and extracurricular activities.

The preparation is quite stressful, and he had to give up many hobbies to prepare for all kinds of exams and participate in various activities, said Xu. "Is it only once?" he recalled his surprise when he took the TOEFL listening test for the first time. "I cannot fall asleep until 3 a.m. before the exam."

Pros and cons of studying abroad

When asked about differences of the undergraduate education between domestic and overseas universities, Yin said one of them is the student assessment method. The final exam is the most important part in most domestic universities while overseas universities will consider not only final exams but also daily assignments, experiments scores and class presentations.

He also mentioned that overseas universities are more "market-oriented" with practical courses. And the background of teachers and students are highly internationalized.

Yang described her university life has broadened her horizon by embracing a totally different culture. She said the courses are diverse in her university, and small classes give everyone a chance to express their ideas.

However, there are also difficulties in studying abroad.

"There are a lot of school associations but because of difficulties in communication, you may not get out of your comfort zone to do what you really like," Yang said, adding that even in class, you may not have a deep discussion with your teacher and classmates because of the language problem. "Actually, my ideal university life is that several good friends living in the same dormitory and having class together."

"It is easier to make friends in domestic universities," Xu said. He said he feels lonely because there are few Chinese students in his school and he really misses Chinese cuisine.

Will they come back?

More and more Chinese students are going abroad to pursue their academic dreams. At the same time, the number of returning students is increasing as well.

The number of outbound students in 2018 increased nearly three times compared with 2009, but the number of returning students increased nearly five times.

Yin observed that a great number of entrepreneurial opportunities and some talent programs in China are attractive. What's more, the gap between China and other developed countries is narrowing.

As a US college student, Xu is not sure whether he will come back after graduation because it is too early for him to decide. But Deng, who hasn't been to the US yet, expressed her wish to come back because of the sense of belonging.

"I came back because my family and friends are here," Yang said. "If I have one more chance, I would like to go abroad for a master's degree other than a bachelor's one."

Words and Expressions

alternative	[ɔːlˈtɜːnətɪv]	n.	one of a number of things from which only one can be chosen(供替代的)选择；两者择一
outbound	[ˈaʊtbaʊnd]	a.	that is going out or leaving 去往外地的；去往外国的
expense	[ɪkˈspens]	n.	money spent in doing sth. 消费；开支
yearn (for)	[jɜːn]	v.	long for or desire 渴望；盼望
stand-up		a.	requiring a standing position 单人表演的
intensity	[ɪnˈtensəti]	n.	a high level or degree; the property of being intense 强度；强烈
assessment	[əˈsesmənt]	n.	the act of judging or assessing a person or situation 评价；评估
embrace	[ɪmˈbreɪs]	v.	accept 接受
entrepreneurial	[ˌɒntrəprəˈnɜːriəl]	a.	of or relating to an entrepreneur 企业家的；创业者的

 Discussion Questions

1. According to China's Ministry of Education, about 10 million students this year participated in the exam, reaching a record high. Meanwhile, more and more Chinese students are going abroad to pursue their academic dreams. Why has the number of Chinese outbound students kept increasing in the past 10 years?
2. What are the difficulties that Chinese outbound students may encounter?
3. Why is the number of returning students increasing?

Part 4　Topical Vocabulary

compulsory education 义务教育
quality education 素质教育
test-oriented education 应试型教育

Unit 1 Education

adult education 成人教育
distance education 远程教育
universal education 普及教育；全民教育
compulsory course / required course 必修课
optional course / selective course 选修课
specialized course 专业课
rote learning 死记硬背
cram for examinations 突击考试
test-taking techniques 应试技巧
critical thinking 评判性思维；批判性思考
academic performance / academic record 学习成绩
academic activities 学术活动
a sense of accomplishment 成就感
open admission 免试入学制
school of Arts and Sciences 文理学院
graduate school 研究生院
alma mater 母校
orientation program 新生训练
assistantship 助学金
scholarship 奖学金
period of schooling 学习年限，学习期限
credit system 学分制
schedule / school timetable 课程表
individual study 自习；个性化学习
take an examination / sit for an examination 参加一场考试
convocation notice 会议通知
office hour 教授与学生面谈时间
thesis / dissertation 毕业论文
graduation appraisal 毕业鉴定；毕业评估
graduation ceremony / commencement 毕业典礼
diploma / graduation certificate 毕业证书
supervisor 论文导师
report card / school report / transcript 成绩单
combine ability with character / equal stress on integrity and ability 德才兼备
national expenditure on education 国家教育经费

extracurricular activities 课外活动
confer a degree on sb. 授予某人学位
professional ethics 职业道德
key university 重点大学
develop morally, intellectually, physically and aesthetically 德、智、体、美全面发展
competition for qualified human resources 人才竞争
optimize the education structure 优化教育结构
excellent in character and learning 品学兼优
individualized instruction 因材施教
interdisciplinary talent 复合型人才

Unit 2

Culture and Society

Part 1 Learning Before Class

- **Listening**

Asians Celebrate the Lunar New Year Around the World

Directions: Listen to the news and answer the questions.

1. With what performance did several hundred Asian-Americans in northern Virginia celebrate the Lunar New Year?
2. How many years have the members of the Hai Hau Community Center gathered to celebrate the Lunar New Year?
3. When does the Chinese New Year usually begin?
4. What other performances can the Asian-Americans in northern Virginia enjoy in addition to more traditional performances?

- **Watching and Thinking**

Couples Enjoy Romantic Evening at Beijing's Capital Museum on the Qixi Festival

Directions: Watch the video and discuss the questions with your partner.

1. Where was the traditional Qixi Festival celebrated this year?
2. On which day is the Qixi Festival celebrated in China?
3. Which animal symbolizes love in the traditional Chinese culture?

4. What is the theme of the traditional opera *Tianxianpei*?

• **Reading and Discussing**

Cultural Differences Start Early

By Alison Gopnik
July 13, 2019
The Wall Street Journal ①

    Do our culture and language shape the way we think? A new paper in the Proceedings of the National Academy of Sciences, by Caren Walker at the University of California at San Diego, Alex Carstensen at Stanford and their colleagues, tried to answer this ancient question. The researchers discovered that very young Chinese and American toddlers start out thinking about the world in similar ways. But by the time they are 3 years old, they are already showing differences based on their cultures.

    Dr. Walker's research took off from earlier work that she and I did together at the University of California at Berkeley. We wanted to know whether children could understand abstract relationships such as "same" and "different". We showed children of various ages a machine that lights up when you put a block of a certain color and shape on it. Even toddlers can easily figure out that a green block makes the machine go while a blue block doesn't.

    But what if the children saw that two objects that were the same—say, two red square blocks—made the machine light up, while two objects that were different didn't? We showed children this pattern and asked them to make the machine light up, giving them a choice between a tray with two new identical objects—say, two blue round blocks—or another tray with two different objects.

    At 18 months old, toddlers had no trouble figuring out that the relationship between the blocks was the important thing: They put the two similar objects on the machine. But much to our surprise, older children did worse. Three-year-olds had a hard time figuring out that the relationship between the blocks was what mattered. The 3-year-olds had actually learned that the individual objects were more important than the relationships

---

① *The Wall Street Journal* is a US business-focused, English-language international daily newspaper based in New York City. The journal, along with its Asian and European editions, is published six days a week by Dow Jones & Company, a division of News Corp. The newspaper is published in the broadsheet format and online. The journal has been printed continuously since its inception on July 8, 1889, by Charles Dow, Edward Jones and Charles Bergstresser. A complement to the print newspaper, *The Wall Street Journal* Online, was launched in 1996.

between them.

But these were all American children. Dr. Walker and her colleagues repeated the machine experiment with children in China and found a different result. The Chinese toddlers, like the toddlers in the US, were really good at learning the relationships; but so were the 3-year-olds. Unlike the American children, they hadn't developed a bias toward objects.

In fact, when they saw an ambiguous pattern, which could either be due to something about the individual objects or something about the relationships between them, the Chinese preschoolers actually preferred to focus on the relationships. The American children focused on the objects.

The toddlers in both cultures seemed to be equally open to different ways of thinking. But by age 3, something about their everyday experiences had already pushed them to focus on different aspects of the world. Language could be part of the answer: English emphasizes nouns much more than Chinese does, which might affect the way speakers of each language think about objects.

Of course, individuals and relationships are both important in the social and physical worlds. And cultural conditioning isn't absolute: American adults can reason about relationships, just as Chinese adults can reason about objects. But the differences in focus and attention, in what seems obvious and what seems unusual, may play out in all sorts of subtle differences in the way we think, reason and act. And those differences may start to emerge when we are very young children.

Directions: *Read the passage and discuss the questions with your partner.*

Questions:

1. According to the researchers, when do Chinese and American toddlers start thinking about the world in different ways?
2. To the mind of the American 3-year-olds, which were more important, the individual objects or the relationships between them?
3. Why were the Chinese 3-year-olds good at learning the relationships between individual objects?
4. How do American adults differ from Chinese adults in terms of reasoning?

Part 2　Learning in Class

Warm Up

Why China Can Be Culturally Confident?

May 20, 2019
CGTN

Among the four major ancient civilizations, China is the only country to have adopted ideograms and continued their use without interruption to date.

To achieve that is never an easy task, especially with the rapid modernization and globalization of the world's second-largest economy.

Museums in China have played an active role in reviving the country's traditional culture in recent years. With "Museum and Cultural Fever" sweeping across the country, TV and Internet shows about museums and cultural artifacts are springing up like mushrooms.

In 2018, over 20,000 exhibitions took place in museums across China and received one billion visitors. With the help of technology, many interactive platforms and digital communities have been built to make the artifacts come to life and offer more fun to visitors.

More and more young people have become fans of Chinese traditional culture.

According to Palace Museum data, the post-80s and the post-90s have become the main focus of Palace Museum tourists, and people under the age of 30 account for 40 percent of visitors.

The protection of intangible cultural heritage is another crucial way to protect and pass on the country's ancient culture. China introduced an Intangible Cultural Heritage Law in 2011. By 2018, 40 Chinese intangible cultural heritage items have been included in UNESCO's Intangible Heritage Representative List. Local artisans of intangible cultural heritage are receiving due attention as well.

China has also made great progress in spreading Chinese culture on the world stage. The Disney blockbuster *Kung Fu Panda*, for example, explained quite well to the world about China's martial arts. The Confucius Institutes around the globe also play very important roles in teaching international people Chinese.

As traditional Chinese culture gains worldwide recognition, China's international influence also expands and civilizations are therefore colorful because of cross-cultural communication.

Addressing the opening ceremony of the Conference on Dialogue of Asian Civilizations in mid-May, Chinese President Xi Jinping said that each civilization is the crystallization of human creation, and each is beautiful in its own way.

Xi also said that Asian nations may build on the rich heritage of their forefathers, stay engaged with other civilizations and increase mutual learning.

Directions: *Read the passage and discuss the questions with your partner.*

1. Why did one billion people visit more than 20,000 exhibitions held in museums across China in 2018?
2. In which aspect has China made great progress in spreading Chinese culture on the world stage?
3. Why is the protection of intangible cultural heritage very crucial to protect and pass on China's ancient culture?
4. What are the possible factors for the long existence of China's civilization?

 Text A

No Way to Turn the Cultural Clock Back

By Zhou Shuchun
July 16, 2019
China Daily ①

Based on what we see happening in and to the world, and despite the positive signs we read into the G20 Summit in Osaka, we can probably say we have reached a new crossroad in history, where the international community faces a set of "to be or not to be" dilemmas, which has far-reaching implications.

The real problems or contradictions of the world are not between civilizations,

---

① *China Daily*, established in 1981 as the national English-language newspaper, has developed into a multi-media information platform combining newspapers, websites and apps with a strong presence on Facebook, Twitter, Sina Weibo and WeChat. It serves more than 200 million readers all over the world and is a default choice for people who read about China in English. The group plays an important role as a channel for information exchanges between China and the rest of the world.

contrary to what some people claim. Yet we can use a cultural perspective to analyze the challenges facing the world and promote inter-civilization dialogue to guide human progress worldwide.

The question is whether we can undo the inter-dependency built among the economies across the world over the past centuries. Indeed there are some people who try hard to halt the momentum of economic globalization and disrupt the global division of labor.

As a result of globalization, most modern products of the world are results of international industrial collaboration. The market plays a decisive role in allocating resources and capital efficiently, making it possible for people worldwide to enjoy quality commodities and services at affordable prices.

There are problems that have come along with globalization, the growing wealth gap for one, and it makes sense to improve the global governance system for the process to be more open, inclusive, balanced and equal, so that more people can enjoy the fruits of globalization.

But it is ridiculous to give up eating for fear of choking. Trying to dismantle the globalized economic system—to overthrow all economic and trade theories since Adam Smith ① and David Ricardo ②—is nothing but a fool's errand.

It is impossible to artificially sever the flows of capital, technologies, commodities and talents, and for the ocean of the world economy to recede into isolated lakes and rivers, to borrow an analogy from President Xi Jinping's speech at an international economic forum in St. Petersburg, Russia, last month.

In the traditional sense, international politics is a theory of survival, and international relations today are not much different from those of the past. Zero-sum ③ is the name of the game. It's akin to the notion of "you lose, I win", or "you die, I live".

But the world has undergone dramatic changes. The fundamental difference, lies in the ever-increasing inter-dependency among the international players and consequently, the emerging community of interests.

If you make other people unsafe, you put yourself in danger. The new philosophy of the new era lies in good implementation of the idea of living and letting others live, or developing and letting others develop.

---

① Adam Smith was a Scottish philosopher and political economist in the 18th century.
② David Ricardo was a British politician, economist and broker.
③ Zero-sum is a situation in which each participant receives as much money or advantages as he gives away.

Unit 2　Culture and Society

The way to move further away from the woods of primitive society is to seek common prosperity and common security. Intensifying changes across the world call for concerted efforts from all countries.

The great patriotic pioneer of democratic revolution, Sun Yat-sen, said, "While competition is the principle of other species, human beings consider mutual assistance as their principle. They will prosper if they follow this principle, and perish if they don't." In a sense, China's proposal to build a community with a shared future for mankind, which draws inspiration from such traditional Chinese values as the "great harmony of the world".

And such a truly international theory serves to address the pressing issues of the contemporary world and follow the trend of history. That is why the proposal put forth by President Xi has been written into several United Nations documents over the past few years, which bodes well for the future of the world.

Early last year, *The China Questions—Critical Insights into a Rising Power*, a book published by Harvard University Press, drew wide attention in and outside the United States. The book is compiled by the Fairbank Center for Chinese Studies at Harvard University and written by 36 experts on China.

We don't have to agree with all that's said about China in the book, but I was impressed by some parts of the Introduction. For instance, the Preface starts by saying that, "If you've picked up this book, you have probably already accepted the premise that China matters, and therefore understanding China matters", "China has always mattered and always will", "but today China matters not only to the Chinese people themselves but also to Americans and to the entire world in some new, unexpected, and interesting ways".

What I'm saying is that we have to agree that there is a worrisome deficit of understanding among countries, and in the case of China and the US, or the West for that matter, misunderstandings, even prejudice abound. The question is not whether there is a lack of understanding; the question is how to get rid of or reduce such misunderstandings.

Except for intentions borne out of ulterior motives, misunderstandings largely arise from differences. People have always had the tendency to misread those who are different from them, owing to a lack of knowledge or confidence.

Isaiah Berlin, the late British philosopher and historian, said that all racial or ethnic conflicts arise from the pursuit of a monistic world. Recent history shows that stressing the superiority of one society or culture causes tragedies to humankind.

How to evaluate the differences between and among civilizations and cultures remains a central theme of human development and progress for the modern world.

To hear the argument today that a country's rise is dangerous and will pose a threat to some parts of the world because it's a different civilization is tantamount to experiencing the shock of traveling back in time to the dark ages.

The 21st century is not only multipolar but also multi-conceptual. In a global village where the advancement of transportation and communication has reduced geographical distances, powers continue to interact while civilizations and cultures need to coexist, or live together as parts of a biosystem, to borrow the concept put forth by 19th century German biologist Henrich Anton de Bary.

In fact, mutual learning among civilizations is the very source of human progress. And in a world of **unprecedented** changes, it's imperative to reaffirm convergence rather than clashes between civilizations.

A renewed intercultural dialogue between the West and the East, China in particular, will only reveal that there are profound elements of convergence between different traditions which, contrary to what the considerations and interpretations of Samuel Huntington① suggest, are not destined to clash.

Addressing the opening ceremony of the Shanghai Import Expo last autumn, Christine Lagarde, chief of the International Monetary Fund, referred to the Huangpu River which, as we know, runs across Shanghai, and talked about the Chinese wisdom and craftsmanship of building the best bridges in the world since ancient times.

In cultural and philosophical terms, the Chinese spirit of building bridges is best expressed in the notion of harmony of differences.

In a world undergoing drastic changes where people could be jolted from their habitual comfort zones, it's especially important to have maximum exchanges between and among different groups and communities as a way to guard against the possible resurgence of cultural hostility.

The idea is to consolidate the "cultural foundation" of the global community of a shared future. This discourse of ours, I presume, represents a small but meaningful and worthwhile part of the general efforts to build bridges and pull down walls.

This year could prove to be an important turning point in the history of the world, as it could decide whether we go forward or move backward, stick to the right course or go astray, depending on how we handle the emerging challenges, some of which are

---

① Samuel Huntington (1927 – 2008) was a famous American political scientist and the founder of the theory Clash of Civilizations.

unprecedented.

Political leaders across the globe, especially those of major countries, therefore need to have an acute sense of historical responsibility, for the fate and future of millions are in their hands. As for intellectuals, they should be aware of where the world is headed to from here, and work together to facilitate reason to prevail over anti-reason.

To conclude, as Audrey Azoulay, director-general of UNESCO ①, said at the Conference on Dialogue of Asian Civilizations earlier this year in Beijing that, in face of the current situation of the world, we need to adopt the correct approach to the issue of civilizations as a way to safeguard world peace.

 Words and Expressions

dilemma	[dɪ'lemə]	n.	a situation in which a difficult choice has to be made between two or more alternatives, especially equally undesirable ones 窘境
momentum	[mə'mentəm]	n.	the ability to keep increasing or developing 推进力；动力
governance	['gʌvənəns]	n.	the action or manner of governing 管理；支配
dismantle	[dɪs'mæntl]	v.	take (a machine or structure) to pieces 解散；拆除
sever	['sevə(r)]	v.	divide by cutting or slicing, especially suddenly and forcibly 割断；断绝
recede	[rɪ'siːd]	v.	go or move back or further away from a previous position 逐渐远离；退去
implementation	[ˌɪmplɪmen'teɪʃn]	n.	the process of putting a decision or plan into effect; execution 执行；实施
concerted	[kən'sɜːtɪd]	a.	jointly arranged, planned, or carried out 同心协力的
ulterior	[ʌl'tɪəriə(r)]	a.	existing beyond what is obvious or admitted; intentionally hidden 隐秘的；不可告人的
monistic	[mɒ'nɪstɪk]	a.	consisting of a single basic substance or element 一元论的

---

① UNESCO is short for United Nations Educational, Scientific and Cultural Organization.

tantamount	[ˈtæntəmaʊnt]	a.	equivalent in seriousness to; virtually the same as 等于
convergence	[kənˈvɜːdʒəns]	n.	the occurrence of two or more things coming together 聚集
resurgence	[rɪˈsɜːdʒəns]	n.	the return and growth of an activity that had stopped 再现
facilitate	[fəˈsɪlɪteɪt]	v.	make (an action or process) easy or easier 促进;使便利

 Exercises

- **Multiple Choice**

Select the most appropriate answer for each of the following questions.

1. Which of the following is TRUE according to this passage?

    A) People in different countries should undo the inter-dependency among the economies across the world.

    B) In this multipolar 21st century, powers continue to interact while civilizations and cultures need to coexist.

    C) The real problems or contradictions of the world are between civilizations.

    D) Stressing the superiority of one society or culture helps humankind make process.

2. The people in the world can enjoy quality commodities and services at affordable prices because of _____.

    A) the zero-sum game   B) the fierce competition

    C) the decisive role of the market   D) the monistic world

3. It can be inferred that economic globalization can _____.

    A) benefit more people in the world

    B) cause a growing wealth gap

    C) halt the world economic development

    D) lead to clashes between civilizations

4. The author argues that for the sake of human development and global progress it is essential to _____.

    A) assess the differences between civilizations and cultures

    B) travel back in time to the dark ages

    C) carry out competition among different societies

    D) reduce the changes across the world

5. The underlined word "unprecedented" in Paragraph 22 is closest in meaning to _____.

   A) unexceptional B) unexpired
   C) unprovoked D) unparalleled

6. All the following are mentioned in the passage EXCEPT _____.

   A) international industrial collaboration turns out most modern products of the world
   B) the developed economies benefit most from the process of globalization
   C) it is necessary to reduce misunderstandings among different countries
   D) it's imperative to reaffirm convergence rather than clashes between civilizations

7. A possible means of preventing cultural hostility from growing is _____.

   A) to stop economic globalization and disrupt the global division labor
   B) to move back to the woods of primitive society
   C) to pull down bridges between different societies of the world
   D) to have as many exchanges as possible among different groups and communities

8. This passage is most probably an excerpt from a(n) _____.

   A) report B) review C) speech D) interview

- **Sentence Completion**

Complete the sentences below with words taken from Text A. Use NO MORE THAN THREE WORDS for each answer.

1. The author believes that the market plays a decisive role in allocating _____ efficiently.

2. It makes sense to improve the _____ for the process to be more open, inclusive, balanced and equal, so that more people can enjoy the fruits of globalization.

3. It is impossible to artificially _____ of capital, technologies, commodities and talents, and for the ocean of the world economy to recede into isolated lakes and rivers.

4. In the traditional sense, international politics is _____, and international relations today are not much different from those of the past.

5. In cultural and philosophical terms, the Chinese spirit of building bridges is best expressed in the notion of _____.

- **Discussion Questions**

1. The book *The China Questions—Critical Insights into a Rising Power* says that China today is important to the Chinese people and the entire world. Do you think so? Why or why not?

2. The new philosophy of the new era lies in good implementation of the idea of living and

letting others live, or developing and letting others develop. How do you understand this statement?
3. What do you think of China's proposal to build a community with a shared future for mankind?

- **Writing**

Many people believe that globalization is in line with the interests of all the countries. However, some other people think that globalization brings about some problems to this world. What is your idea of globalization? Write an essay of no less than 300 words to comment on these ideas.

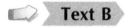 Text B

Different Cultures, Different Temperaments for Kids

By Samuel Putnam & Masha A. Gartstein
January 15, 2019
The Washington Post ①

As early as the fifth century B.C., the Greek historian Thucydides contrasted the self-control and stoicism of Spartans with the more indulgent and free thinking citizens of Athens.

Today, unique behaviors and characteristics seem ingrained in certain cultures.

Italians wildly gesticulate when they talk. Dutch children are notably easy-going and less fussy. Russians rarely smile in public. As developmental psychologists, we're fascinated by these differences, how they take shape and how they get passed along from one generation to the next.

Our work explores the way a society's values influences the choices parents make—and how this, in turn, influences who their kids become. Although genetics certainly matter, the way you behave isn't hard-wired.

In the past two decades, researchers have shown how culture can shape your personality. In 2005, psychologist Robert McCrae and his colleagues were able to document pronounced differences in the personalities of people living in different parts of

---

① *The Washington Post* is a large American daily newspaper founded and continuously published in Washington, D. C. since 1877. This broadsheet newspaper is well-known both in the USA and abroad for its reports on American political developments and international affairs.

the world. For example, adults from European cultures tended to be more outgoing and open to new experiences than those from Asian cultures. Within Europe, they found that people from Northern Europe were more conscientious than their peers in Southern Europe.

Recently, we've been able to trace some of these differences to early childhood. Parenting—perhaps not surprisingly—played a role. Working with colleagues from 14 countries, we looked at the way broad societal values influenced how parents raise their children. We then studied how these different parenting styles shaped the behavior and personality of kids. (Our book, *Toddlers, Parents, and Culture*, was published in November.)

We did this primarily by administering questionnaires to parents around the world, asking them to describe their daily routines, hopes for their kids and methods of discipline. We then asked them to detail the behaviors of their children.

We also relied on the work of Dutch social psychologist Geert Hofstede, who, in the 1970s, asked IBM employees around the world about factors that led to work satisfaction. We were able to compare his findings to ours, and we were surprised to see that his results correlated with our own. The cultural values that were revealed through work preferences in the 1970s could be seen in parenting practices and child temperament 40 years later.

This is important: It shows cultural values are relatively enduring, and seem to have an effect on how kids develop over time. Perhaps the most well-known of these broad cultural values are individualism and collectivism.

In some societies, such as the United States and Netherlands, people are largely driven by pursuits that benefit themselves. They're expected to seek personal recognition and boost their own social or financial status. In more collectivist societies, such as South Korea and Chile, high value is placed on the wellbeing of the larger group—typically their family, but also their workplace or country.

We found that the way parents discipline their children is strongly influenced by these social values, and probably serves to perpetuate these values from one generation to the next. For example, compared with parents in individualist cultures, collectivist parents are much more likely, when reprimanding their kids, to direct them to "think about" their misbehavior, and how it might negatively impact those around them.

This seems to promote group harmony and prepare a child to thrive in a collectivist society. At the same time, if you're constantly being told to think about how your actions impact others, you might also be more likely to feel anxiety, guilt and shame. Indeed, we've found that kids in collectivist cultures tend to express higher levels of sadness, fear and discomfort than children growing up in individualist societies.

A second set of values we studied was indulgence *vs.* restraint. Some cultures, such as the United States, Mexico and Chile, tend to permit and promote self-gratification. Others—such as South Korea, Belgium and Russia—encourage restraint in the face of temptation.

These values seem to be connected to a specific set of parenting goals. In particular, parents in indulgent societies tend to emphasize the importance of developing self-esteem and independence. For example, they expect children to entertain themselves and fall asleep on their own. When one of their kids misbehaves, they'll often suggest ways he or she can make amends and try to repair the damage.

The message kids may get from this kind of treatment is that they're the ones in control of their happiness, and that they should be able to fix their own mistakes. At the same time, when kids are expected to pursue gratification, they may be more likely to impulsively seek immediate rewards—whether it's eating candy before dinner or grabbing a toy off a shelf at a store—before getting permission.

Meanwhile, in societies that prioritize restraint, parents were more likely to shout or swear when disciplining their children. This might make them more obedient. But it might also cause children to be less optimistic and less likely to enjoy themselves.

Parents seem to be motivated to best prepare their kids for the world they're likely to inhabit, and what works in one culture might not necessarily work well in another. But as our world becomes more interconnected, this diversity of parenting approaches may dwindle. Most countries have become more individualistic over the past 50 years—a shift that's most pronounced in countries that have experienced the most economic development.

Nonetheless, there's still a huge difference in parenting styles and childhood development across cultures—a testament to the enduring influence of societal values.

Words and Expressions

stoicism	[ˈstəʊɪsɪzəm]	*n.*	the endurance of pain or hardship without the display of feelings and without complaint 默默忍受；坚忍
ingrain	[ɪnˈɡreɪn]	*v.*	firmly fix or establish (a habit, belief, or attitude) in a person 使根深蒂固

gesticulate	[dʒeˈstɪkjuleɪt]	v.	use gestures, especially dramatic ones, instead of speaking to emphasize one's words 做手势；用手势表达
hard-wired	[hɑːdˈwaɪəd]	a.	make (a pattern of behavior or belief) standard or instinctive 无法改变的；天生的
conscientious	[ˌkɒnʃɪˈenʃəs]	a.	taking care to do things carefully and correctly 勤勉认真的
administer	[ədˈmɪnɪstə(r)]	v.	give or provide sth. 给予；提供
discipline	[ˈdɪsəplɪn]	v.	train sb., especially a child, to obey particular rules and control the way they behave 训导；管教
reprimand	[ˈreprɪmɑːnd]	v.	tell sb. officially that you do not approve of them or their actions 训斥；斥责
indulgence	[ɪnˈdʌldʒəns]	n.	the state of allowing sb. to have or do whatever they want 放纵，纵容
prioritize	[praɪˈɒrətaɪz]	v.	treat sth. as being more important than other things 优先处理
dwindle	[ˈdwɪndl]	v.	become gradually less or smaller (逐渐)减少，变小

 Exercises

- **True / False / Not Given**

Do the following statements agree with the information given in Text B?

In Blanks 1-10 write

True	if the statement is true
False	if the statement is false
Not Given	if the information is not given in Text B

_____ 1. It seems that unique behaviors and characteristics are fixed in certain cultures.

_____ 2. In 2005, psychologist Robert McCrae and his colleagues were able to document pronounced differences in the personalities of people living in similar parts of the world.

_____ 3. In cooperation with colleagues from 14 countries, the psychologists studied how different parenting styles shaped the behavior and personality of kids.

_____ 4. The researchers interviewed parents around the world to know their daily routines, hopes for their kids and methods of discipline.

_____ 5. Surprisingly the results of a Dutch social psychologist's work in the 1970s were closely connected with those of the researchers.

_____ 6. In some societies like the US and Netherlands, people, who are largely driven by pursuits that benefit themselves, are expected to seek personal recognition and boost their own social or financial status.

_____ 7. The researchers found that the way parents discipline their children is hardly influenced by their social values.

_____ 8. The findings show that children growing up in individualist societies tend to express lower levels of sadness, fear and discomfort than kids in collectivist cultures.

_____ 9. Parents in indulgent societies tend to emphasize the importance of developing self-esteem and independence.

_____ 10. The countries that have experienced the most economic development have become more individualistic in the past five decades.

- **Summary**

Complete the summary below with appropriate words taken from Text B. Use ONLY ONE WORD for each answer.

Developmental (1) _____ explore how parents and societies mold their children's personalities in early childhood. Working with colleagues from 14 countries, Samuel and Masha studied the way social values (2) _____ how parents raise their children and how these different (3) _____ styles shaped the behavior and personality of kids by (4) _____ questionnaires to parents around the world. Their results show that cultural values seem to have an effect on how kids develop over time. In some (5) _____ societies, people are largely driven by (6) _____ that benefit themselves and they are expected to seek personal recognition and boost their own social or financial status whereas in more (7) _____ societies, high value is placed on the well-being of the larger group. Besides, parents in (8) _____ societies tend to emphasize the importance of developing self-esteem and independence. However, in societies that (9) _____ restraint, parents are more likely to shout or swear when (10) _____ their children, which might make them more obedient and less optimistic.

- **Short Answer Questions**

1. According to the text, what seems established in certain cultures?
2. According to Robert McCrae and his colleagues, who tended to be more outgoing and open to new experiences than those from Asian cultures?
3. What is the most well-known of the broad cultural values?
4. How might children feel if they are constantly being told to think about how their actions impact others?

5. When are children more likely to seek immediate rewards?

- **Discussion Questions**

1. What factors can shape children's personality?
2. What are the different behaviors and performances of children in individualist cultures and collectivist cultures?
3. How do indulgent and restrained societies influence the way parents raise their children?

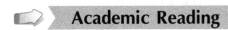

Academic Reading

Understanding Vocabulary (2)

Learning Objective

In the section, you will learn to use word parts to uncover word meanings.

Using Word Parts: Roots, Prefixes, Suffixes

Your knowledge of word parts (roots, prefixes, suffixes) can help you determine the meanings of unfamiliar words. A **root** is the basic part, or stem, from which words are derived. For example, the root tang means "touch", and the word tangible is formed from it. A **prefix** is a word part or group of letters added before a root or word to change its meaning or to create a new word. For instance, if we add the prefix in—which means "not"—to tangible, we get intangible. Thus, we change the meaning from touchable to untouchable. Finally, a **suffix** is a word part or group of letters added after a root or word to create another word or to affect the way a word is used in a sentence. As you saw in the example above, the suffix-ible, meaning "capable of being", can be added to the root tang-to form tangible or intangible. Thus, the word "intangible" is made up of the prefix in-(not), the root tang-(touch), and the suffix-ible (capable of being), which add up to the literal meaning "not capable of being touched". The more roots, prefixes and suffixes that you know, the greater the likelihood that you will be able to use at least some of them to figure out word meanings.

ROOTS		
Root	Meaning	Example
audi	hear	audible
auto	self	autobiography
bene	good, well	benign
bio	life	biography

(To be continued)

chron	time	synchronize
cred	believe	credible
culp	blame	culprit
derm	skin	dermatology
dict, dic	to speak	diction
geo	earth	geology
graph	to write	polygraph
log	speech	dialog
micro	small	microbiology
mit, miss	to send	mission
mort	death	mortal
path	feeling	sympathy
ped	foot	pedicure
phon	sound	phonics
poly	many	polygamy
port	to carry	transport
pseud	false	pseudonym
psych	mind	psychology
script	to write	scripture
spec	to look	spectacles
therm	heat	hyperthermia

PREFIXES		
Prefix	**Meaning**	**Example**
a-	not, without	asymmetrical
ante-	before, in front of	anterior
anti-	against, opposite	antiseptic
bi-	two	bilingual
circum-	around	circumference
col-, com-, con-	together, with	congregate
contra-	against	contraception
de-	away from	deploy
dis-	not, apart, away	disable
extra-	more than	extraterrestrial

(To be continued)

hyper-	over	hyperactive
hypo-	under	hypodermic
il-	not	illogical
im-	not	immobile
in-	not	inoperative
inter-	between	interstate
intra-	within	intrastate
ir-	not	irrational
mal-	bad	malignant
mis-	wrong	misadvise
mono-	one	monologue
non-	not	nonprofit
poly-	many	polygon
post-	after	posterior
pre-	before	prejudice
pro-	for	proponent
re-	back, again	recede
retro-	backward	retroactive
semi-	half	semiconscious
sub-	under	subway
super-	over	supernatural
tele-	far	telescope
trans-	across	transfer
tri-	three	tripod
un-	not	uncivil

SUFFIXES		
Suffix	Meaning	Example
-able	capable of	readable
-ar	relating to	solar
-en	made of	golden
-er	person who	adviser
-ful	full of	plentiful
-fy	to make	pacify

(To be continued)

-hood	condition	bachelorhood
-ible	capable of	edible
-ize	to make	sterilize
-less	without	penniless
-logy	study of	sociology
-ment	state of being	harassment
-or	person who	conductor
-ward	direction	westward

Directions: *Using word parts, try to figure out the meanings of the words listed below.*

1. aquanaut: _____
2. inaudible: _____
3. biology: _____
4. antechamber: _____
5. circumscribe: _____
6. contradiction: _____
7. monosyllable: _____
8. telepathy: _____
9. immortal: _____
10. retrospect: _____
11. polysyllable: _____
12. hypothermia: _____
13. malcontent: _____
14. hyperextend: _____
15. bisect: _____
16. substandard: _____
17. pathology: _____
18. dictation: _____
19. impediment: _____
20. transcription: _____

Part 3　Learning After Class

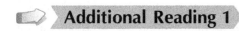

Intl Mother Language Day 2019: Revitalizing Languages, Cultures

February 21, 2019
CGTN

"When a language disappears, the community and, in turn, the world, loses generations of knowledge that have been preserved," said Kristen Tcherneshoff, who works at Wikitongues, a New York-based non-profit organization focused on language preservation.

"Language is the artistic, intellectual, and spiritual expression of the full complexity and diversity of the human experience," she told CGTN.

February 21 marks the International Mother Language Day, celebrated this year under the theme "indigenous languages matter for development, peace building and reconciliation". The day aims at promoting the preservation and protection of languages amid increased threat to linguistic diversity.

According to UNESCO statistics, around 40 percent of the estimated 7,000 languages around the world are endangered, most of which are indigenous languages. Furthermore, one language disappears every two weeks, together with its entire cultural and intellectual heritage. Some linguists hold the view that nearly half of the world's current stock of languages may disappear within the next century.

In order to bring the issue to light, the UN officially launched the Year of Indigenous Languages on February 1 this year.

"Each indigenous language has an incalculable value for humankind," said UN General Assembly President María Fernanda Espinosa Garcés at the event. "They are much more than tools for communication. They are channels for human legacies to be handed down."

A language is closely related to its unique culture

Polyglots can relate to the struggle sometimes of not being able to find two words in two different languages that would mean the exact same thing.

Tuvan, one of the many small languages used in Russia, has a unique word "khoj özeeri" (a local method of killing a sheep), which is untranslatable into English or Russian. Slaughtering livestock can be part of human communities' evolving culture, and "khoj özeeri" is one of its unique versions.

Different languages highlight various human interpretations and perceptions of the world. Members of the Amazonian tribe Pirahã only use words like "few" or "many" instead of numerical terms, which indicates that assigning numbers may be a cultural product rather than an innate preference.

Reasons to save endangered languages

We all have our own ways to describe what we see, but can you imagine what would happen if the language we speak every day out of a sudden disappeared?

For languages like Aka, spoken by people from a remote state in northeastern India, the death of their language shook the fundamental foundations of the tribe. As one villager put it, Aka represents their identities.

When asked why we need to protect endangered languages, Dr. Lisa Lim, associate professor in Linguistics at the University of Sydney, told CGTN that languages (including traditional storytelling and songs) are a central part of intangible cultural heritage.

"A lot of Traditional Ecological Knowledge (TEK) is embodied or conveyed through indigenous languages," Lim said, giving Tanka boat-dwellers in Hong Kong as an example. Their language and songs convey their intimate knowledge of the ecology of the sea, such as fish species, and fishing.

Tcherneshoff thinks that a language is a tool to share our thoughts, beliefs, and emotions, yet it encompasses much more: It is a cultural expression, an archive of knowledge.

When a language dies, it could take away all memories related to it.

What can we do to preserve "ancestral tongues"?

Why does a language become endangered or even vanish? Some languages disappear with the death of their last speaker, while others gradually disappear in bilingual or multilingual cultures as indigenous tongues take the back seat at school and on television. Another reason could be the lack of written form for some languages, which are difficult to preserve but easily forgotten.

Last but not the least, an increasingly globalized and connected world makes languages characteristics of remote places no longer protected by national borders or natural boundaries. For better communication and better development, we start to learn and use a widespread language like English.

The trend of globalization is unstoppable, but what can we do? Dr. Lim says we need to find a way for such indigenous languages to have not only cultural and symbolic and social dimensions, but also find the capital that would help their survival.

When talking about the difficulties of her organization, Tcherneshoff said, "The main issue we encounter is funding." Wikitongues is a non-profit organization that aims to build a public archive of every language in the world. They have thousands of volunteers from all over the world.

She shared a story of a volunteer from the Democratic Republic of Congo named Hangi who insists on recording videos of his mother tongue Kihunde even when it is difficult to access the Internet. He is also currently working on a phrasebook in Kihunde and has begun translating classical poetry works into Kihunde.

Tcherneshoff suggests that anyone can contribute by researching the area where they are from. "What languages are indigenous to the region? Are they still in use, or are they inactive?" Lim and Tcherneshoff both agree that social media is a successful tool in language preservation nowadays.

"Such platforms make the language relevant for our world today—not only a language for 'traditional' topics or rituals—with new vocabulary being developed, and making it attractive for young people to use, which is a key to maintaining a language," Dr. Lim said.

Actions to hear vanishing voices

The diversity of languages is threatened, but luckily, people are taking action. Organization like Wikitongues count on volunteers to save languages. There are young language activists who create new generations of language learners through mobile apps in the form of games and dictionaries.

Governments are participating as well. Canada passed the Indigenous Languages bill earlier this month. Several universities in the US have started offering courses in Native American languages. Indigenous children in 181 of India's state primary schools will have access to literacy education in their own languages.

China is also doing its share. In January, UNESCO officially announced the Yuelu Proclamation on the protection of linguistic diversity, which was discussed and passed at an international conference held in the city of Changsha last year. China also has a language project in place to preserve its various dialects.

Some languages are vanishing, but the future lies in our hands. Every one of us can make a difference. Like Tcherneshoff says, maybe we should move forward optimistically.

Words and Expressions

indigenous	[ɪnˈdɪdʒənəs]	a.	originating or occurring naturally in a particular place; native 土生土长的; 本地的
reconciliation	[ˌrekənsɪlɪˈeɪʃn]	n.	the restoration of friendly relations 和解; 调解
polyglot	[ˈpɒliɡlɒt]	n.	a person who knows and is able to use several languages 通晓多种语言的人
livestock	[ˈlaɪvstɒk]	n.	farm animals regarded as an asset 家畜; 牲畜
intangible	[ɪnˈtændʒəbl]	a.	unable to be touched or grasped; not having physical presence 无形的, 触摸不到的
encompass	[ɪnˈkʌmpəs]	v.	include a large number or range of things 包含, 涉及
archive	[ˈɑːkaɪv]	n.	a collection of historical documents or records 档案(库); 档案文件
proclamation	[ˌprɒkləˈmeɪʃn]	n.	the public or official announcement of an important matter 公告; 申明

Discussion Questions

1. According to UNESCO statistics, about 40 percent of the estimated 7,000 languages around the world are endangered. Why should the endangered languages be protected?
2. What measures should the governments and people take to prevent the indigenous languages from disappearing?

Additional Reading 2

A Holiday of Dread for China's Single Women

By Anna Fifield, Liu Yang & Wang Yuan
January 31, 2019
The Washington Post

Beijing—Spare a thought for the single Chinese woman this Lunar New Year holiday.

The remonstrations over their unwed status and the pressure on them to get married are so intense that some of these "leftover women"—the name for women not married by their late 20s—are searching for ways to avoid this family badgering.

Some are asking their bosses for extra work during China's biggest holiday, which falls on Feb. 5 this year. Others are inventing boyfriends. But still, the pressure mounts. Hospitals are reporting a spike in young people seeking treatment for anxiety.

"I was so afraid last year that I didn't go home. I don't want to go home this year either, but there's no way to avoid going back," said Emily Liu, a 31-year-old who works at a state-owned enterprise and will return to her hometown of Dalian next month.

"My parents say, 'Your classmates have children. You don't even have a boyfriend,'" she said. "This is the only topic when I am back home, and they even mobilize all the relatives. The pressure is too great."

Women are considered "leftover" in many parts of Asia if they haven't married by their mid-20s. But China's economic gains over the past few decades and the creation of a huge middle class have led many women to pursue careers instead of getting married early. Or at all.

This is contributing to a rapid decline in the number of births in China. There were 15.2 million live births in China last year, an astonishing 2 million fewer than the previous year, according to official statistics released last week.

The Chinese government, concerned that this is creating a demographic time bomb as the population ages, abandoned its one-child policy several years ago in an effort to encourage bigger families.

Despite the fact that there are about 33 million more men than women in China, the result of a preference for boys exacerbated by the one-child policy. It is the women who are considered "leftover" rather than the men.

Just as the government campaign to nudge up the birthrate has yet to show much progress, the government—and parents—haven't had much success in encouraging young women to get hitched early. The number of weddings in China has fallen for five years straight. There are 200 million single adults in China.

Now, some companies are joining the effort to change that. They are encouraging female workers to date and, maybe, tie the knot.

Two companies that run Song Dynasty Town, a tourist attraction in Hangzhou, south of Shanghai, have given an extra eight days' holiday to their single female employees over the age of 30, specifically so they can date over the New Year holiday, the peak season for blind dating in China. That will give them a total of 15 days off. If any of these women get married before the end of 2019, they will receive double their usual annual bonus.

The two companies say they are offering this "dating leave" as a sign of how much they care for their employees. "Some of our staff are quite busy with work, so we think it's a good idea to give them some extra time for dating," said the companies' human resources manager, Huang Lei.

Elsewhere in Hangzhou, a middle school is offering teachers two half days of "love leave" each month. About 40 percent of the school's teachers are unmarried, so the school introduced the "love leave" to help them, the principal told local media. For both genders, married teachers without children can also apply for the time off as "family leave" or "happiness leave". Some single women are intrigued by the idea—even as some commentators online have complained about discrimination against single men.

"It's good for some employees who are too busy to date," said Peng Mei, a 38-year-old office worker in Chengdu. But she sees other benefits. "Or they can simply take the leave and use it for vacation since the company doesn't require the details of the dating." She did wonder, however, who the women were supposed to be dating on their days off, because men weren't being given time off, too.

Many single women over the age of 25 dread the idea of returning home for the holiday and being hectored about being single and enduring relentless match-making efforts. Some 85 percent of 26-to-30-year-old singletons say their parents have urged them to hurry up and get married, according to a survey last year by Zhenai.com, a popular dating site.

Shen, a 25-year-old woman from Ningbo who gave only her last name, went to great lengths to avoid this browbeating: She spent a month photo-editing 10 pictures to show herself with a famous actor called Liu Haoran.

She sent them to her parents, presenting the young man as her boyfriend. They were overjoyed. Then she saw that one of her father's friends had posted about the news on

WeChat, the ubiquitous social media app.

"Last night, I dreamed that my daughter was married. I cried so much and woke up for several times," Shen's father said, according to his friend. "I've started practicing the speech for my daughter's wedding day."

When Shen saw the post, she was overcome with guilt and admitted on Weibo, China's answer to Twitter, what she'd done. Her confession struck a chord with millions of singles in the same position.

Her parents, clearly missing the point, told her not to worry about the fabrication and to just get on with blind dating, Shen told Pear Video, a popular short-video platform, after her messages went viral. The video was watched more than 200 million times in the 24 hours after it was posted.

A 35-year-old woman with a doctorate, identified only as Dong, was also trying to avoid her parents and their nagging. She's not only a "leftover woman". She also falls into the category of "three highs"—high level of education, high level of income and high age.

She's sick of being "besieged" by relatives and other busybodies over the holiday, so she hoped to escape into her job, Dong told the Qianjiang Evening News in Hangzhou. She asked her boss to let her work over the Lunar New Year holiday.

Her boss declined her request. She had more-urgent business to attend to, he said. He is about the same age as her parents and clearly sympathized with them, not with his employee.

"Escaping won't change the reality. You can solve your problems only by confronting them," Dong quoted him as saying. "The holiday is a good opportunity for socializing and you should try to meet more people, keep your eyes open, take the initiative to reach out, and you'll probably find your Mr. Right."

Turning on the television won't necessarily provide respite. Many popular dating shows involve parents on the stage choosing potential spouses for their children.

A new show that debuted in Hunan Province this week, called "Meeting Mr. Right", shows fathers watching videos of their daughters going out with men and commenting on their dating techniques.

A popular reality show with a similar concept—moms and dads commenting on footage of their daughters—showed parents urging their daughters to marry 23 times in the space of three episodes, according to a count by the Beijing News. The program was "producing anxiety", one TV critic said.

Words and Expressions

remonstration	[ˌremən'streɪʃn]	n.	protest or complaint about sth/sb 规劝，抗议
badger	['bædʒə]	v.	put pressure on sb. by repeatedly asking them to do sth. 烦扰，纠缠
demographic	[ˌdemə'græfik]	a.	relating to the structure of populations 人口统计的
exacerbate	[ɪɡ'zæsəbeɪt]	v.	make sth. worse, especially a problem 使恶化；使加剧
nudge (up)	[nʌdʒ]	v.	push sth. gradually in a particular direction 推动
get hitched			get married 结婚
intrigue	[ɪn'triːɡ]	v.	arouse the curiosity or interest of 引发……的好奇心；激起……的兴趣
hector	['hektə(r)]	v.	try to make sb. do sth. by talking or behaving in an aggressive way 威逼；威吓
singleton	['sɪŋɡltən]	n.	a single person 单身；独身
browbeat	['braʊbiːt]	v.	frighten or threaten sb. in order to make him/her do sth. 威逼；恫吓
ubiquitous	[juː'bɪkwɪtəs]	a.	seeming to be everywhere; very common 似乎无处不在的；普遍存在的
fabrication	[ˌfæbrɪ'keɪʃn]	n.	the action or process of manufacturing or inventing something 编造；虚构
besiege	[bɪ'siːdʒ]	v.	surround sb./sth. in large numbers; bother 团团围住；烦扰
busybody	['bɪzɪbɒdi]	n.	a meddling or prying person 爱管闲事者；好事的人
respite	['respaɪt]	n.	a short break or escape from sth. difficult or unpleasant 暂停；暂缓
debut	['deɪbjuː]	v.	first appearance or performance 初次露相；首次登台
footage	['fʊtɪdʒ]	n.	part of a film showing a particular event 连续镜头，片段
episode	['epɪsəʊd]	n.	an incident in the course of a series of events, in sb.'s life or experience 片段；一集

Unit 2 Culture and Society

  Discussion Questions

1. Many Chinese women in their late 20s or early 30s are still not married. What factors do you believe account for their late marriage?
2. Many popular dating shows involve parents on the stage choosing potential spouses for their children. What do you think of this phenomenon?

Additional Reading 3

The Biggest Lie We Tell on the Internet Is Ourselves

By Chris Taylor
June 23, 2019
Mashable

If you and the version of yourself that you present to the world online went for a drink together, would you even know each other?

Let's be honest: In this vast anonymizing realm we call the Internet, we all lie a little. Not just on the small stuff, though there is a lot of that; we also tell more intangible lies about the biggest thing we have to talk about, our identity. We smooth over nuance to fit ourselves into checkboxes. We adhere to our "personal brand", which doesn't always reflect our truths. On Facebook we tell many lies of omission, often without realizing.

Even those of us who are scrupulous about calling out Trumpian "alternative facts" when we see them are not immune to the desire to show our best face—a face that eventually hardens into a mask.

The lies start young, often when we encounter our first age-related barriers to being extremely online. According to one 2013 survey by the UK's Advertising Standards Authority, an eye-popping 83 percent of those 11 to 15 had registered at least one social media account with a false age. A more recent survey found 61 percent of children in the country had social media accounts by age 12.

It's almost a rite of passage, it seems, the modern equivalent of getting a fake ID for underage drinking—except in this case, we're more likely to fudge our age with parental approval. Another UK survey, in 2017, found that 60 percent of parents were happy to let their kids lie about their age to get on popular social media sites (most of which have a minimum age of 13, though it varies, due to online privacy laws).

You may well ask: so what? Kids are always going to act older than they really are, or go places they're officially not allowed; far better that they do so with full parental awareness. And you'd be right. But it's telling that the very first lesson of so many social media lives is this: It's okay to tell little lies about myself, if it gets me to a place I want to go.

The next focal point for little lies comes with our first online dating profile. Here too, we might lie about our age, to make us seem more mature. More likely, we lie about our weight. A 2008 study that looked at the profiles of 80 Match. com users—then weighed and measured them in person—found that they were off by an average of about 5 pounds. Their reported height was more accurate (a third of an inch was the average deviation). But if the anecdotal evidence of dating horror stories and this April Fools' joke is any guide, the height fib is more prevalent in the Tinder era.

We stretch the truth about our hobbies to sound more interesting. We lie about what books we've read—or more commonly, what books we actually finished—in order to sound smarter. We skim headlines and pretend we've read the article. We smooth our skin and otherwise touch up our photos to meet what we think is the definition of beauty; apps make that process easier by the day. Again, we're not talking about the big and malicious lies, the deepfake video, the catfishing profile, the troll, the Twitter bot. This is just the slow, daily erosion of sincere online truth.

We may be more reluctant to share stuff on Facebook in the wake of its various privacy scandals: in a 2019 Consumer Reports survey, 74 percent of respondents said they'd altered their behavior on the service. But in practice, that likely means the stuff we share is more anodyne. We're even less likely now to talk about the difficult stuff (our depression, our loneliness, our grief) for fear of which advertisers, marketers, employers, or health insurers might be listening.

Those who push a professional or personal brand aren't exactly lying. They're just being selective about what they share. They aren't going to post opinions their employers or clients would disagree with, of course. But they're also tweaking the brand based on what garners engagement. If you tweet about a topic and a lot of people retweet it, you're getting a dopamine hit, which makes you more likely to tweet about that topic again. And one more guardrail is erected around the edges of your personality.

It's natural for us to want to know ourselves and show ourselves by our membership in various tribes. Whether you cheer or decry the rise of so-called "identity politics", you can't deny the rising desire for simple, shorthand definitions. We want to slot ourselves into categories based on our gender, our sexuality, our ethnicity, or our political allegiance. And that's all well and good, especially in an age when many of these definitions are under attack from dangerous idiots who would deny them the right to exist.

Trouble is, fitting into those shorthand categories often seems to involve sanding down some of the rough, quirky edges that make us individuals. We act as if identity is monolithic, when it's anything but. We self-stereotype. "I've noticed it with a lot of second-generation Americans who struggle to integrate their parents' cultures into their lives," says my colleague Morgan Sung, who has written about subtle Asian traits groups on Facebook. "A lot of these groups make the entirety of Asian identity about liking boba. I don't like boba and I feel weird about it!"

Perhaps this is an inevitable part of the evolution of the Internet. Just as an MP3 compresses the range of music we can hear in a song, the better to deliver it quickly and efficiently to your devices, we are trying to compress all of human culture into one text- and photo-based medium. In any facsimile of reality, details are going to get lost.

But the weird thing about this online compression of human identity is that it doesn't lose the extreme parts of the sound, the way an MP3 does. In fact, it enhances them, and cuts out the center channels instead. Social media and news ecosystems thrive on controversies that make us choose sides. YouTube's algorithm is designed to push videos that will keep you watching, and extreme viewpoints do that better than anything else.

This will likely not be the case forever. We live in an age of moral crisis and shredded norms where neutrality looks like (and often is) the dumbest position. Issues like Brexit, Trump, and climate change demand that we take a stand. If and when global politics quietens down, online citizens may start to prize negotiation and compromise.

As the Internet expands, there is more room for nuance. Memes based on self-stereotyping have a short shelf life. We get tired of pigeon-holing ourselves just to fit in. Through trial and error, we gain enough courage to share the hard internal battles we're fighting. We stumble across more avenues to non-judgmental support. We learn who our friends really are.

And then maybe, one day, if we're lucky, we look at our online persona and see not a wacky funhouse reflection, but a magic mirror that tells the unvarnished truth.

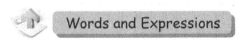

| anonymize | [əˈnɒnɪmaɪz] | v. | remove identifying particulars or details, typically for statistical or other purposes 隐匿 |

smooth over			ease or remove 消除
nuance	[ˈnjuːɑːns]	n.	a subtle difference or variation 细微差别
scrupulous	[ˈskruːpjələs]	a.	careful about paying attention to details 严谨的；小心的
eye-popping	[ˈaɪˌpɒpɪŋ]	a.	astonishing or surprising 使人瞠目的；惊人的
fudge	[fʌdʒ]	v.	avoid giving clear and accurate information 含混其词；回避
catfishing	[ˈkætfɪʃɪŋ]	n.	a type of deceptive activity where a person creates a fake identity on a social network account 网络示夸
anodyne	[ˈænədaɪn]	a.	unlikely to offend anyone 不得罪人的；温和的
tweak	[twiːk]	v.	make slight changes to improve sth. 稍微调整
garner	[ˈɡɑːnə(r)]	v.	obtain or collect sth. such as information, support 获得，收集
dopamine	[ˈdəʊpəmiːn]	n.	a chemical functioning both as a hormone 多巴胺（一种具有激素作用的化学物质）
guardrail	[ˈɡɑːdreɪl]	n.	a rail that prevents people from falling off or being hit by sth. 护栏；栏杆
ethnicity	[eθˈnɪsəti]	n.	the fact of belonging to a particular race 种族渊源
allegiance	[əˈliːdʒəns]	n.	a person's continued support for a political party, etc. 对(政党等的)忠诚
quirky	[ˈkwɜːki]	a.	characterized by peculiar or unexpected traits 诡诈的，离奇的
monolithic	[ˌmɒnəˈlɪθɪk]	a.	large, powerful 巨大的，庞大的
facsimile	[fækˈsɪməli]	n.	an exact copy of sth. 摹本；复制
algorithm	[ˈælɡərɪðəm]	n.	a set of rules that must be followed when solving a particular problem 算法；计算程序
wacky	[ˈwæki]	a.	funny or amusing in a slightly crazy way 古怪的；滑稽可笑的
unvarnished	[ʌnˈvɑːnɪʃt]	a.	with nothing added 不加掩饰的；确凿的

Discussion Questions

1. Why do online citizens all lie a little on the Internet according to the text?
2. What bad effects might kids suffer when they lie about their age to get on to social media sites?

Part 4   Topical Vocabulary

corporate culture 企业文化, 公司文化
counterculture 反文化
cross-cultural communication 跨文化交流
cultural conflict 文化冲突
cultural differences 文化差异
cultural distribution 文化分布
cultural diversity 文化多样性
cultural exchange 文化交流
cultural globalization 文化全球化
cultural heritage 文化遗产
cultural identity 文化身份
cultural pluralism 文化多元论
cultural shock 文化冲击
culture industry 文化产业
ecotourism 生态旅游
enterprise culture 企业文化
fraction in culture 文化断层
historical cultural city 历史文化名城
improve the quality of the population 提高全民文化素质
indigenous culture 本土文化
international culture communication 国际文化交流
local customs and practices 风土人情
mainstream culture 主流文化
material culture 物质文化

multi-cultural society 多元文化社会
national culture 民族文化
non-material cultural heritage 非物质文化遗产
non-profit cultural undertakings 公益性文化事业
popular culture 流行文化;大众文化
population explosion 人口激增
social activities 社交活动,社会活动
social and cultural life 社会文化生活
social benefit 社会公益
social capital 社会资本(指交通、卫生、通信等基本设施)
social culture orientation 社会文化导向
social environment 社会环境
social insurance 社会保险
social issues 社会问题
social life 社交生活,社会生活
social network 社交网络
social news 社会新闻
social order 社会秩序
social responsibility 社会责任
social science 社会科学
social security system 社会保障制度
social security 社会保险;社会保障
social services 社会服务
social status 社会地位
social structure 社会结构
social system 社会制度
social welfare 社会福利
sustainable development 可持续发展
traditional culture 传统文化
traffic congestion 交通拥挤
transmission of culture 文化传递
urban sprawl 城市扩张
urbanization 城市化
ways of consumption 消费方式
Western culture 西方文化
world cultural heritage 世界文化遗产

• Unit 3　Politics •　

Unit 3

Politics

Part 1　Learning Before Class

• **Listening**

British Lawmakers Deal Another Blow to Johnson's EU Plan

Directions: *Listen to the news and answer the questions.*

1. What did British law-makers deny on Wednesday?
2. When must Britain leave the EU according to Johnson?
3. Why do many members of Britain's parliament fear leaving the EU without a deal in place?
4. Why does Johnson need the support of a few Labour members to get enough votes to hold an election?

• **Watching and Thinking**

Tariffs on China: Economics Out, Politics In

Directions: *Watch the video and discuss the questions with your partner.*

1. What does "America dropped bombs again" refer to?
2. Why will most sane economists agree that the trade deficit is a non-issue?
3. What will trade wars cause?
4. What is China's most ambitious social and economic experiment in history?

• Reading and Discussing

Why China Can Lift Hundreds of Millions of People Out of Poverty?

June 25, 2019
CGTN

Lanping Bai and Pumi Autonomous County, in southwest China's Yunnan Province, used to be one of the most impoverished regions in the country. Walking around villages in the county, one saw dilapidated houses with leaking roofs and bumpy dirt roads.

But by the end of 2018, residents in Lanping's rural areas saw their annual income increased from 4,406 *yuan* in 2014 to 6,515 *yuan*, an increase of more than 2,000 *yuan* in four years.

Lanping's transformation reflects the larger socio-economic changes that China has gone through—from an agrarian backwater into an industrial powerhouse. Due to rapid industrialization and persistent poverty alleviation efforts by the government, more than 800 million people have been lifted out of poverty during China's reform and opening-up process. From 1978 to 2018, the number of impoverished people dropped from 770 million to 16.6 million, and the poverty rate dropped from 97.5 percent to 1.7 percent.

"Forty years ago, China's poverty headcount ratio is about 97 percent," said Xu Jin, a professor at the China Institute for South-South Cooperation in Agriculture at China Agricultural University. "If we don't have this poverty reduction process, we cannot imagine what China is like today."

Poverty is most severe in China's geographic margins. The harsh natural conditions, absence of fertile land and lack of access to fresh water in some parts of China's western regions precluded any possibility of economic development through farming, not to mention industrial development.

In the mountainous deep south or the rocky deep north, modernity barely left a trail. This problem plagued Lanping as well. The county is prone to natural disasters and because the population was scattered around the county, the cost of infrastructure development would be too high.

In response, the Chinese government introduced ecological migration in 2000, relocating people from lands distressed by a poor ecological environment to newly built residential communities on more fertile land. Residents in Lanping were relocated to modern apartment complexes with many of their consumer electronics provided free by the local government.

To address various causes of poverty, different measures must be combined to tackle its root causes, said Xu. The Chinese government has introduced six approaches to poverty alleviation: production, migration, ecological conservation, education, minimal allowances, and mass public participation.

In Lanping, apart from migration to more fertile land, residents also tried ecological conservation to promote tourism and boost local revenue.

China vows to eliminate absolute poverty—living on less than 1 dollar a day—by the end of 2020. But achieving the last mile can be difficult since many of those left in poverty are afflicted by physical or mental ailments. To lift the last several million requires no less of an effort than helping the billions whose lives have now been transformed.

Directions: *Read the passage and discuss the questions with your partner.*

1. Why have hundreds of millions of people been lifted out of poverty during China's reform and opening-up process?
2. What did the Chinese government do to lift residents in Lanping out of poverty in 2000?
3. What approaches have been introduced by the Chinese government to alleviate poverty?
4. What did residents in Lanping do to get rid of poverty apart from migration to more fertile land?

Part 2   Learning in Class

Warm Up

The Politics of Human Rights

Directions: *Watch the video and discuss the questions with your partner.*

1. Why do we have to discuss human rights openly and honestly according to the speaker?
2. How is the current situation of human rights in China according to the speaker?
3. What do most Africans want to solve firstly according to the speaker?
4. What is the most serious and gross violation of human rights in the 21st century according to the speaker?

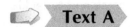

Text A

How to Restore the Damaged US Credibility

June 2, 2019
CGTN

A. Thomas Schelling, a famous American professor of political economy and Nobel laureate, pointed out in his book *Arms and Influence that* "**face** is one of the few things worth fighting over". Americans have always regarded their strong and reliable reputation or credibility as the pillar underpinning the world order, and they even resort to limited wars to establish a firm reputation and increase their bargaining chips in international affairs. However, the credibility of the US has eroded in recent years, because the US government reneged on its commitments in a series of international affairs. Especially after the current president took office, the credibility of the US has dropped to a new low.

B. In fact, the US government has been going back on its words and behaving irresponsibly for a long time. As early as 2001, the Bush administration announced that the "Kyoto Protocol" had "fatal defects" and decided to unilaterally withdraw from it, which greatly reduced the effectiveness of the "Kyoto Protocol". Under Obama, the US government pushed for reconciliation with Iran and finally reached a six-party nuclear agreement, which "set free a tiger back to the mountains" in a way that betrayed the US's closest ally in the Middle East, Saudi Arabia. The "treachery" of the US has gradually deprived it of its influence over Saudi Arabia.

C. Even more reckless and unscrupulous, the current US government reneges on its words with a vengeance. As the main builder and participant of the international economic order and the multilateral system after the World War II, the US should have taken the lead in abiding by multilateral rules, but the US government, advocating "America first", withdraws from international agreements and institutions at every turn: withdrawal from the Paris climate accord, the Iran nuclear deal, the United Nations Educational, Scientific and Cultural Organization, the United Nations Human Rights Council.

D. In the China-US trade war, in defiance of the WTO rules advocated by the US itself and the outcomes of the China-US trade talks over the past year, US President Donald Trump insisted on imposing a 25 percent tariff on 200 billion US dollars of Chinese exports to the US. He even accused the Chinese side of "going back on its words", which once again gives the world a chance to see the true colors the US government as "giving a false account of the facts".

E. In addition, President Trump, who has been prone to "governing the country by tweets", has taken the US further down the road of dishonesty through a large number of "tweets" that have proved to be false.

F. Public opinion polls reported by the US media show that "between two-thirds and three-quarters of Americans do not find Trump trustworthy". According to a 2018 survey by the Pew Research Center of the US, Trump has become the world's least trusted leader of a great power. Americans have more confidence in French President Macron, Japanese Prime Minister Abe and German Chancellor Merkel than Trump in dealing with international affairs. At the same time, traditional US allies, such as the United Kingdom, France, Germany, Saudi Arabia, Japan, South Korea and Australia, have little confidence in the US president.

G. Although the US government does not derive its credibility from the president's words and deeds alone, Trump's failure to keep promises undoubtedly carries serious consequences for the US. His "inconsistency in policy making" and "capriciousness" have led to a sharp decline in the credibility of the US around the world, making it difficult for US allies to trust the commitments made by the US. According to a poll conducted by market research firm YouGov cited by SPUTNIK, a Russian media outlet, on May 13, 45 percent of Europeans believe that the US is no longer a reliable security partner of the European Union.

H. In addition, Trump does not have political experience and does not listen to White House aides. Internationally, he often speaks carelessly and makes remarks that are not in the interests of US foreign policy; domestically, in order to win the general election, he attacks the "dissidents" within the Democratic Party and the Republican Party without any scruple. People no longer believe that he can effectively safeguard the fundamental interests and the strategic intentions of the US, which has led to the decline of the credibility of the US government and the weakening of the US deterrence. The risks of deadly miscalculation will increase.

I. As pointed out by a review in *Foreign Affairs*, a US magazine, "The United States has already paid a significant price for Trump's behavior: the president is no longer considered the ultimate voice on foreign policy. Foreign leaders are turning elsewhere to gauge American intentions. With the US domestic system so polarized and its governing party so fragmented, communicating intent has become more difficult than ever. The more bipartisan and univocal US signaling is, the less likely it is that Trump's damage to American credibility will outlast his tenure."

J. As ancient Chinese philosophers said, "In communication with his subjects, he (a king) rested in good faith", "he who does not keep his promise can hardly act resolutely". As the most powerful country in the world, the US may be used to "conquering" the world with hard power like powerful economy and military prowess. It must not forget that in the information age, soft power, represented by credibility, is more important than ever. If the US is to achieve its goal of "America first", perhaps it should first think about how to restore its perilous credibility.

 Words and Expressions

credibility	[ˌkredəˈbɪləti]	n.	the quality of being believable or trustworthy 信誉；可信度；公信力
underpin	[ˌʌndəˈpɪn]	v.	give strength or support 巩固；加强；支持
bargaining chips			leverage in the form of an inducement or a concession useful in successful negotiations 谈判的筹码；讨价还价的筹码
erode	[ɪˈrəʊd]	v.	become ground down or deteriorate 毁坏；削弱；降低
renege (on)	[rɪˈniːg]	v.	fail to fulfill a promise or obligation 违约；背信；食言
commitment	[kəˈmɪtm(ə)nt]	n.	a thing one has promised to do 承诺，保证
withdraw (from)	[wɪðˈdrɔː]	v.	take back; make a retreat from an earlier commitment or activity 撤回；取消；退出
reconciliation	[ˌrekənsɪliˈeɪkʃn]	n.	the reestablishing of cordial relations 和解；和谐
treachery	[ˈtretʃəri]	n.	showing great disloyalty and deceit 叛变；背叛
reckless	[ˈrekləs]	a.	not caring or worrying about the possibly bad or dangerous results of one's actions 鲁莽的；轻率的；不计后果的
unscrupulous	[ʌnˈskruːpjələs]	a.	not caring about honesty and fairness in getting what one wants; completely without principles 肆无忌惮的；不择手段的；无道德原则的
vengeance	[ˈvendʒəns]	n.	the act of taking revenge 报复；报仇
defiance	[dɪˈfaɪəns]	n.	an intentionally contemptuous behavior or attitude; a hostile challenge 蔑视；违抗；挑衅

inconsistency	[ˌɪnkənˈsɪstənsi]	n.	the quality of being inconsistent and lacking a harmonious uniformity among things or parts 不一致;矛盾
capriciousness	[kəˈprɪʃəsnəs]	n.	the trait of acting unpredictably and more from whim or caprice than from reason or judgment 任性;善变;变化无常
dissident	[ˈdɪsɪdənt]	n.	a person who openly and often strongly disagrees with an opinion, a group, or a government 意见不同的人;持不同政见者
scruple	[ˈskruːpl]	n.	a moral principle which keeps one from doing something; a doubt about the rightness of an action 顾虑;顾忌
deterrence	[dɪˈterəns]	n.	the prevention of something, especially war or crime, by having something such as weapons or punishment to use as a threat 威慑
gauge	[geɪdʒ]	v.	judge tentatively or form an estimate of (quantities or time) 估计;判断
bipartisan	[ˌbaɪpɑːtɪˈzæn]	a.	supported by both sides 得到两党支持的; 代表两党的
univocal	[juːˈnɪvəkl]	a.	admitting of no doubt or misunderstanding 意义明确的
outlast	[aʊtˈlɑːst]	v.	last longer than 比……经久;比……持久
tenure	[ˈtenjə]	n.	a period of office (职位的)任期
resolutely	[ˈrezəluːtli]	adv.	showing firm determination or purpose 坚决地;果断地
prowess	[ˈpraʊəs]	n.	superior ability 杰出的技能;高超的本领
perilous	[ˈperələs]	a.	very dangerous; risky 危险的;冒险的

- **Multiple Choice**

Select the most appropriate answer for each of the following questions.

1. The underlined word "face" in Paragraph A is closest in meaning to "_____".
   A) profile   B) portrait   C) reputation   D) looking
2. The credibility of the US has been damaged in recent years because the US government _____ in a series of international affairs.

A) increases its bargaining chips   B) behaves arrogantly

C) betrays all of its close allies   D) goes back on its words

3. The US government's irresponsible behavior and reneging on its words can be dated back to _____.

   A) the Bush administration   B) the Obama administration

   C) after 2001   D) the current US government

4. As the main builder and participant of the international economic order and the multilateral system after the World War II, the US should not _____.

   A) advocate "America first"   B) withdraw from international institutions

   C) withdraw from international agreements   D) all of the above

5. US President Donald Trump did all of the following in the China-US trade war EXCEPT _____.

   A) defied the WTO rules

   B) withdrew from the WTO

   C) defied the outcomes of the China-US trade talks

   D) accused the Chinese side of going back on its words

6. Which of the following statements is NOT true?

   A) 45 percent of Europeans believe that the US is no longer a reliable security partner of the European Union.

   B) Trump's failure to keep promises undoubtedly carries serious consequences for the US.

   C) Trump is still considered to be the ultimate voice on foreign policy.

   D) Trump does not have political experience and does not listen to White House aides.

7. It can be inferred from the last paragraph that the US government should realize _____.

   A) the US is no longer the most powerful country in the world

   B) Trump can act resolutely if he keeps his promise

   C) US can conquer the world with hard power like powerful economy and military prowess.

   D) restoring its perilous credibility is more important than achieving its goal of "America first"

8. The author's attitude towards the current US president is _____.

   A) hopeful   B) negative   C) positive   D) indifferent

- **Matching**

Which paragraph contains the following information?

1. After the current president took office, the credibility of the US has dropped to a new low.
2. Even more reckless and unscrupulous, the current US government reneges on its words with a vengeance.
3. US President Donald Trump insisted on imposing a 25 percent tariff on 200 billion US dollars of Chinese exports to the US.
4. Public opinion polls reported by the US media show that "between two-thirds and three-quarters of Americans do not find Trump trustworthy".
5. Trump's failure to keep promises undoubtedly carries serious consequences for the US.
6. It must not forget that in the information age, soft power, represented by credibility, is more important than ever.

- **Sentence Completion**

Complete the sentences below with words taken from Text A. Use NO MORE THAN THREE WORDS for each answer.

1. Americans have always regarded their strong and reliable _____ or _____ as the pillar underpinning the world order.
2. The US government has been going back on its words and _____ for a long time.
3. The current US government advocates "America first" and withdraws from _____ _____ and institutions at every turn.
4. People no longer believe that Trump can effectively safeguard the fundamental interests and the _____ of America.
5. With the US domestic system so polarized and its governing party so fragmented, _____ has become more difficult than ever.

- **Writing**

It is undeniable that President Trump has taken the US further down the road dishonesty through a large number of "tweets" that have proved to be false. More and more people question the credibility of media coverage. They hold that inaccurate and even false information may cause more problems than benefits it may bring to the public. Write a composition of no less than 300 words to state your opinions on the credibility of media coverage.

Text B

The Biggest Threat to America Is Us

By Thomas L. Friedman ①

July 3, 2019

The New York Times

  A. Near the close of last Wednesday's Democratic presidential debate, Chuck Todd asked the candidates what he called "a simple question". In "one word," he asked, who or what is the biggest geopolitical threat to America today?

  B. Reflecting on that moment, I asked myself what I would say. It didn't take long to decide. It's not China or Russia or Iran. It's us. We've become the biggest threat to ourselves.

  C. China, Russia, Iran and even North Korea's ② "Little Rocket Man" aren't going to take us down. Only we can take ourselves down. Only we can ensure that the American dream—the core promise we've made to ourselves that each generation will do better than its parents—is not fulfilled, because we fail to adapt in this age of rapidly accelerating changes in technology, markets, climates, the workplace and education.

  D. And that is nearly certain to happen if we don't stop treating politics as entertainment, if we don't get rid of a president who daily undermines truth and trust—the twin fuels needed to collaborate and adapt together—if we don't prevent the far left from pulling the Democrats over a cliff with reckless ideas like erasing the criminal distinction between those who enter America legally and those who don't, and if we fail to forge what political analyst David Rothkopf described in a recent *Daily Beast* essay as "a new American majority".

  E. That's a majority that can not only win the next election but can actually govern the morning after, actually enable us to do big hard things, because we have so many big hard things that need to be addressed—and big hard adaptations can only be done quickly together.

  F. Sounds naïve? No, here's what's naïve. Thinking we're going to be OK if we keep ignoring the big challenges barreling down on us, if we just keep taking turns having one

---

① Thomas L. Friedman is the foreign affairs Op-Ed columnist. He joined the paper in 1981, and has won three Pulitzer Prizes. He is the author of seven books, including *From Beirut to Jerusalem*, which won the National Book Award.

② North Korea 规范名称为 Democratic People's Republic Korea, 尊重原文,下文不再作说明。

party rule and the other obstruct—with the result that no big, long-term and well-thought-out adaptations get built.

G. Indeed, this moment reminds me of something that Mark Mykleby, a retired Marine colonel, said in a book I co-authored in 2011 with Michael Mandelbaum, *That Used to Be Us: How America Fell Behind in the World It Invented and How We Can Come Back*: "At no time in our history have our national challenges been as complex and long-term as those we face today." But, he said, the most salient feature of our politics of late has been our inability "to respond coherently and effectively to obvious problems before they become crises … If we can't even have an 'adult' conversation, how will we fulfill the promise of and our obligation to the Preamble of our Constitution—to 'secure the blessings of liberty to ourselves and our posterity'?" How indeed?

H. Here are just a few of the challenges coming head-on: First, if we have four more years of Trump, we'll probably lose any chance of keeping the global average temperature from rising only 1.5 degrees Celsius instead of 2 degrees—which scientists believe is the difference between being able to manage the now unavoidable climate-related weather extremes and avoiding the unmanageable ones.

I. Second, as Ray Dalio, the founder of the Bridgewater hedge fund, recently pointed out, there has been "little or no real income growth for most people for decades. Prime-age workers in the bottom 60 percent have had no real income growth since 1980". In that same time frame, the "incomes for the top 10 percent have doubled and those of the top 1 percent have tripled. The percentage of children who grow up to earn more than their parents has fallen from 90 percent in 1970 to 50 percent today. That's for the population as a whole. For most of those in the lower 60 percent, the prospects are worse". The anger over that is surely one of the things that propelled Trump into office and, if not addressed, could propel someone even worse, like Donald Trump Jr., in the future.

J. Third, technology is propelling social networks and cybertools deeper and deeper into our lives, our privacy and our politics, so that many more people can erode truth and trust. But the gap between the speed at which these technologies are going deep and the ability of our analog politics to develop the rules, norms and laws to govern them is getting wider, not narrower. That gap has to be closed to preserve our democracy.

K. Fourth, today's workplace is distinguished by one overriding new reality, argues Heather McGowan, an expert on the future of work: "The pace of change is accelerating at the exact same time that people's work lives are elongating."

L. When the efficient steam engine was developed in the 1700s, McGowan explains, average life expectancy was 37 years and steam was the driving force in industry and business for around 100 years. When the combustion engine and electricity were harnessed in the mid-1800s, life expectancy was around 40 years and these technologies dominated the workplace for about another century. So in both eras, notes McGowan, "You had multiple generations to absorb a single big change in the workplace."

M. In today's digital information age, "You have multiple changes in the nature of work within a generation," McGowan says. This dramatically increases the need for lifelong learning. "The old model was that you learned once in order to work, and now we must work in order to learn continuously," she contends. So we're going from a model of "learn, work, retire" to a model of "learn, work, learn, work, learn, work".

N. In that kind of world, the new social contract has to be that government makes sure that the safety nets and all the tools for lifelong learning are available to every American—but it's on each citizen to use them. This moment "is not about who to blame or what to bring back or what to give away", concludes McGowan. "It is about how to create a new deal that engages the American people to 'take longer strides'," as President John F. Kennedy said in seeking funding for NASA. But more of that striding will be on you for more of your life.

O. Fortunately, the mid-term elections showed us that there is a potential new American majority out there to be assembled to meet these challenges. After all, it was the independent voters, suburban women and moderate Republicans—who shifted their votes to Democrats, because they were appalled by Trump's lying, racist-tinge nationalism and divisiveness—who enabled the Democrats to win back the House of Representatives.

P. If Democrats can choose a nominee who speaks to our impending challenges, but who doesn't say irresponsible stuff about immigration or promise free stuff we can't afford, who defines new ways to work with business and energize job-creators, who treats with dignity the frightened white working-class voters who abandoned them for Trump—and who understands that many, many Americans are worried that we're on the verge of a political civil war and want someone to pull us together—I think he or she will find a new American majority waiting to be assembled and empowered.

Unit 3 Politics

  Words and Expressions

accelerate	[ækˈseləreɪt]	v.	(cause to) move faster 加速；使……加速
undermine	[ˌʌndəˈmaɪn]	v.	weaken or destroy gradually 逐渐削弱；暗中损害
fuel	[fjuːəl]	n.	anything that keeps people's ideas or feelings active, or makes them stronger 刺激因素；动力
collaborate	[kəˈlæbəreɪt]	v.	work together on a common enterprise of project 合作，协作
address	[əˈdres]	v.	deal with; tackle 处理；设法解决
barrel	[ˈbærəl]	v.	move very fast 高速行驶；飞驰
obstruct	[əbˈstrʌkt]	v.	hinder or prevent the progress or accomplishment of 阻碍；妨碍
well-thought-out		a.	resulting from careful thought 经过深思熟虑的；精心策划的
salient	[ˈseɪliənt]	a.	having a quality that thrusts itself into attention 显著的；突出的
coherently	[kəʊˈhɪərəntli]	adv.	naturally or reasonably connected and therefore easy to understand 有条理地；一致地
preamble	[priˈæmbl]	n.	a preliminary introduction to a statute or constitution (usually explaining its purpose) 前言；序文
constitution	[ˌkɒnstɪˈtjuːʃn]	n.	a law determining the fundamental political principles of a government 宪法
posterity	[pɒˈsterəti]	n.	offsprings; all future generations 子孙；后代
hedge fund			an investment fund that invests large amounts of money using methods that involve a lot of risk 对冲基金
prime	[praɪm]	a.	the most important, or of the very best quality 首要的；最好的
propel	[prəˈpel]	v.	cause to move forward with force 推进；促使

115

analog	[ˈænəlɒg]	n.	something having the property of being analogous to something else 模拟
		a.	of a circuit or device having an output that is proportional to the input 模拟的;类比的
elongate	[ˈiːlɒŋgeɪt]	v.	make long or longer by pulling and stretching (使)拉长;(使)延长
combustion	[kəmˈbʌstʃn]	n.	a process in which a substance reacts with oxygen to give heat and light 燃烧
harness	[ˈhɑːnɪs]	v.	control; use 控制;利用
contend	[kənˈtend]	v.	debate; claim 争论;据理力争;坚决主张
assemble	[əˈsembl]	v.	get people together 集合;召集,聚集
appall	[əˈpɔːl]	v.	cause to be unpleasantly surprised 使惊骇;使大吃一惊
tinge	[tɪndʒ]	n.	a hint of sth. 一丝痕迹
impending	[ɪmˈpendɪŋ]	a.	close in time; about to occur 即将发生的;迫在眉睫的
energize	[ˈenədʒaɪz]	v.	cause to be alert and energetic 赋予能量;激励

- **True / False / Not Given**

Do the following statements agree with the information given in Text B?

In Blanks 1-10 write

 True   if the statement is true

 False   if the statement is false

 Not Given if the information is not given in Text B

_____ 1. According to the author, the biggest geopolitical threat to America today is Americans themselves.

_____ 2. The author thinks that the US fails to adapt in the age of rapidly accelerating changes in technology, markets, climates, the workplace and education.

_____ 3. The current president of the US has given a large number of false remarks, which are undermining truth and trust.

_____ 4. The author hopes a new American majority can win the next election and can actually govern the country.

_____ 5. The government's ignoring the big hard challenges results in the lack of long-term and well-thought-out adaptations.

_____ 6. Ray Dalio pointed out prime-age workers in the bottom 60 percent had had a little income growth since 1980.

_____ 7. Incomes for the top 1 percent have tripled since 1970.

_____ 8. In today's digital information age, multiple changes in the nature of work within multiple generations dramatically increase the need for lifelong learning.

- **Sentence Completion**

Complete the sentences below with words taken from Text A. Use NO MORE THAN THREE WORDS for each answer.

1. That is nearly certain to happen if Americans fail to forge "a new America _____ _____".

2. We have so many big hard things that need to be addressed, and big hard _____ _____ can only be done quickly together.

3. At no time in our history have our _____ been as complex and long-term as those we face today.

4. The most salient feature of our politics of late has been our inability "to _____ _____ and effectively to obvious problems before they become crises".

5. Technology is _____ social networks and cybertools deeper and deeper into our lives, our privacy and our politics.

6. The pace of change is _____ at the exact same time that people's work lives are elongating.

- **Matching**

Which paragraph contains the following information?

1. That is nearly certain to happen if we don't stop treating politics as entertainment.

2. If we can't even have an adult conversation, how will we fulfill the promise of and our obligation to the Preamble of our Constitution?

3. If we have four more years of Trump, we'll probably lose any chance of keeping the global average temperature from rising only 1.5 degrees Celsius instead of 2 degrees.

4. There has been little or no real income growth for most people for decades. For most of those in the lower 60 percent, the prospects are worse.

5. McGowan contends that the old model was that you learned once in order to work, and now we must work in order to learn continuously.

6. "It is about how to create a new deal that engages the American people to 'take longer strides'", as President John F. Kennedy said in seeking funding for NASA.

7. The mid-term elections showed us that there is a potential new American majority out there to be assembled to meet these challenges.

8. Many Americans are worried that we're on the verge of a political civil war and want someone to pull us together.

- **Writing**

Most people agree that multiple changes in the nature of work within a generation greatly increase the need for lifelong learning. We are changing from an old model of "learn, work, retire" to a new model of "learn, work, learn, work, learn, work". Write a composition of no less than 300 words to state your opinions on the lifelong learning.

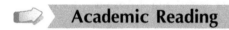

Understanding What You Read (1)

Learning Objective

In the section, you will learn to distinguish topics, main ideas, major details, minor details, and unstated main ideas.

In addition to uncovering word meanings, being able to differentiate among topics, main ideas, major details, and minor details is an extremely important skill because it contributes to a much better understanding of what you are reading. Read the following paragraph, and then answer the question "What is this about?"

One way to recover the past is through music. Popular songs not only provide insight into attitudes and beliefs but also quickly convey the mood and feelings of an era. Through their lyrics, songwriters express the hopes and fears of a people and the emotional tone of an age. Consider, for example, the powerful message conveyed in the Democratic party adoption of "Happy Days Are Here Again" as a campaign theme during the Great Depression. The decline of pop music and the rise of rock and roll in the 1950s tells historians a great deal about the mood of that period. Similarly, the popularity of both folk music and rock in the 1960s provides another way of following social change in that turbulent decade.

If your answer to the question was "music", you are correct: Virtually all of the sentences in the paragraph deal with that particular topic. **The topic** is the subject of a given paragraph, and it can usually be expressed in a word or phrase that can serve as a title. Now reread the same paragraph, and try to answer the following question: "What is the overall message the writer is communicating about the topic?" The answer to that question can be found in the first sentence, which states: "One way to recover the past is through music." That sentence is **the main idea** of the paragraph because it lets you know in a general sense what the writer wants to say about the topic, and it sums up all or most of the remaining sentences. In fact, the main idea always mentions the topic, which explains why the main idea—when it is stated—is also referred to as **the topic sentence**. The rest of the paragraph then consists of **details** that provide more information in order to make the main idea clearer.

Not all details, however, are of equal importance. Some lend direct support to the main idea and are called **major details**. Others, called **minor details**, lend direct support to the major details but only indirect support to the main idea. In other words, major details explain main ideas more specifically, and minor details explain the major details more specifically. For instance, the second and third sentences in the following paragraph on music are the major details because they support the main idea directly by telling you specifically how or why the past can be recovered through music. In short, they supply more information to help make the main idea clearer. The remaining sentences are minor details that further explain the major details by providing very specific examples. Look again at the paragraph, and take note of the topic, main idea, major details, and minor details.

<u>One way to recover the past is through music.</u> Popular songs not only provide insight into attitudes and beliefs but also quickly convey the mood and feelings of an era. Through their lyrics, songwriters express the hopes and fears of a people and the emotional tone of an age. Consider, for example, the powerful message conveyed in the Democratic party adoption of "Happy Days Are Here Again" as a campaign theme during the Great Depression. The decline of pop music and the rise of rock and roll in the 1950s tells historians a great deal about the mood of that period. Similarly, the popularity of both folk music and rock in the 1960s provides another way of following social change in that turbulent decade.

It is very important for you, as a reader, to be aware of the main idea of every paragraph that you encounter, because the main idea sums up the other sentences and focuses on the overall message that the writer is trying to convey about a given topic. Details give you additional information that make it easier for you to understand the main idea.

When the main idea is stated, as in the example on music, it can be found anywhere in a paragraph—**at the beginning, at the end, or somewhere in between**. In addition, sometimes a paragraph will have a main idea expressed in more than one sentence. Look at the following examples, and pay particular attention to the topics, main ideas, major details, and minor details.

The total number of insect species is greater than the total of all other species combined. About a million insect species are known today, and researchers estimate that at least twice this many exist (mostly in tropical forests) but have not yet been discovered. Insects have been prominent on land for the last 400 million years. They have been much less successful in aquatic environments; there are only about 20,000 species in freshwater habitats and far fewer in the sea.

Throughout US history, various groups that believed the government would not respond to their needs have resorted to some form of violence. Analyzing fifty-three US protest movements, William Gamson (1975) found that 75 percent of the groups that used violence got what they wanted, compared with only 53 percent of those that were nonviolent. Violence, it seems, can pay off.

Twenty or thirty years ago, high school health and safety courses may have mentioned some of the hazards of sustained alcohol abuse but with that exception, drug education would not have been found in the high school curriculum. Today, one would be hard-pressed to find a single school in America that does not offer anti-drug education as part of its basic curriculum. Usually, anti-drug programming begins in the elementary grades and intensifies in junior high and high school. In addition to school-based programs, the Partnership for a Drug-Free America and other advocacy groups have sponsored national anti-drug media campaigns targeted mainly at youth. Contemporary youth are bombarded with messages about the evils of drugs and exhortations to avoid their use. If American children watch as much television as alleged, the average teenager is exposed to anti-drug messages several times each day.

Occasionally, certain phrases and words, such as "in short", "in brief", "in summary", "in fact", "clearly", "thus", "yes" and "as these examples show", introduce **the main idea**. Be on the lookout for them. **Major and minor details** are sometimes preceded by the words "for example" or "for instance", because details generally are examples or instances of something. Look carefully for the main idea directly above those words! Finally, simple lists of sentences that begin with such words as "first", "second", "third" and "finally" are often major details, and you usually can find the main idea just before the first item on those lists. A simple listing of facts is a common pattern of organization.

Unstated Main Ideas

Sometimes a paragraph will consist of just details with no topic sentence or stated main idea. However, that does not mean that there is no overall message regarding the topic. It is simply unstated and therefore cannot be found in the paragraph. When that occurs, the details should point you in the direction of the message, which you can then put into your own words. Look at this example:

The average American consumer eats 21 pounds of snack foods in a year, but people in the West Central part of the country consume the most (24 pounds per person), whereas those in the Pacific and Southeast regions eat "only" 19 pounds per person. Pretzels are the most popular snack in the mid-Atlantic area, pork rinds are most likely to be eaten in the South, and multigrain chips turn up as a favorite in the West. Not surprisingly, the Hispanic influence in the Southwest has influenced snacking preferences—consumers in that part of the United States eat about 50 percent more tortilla chips than do people elsewhere.

The topic of the paragraph has to do with snack foods that Americans eat. Although no sentence expresses the overall message regarding the topic, a number of details provide examples. The average American eats 21 pounds of snack food in a year. People in the West Central part of the United States eat the most. People in the Pacific and Southeast regions consume the least. Pretzels are popular in the mid-Atlantic area. Pork rinds are popular in the South. Multigrain chips are the favorite in the West. And tortilla chips are consumed in the Southwest. If you take all of these details together and look for one general idea, it would be "**Americans differ in their preferences for snack foods according to where they live**".

Every paragraph has a topic or subject and an overall message about the topic that is expressed as the main idea. When there is no stated main idea, remember to consider carefully what most or all of the major details in a paragraph have in common, which should then help you figure out **the unstated main idea**. Remember that major details further explain main ideas, while minor details provide more information about major details. Whether the main idea is stated or not, be sure to come away from each paragraph that you read with the overall message clearly in mind.

Part 3 Learning After Class

Additional Reading 1

British Prime Minister, Theresa May Resigns

Theresa May will step down as Conservative party leader on June 7, and pave the way for a new prime minister to take over in the summer. This is the full text of her speech outside Downing Street.

By Theresa May

May 24, 2019

The Guardian [1]

Ever since I first stepped through the door behind me as prime minister, I have striven to make the United Kingdom a country that works not just for a privileged few, but for everyone, and to honour the result of the EU referendum. Back in 2016, we gave the British people a choice. Against all predictions, the British people voted to leave the European Union. I feel as certain today as I did three years ago that in a democracy, if you give people a choice you have a duty to implement what they decide. I have done my best to do that.

I negotiated the terms of our exit, and a new relationship with our closest neighbours that protects jobs, our security and our union. I have done everything I can to convince MPs to back that deal. Sadly, I have not been able to do so. I tried three times. I believe it was right to persevere even when the odds against success seemed high. But it is now clear to me that it is in the best interests of the country for a new prime minister to lead effort. So I am today announcing that I will resign as leader of the Conservative and Unionist Party on Friday 7th of June, so that a successor can be chosen. I have agreed

---

[1] *The Guardian*, formerly known as *The Manchester Guardian* (founded in 1821), is a British national daily newspaper. Currently edited by Alan Rusbridger, it has grown from nineteenth century local paper to a national paper associated with a complex organisational structure and international multimedia presence with sister papers *The Observer* (British Sunday paper) and *The Guardian Weekly*, as well as a large web presence. According to its editor, *The Guardian* has the second largest online readership of any English-language newspaper in the world, after *The New York Times*.

with the party chairman and with the chairman of the 1922 committee that the process for electing a new leader should begin in the following week. I have kept Her Majesty the queen fully informed of my intentions, and I will continue to serve as her Prime Minister until the process has concluded. It is and will always remain a matter of deep regret to me that I have not been able to deliver Brexit. It will be for my successor to seek a way forward that honours the result of the referendum. To succeed, he or she will have to find consensus in Parliament where I have not.

Such a consensus can only be reached if those on all sides of the debate are willing to compromise. For many years, the great humanitarian, Sir Nicholas Winton, who saved the lives of hundreds of children by arranging their evacuation from Nazi-occupied Czechoslovakia through the Kindertransport, was my constituent in Maidenhead. At another time of political controversy a few years before his death, he took me to one side at a local event and gave me a piece of advice. He said, "Never forget that compromise is not a dirty word. Life depends on compromise." He was right. As we strive to find the compromises, we need in our politics whether to deliver Brexit or to restore devolved government in Northern Ireland. We must remember what brought us here. Because the referendum was not just a call to leave the EU, but for profound change in our country, a call to make the United Kingdom a country that truly works for everyone.

I'm proud of the progress we have made over the last three years. We have completed the work that David Cameron and George Osborne started. The deficit is almost eliminated. Our national debt is falling and we are bringing an end to austerity. My focus has been on ensuring that the good jobs of the future will be created in communities across the whole country not just in London and the South East, through our modern industrial strategy. We have helped more people than ever enjoy the security of a job. We are building more homes, and helping first-time buyers onto the housing ladder, so young people can enjoy the opportunities their parents did. And we are protecting environment, eliminating plastic waste, tackling climate change, and improving air quality. This is what a decent, moderate and patriotic Conservative government on the common ground of British politics can achieve, even as we tackle the biggest peacetime challenge any government has faced.

I know that the Conservative Party can renew itself in the years ahead, that we can deliver Brexit and serve the British people with policies inspired by our values. Security, freedom and opportunity, those values have guided me throughout my career. But the unique privilege of this office, is to use this platform to give a voice to the voiceless, to fight the burning injustices that still scar our society. That is why I put proper funding for mental health at the heart of our NHS long-term plan. It's why I'm ending the postcode lottery for survivors of domestic abuse. It is why the race disparity audit and gender pay reporting are shining a light on inequality, so it has nowhere to hide. And it is why I set up the independent publicing inquiry into the tragedy at Grenfell Tower to search for the truth, so nothing like it can ever happen again, and so the people who lost their lives that night are never forgotten.

Because this country is a union, not just a family of four nations, but a union of people, all of us. Whatever our background, the colour of our skin or who we love, we stand together, and together we have a great future. Our politics may be under strain but there is so much that is good about this country, so much to be proud of, so much to be optimistic about. I will shortly leave the job that it has been the honour of my life to hold. The second female prime minister, but certainly not the last. I do so with no ill will, but with enormous and enduring gratitude, to have had the opportunity, to serve the country I love.

 Words and Expressions

strive	[straɪv]	v.	make a great effort, especially to gain sth. 努力；力求
privileged	[ˈprɪvəlɪdʒd]	a.	having an advantage or opportunity that most other people do not have 享有特权的
referendum	[ˌrefəˈrendəm]	n.	asking the people to vote on the policy and show whether or not they agree with it 公民投票；全民公决
implement	[ˈɪmplɪm(ə)nt]	v.	carry out or put into practice 实施；实现；使生效
consensus	[kənˈsensəs]	n.	a general agreement among a group of people 一致；共识
constituent	[kənˈstɪtjuənt]	n.	a voter; a member of a constituency 选民
compromise	[ˈkɒmprəmaɪz]	n.	an agreement with another person or group, when you both do part of what the other person or group wants 妥协；折衷；和解
devolve	[dɪˈvɒlv]	v.	pass on or delegate to another 委任；移交
eliminate	[ɪˈlɪmɪneɪt]	v.	get rid of; remove 消除；排除

postcode lottery			a situation in which the standard of medical care, education, etc, received by the public varies from area to area, depending on the funding policies of various health boards, local authorities 邮编彩票(指公众因所居住地区不同而享受到不同的医疗、教育标准)
disparity	[dɪˈspærəti]	n.	inequality or difference in some respect 明显差异;悬殊差别
audit	[ˈɔːdɪt]	n.	official examination of business and financial records to see that they are true and correct 审计;账目的检查

Discussion Questions

1. Theresa May quoted a piece of advice given by Sir Nicholas Winton, "Never forget that compromise is not a dirty word. Life depends on compromise." Do you agree with this idea? Why or why not?
2. What progresses have been made by the Conservative Government over the last three years according to Theresa May? What do you think is the most important progress?

Additional Reading 2

China Is Not the Source of Our Economic Problems—Corporate Greed Is

The author elaborated on the falsehood of blaming China as the "enemy", sharply pointed out how the trade tension was created out of the greed of Washington policies, and that "there will be no winners in such a conflict". In a word, he said the US should find its own way out, using homegrown solutions, rather than finding a scapegoat.

By Jeffrey Sachs ①
May 27, 2019
CNN ②

China is not an enemy

It is a nation trying to raise its living standards through education, international trade, infrastructure investment, and improved technologies. In short, it is doing what any country should do when confronted with the historical reality of being poor and far behind more powerful countries. Yet the Trump administration is now aiming to stop China's development, which could prove to be disastrous for both the United States and the entire world.

China is being made a scapegoat for rising inequality in the United States. While US trade relations with China have been mutually beneficial over the years, some US workers have been left behind, notably midwestern factory workers facing competition due to rising productivity and comparatively low labor costs in China. Instead of blaming China for this normal phenomenon of market competition, we should be taxing the soaring corporate profits of our own multinational corporations and using the revenues to help working-class households, rebuild crumbling infrastructure, promote new job skills and invest in cutting-edge science and technology.

We should understand that China is merely trying to make up for lost time after a very long period of geopolitical setbacks and related economic failures. While China has seen incredible growth in the past four decades, the legacy of more than a century of poverty, instability, invasion and foreign threats still looms large. Chinese leaders would like to get things right this time, and that means they are unwilling to bow to the United States or other Western powers again.

China is now the second-largest economy in the world, when GDP is measured at market prices. Yet it is a country still in the process of catching up from poverty. In 1980, according to IMF data, China's GDP per capita was a mere 2.5 percent of the United States, and by 2018 had reached only 15.3 percent of the US level.

---

① Jeffrey Sachs is an American economist, public policy analyst and former director of the Earth Institute at Columbia University. He is known as one of the world's leading experts on economic development and the fight against poverty.

② CNN (Cable News Network) is an American news-based pay television channel owned by AT&T's WarnerMedia. CNN was founded in 1980 by American media proprietor Ted Turner as a 24-hour cable news channel. Upon its launch, CNN was the first television channel to provide 24-hour news coverage, and was the first all-news television channel in the United States. CNN Digital is the world leader in online news and information and seeks to inform, engage and empower the world. Staffed 24 hours, seven days a week by a dedicated team in CNN bureaus around the world, CNN's digital platforms deliver news from almost 4,000 journalists in every corner of the globe.

The constant US refrain that China "steals" technologies is highly simplistic.

China has roughly followed the same development strategy as Japan, South Korea and Singapore before it. From an economic standpoint, it is not doing anything particularly unusual for a country that is playing catch up.

Countries that are lagging behind upgrade their technologies in many ways, through study, imitation, purchases, mergers, foreign investments, extensive use of off-patent knowledge and, yes, copying. And with any fast-changing technologies, there are always running battles over intellectual property. That's true even among US companies today—this kind of competition is simply a part of the global economic system. Technology leaders know they shouldn't count on keeping their lead through protection, but through continued innovation.

The United States relentlessly adopted British technologies in the early 19th century. And when any country wants to close a technology gap, it recruits know-how from abroad. The US ballistic missile program, as it is well-known, was built with the help of former Nazi rocket scientists recruited to the United States after World War II.

If China were a less populous Asian country, say like South Korea, with a little more than 50 million people, it would simply be hailed by the United States as a great development success story—which it is. But because it is so big, China refutes America's pretensions to run the world. The United States, after all, is a mere 4.2 percent of the world's population, less than a fourth of China's. The truth is that neither country is in a position to dominate the world today, as technologies and know-how are spreading more quickly across the globe than ever before.

To accuse China of unfairness in trade is wrong.

Trade with China provides the United States with low-cost consumer goods and increasingly high-quality products. It also causes job losses in sectors such as manufacturing that compete directly with China. That is how trade works.

Plenty of American companies have reaped the benefits of manufacturing in China or exporting goods there. And US consumers enjoy higher living standards as a result of China's low-cost goods. The US and China should continue to negotiate and develop improved rules for bilateral and multilateral trade instead of stoking a trade war with one-sided threats and over-the-top accusations.

The most basic lesson of trade theory, practice and policy is not to stop trade—which would lead to falling living standards, economic crisis and conflict. Instead, we should share the benefits of economic growth so that the winners who benefit compensate the losers.

Yet under American capitalism, which has long strayed from the cooperative spirit of the New Deal era, today's winners flat-out reject sharing their winnings. As a result of this lack of sharing, American politics are fraught with conflicts over trade. Greed comprehensively dominates Washington policies.

The real battle is not with China but with America's own giant companies.

Many of which are raking in fortunes while failing to pay their own workers' decent wages. America's business leaders and the mega-rich push for tax cuts, more monopoly power and offshoring—anything to make a bigger profit—while rejecting any policies to make American society fairer.

Trump is lashing out against China, ostensibly believing that it will once again bow to a Western power. It is willfully trying to crush successful companies like Huawei by changing the rules of international trade abruptly and unilaterally. China has been playing by Western rules for the past 40 years, gradually catching up the way that America's Asian allies did in the past. Now the United States is trying to pull the rug out from under China by launching a new Cold War.

Unless some greater wisdom prevails, we could spin toward conflict with China, first economically, then geopolitically and militarily, with utter disaster for all. There will be no winners in such a conflict. Yet such is the profound shallowness and corruption of US politics today that we are on such a path.

A trade war with China won't solve our economic problems. Instead we need homegrown solutions: affordable health care, better schools, modernized infrastructure, higher minimum wages and a crackdown on corporate greed. In the process, we would also learn that we have far more to gain through cooperation with China rather than reckless and unfair provocation.

Words and Expressions

confront with			force to deal with 使面临；使面对
soar	[sɔː]	v.	rise rapidly 剧增；猛增
crumbling	[ˈkrʌmblɪŋ]	a.	falling apart into fragments; falling into decay or ruin 破碎的；崩溃的；摇摇欲坠的
cutting-edge	[ˈkʌtɪŋˈedʒ]	a.	in accord with the most fashionable ideas or style 领先的，尖端的
recruit	[rɪˈkruːt]	v.	register formally as a participant or member 聘用；通过招募组建

ballistic	[bəˈlɪstɪk]	a.	relating to or characteristic of the motion of objects moving under their own momentum and the force of gravity 弹道的;射击的
refute	[rɪˈfjuːt]	v.	overthrow by argument, evidence, or proof 驳斥;驳倒
pretension	[prɪˈtenʃn]	n.	a false or unsupportable quality 自负,狂妄;声称,标榜
fraught	[frɔːt]	a.	filled with or attended with 充满……的
abruptly	[əˈbrʌptli]	adv.	quickly and without warning 突然地;唐突地
spin	[spɪn]	v.	revolve quickly and repeatedly around one's own axis 旋转;疾驰
crackdown	[ˈkrækdaʊn]	n.	strong official action taken to punish people who break laws 制裁;惩罚
provocation	[ˌprɒvəˈkeɪʃn]	n.	unfriendly behavior that causes anger or resentment 挑衅;激怒

 Discussion Questions

1. What homegrown solutions should be used by the US to solve its economic problems according to Jeffrey Sachs?
2. Jeffrey Sachs points out that, "The constant US refrain that China 'steals' technologies is highly simplistic." Do you agree with this idea? Why or why not?

Additional Reading 3

EU Elections: Will Young People Turn Up?

May 26, 2019
CGTN

European elections have long suffered a voter turnout problem. Disinterest has been especially severe among young people.

Ahead of this weekend's vote, political parties and campaign groups have done their best to motivate young voters to head to the polls. Meanwhile, school children and students worldwide have taken to the streets to demand action against climate change. So can we expect higher youth turnout this year, and what could this mean for the next EU parliament?

A persistent turnout problem

Voter participation in European elections has dropped steadily since 1979. From 61.99 percent, it fell to just 42.61 percent in the last election in 2014.

And the proportion of young voters was dismal. A post-election survey by the European parliament in 2014 found less than 28 percent of those aged 18 to 24 had bothered to head to the polls. This compared to 51 percent of those aged 55 and above.

Young voters have often been dismissed as apathetic. Campaigners meanwhile blame politicians for doing too little to get young people interested and failing to address their concerns. Ahead of elections on May 23 – 26, efforts to get young voters to the polls seemed to show a new recognition that their votes count too.

YouTube, Instagram and Spotify

Austria made a first move to get more young people involved in 2007 when it lowered the voting age to 16. Greece and Malta have since followed suit. French President Emmanuel Macron took part in a live chat on Friday with a young YouTube star in a last-minute attempt to drum up support for the elections.

The European parliament meanwhile recruited so-called "influencers" with millions of followers on Instagram, Facebook or Twitter to get the message out and help explain how the European parliament works and how to register to vote.

Creative projects and groups with names like Vote Together, This Time I'm Voting and Your Vote Matters sprang up, with more or less backing from EU organizations, to urge people to "Go Vote".

In perhaps the most unusual campaign move, music streaming service Spotify sent users messages urging them to vote and even released an EU election playlist, labeled "Get Vocal Europe" and featuring artists from every member country.

Shaping the next European parliament

But it's not just about turnout figures and statistics. Young voters tend to be more pro-European than their elders: a recent survey by the Pew Research Center found as much as a 30-point gap in some countries between the percentage of 18 – 29-year-olds who favor the European Union, and those aged 50 or over.

With experts predicting wins for populist, nationalist and eurosceptic parties at these elections—and with Brexit looming over the bloc, prompting fears of further disintegration—youth votes are more crucial than ever.

On issues too, young voters' priorities differ greatly from their parents. Among their main concerns: climate change, digital rights, migration and youth unemployment, rather than pensions and the economy.

Parties that put an accent on these issues, such as the environmental Greens, could thus benefit from a high youth turnout, impacting the make-up and policies of the European parliament for the next five years.

Parties with younger candidates—including the far-right, which has been actively courting the youth vote—also look to profit: at the moment, the average age among MEPs is 55, with just one deputy aged under 30, while the oldest is 90.

"We want a say."

On Friday, school children and students worldwide ditched class again as part of a massive movement demanding action against climate change.

From the environment to Brexit, young people have been vocal about issues that will directly affect them in the near future. In that, this election differs from previous ones: young people have a clear stake in the outcome and have been demanding a say at the policy-making level, exasperated that politicians who will not have to suffer the consequences are the ones making decisions.

As Our Future Our Choice, a group campaigning to register young voters in the UK, noted ahead of the vote: "We shouldn't have to live with something we don't want."

"On May 26, you have the chance to vote and make some fundamental change: to elect the people who will be responsible for our present, and most importantly our future," German "influencer" Alex Boehm urged in a YouTube video entitled "Go Vote, dammit" that was viewed over 200,000 times.

Will they, won't they?

Young voters tend to decide late who they will vote for, and with 28 countries heading to the polls, predictions are tricky.

Already, the Netherlands—which voted on Thursday—has caused a sensation, with exit polls predicting a win for pro-EU parties there, against analysts' expectations.

So far, every member state that has headed to the polls, except Lithuania, has reported higher early voting turnout than in 2014, according to poll forecaster Europe Elects. The youth vote could still create a surprise when final results come in on Sunday.

Words and Expressions

turnout	[ˈtɜːnaʊt]	n.	attendance 出席者；参加人数
motivate	[ˈməʊtɪveɪt]	v.	give an incentive for action 使有动机，激发积极性
parliament	[ˈpɑːləmənt]	n.	(in some countries) the main law-making body, made up of members wholly or partly elected by the people of the country 议会；国会
dismal	[ˈdɪzməl]	a.	gloomy; causing dejection 令人沮丧的；忧郁的，压抑的
spring up			appear or develop quickly and/or suddenly 迅速出现；突然兴起
eurosceptic	[ˌjʊərəʊˈskeptɪk]	n.	someone, especially a politician, who is opposed to closer links between Britain and the European Union 欧洲怀疑论者（指反对英国与欧盟关系密切的人）
pension	[ˈpenʃn]	a.	an amount of money paid regularly, especially by a government or company, to sb. who can no longer earn money by working, especially because of old age or illness 退休金；抚恤金
ditch		v.	abandon or get rid of 摆脱，抛弃

Discussion Questions

1. Why should young adults care about politics?
2. Young voters from European countries focus on the issues such as climate change, digital rights, migration and youth unemployment. What issues do you concern about most as a young adult?

Part 4　Topical Vocabulary

one-country-two-system policy "一国两制"的政策
be honest in performing one's official duties 廉洁奉公
build a clean and honest government; construction of a clean government 廉政建设
fight corruption and build a clean government 反腐倡廉
distribution according to one's performance 按劳分配
maintain steady and rapid growth 保持平稳较快增长
socialism with Chinese characteristics 中国特色社会主义

the cohesiveness of our nation 民族凝聚力　　cast a ballot 投票
polling day 投票日　　count of votes 计票
electoral procedure 选举程序　　primary election 初选
general election 普选　　mid-term election 中期选举
secret vote / anonymous ballot 不记名投票　　soliciting votes 拉票
public opinion poll 民意测验　　approval rating 支持率
Constitution 宪法　　legislation 立法
the ruling party 执政党　　Amendment 修正案
Democrat 民主党党员　　Republican 共和党党员
Congress 美国国会　　Senate 参议院
the House of Representatives 众议院　　veto power 否决权
national sovereignty 国家主权　　diplomatic dispute 外交纷争
overall national strength 综合国力　　boundary negotiation 边界谈判
international waters 国际水域　　territorial integrity 领土完整
press conference 新闻发布会　　anti-corruption 反腐败
peace-keeping force 维和部队　　China's actual conditions 中国国情
long-standing issue 由来已久的问题　　Comfortable Housing Project 安居工程
revitalizing key industry 重点产业振兴
deep-rooted social problem 根深蒂固的社会问题

Unit 4

Economy

Part 1 Learning Before Class

• Listening

China Launches Tech Hub Megalopolis to Rival Silicon Valley

Directions: *Listen to the news and answer the questions.*

1. In this news, China announced a long-awaited plan. What is the plan?
2. Why did China make such a grand plan?
3. Can you analyze the economic significance of the plan?

• Watching and Thinking

Global Firms Welcome China's First Foreign Investment Law

Directions: *Watch the video and discuss the questions with your partner.*

1. What were the main concerns of foreign investors when they expanded their investment in China?
2. China's first Foreign Investment Law is, undoubtedly, of great significance for domestic economy, foreign investors and even the world trade growth. What do you think of this far-reaching law?
3. What is the relationship between China's first Foreign Investment Law and China's reform and opening-up policy?

Unit 4　Economy

● Reading and Discussing

World Economy Facing Delicate Moment, IMF Says

By Andrew Walker
April 9, 2019
BBC News ①

　　The global economy is at what the International Monetary Fund's chief economist calls a "delicate moment". Gita Gopinath ② says that while she does not predict a global recession, "there are many downside risks".

　　The IMF has released its regular assessment of the World Economic Outlook, which forecasts global growth of 3.3% this year and 3.6% in 2020. That would be slower growth than last year—and for 2019, a downgrade compared with the previous forecast. The downward revision of 0.2 percentage points for global growth is spread widely.

　　Developed economies affected include the US, the UK and the Eurozone. The UK economy is predicted to grow by 1.2% in 2019, down 0.3% from the IMF forecast in January. Growth in 2020 has also been revised down. The revisions are especially marked for Germany and Italy, which is already in recession.

　　The IMF expects weaker performance in Latin America, as well as in the Middle East and North Africa. For China, there are small revisions, upward for this year and downward for next. The slowdown there, which began at the start of the decade, is expected to continue.

"Precarious" recovery

　　The weakness in the forecast reflects a slowdown in the latter part of 2018, which the IMF expects to continue in the first half of this year. After that, growth should pick up more paces, with the additional momentum continuing into next year.

---

　　① BBC News is an operational business division of the British Broadcasting Corporation (BBC) responsible for the gathering and broadcasting of news and current affairs. The department is the world's largest broadcast news organization. It is a British free-to-air television news channel. It was launched as BBC News 24 on 9 November, 1997 at 5:30 pm as part of the BBC's foray into digital domestic television channels, becoming the first competitor to Sky News, which had been running since 1989.

　　② Gita Gopinath is a professor of International Studies and of Economics at Harvard University. She is currently on leave of public service from the economics department to serve as the Chief Economist of the International Monetary Fund (IMF). Her research focuses on International Finance and Macroeconomics. She is the co-editor of the current *Handbook of International Economics* and was earlier the co-editor of the *American Economic Review*, managing editor of the *Review of Economic Studies*.

But Ms. Gopinath describes that recovery as "precarious". She says it depends on a recovery in a number of developing economies that are stressed, notably Turkey and Argentina. Ms. Gopinath also expects a partial recovery in the Eurozone. The US, however, is likely to slow further, growing by slightly less than 2% next year as the impact of President Donald Trump's tax cuts fades. There is no sign in her blog, or in the IMF's report, of any sympathy for President Trump's view that the main thing holding back the US economy is the Federal Reserve's increases in interest rates over the last two years.

Flare of disruption?

The risks that Ms. Gopinath warns about include some familiar ones.

The first she mentions is the possibility that global trade tensions could flare up again and spread into new areas. She refers to cars in particular, an area where President Trump is considering new tariffs on imported goods. That, she suggests, could lead to "large disruptions to global supply chains". She says the escalation of US-China trade tensions contributed to last year's slowdown.

She also mentions risks associated with Brexit. The forecasts for the UK are based on the expectation of an orderly departure—with a deal—from the EU later this year. A no-deal Brexit would be more costly.

Other risks include the possibility of deterioration in financial markets, leading to higher borrowing costs, including for governments. That raises the possibility of what she calls sovereign/bank doom loops. That was a particular problem in the euro-area financial crisis, when financial problems for governments and banks reinforced one another.

Directions: *Read the passage and discuss the questions with your partner.*

1. The global economy is at what the International Monetary Fund's chief economist calls a "delicate moment". How do you interpret such a delicate moment?
2. Why does Ms. Gopinath think the recovery of 2019 world economy is precarious?
3. Considering the risks that the world economic growth is facing, what do you think of the relationships of regional economic cooperation and world economic development?

Part 2 Learning in Class

Warm Up

US-China Tariff Dispute Threatens to Cause Economic Damage on All Sides

Directions: Watch the video and discuss the questions with your partner.

1. What is a tariff?
2. How does a higher tariff affect the livelihood of domestic average people?
3. Is there a real winner of a trade war? Why or why not?

Text A

Forget China—It's America's Own Economic System That's Broken

By Robert Reich [1]

Jun. 23, 2019

The Guardian

US weakness is inbuilt—the big 500 companies owe loyalty only to themselves and the public is shut out from prosperity. Xi Jinping might possibly agree next weekend on further steps to bring down China's trade imbalance with the US, giving Donald Trump a face-saving way of ending his trade war. But Xi won't agree to change China's economic system. Why should he?

The American economic system is focused on maximizing shareholder returns. And it's achieving that goal: on Friday, the S & P 500 notched a new all-time high. But average Americans have seen no significant gains in their incomes for four decades, adjusted for inflation. China's economic system, by contrast, is focused on maximizing China. And it's achieving that goal. Forty years ago China was still backward and agrarian. Today it's the world's second-largest economy, home to the world's biggest auto

---

[1] Robert Reich, a former US secretary of labor, is professor of public policy at the University of California at Berkeley and the author of *Saving Capitalism: For the Many, Not the Few and the Common Good*. He is also a columnist for *Guardian US*.

industry and some of the world's most powerful technology companies. Over the last four decades, hundreds of millions of Chinese people have been lifted out of poverty.

The two systems are fundamentally different. At the core of the American system are 500 giant companies headquartered in the US but making, buying and selling things all over the world. Half of their employees are non-American, located outside the US. A third of their shareholders are non-American. These giant corporations have no particular allegiance to America. Their only allegiance and responsibility is to their shareholders. They'll do whatever is necessary to get their share prices as high as possible—including keeping wages down, fighting unions, reclassifying employees as independent contractors, outsourcing anywhere around world where parts are the cheapest, shifting their profits around the world wherever taxes are the lowest, and paying their top CEOs ludicrous sums.

At the core of China's economy, by contrast, are state-owned companies that borrow from state banks at artificially low rates. These state firms balance the ups and downs of the economy, spending more when private companies are reluctant to do so. They're also engines of economic growth making the capital-intensive investments China needs to prosper, including investments in leading-edge technologies. China's core planners and state-owned companies will do whatever is necessary both to improve the well-being of the Chinese people and become the world's largest and most powerful economy. Since 1978, the Chinese economy has grown by an average of more than 9% per year. Growth has slowed recently, and American tariffs could bring it down to 6% or 7%, but that's still faster than almost any other economy in the world, including the US.

The American system relies on taxes, subsidies and regulations to coax corporations to act in the interest of the American public. But these levers have proven weak relative to the overriding corporate goal of maximizing shareholder returns. Last week, for example, Wal-Mart, American's largest employer, announced it would lay off 570 employees despite taking home more than $2bn **courtesy** of Trump and the Republican corporate tax cuts. Last year, the company closed dozens of Sam's Club stores, leaving thousands of Americans out of work. At the same time, Wal-Mart has plowed more than $20bn into buying back shares of its own stock, which boosts the pay of Wal-Mart executives and enriches wealthy investors but does nothing for the economy.

It should be noted that Wal-Mart is a global company, not adverse to bribing foreign officials to get its way. On Thursday it agreed to pay $282m to settle federal allegations of overseas corruption, including channeling more than $500,000 to an intermediary in Brazil known as a "sorceress" for her ability to make construction permit problems disappear.

Across the American economy, the Trump tax cut did squat for jobs and wages but did nicely for corporate executives and big investors. Instead of reinvesting the savings into their businesses, the International Monetary Fund reports that companies used it to buy back stock.

But wait. America is a democracy. True, but most Americans have little or no influence on public policy—which is why the Trump tax cut did so little for them. That's the conclusion of professors Martin Gilens of Princeton and Benjamin Page of Northwestern, who analyzed 1,799 policy issues before Congress and found that "the preferences of the average American appear to have only a minuscule, near-zero, statistically non-significant impact upon public policy". Instead, American law-makers respond to the demands of wealthy individuals (typically corporate executives and Wall Street moguls) and of big corporations, those with the most lobbying prowess and deepest pockets to bankroll campaigns.

Don't blame American corporations. They're in business to make profits and maximize their share prices, not to serve America. But because of their dominance in American politics and their commitment to share prices instead of the well-being of Americans, it's folly to count on them to create good American jobs or improve American competitiveness.

I'm not suggesting we emulate the Chinese economic system. I am suggesting that we not be smug about the American economic system. Instead of trying to get China to change, we should lessen the dominance of big American corporations over American policy. China isn't the reason half of America hasn't had a raise in four decades. The simple fact is Americans cannot thrive within a system run largely by big American corporations, organized to boost their share prices but not boost Americans.

Words and Expressions

agrarian	[əˈgreərɪən]	a.	connected with farming and the use of land for farming 农业的；农村的
fundamentally	[ˌfʌndəˈmentəli]	adv.	indicating that something affects or relates to the deep, basic nature of something 从根本上；基本地
allegiance	[əˈliːdʒəns]	n.	support for and loyalty to a particular group, or belief 忠诚；拥护

contractor	[kənˈtræktə(r)]	n.	a person or company that arranges to supply materials or workers to other people or organizations 承包人;承包商
outsource	[ˈaʊtsɔːs]	v.	obtain goods or services from an outside supplier 外包
ludicrous	[ˈluːdɪkrəs]	a.	stupid, unreasonable and deserving to be laughed at 荒谬的;可笑的
subsidy	[ˈsʌbsədi]	n.	money that is paid by a government or an organization to reduce the costs of services or of producing goods so that their prices can be kept low 补贴
coax	[kəʊks]	v.	gently try to persuade sb. to do 劝诱
adverse	[ˈædvɜːs]	a.	having a negative, harmful or unfavorable effect on 不利的;有害的
allegation	[ˌæləˈɡeɪʃn]	n.	accusing somebody of doing something wrong or illegal 指控
intermediary	[ˌɪntəˈmiːdiəri]	n.	someone who carries messages between people who are unwilling or unable to meet 仲裁者;调解者
squat	[skwɒt]	v.	蹲下,蹲坐
democracy	[dɪˈmɒkrəsi]	n.	the belief in freedom and equality between people, or a system of government based on this belief, in which power is either held by elected representatives or directly by the people themselves 民主;民主思想;民主政体
minuscule	[ˈmɪnəskjuːl]	a.	extremely small 非常小的;极不重要的
mogul	[ˈməʊɡl]	n.	an important person who is very rich or powerful 显要人物;有权势的人
lobby	[ˈlɒbi]	v.	try to persuade (a politician, an official or an official group) that a particular thing should or should not happen 游说
prowess	[ˈpraʊəs]	n.	great skill 高超技艺
bankroll	[ˈbæŋkrəʊl]	v.	support a person or activity financially 提供资金
commitment	[kəˈmɪtmənt]	n.	a willingness to give your time and energy to something that you believe in, or a promise or firm decision to do something 忠诚;奉献;承诺

Unit 4　Economy

emulate	[ˈemjuleɪt]	v.	copy; imitate 效仿;模仿
smug	[smʌg]	a.	too pleased or satisfied about sth. you have achieved or sth. you know 沾沾自喜的;自鸣得意的
dominance	[ˈdɒmɪnəns]	n.	the situation in which one company, product, etc. has more power, influence, or success than others 支配;控制
boost	[buːst]	v.	improve or increase sth. 提高;增强;推动

- **Multiple Choice**

Select the most appropriate answer for each of the following questions.

1. From this sentence "the big 500 companies owe loyalty only to themselves" (Paragraph 1), we can infer that _____.

   A) American commercial magnates enjoy an exclusionary community solidarity

   B) shareholders are the priority of American giant corporations

   C) the US big companies need to strengthen the economic bond between them

   D) closer cooperation is really critical to American big businesses

2. According to the author, the fundamental difference between US-China economic systems lies in _____.

   A) what they focus on maximizing

   B) their different economic structure

   C) their different commitments of dominant businesses to the public

   D) the relationship between their corporations and government

3. In Paragraph 5, Wal-Mart is taken as an example to demonstrate _____.

   A) Wal-Mart is one of the giant corporations with the abundant financial bankroll

   B) the maximization of shareholder returns is the overwhelming goal of US corporations

   C) the functions of US economic levers are impotent in their regulating the operating of businesses

   D) the American corporations fail to benefit adequately from US economic system

4. The underlined word "**courtesy**" in Paragraph 5 is closest in meaning to "_____".

   A) politeness   B) preferential service

   C) complimentary service   D) privilege

5. Which of the following is TRUE according to this passage?

141

A) American economic system is on the edge of disintegration.

B) Average Americans are basking in the boom of US economy.

C) American giant corporations have conventionally maintained their dominance over US economy.

D) Big American corporations exert considerable influence on the boosting of US economy.

6. What is the author's tone about the analysis of American and Chinese systems of economy?

A) Ambiguous. B) Contemptuous.

C) Detached. D) Radical.

- **True /False**

Do the following statements agree with the information given in Text A?

In Blanks 1-6 write

True   if the statement is true

False   if the statement is false

_____ 1. Economically interests-oriented difference results in different main beneficiaries of the US and China.

_____ 2. China's state-owned companies act as a drive of its economic growth.

_____ 3. American businesses are inextricably linked with US national policies.

_____ 4. It is not advisable to depend on the US giant corporations to achieve adequate employment and improve American competitiveness.

_____ 5. Despite the validity of US giant corporations' pursuit of profits and share prices, it is not necessarily unreasonable for them to take account of the well-being of the public.

_____ 6. The US economic system is fundamentally organized largely by American giant corporations.

- **Short Answer Questions**

1. What is the only allegiance and responsibility of US giant corporations?
2. How do US giant corporations maximize their shareholder returns?
3. What is the goal of the state-owned companies and core planners in China?
4. What is the status of US giant corporations, economically and politically?
5. What are the main levers adopted by the American system to adjust the operation of big corporations?

Discussion Questions

1. What are the different focuses of US and China economic systems?
2. Over the last four decades, the majority of Chinese people have been lifted out of poverty, while average American have seen no significant gains in their incomes. What do you think is the fundamental reason behind the difference?

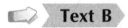

Tariffs Will Ultimately Harm US Economy

By Dong Yan & Zeng Chenwei [1]

June 27, 2019

China Daily

That Vice Premier Liu He talked with US Trade Representative Robert Lighthizer and US Treasury Secretary Steven Mnuchin on the phone on Monday raises hope that China and the United States would resume the bilateral trade negotiations. However, the negotiations, if they resume, are not likely to be smooth. On June 18, Lighthizer threatened to impose punitive tariffs on Chinese imports if certain issues were not resolved to the US' satisfaction. The US has been constantly pressuring China and has slapped 25 percent tariffs on about $250 billion of Chinese goods even though US President Donald Trump called President Xi Jinping on the phone recently and said that he would restart the trade negotiations on the sidelines of the G20 Summit in Osaka, Japan, later this week. US trade war hawks believe Washington can win the tussle with Beijing because they either indulge in self-deception or are ignorant enough to gloss over the US' loss in the trade war it has started. In March last year, the White House claimed it is easy to win a trade war, with the US administration stressing that a trade war will deal a serious blow to the Chinese economy despite basic economic principles and scientific data analysis suggesting otherwise.

US consumers forced to pay more for goods

Theoretically speaking, the distribution of tariff cost depends on the relative value of

---

[1] Dong Yan is a research fellow at the Institute of World Economics and Politics, Chinese Academy of Social Sciences. And Zang Chengwei is a postdoctoral scholar at the same institute.

US consumers' demand elasticity to the supply elasticity of vendors that export to the US. The lesser the demand elasticity and greater the supply elasticity, the higher the cost of tariff the US is expected to pay. Independent studies conducted by multiple scholars in the US show the tariffs would increase the price US consumers pay for a product while the supply price of Chinese vendors remains nearly unaffected. Chinese Academy of Social Sciences, too, has said that more than 90 percent of the tariffs would have to be paid by the US. And an International Monetary Fund report, issued in May indicated the US would shoulder most of the cost of the tariff hike.

The tariff hike would also deal a blow to the US economy and welfare. According to the US National Bureau of Economic Research, the welfare loss on the consumers' and producers' side due to the 2018 tariff policy would total 0.7 percent of GDP, while the Center for Economic and Policy Research, a Washington-based economic policy think tank, predicted the tariff policy would cause a monthly loss of $14 billion to the US.

Thanks to the negative effects of the trade disputes with multiple countries, the US did not achieve the expected GDP growth rate of 3 percent in 2018.

Some in US fantasizing about "winning" trade war

The US' unexpected 3.2 percent GDP growth in the first quarter this year might have prompted certain people including politicians to fantasize that Washington is "winning" the trade war. Yet the temporary recovery of the US economy can be attributed to a series of economic stimulus, including tax reduction and increase in public spending which for the time being appears to offset the negative influences of the trade war on the US economy.

The fact is, the US could have registered a much higher growth rate had it not launched a trade war against China. That institutions including JPMorgan Chase and Goldman Sachs have all lowered the forecasts for US growth suggests their White House has squandered the chance to bolster US economic growth by imposing punitive tariffs on imports, especially from China.

A simulation test conducted by Chinese Academy of Social Sciences shows the US would lose 0.004 percent of GDP for hiking tariffs and 0.067 percent of GDP because of China's counter-measures. Also, the US manufacturing sector employment would decline by 0.652 percent due to the 25 percent tariffs it has imposed on Chinese goods and another 0.907 percent due to China's counter-measures, which means the tariff hike will harm American people's livelihoods.

The US daydreaming that it can win trade war

The US administration is free to use its imaginary achievements to beat its chest, but it must be daydreaming to believe it can win the trade war. At the very least, the US' huge economic loss would make the trade war a bad bargain even if it succeeded in realizing some of its objectives. According to scholars including Mary Amiti, assistant vice-president of the Federal Reserve Bank of New York, even if a trade negotiation increases the royalties China pays to the US by 25 percent, it would take three years of these higher royalties to cancel out the deadweight welfare loss ① caused by the US-triggered trade war. On the other hand, even if the trade war helps create 35,400 manufacturing jobs—the number of steel and aluminum sector jobs lost in the last 10 years—the deadweight welfare loss per job saved would be $195,000, which is almost four times the average annual wage of a steel worker $52,500.

Since the US first slapped punitive tariffs on Chinese goods in 2018, their full impact on global trade is not yet known. And although Chinese enterprises couldn't immediately find substitute trade partners, they will certainly achieve a smooth transfer of production and trade with the passage of time. For instance, Harley Davidson, once hailed by the White House as a model of "Made in America", has shifted part of its production unit and even started cooperation with Qianjiang Motorcycle to produce motorbikes in China. The trade protectionism policy that the US administration claimed would create jobs for Americans is instead bringing quality investment to China.

In the short term, the US can neither claim victory in the trade war nor say China alone is paying the hiked tariffs. And in the long run, at a time when developed economies are struggling to boost growth, and populism and protectionism are rising, the US, rather than making its due contribution to improve the global economy, is continuing to intensify Sino-US disputes. And by so doing, the US is soiling its global image and overdrawing on its long-term global competitiveness.

---

① Deadweight loss is a cost to society created by market inefficiency, which occurs when supply and demand are out of equilibrium. It is the loss of total welfare or the social surplus due to reasons like taxes or subsidies, price ceilings or floors, externalities and monopoly pricing. It is the excess burden created due to loss of benefit to the participants in trade which are individuals as consumers, producers or the government.

Words and Expressions

punitive	[ˈpjuːnətɪv]	a.	intended as a punishment 处罚的；惩罚性的
tussle	[ˈtʌsl]	v.	have difficult disagreements or strong arguments （激烈地）争执，争辩
indulge	[ɪnˈdʌldʒ]	v.	allow yourself to have or do something that you like, especially something that is considered bad for you 沉溺于
ignorant	[ˈɪɡnərənt]	a.	lacking knowledge or information about something 无知的；愚昧的
elasticity	[ˌiːlæˈstɪsəti]	n.	the ability to stretch, change 弹性；灵活性
fantasize	[ˈfæntəsaɪz]	v.	think about something very pleasant that is unlikely to happen 想象；幻想
squander	[ˈskwɒndə(r)]	v.	waste money, time, etc. in a stupid or careless way 浪费，挥霍
bolster	[ˈbəʊlstə(r)]	v.	support or improve, or make stronger 支持，鼓励
countermeasure	[ˌkaʊntəˈmeʒə]	n.	an action taken against an unwanted action or situation 对策；应对措施
impose	[ɪmˈpəʊz]	v.	officially force a rule, tax, punishment, etc. to be obeyed or received 推行；强制实行
livelihood	[ˈlaɪvlihʊd]	n.	生计；营生；生活
royalty	[ˈrɔɪəlti]	n.	a sum of money paid to writers, people who have invented things, owners of property, etc. every time their books, devices, land, etc. are bought or used by others（专利）使用费；（著作的）版税
aluminum	[əˈluːmɪnəm]	n.	a chemical element 铝
enterprise	[ˈentəpraɪz]	n.	an organization, especially a business 公司，企业
substitute	[ˈsʌbstɪtjuːt]	n.	a thing or person that is used instead of another thing or person 代替者
populism	[ˈpɒpjəlɪzəm]	n.	political ideas that are intended to get the support of ordinary people by giving them what they want 民粹主义
overdraw	[ˌəʊvəˈdrɔː]	v.	take out more money from a bank account than it contains 透支

Exercises

- **Multiple Choice**

Select the most appropriate answer for each of the following questions.

1. Which of the following is the economic stimuli that brought about the US slight boom early this year?
   A) Tax cut and tariff hike.
   B) Public spending increase.
   C) Royalty increase.
   D) Tax cut and public spending increase.

2. The word "hike" in the sentence "the US would shoulder most of the cost of the tariff hike" is closest in meaning to "_____".
   A) saunter   B) tramp   C) increase   D) ramble

3. According to this passage, which of the following is TRUE about Sino-US trade disputes?
   A) A slim chance can be forecast that the bilateral trade negotiations between the US and China will bear fruits in a short time.
   B) The punitive tariffs imposed by the White House on Chinese imports have coerced China into resolving certain issues for the sake of America.
   C) The world economy has been suffering the full impact of trade war between the US and China.
   D) The recent recovery of the US economy has benefited significantly from its tariffs as a means of economic stimulus.

4. The instance of "Harley Davidson" in this passage illustrates that _____.
   A) the trade protectionism failed to achieve certain objectives that the US administration had expected
   B) the US-triggered trade war resulted in quality investment pouring into China
   C) the corporation, Harley Davidson, once took the lead in the American business
   D) the US administration has lost control over its oversea capital

5. Based on the analysis made in this passage, we can draw a safe conclusion that _____.
   A) in the world trade, the dominant economic position of the United States remains untouched
   B) in the US-triggered trade war, China has taken positive actions to safeguard its national interests
   C) American global competitiveness is to be increasingly elevated regardless of this trade war
   D) US trade war hawks feel confident of its constant GDP growth

6. The following are the consequences resulting from American tariffs on Chinese imports in the US trade war against China EXCEPT _____.

   A) an increase in the prices US consumers pay for a product
   B) the welfare loss on the consumers' and producers' side
   C) the harm to American average people's livelihood
   D) the change of world economic pattern

- **Sentence Completion**

Complete the sentences below with words taken from Text B. Use NO MORE THAN THREE WORDS for each answer.

1. US hawks hold the belief that Washington can win the trade war against China just because of their _____ or being _____ enough to gloss over the US' loss in the ongoing trade war.

2. The tariff hike by the US administration would also _____ a serious blow to the US economy and welfare.

3. Early this year, the temporary recovery of the US economy can be _____ to a series of economic stimulus. But if it had not launched a trade war against, the US could have _____ a much higher growth rate.

4. Even though the US administration is blindly taking advantage of its _____ to beat its chest, but it must be a daydream of its being a winner in the US-triggered trade war.

5. In the long run, the US' continuing to intensify Sino-US disputes will be _____ _____ its global image and _____ on its long-term global competitiveness.

- **Short Answer Questions**

1. Under what circumstance did Lighthizer threaten to impose punitive tariffs on Chinese imports?
2. What did an International Monetary Fund report issued in May indicate?
3. Some influential institutions including JPMorgan Chase and Goldman Sachs have all lowered the forecasts for US economic growth. What did it suggest?
4. If the US administration succeeded in realizing some of its objectives in the trade war against China, who would suffer hugely?
5. Who would be the main victims in America if the trade war helps it create 35,400 manufacturing jobs?

Unit 4 Economy

Discussion Questions

1. What's your understanding of the term "protectionism"?
2. As two big economies, both America and China play an essential part in world economy. How do you comment on "a great power is supposed to make its due contribution to improve the global economy"?
3. Economic globalization is a world phenomenon wherein countries' economic situation can depend significantly on other countries. In such an international context, what do you think of this US-triggered trade war against China?

Academic Reading

Understanding What You Read (2)

Learning Objective

In the section, you will learn to recognize patterns of organization: simple listing of facts, time sequence, comparison and contrast, cause and effect.

Recognizing Patterns of Organization

Look carefully at this sequence of numbers: 16-1-20-20-5-18-14-19 1-18-5 8-5-12-16-6-21-12.

Does this mean anything to you? Can you see a message? Probably not. What if you were told that each number corresponds to a letter in the alphabet, numbered in order from 1 to 26? Is that better? After a few minutes, you should be able to figure out that the message is "Patterns are helpful"!

Once you determine the arrangement or pattern of something, the message is much easier to understand. Have you ever heard someone say, "I am starting to see a pattern here?" That comment usually means that several pieces of similar information are enabling the person to come to a particular conclusion. For example, if Jonathan has consistently arrived late for a psychology class during the first three weeks of the semester, his instructor would see a pattern and might conclude that Jonathan is not a very responsible student. Again, patterns can be useful by adding meaning to given situations.

Writers often help readers recognize important details by arranging them in a certain way. These arrangements of details are called **patterns of organization**, and there are four major ones: **simple listing of facts, time sequence, comparison and contrast, and cause** and effect. When reading material is organized using one or more of these patterns, you will more easily see not only details but also the main idea. Or the main idea may tip you off to the presence of a specific pattern of organization. So it is a two-way process. Let us take a look at each of the patterns.

(1) **Simple Listing of Facts**

This pattern involves a list of details that could include the causes, characteristics, examples, or types of something. Writers will often use **transition words** such as the following to help you recognize this pattern: also, another, examples, factors, finally, following, in addition, last, list, many, numbers (first, second, etc.), other, several, types, next, moreover, further, furthermore.

Look at the following example:

> The Internet is a powerful tool for advertisers. Click-through rates are one measure of effectiveness. Another trend is paid search advertising. New products and services spawned by the digital revolution include: broadband, which permits transmission of streaming media over the Internet; mobile commerce (m-commerce) which is made possible by Wi-Fi, Bluetooth, WiMax, and other forms of wireless connectivity; telematics and global positioning systems (GPS); and short message service (SMS). Smart phones are creating new markets for mobile music downloads, including ringtones, truetones, and full-track music files; they can also be used for mobile gaming and Internet phone service using VoIP.

Notice how the main idea "The Internet is a powerful tool for advertisers" covers a number of products, which you may or may not be familiar with. The main idea is in the first sentence. The list of products uses transition words such as **one measure**, **another trend**, **including**, **and also**. The list also includes punctuation such as the colon and the semicolon to let you know there will be a list of Internet-advertising trends.

Another example of a simple listing of facts or details does not have the main idea in the first sentence. Read the following example:

> America can be fairly called a "drug culture" in the sense that nearly everyone uses drugs of one sort or another. When we are ailing, we expect to be given some drug that will make us feel better. If we have trouble sleeping, we take sleeping medications, whether over-the-counter or prescribed. If we feel anxious, we want anti-anxiety drugs, and if we feel depressed, we seek antidepressants. The use of drugs to make one feel better or to solve one's problems, whatever they might be, is deeply entrenched in our culture and our expectations.

In this example, the main idea is stated in both the first and last sentences, which convey just about the same overall message. Writers will sometimes repeat the same—or close to the same—main idea in the first and last sentences of a paragraph, which makes it easier to spot. All the rest of the sentences in the paragraph are major details that list the kinds of drugs people take and their reasons for taking them. Although there is no numbering, you are helped to recognize the presence of the list by the repetition of the words **when we** and **if we**.

(2) **Time Sequence**

This pattern involves details placed in the order in which they occur in time. Transition words often found in time sequence include these: after, before, beginning, dates, finally, first, last, later, next, once, prior, repeat, steps, then, thereafter, times of day, when, year, previously, now, following, immediately, while, during, often, until, soon.

Historical and other material with dated events or times of the day are the most obvious place to find this pattern, as in the following example:

> The population of the United States has been shifting to the South and the West, the region known as the Sunbelt, and away from the Northeast and Midwest, the Frostbelt. In 1970, a majority of the nation's population, 52 percent, lived in the Frostbelt. The population has subsequently shifted steadily to the South and West. In 2000, 58 percent of Americans lived in the Sunbelt. The Sunbelt population is growing because of relatively higher birthrates in the region, immigration from abroad, and intrastate migration from the Frostbelt.

Once again, the main idea is stated in the first sentence, which informs you that the time sequence organizes details that illustrate how "the population has shifted". The dates make it easy to identify the major details that directly support the overall message.

This pattern can also include the steps in a process, directions, or anything else that is accomplished in a definite time order, as in the example below:

> In courtship, a male and female loon swim side by side while performing a series of displays. (1) The courting birds frequently turn their heads away from each other. (In sharp contrast, a male loon defending his territory often charges at an intruder with his beak pointed straight ahead.) (2) The birds then dip their beaks in the water, and (3) submerge their heads and necks. Prior to copulation, the male invites the female onto land by (4) turning his head backward with his beak held downward. There, (5) they copulate.

The main idea is stated in the first sentence, which tells you that "In courtship, a male and female loon swim side by side while performing a series of displays". That sentence, along with the transition words series, **then**, and **prior**, lets you know that behavior is being traced that must be accomplished in a definite sequence. The rest of the sentences, with the exception of the one in parentheses, are major details that trace the steps in the process. Although the major details are numbered, the pattern of organization here is time sequence rather than a simple listing of facts because the steps in the process must be done in that order. In other words, Step 1 must be accomplished before Step 2, Step 2 must be accomplished before Step 3, Step 3 must be accomplished before Step 4, and Step 4 must be accomplished before Step 5. With a simple listing, the items on a given list are not in any specific time order. This is the key difference between those two patterns.

(3) **Comparison and Contrast**

This pattern organizes details that deal with the similarities (comparison) and differences (contrast) between persons, events, ideas, or things. Transition words that are often found with comparison and contrast include these: alike, between, common, commonalities, compare, contrast, debate, difference, disagree, distinction, distinguish, like, likeness, on the other hand, same, similarity, unlike, whereas.

Also, the main idea usually tells you exactly what is being compared or contrasted. Read the following example:

> 1. Think of all the ways that human beings are alike. Everywhere, no matter what their backgrounds or where they live, people love, work, argue, dance, sing, complain, and gossip. They rear families, celebrate marriages, and mourn losses. They reminisce about the past and plan for the future. They help their friends and fight with their enemies. They smile with amusement, frown with displeasure, and glare in anger. Where do all these commonalities come from?
>
> 2. Think of all the ways that human beings differ. Some of us are extroverts, always ready to throw a party, make a new friend, or speak up in a crowd; others are shy and introverted, preferring the safe and familiar. Some are trailblazers, ambitious and enterprising; others are placid, content with the way things are. Some take to book learning like a cat to catnip; others don't do so well in school but have lots of street smarts and practical know-how. Some are overwhelmed by even the most petty of problems; others, faced with severe difficulties, remain calm and resilient. Where do all these differences come from?

The first paragraph deals with how human beings are similar as stated by the main idea: "Think of all the ways that human beings are alike." The transition words **alike** and **commonalities** help you recognize the pattern. All of the remaining sentences, with the exception of the last one, are major details that directly support the overall message by giving examples of similarities. The main idea of the second paragraph—"Think of all the ways that human beings differ"—tells you that it is concerned with how human beings are different, and the transition words **differ** and **differences** are also revealing. Again, the rest of the sentences in the paragraph, except the last one, are major details that directly support the overall message by providing examples of differences. Do you notice that there is an additional pattern of organization in both paragraphs? There is also a simple listing of facts. The repetition of the word **they** in the first paragraph and **some** and **others** in the second one gives strong indication that lists are present. As you can see, writers sometimes use a combination of patterns, which is very helpful to you, because it gives you more than one opportunity to recognize important details and thus better understand what you are reading.

(4) **Cause and Effect**

This pattern organizes details that present causes or reasons along with their effects or results. In other words, this pattern explains why something has happened. For example, if one of your classmates asked you how you got an A+ on the last history test (**effect**), you might proceed to explain that you attended all classes (**cause**), took down every word the professor had said (**cause**), read all the assignments (**cause**), and studied on a daily basis (**cause**). In essence, you would be using the cause-and-effect pattern to give the reasons why you earned such a high grade. Transition words to look for when this pattern is present include these: affects, because, brings out, cause, consequences, contributed, create, effect, leads to, reaction, reason, result, therefore, whereas, due to, accordingly, since, if … then, thus.

Sometimes the causes are stated first, as in the following example:

> During the late 1980s, news articles, TV shows, and radio commentaries proclaimed that the nation was facing a shortage of scientists. The growth in high-tech industries was going to create demands for scientists and engineers that would not be met. The government even suggested that this shortage would endanger national security. The result was an increase in the number of students seeking postgraduate education, especially doctoral degrees in engineering, the sciences, mathematics, and computer science. For example, in 1981 – 1982, a total of 2,621 PhDs were granted in engineering; by 1991 – 1992, the number had more than doubled, to 5,488. Similar, though less dramatic, increases were seen in the number of doctorates awarded in the sciences and mathematics.

The first three sentences in the paragraph provide causes:

• "During the late 1980s, news articles, TV shows, and radio commentaries

proclaimed that the nation was facing a shortage of scientists."
- "The growth in high-tech industries was going to create demands for scientists and engineers that would not be met."
- "The government even suggested that this shortage would endanger national security."

The fourth sentence states the effect:
- "The result was an increase in the number of students seeking postgraduate education, especially doctoral degrees in the engineering, sciences, mathematics, and computer science."

More specific information, which directly supports the effect, is found in the remaining sentences, preceded by the words **for example**. Notice the two transition words create and result, which help you recognize the pattern. The main idea, which for the most part is unstated, would read something like this: "There was an increase in the number of students seeking postgraduate education in engineering, sciences, mathematics, and computer science as a result of national concern in the late 1980s that there was a serious shortage of scientists and engineers."

This pattern sometimes presents effects first, followed by causes, as in the following example:

> People became homeless for a variety of reasons. Some started life in seriously disturbed families. Others fell prey to alcohol and drugs. Still others had health or learning problems that eroded the possibility of a stable life. For millions of working Americans, homelessness was just a serious and unaffordable illness away. Though many Americans initially regarded the homeless as "bag ladies, winos, and junkies", they gradually came to realize that the underclass category included others as well.

The first sentence—"People became homeless for a variety of reasons"—has the transition word **reasons** and also lets you know that homelessness is the **effect**. **Causes** are presented in the second, third, and fourth sentences, which are the major details:
- "Some started life in seriously disturbed families."
- "Others fell prey to alcohol and drugs."
- "Still others had health or learning problems that eroded the possibility of a stable life."

Did you notice a second pattern of organization? The words **some**, **others**, and still others indicate that the causes are also organized in a simple listing of facts. When you read, recognizing one or more than one pattern of organization enables you to focus on important information and thus helps you comprehend better.

Part 3 Learning After Class

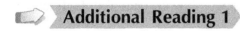

Whoever Runs the World Bank Needs a Plan for Emerging Markets

Robert Zoellick [1]
February 6, 2019
The Financial Times [2]

Governments are now selecting a new president of the World Bank. In doing so, they should be considering the strategic economic context in which the bank will operate. The retrospectives 10 years after the global financial crisis dramatized events in the US and Europe, but rarely cast an eye on developing economies. The next World Bank president needs a better grasp of that history and must know what his or her institution and others should be doing now to prepare for the next downturn.

If policy-makers overlook the experience of developing countries during the crisis, they are less likely to consider emerging market dynamics, understand developing economies' sources of resilience and appreciate vulnerabilities. Given the attention accorded to developing economies in earlier crises, it would be ironic to ignore their roles during the "great recession". The consequences of skewed history could be dire.

Multiple poles of growth are a source of strength for the global economy. Breakdowns in developing markets, in contrast, harm the most desperate. Migrations to Europe and North America reveal the human cost for all societies of failures in poor countries.

The firefighters of 2008 recognized that the world had changed: they shifted from the G7 to the G20. In the immediate aftermath of the financial shocks, developing economies accounted for about half of the world's growth. Emerging markets led the recovery in world trade, with demand for imports rising twice as fast as in wealthier countries.

---

[1] Robert Zoellick is a former president of the World Bank, US Trade Representative and Deputy Secretary of State.

[2] *The Financial Times* is an English-language international daily newspaper headquartered in London, with a special emphasis on business and economic news. The paper was founded in 1888 by James Sheridan and Horatio Bottomley, and merged in 1945 with its closest rival, *The Financial News* (which was founded in 1884).

Developing economies were even net exporters of capital to high income estates. South-south linkages assumed greater importance, representing one third of global trade and foreign direct investment.

The developing economy story suggests five lessons. First, emerging markets were not spared the costs of crisis. Their average growth rate of about 7 percent in the five years preceding the crisis fell to 1.6 per cent in 2009, knocking an estimated 64m people into extreme poverty. Excluding China and India, average growth rates fell from about 6 per cent to almost minus 2 per cent.

Second, China's huge stimulus offered a critical boost to a tumbling world economy and especially to commodity exporters. Policy-makers who claim that Beijing harms global markets and who want to "decouple" China from the world economy, should take note. India and Indonesia also demonstrated resilience when most needed.

Third, trade disruptions were more likely to harm poor countries than were financial shocks. Global trade plum meted promptly, with trade in the first quarter of 2009 down about 30 per cent from the prior year. Resistance against protectionism proved vital. The World Trade Organization and World Bank had to press G20 central bankers not to strangle trade finance. The current tariff wars—plus a creeping movement in recent years towards temporary trade barriers for intermediate as well as retail goods—will undermine resilience in the next downturn.

Fourth, developing countries' structural reforms before the storm created room for timely fiscal expansion. Many governments could rely on well-designed-programs for healthcare, education, social safety nets and infrastructure, even though they had to slow spending growth. They tried to protect their primary productive "asset": human capital and skills.

In the face of a harsh reprising of risk and the pullback of international banks, some countries could mobilize domestic financial resources, including private investment, because they had developed local currency securities markets and inclusive finance for smaller enterprises. Developed economies can help themselves in the future if they assist developing economies to prepare today.

Finally, the multilateral development banks complemented the IMF's countercyclical support with $158bn of commitments between July 2008 and December 2009, $88bn of which came from the World Bank. The policies the development banks catalyzed were as important as the money. They supplied critical farm inputs and resisted export bans during the food price surge 2008.

Meanwhile, development funds enabled countries to maintain safety nets and to offer innovative finance for groups at risk. The European Bank for Reconstruction and Development and the World Bank persuaded western European commercial banks to keep capital in eastern European subsidiaries, avoiding a countercyclical contraction.

The lessons from the financial crisis of 2008 extend far beyond central bank interventions, bank bailouts and supervision. When the next downturn or financial crisis hits, emerging markets are likely to prove even more important than they were a decade ago. The new World Bank president should help developing countries to prepare now.

Words and Expressions

retrospective	[ˌretrəˈspektɪv]	n.	a show of the work an artist has done in their life so far 回顾展
dramatize	[ˈdræmətaɪz]	v.	make something seem more exciting or important than it really is 戏剧化；夸张；渲染
resilience	[rɪˈzɪliəns]	n.	the quality of being able to return quickly to a previous good condition after problems 适应性
vulnerability	[ˌvʌlnərəˈbɪləti]	n.	the quality of being weak and easily hurt physically or emotionally 弱点；易受攻击；脆弱性
skew	[skjuː]	v.	twist or distort 使歪斜
dire	[ˈdaɪə]	a.	very serious or extreme 严重的；极其的
aftermath	[ˈɑːftəmæθ]	n.	the period that follows an unpleasant event or accident, and the effects that it causes 后果
tumble	[ˈtʌmbl]	v.	fall a lot in value in a short time (价值)暴跌，骤降
disruption	[dɪsˈrʌpʃn]	n.	an interruption in the usual way that a system or process works 分裂；破裂
plum	[plʌm]	n.	something good and worth having 美事
mete	[miːt]	v.	make someone receive unfair treatment 使受不公正对待
infrastructure	[ˈɪnfrəstrʌktʃə]	n.	the basic systems and services, such as transport and power supplies 基础设施
reprise	[rɪˈpriːz]	n.	a repeat of something, especially a piece of music 重奏

countercyclical	[ˌkaʊntəˈsaɪklɪkəl]	a.	countercyclical activities do not follow the pattern which is normal in business or the economy 反周期的
catalyze	[ˈkætəlaɪz]	v.	make something start happening or start being successful 催化；催动……发生（或成功）
subsidiary	[səbˈsɪdiəri]	n.	a company that is owned or controlled by a larger company 子公司
bailout	[ˈbeɪlaʊt]	n.	an act of giving money to a company, a foreign country, etc. that has very serious financial problems 紧急（财政）援助
migration	[maɪˈɡreɪʃn]	n.	the movement from one region to another 移民；移往
commodity	[kəˈmɒdəti]	n.	a substance or product that can be traded, bought, or sold 商品，货物
estate	[ɪˈsteɪt]	n.	a large area of land developed for a specific purpose 土地；地产，房产
preceding	[prɪˈsiːdɪŋ]	a.	existing or happening before someone or something 在前的，在先的；前面的

 Discussion Questions

1. According to the author, it would be ironic to overlook the important roles of developing economies during the recovery of world trade after the global financial crisis. What are the reasons?

2. What lessons do developing economies suggest when functioning significantly in the global economic growth?

• Unit 4　Economy •

Additional Reading 2

Xi Jinping's Second Belt and Road Forum: The Key Takeaways

April 27, 2019

Bloomberg News [1]

Chinese President Xi Jinping hosted some 5,000 delegates from across the globe at the Belt and Road forum in Beijing last week to discuss his signature infrastructure project, which began in 2013 to rebuild ancient trading routes across Eurasia. This year's gathering eschewed the pageantry of the inaugural summit in 2017. Here are three takeaways from the summit.

At the forum, People's Bank of China Governor Yi Gang said the central bank would "build an open, market-oriented financing and investment system", and the government released its analysis framework for debt sustainability.

Xi didn't announce new numbers on upcoming investment into the program, though he said $64 billion worth of deals were signed at last week's forum. In 2017, he said China would add 100 billion *yuan* (about $14.8 billion) to the Silk Road Fund and two state-owned banks would provide special loans for BRI (Belt and Road) projects worth 380 billion *yuan* in total.

This year's joint statement—released after Xi chaired a round table with participating leaders—repeatedly called for "high-quality" projects and standards. The 2017 communiqué didn't use the phrase. The document also encouraged developed nations to invest in "connectivity projects" in developing countries, and said cooperation "will be open, green and clean".

"International lenders will not invest in a project that has not been derisked or is not financially viable," said Daniel Russel, vice president for international security and diplomacy at the Asia Society Policy Institute. "China's challenge now is to demonstrate that the 'Green BRI' and 'Clean BRI' have been translated into action throughout the Belt and Road." China's efforts to rehabilitate the Belt and Road's image did have some success, drawing eight more heads of state to this year's conference.

Malaysian Prime Minister Mahathir Mohamad, previously one of the biggest critics of the initiative in Southeast Asia, said his country is fully supportive and stands to benefit

---

[1] Bloomberg News, an international news agency headquartered in New York.

from its BRI project. Earlier this month, Malaysia struck a deal with China to resume the East Coast Rail Link project for 44 billion ringgit—down from 65.5 billion ringgit—after deciding to terminate it in January.

In March, Italy became the first Group of 7 countries to sign up for the BRI, a big win for Beijing. At last week's forum, developed countries including Austria, Switzerland and Singapore signed up for the third-party market cooperation. Japan, France, Canada, Spain, the Netherlands, Belgium, Italy and Australia have already signed the document, agreeing to help build infrastructure in developing countries.

"The attendance of some EU countries leaders show the projects are attractive to some developed countries which also have their own domestic economic issues," said Suisheng Zhao, executive director of the Center for China-US Cooperation at the University of Denver's Graduate School of International Studies. "Since the trade war with the US broke out, China has reexamined its leverage in its relations with major countries and readjusted some accordingly."

While Xi made no mention of the ongoing trade war with the US in his speech on Friday, a large part of it alluded to the major issues in negotiations—such as cleaning up state subsidies, reducing non-tariff barriers, boosting imports and protecting intellectual property.

China won't engage in currency devaluation that "harms others", Xi said in the speech. The phrase mirrors language he's used to describe China's diplomatic policies. Bloomberg News reported earlier that the US was asking China to keep the value of the yuan stable to neutralize any effort to soften the blow of US tariffs.

While he reiterated Chinese talking points about opening up, Xi specifically highlighted the significance of implementation, another sticking point in the China-US trade talks. "We will establish a binding enforcement system for international agreements," Xi told the forum. US Treasury Secretary Steven Mnuchin has said the two sides have "pretty much agreed on" a mechanism for sticking to the trade deal.

"It's clear that Xi sought to use this year's Belt and Road Forum as a platform to pursue multiple objectives: to rebrand the Belt and Road and also to telegraph to the United States that he is prepared—at least—to address American concerns that have led to the current trade confrontation," said Daniel Kliman, senior fellow in the Asia-Pacific Security Program at the Centre for a New American Security.

Unit 4　Economy

 Words and Expressions

takeaway	[ˈteɪkəweɪ]	n.	conclusions, impressions or action points resulting from a meeting discussions, presentation, etc. 从……中了解到的主要信息
eschew	[ɪsˈtʃuː]	v.	avoid something intentionally, or give something up 避开；放弃
pageantry	[ˈpædʒəntri]	n.	impressive and colorful ceremonies 盛典；盛况
inaugural	[ɪˈnɔːgjərəl]	a.	that is the first in a series of planned events 首次的，初始的
sustainability	[səˌsteɪnəˈbɪləti]	n.	持续性，可持续性
communiqué	[kəˈmjuːnɪkeɪ]	n.	an official piece of news or an announcement, especially to the public or newspapers 公报
viable	[ˈvaɪəbl]	a.	able to work as intended or able to succeed 可以实施的；可望成功的
demonstrate	[ˈdemənstreɪt]	v.	show or make something clear 显示；表明
rehabilitate	[ˌriːəˈbɪlɪteɪt]	v.	return to the previous good condition 使恢复；修复
terminate	[ˈtɜːmɪneɪt]	v.	end or stop (使……)结束；终止
forum	[ˈfɔːrəm]	n.	a meeting in which people can talk about a problem or matter especially of public interest 论坛，讨论会
allude	[əˈluːd]	v.	mention directly 暗指
devaluation	[ˌdiːˌvæljuˈeɪʃn]	n.	the action of reducing the rate at which money can be exchanged for foreign money (货币)贬值
diplomatic	[ˌdɪpləˈmætɪk]	a.	connected with managing relations between countries 外交的
neutralize	[ˈnjuːtrəlaɪz]	v.	make something neutral 使中立
reiterate	[riˈɪtəreɪt]	v.	repeat something that you have already said, especially to emphasize it 重申
implementation	[ˌɪmplɪmenˈteɪʃn]	n.	putting a plan into action 成就；贯彻
confrontation	[ˌkɒnfrʌnˈteɪʃn]	n.	a fight or argument 冲突；争论

Discussion Questions

1. According to this passage, what are the main characteristics of the Belt and Road initiative?
2. At the Second Belt and Road Forum, many countries, including some big economies like Italy, France, Japan and Australia, have signed the document, agreeing to support this great project. What are the reasons?

Additional Reading 3

Global Economy Emerges from Gloom into a Bright Spring

By Chris Giles

May 6, 2019

The Financial Times

Less than a month ago in the IMFs imposing HQ2 building in Washington Gita Gopinath, its new chief economist, had a bleak message for the world. Disappointing data had led the fund to cut its forecasts for global growth yet again, any recovery penciled in for the second half of this year was "precarious", and this toxic combination meant that spring 2019 was a "delicate moment" for the global economy.

But the IMF's message appears to have been far too gloomy. Over the past few days the three largest economic blocs in the world—the EU, the US and China, comprising almost half of global output—have published first-quarter estimates and all three have been stronger than expected.

On the latest data, at least the slowdown of late 2018 has already ended.

In Europe, the eurozone grew 0.4 per cent in the first quarter, according to preliminary estimates, significantly higher than expected. Italy has emerged from recession and Germany, which has published its figures yet, is also likely to show improved performance.

Outside the eurozone, growth has been stronger still, with the EU economy as a whole growing at an above-average rate of 0.5 per cent. The Bank of England last week upgraded its forecast for the UK's performance this year from 1.2 per cent growth to 1.5 per cent, with Governor Mark Carney saying the global outlook had become "more benign".

Unit 4　Economy

Europe's above-trend performance has been eclipsed by even stronger data from the US first-quarter growth of 0.8 per cent—the US reports this 3.2 per cent on an annualized basis—was far higher than expected for a quarter that started with a prolonged government shutdown. Although the details suggested that strength might be partly temporary, the figures still indicated considerable momentum.

In China, growth stabilized at annual rate of 6.4 per cent and more up-to-date figures suggested the government's infrastructure stimulus was having its desired effect, with industrial production rising at an annual rate of 8.5 per cent in March—much stronger.

Catherine Mann at Citi said the outlook was still fragile but "growth has stabilized", adding that "prospects (have) changed from the IMF's 'glass half empty' to 'glass half full'".

In London, the National Institute of Economic and Social Research suggests 3.4 per cent global growth this year, compared with the IMF's 3.3 per cent forecast Jagjit Chadha, its director, criticized the fund's "caustic" message.

"This decade will probably be seen as one of remarkably sustained economic growth," Prof Chadha said. "Whilst there are clear risks from the build-up of public and private debt, the data has not and does not yet support the IMF's view of highly precarious world growth."

There are some dark spots in the global outlook and economies that were weak in the first quarter, but these are the exception rather than the rule. Iran is suffering from sanctions, South Korea's economy contracted in the first quarter on the back of a drop in exports to China, and Turkey appears increasingly vulnerable to further capital flight as it struggles to deal with a recession.

Equity markets sensed the change in mood long before economists, the MSCI World equity index has risen 21 per cent since it troughed on Christmas Day, and the question now occupying analysts is why the global economy has turned the corner so much earlier than expected. Kevin Daly at Goldman Sachs said the slowdown was largely caused by rising US rates, which tightened global financial conditions, combined with concerns over a trade war and rising oil prices. "The improvement this year is due to the partial reversal of those factors."

Ms. Mann added that the continued resilience of the service sector a strong labor markets had boosted incomes and there had been a helping hand from the Chinese fiscal stimulus.

The gloomy forecasts were largely driven by trade and manufacturing woes, and arguably paid insufficient attention to household income growth, low unemployment and strength in services. As a result, some forecasters have begun to edge their economic forecasts higher; Citi has just raised its global economic growth estimates for the first time since February, 2018.

However, concerns remain that the rebound will peter out, particularly as global goods trade volumes over the past three months fell year on year for the first time since the financial crisis a decade ago. "Growth has stabilized but the slide in imports has not," warned Janet Henry, chief economist of HSBC.

Leading economic indicators, such as those produced by the OECD, are still flashing warning signs. And there are concerns about the nature of growth, with consumption doing most of the heavy lifting and business investment in the doldrums almost everywhere. This pointed to "stabilization rather than a rapid revival", said Ms. Henry. And there are big risks on the horizon.

Few expect US president Donald Trump's rapprochement with China to end the talk of trade wars, and many fear an escalation with the EU once an agreement has been forged with Beijing. Momentum in the US economy is also potentially dependent on further fiscal tumulus, which is far from guaranteed.

So 2019's bright spring is not guaranteed to turn into a hot summer. But economists and financial markets increasingly agree there is no longer a need to talk of a global economy on the slide.

Words and Expressions

bleak	[bliːk]	a.	(of a situation) not encouraging or giving little or no hope for the future (境况)惨淡的；无希望的
precarious	[prɪˈkeərɪəs]	a.	(a situation) likely to get worse (情势)不稳定的，危险的
toxic	[ˈtɒksɪk]	a.	poisonous 有毒的，引起中毒的
preliminary	[prɪˈlɪmɪnəri]	a.	happening before a more important action or event 初步的；开始的
stabilize	[ˈsteɪbəlaɪz]	v.	(cause it to) become fixed (使)稳定；(使)稳固
fragile	[ˈfrædʒaɪl]	a.	easily damaged, broken, or harmed 易损坏；易碎的；脆弱的

caustic	[ˈkɔːstɪk]	a.	(of a chemical substance) able to destroy or dissolve other substances; critical in a bitter or sarcastic way 腐蚀性;刻薄的
sustain	[səˈsteɪn]	v.	cause or allow something to continue 保持,维持;使继续
sanction	[ˈsæŋkʃn]	n.	an official order, such as the stopping of trade that is taken against a country in order to make it obey the international law 制裁
equity	[ˈekwəti]	n.	the value of a company's shares; the value of a property after all charges and debts have been paid (公司)股本;股票值;股票
reversal	[rɪˈvɜːsl]	n.	the act of changing or making something change to its opposite; a problem or failure 翻转,倒转,反转
fiscal	[ˈfɪskl]	a.	connected with government or public money, especially taxes 财政的;国库的
peter out			gradually stop or disappear 逐渐停止;慢慢消失
doldrums	[ˈdɒldrəmz]	a.	(informal) unsuccessful or showing no activity or improvement 停滞的;没有进展的
rapprochement	[ræˈprɒʃmənt]	n.	an agreement reached by opposing groups or people 和解;恢复友好关系
tumulus	[ˈtjuːmjələs]	n.	a large pile of earth built over the grave of an important person in ancient times 冢;古墓

 Discussion Questions

1. Why does the author conclude that the IMF's message appears to have been far too gloomy?
2. According to this passage, what factors drove the global economic forecast from gloom to stable growth?

Part 4 Topical Vocabulary

wholly foreign-owned enterprise 外商独资企业
liberal economy 自由经济
purchasing power / buying power 购买力
reserve / reserve fund 准备金,储备金
devaluation (货币)贬值
quotation 报价,牌价
value added tax 增值税
tax exemption 免税
real estate 不动产
collateralize 担保
broker 经纪人
money market 货币市场
underwrite 认购
principal 本金
holding company 控股公司
shareholder/stockholder 股东
the Federal Reserve Board 美国联邦储备委员会
New York Stock Exchange/NYSE 纽约证券交易所
foreign direct investment (FDI) 外商直接投资
Chinese-foreign contractual joint venture 中外合作经营企业
Chinese-foreign equity joint venture 中外合资经营企业

planned economy 计划经济
economic fluctuation 经济波动
treasury bills 国库券
reserve ratio 准备金比率
deflation 通货紧缩
progressive taxation 累进税制
income tax 所得税
liquid assets 流动资产
auction 拍卖
dealer 交易员
floating-rate 浮动比率
capital market 资本市场
endorsement 背书
speculation 投机
share 股份,股票
raising limit 涨停板
outbound investment 境外投资
eurobond market 欧洲债券市场
London Stock Market 伦敦股票市场

Unit 5

Science and Technology

Part 1 Learning Before Class

- **Listening**

High School Cheaters Nabbed by Neural Network

Directions: *Listen to the news and answer the questions.*

1. Why is the program Ghostwriter created?
2. What is at the core of this program?
3. According to the article, what else can the program do apart from detecting cheats?
4. What do you think of such a program?

- **Watching and Thinking**

AI Is Monitoring Your Right Now and Here's How They're Using Your Data

Directions: *Watch the video and discuss the questions with your partner.*

1. What is EMBERS? What does it mine data for?
2. What are EMBERS' limits mentioned in the video?
3. What are Dr. Mubarak Shah and his team using to track and predict the movements of dense crowds and the individuals in those crowds?
4. What is the downside or disadvantage mentioned in the video? What do you think of this problem?

• Reading and Discussing

How Best to Use AI for Human Development

By Michael Chui & Martin Harrysson ①

January 14, 2019

China Daily

The excitement surrounding artificial intelligence (AI) today reflects not only how AI applications could transform businesses and economies, but also the hope that they can address challenges such as cancer and climate change. The idea that AI could revolutionize people's well-being is obviously appealing.

But just how realistic is it? To answer that question, we (at McKinsey Global Institute②) examined more than 150 scenarios in which AI is being applied or could be applied for social good. What we found is that AI could make a powerful contribution to resolving many types of societal challenges, but it is not a silver bullet. While AI's reach is broad, development bottlenecks and application risks must be overcome before the benefits can be realized on a global scale.

AI is already changing how we tackle human development challenges. In 2017, for example, object-detection software and satellite imagery aided rescuers in Houston as they navigated the aftermath of Hurricane Harvey. In Africa, algorithms have helped reduce poaching in wildlife parks. In Denmark, voice-recognition programs are used in emergency calls to detect whether callers are experiencing cardiac arrest. And at the Massachusetts Institute of Technology Media Lab near Boston, researchers have used "reinforcement learning" in simulated clinical trials involving patients with glioblastoma, the most aggressive form of brain cancer, to reduce chemotherapy doses.

Moreover, this is only a fraction of what is possible. AI can already detect early signs of diabetes from heart rate sensor data, help children with autism manage their emotions, and guide the visually impaired. If these innovations were widely available and used, the health and social benefits would be immense. In fact, our assessment concludes that AI

---

① Michael Chui is a partner at the McKinsey Global Institute, and Martin Harrysson is a partner in McKinsey & Company's Silicon Valley office.

② McKinsey Global Institute (MGI), the business and economics research arm of McKinsey, was established in 1990 to develop a deeper understanding of the evolving global economy. MGI's mission is to provide leaders in the commercial, public, and social sectors with the facts and insights on which to base management and policy decisions.

technologies could accelerate progress on each of the 17 UN Sustainable Development Goals ① .

But if any of these AI solutions are to make a difference globally, their use must be scaled up dramatically. To do that, we must first address developmental obstacles and mitigate risks that could render AI technologies more harmful than helpful.

On the development side, data accessibility is among the most significant hurdles. In many cases, sensitive or commercially viable data that have societal applications are privately owned and not accessible to nongovernmental organizations. In other cases, bureaucratic inertia keeps otherwise useful data locked up.

So-called last-mile implementation challenges are another common problem. Even in cases where data are available and the technology is mature, the dearth of data scientists can make it difficult to apply AI solutions locally. One way to address the shortage of workers with the skills needed to strengthen and implement AI capabilities is for companies that employ such workers to devote more time and resources to beneficial causes. They should encourage AI experts to take on pro bono projects and reward them for doing so.

There are of course risks. AI's tools and techniques can be misused, intentionally or inadvertently. For example, biases can be embedded in AI algorithms or datasets, which in turn can amplify existing inequalities when the applications are used. According to one academic study, error rates for facial analysis software are less than 1 percent for light-skinned men, but as high as 35 percent for dark-skinned women, which raises important questions about how to account for human prejudice in AI programming. Another obvious risk is misuse of AI by those intent on threatening individuals' physical, digital, financial and emotional security.

Stakeholders from the private and public sectors must work together to address these issues. To increase the availability of data, for example, public officials and private actors should grant broader access to those seeking to use data for initiatives that serve the public good. Already, satellite companies have participated in an international agreement that commits them to provide open access during emergencies. Such data-dependent partnerships must be expanded so that it becomes a feature of companies' operational routines.

---

① Sustainable Development Goals are the blueprint to achieve a better and more sustainable future for all. They address the global challenges we face, including those related to poverty, inequality, climate, environmental degradation, prosperity, and peace and justice. The goals interconnect and in order to leave no one behind, it is important that we achieve each goal and target by 2030. The 17 goals are: end poverty in all its forms; zero hunger; health; education; gender equality and women's empowerment; water and sanitation; energy; economic growth; infrastructure and industrialization; inequality; cities; sustainable consumption and production; climate change; oceans; biodiversity, forests and desertification; peace, justice and strong institutions; partnerships.

AI is fast becoming an invaluable part of the human development toolkit. But if AI's potential to do good globally is to be fully realized, proponents must focus less on the hype and make more efforts to removes the hurdles preventing its uptake.

Directions: *Read the passage and discuss the questions with your partner.*

1. According to the writers, what human development challenges has AI helped to resolve? What other challenges can you name which AI can help resolve?
2. What are the obstacles and risks mentioned in the article which may hinder or harm human development?
3. Do the writers propose any suggestions on how to solve the problems? What suggestions can you come up with to make AI serve humans better?

Part 2　Learning in Class

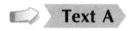

How a Driverless Car Sees the Road

Directions: *Watch the video and discuss the questions with your partner.*

1. According to the speaker, why is the application of self-driving cars urgent?
2. What aspects of self-driving cars has the speaker introduced in this speech?
3. What do you think of self-driving cars? What may be the risks of self-driving cars?

Text A

As Cars Become Computers on Wheels, Drivers Need to Lock More than Just the Doors

By Jim Motovalli

March 10, 2019

The Global and Mail ①

---

① *The Globe and Mail* is a Canadian newspaper printed in five cities in western and central Canada. With a weekly readership of 2,018,923 in 2015, it is Canada's most widely read newspaper on weekdays and Saturdays, although it falls slightly behind *The Toronto Star* in overall weekly circulation because *The Toronto Star* publishes a Sunday edition while *The Globe and Mail* does not.

Going back at least a decade, cars have been targeted by hackers, some who ended up working with the industry, others acting maliciously. But vehicles now carry far more electronic equipment, and autonomous driving, relying on sensors, cameras and radar, is on the horizon, with all kinds of ripe new targets.

Concern that cars could be seriously hacked—by criminals, terrorists or even rogue governments—has prompted a new round of security efforts on the part of the auto industry.

As far back as 2010, a disgruntled former employee at Texas Auto Center in Austin used a co-worker's account to log into company software used for car repossession. He disabled over 100 cars, and owners who were up to date on their payments suddenly found their vehicles honking furiously, and unable to start.

In 2015, a veteran hacker named Samy Kamkar built a device for under $100 that he said could find, unlock and remotely start any General Motors car equipped with the OnStar communications system. Luckily, Kamkar was acting as a "white hat", and not selling his OwnStar device to unscrupulous hackers.

"I worked with GM to resolve that issue," he said, and that particular vulnerability is gone. "Cars are getting more secure, but it's a long cycle to get the necessary new software and hardware installed."

Dan Flores, a GM cybersecurity and safety spokesman, confirmed the collaboration with Kamkar. "We recognize the importance of the work that researchers, like Samy, do to help advance the work in this area," he said in an e-mail.

Securing cars is a big challenge, which is why some companies that traditionally prefer to go it alone have teamed up to share best practices.

Digital threats to self-driving cars, according to a 2018 University of Michigan report, "include hackers who would try to take control over or shut down a vehicle, criminals who could try to ransom a vehicle or its passengers and thieves who would direct a self-driving car to relocate itself to the local chop-shop."

The average car has over 150 million lines of computer code, and some have even more than a Boeing 787, according to a 2018 KPMG ① report. That complexity, the report said, "creates a real risk of cyberattack—a risk we fear many companies in the automotive industry may be underestimating."

---

① KPMG is a global network of independent member firms operating in 153 countries and collectively employing more than 207,000 people. They serve the needs of business, governments, public-sector agencies, not-for-profits and through member firms' audit and assurance practices, the capital markets, helping other organizations mitigate risks and grasp opportunities.

That view is widespread. "From my perspective, automakers were a little surprised and caught off guard by this threat," said Doug Newcomb, a senior industry analyst at Wards Intelligence ①. "They added all this connectivity, but got ahead of themselves and don't always think of the vulnerabilities that exist. It's an ongoing issue, not a fix-it-and-forget-it thing."

Once a car is out of warranty, automakers are used to cutting or at least loosening their ties. But hacking issues mean that protection will most likely require factory-to-junkyard monitoring.

In 2015, Fiat Chrysler recalled 1.4 million cars and trucks after Chris Valasek and Charlie Miller demonstrated, in a *Wired* ② magazine article, that they could remotely control a Jeep Cherokee's brakes, radio, wipers and other functions by gaining access through its UConnect infotainment system. The company declined to comment on any subsequent security changes.

André Weimerskirch, vice president for cybersecurity and functional safety at Lear Corp., said that automakers had made "huge improvements" in recent years, and that joint efforts involving the industry, academia and standards organizations had also led to gains.

Most car hackers have been wearing those white hats, with no criminal intent, but imagining what could happen led to the 2015 formation of the Automotive Information Sharing and Analysis Center, known as Auto-ISAC. Most of the world's automakers are members.

Faye Francy, the center's executive director, described the Jeep episode as "a good wake-up call for the industry". "The hackers are smart guys, very educated," she said. "It's not simple to do what they did. We're fortunate that there hasn't been another breach, but it's not impossible."

Not impossible, but still difficult. Ron Plesco, a principal at KPMG Cyber Security Services, agrees that hacking into a car's driver controls requires "a lot of knowledge and effort". "It's not as easy as Hollywood claims it is," he said.

That's one reason we haven't seen more major attacks. But Plesco argues that today there isn't much incentive for thieves, since the identity information stored onboard vehicles is fairly limited. "But," he added, "that's about to change as we do more

---

① Wards Intelligence has, since 1924, provided business intelligence about the automotive industry for its key players and the financial community investing in it. Today, Wards Intelligence reliably tracks and interprets market size, trends and movements, delivering forward-looking intelligence, statistics and insight.

② *Wired* is a monthly American magazine, published in print and online editions, which focuses on how emerging technologies affect culture, economy and politics.

purchasing through the dashboard of the car. The automobile is becoming another computer that can be hacked."

New infotainment and autonomous features are important selling points, but because most consumers assume their cars are safe, automakers tend to keep cybersecurity news in the background. Much is happening behind the curtain, however. Some private security firms say they are signing on with major automakers to provide expert protection.

"There are multiple ways for hackers to get in, and it's the job of the whole industry to defend against it," said Dan Sahar, a vice president at Upstream Security in Israel. "Just one hack can cost a manufacturer tens of millions of dollars, and that doesn't include the brand damage. And the threat is getting more serious."

According to Sahar, "2018 saw more than 60 documented automotive-related cybersecurity incidents, a sixfold increase in just four years."

Upstream is working with "a handful" of manufacturers, Sahar said. "Automakers are focused on cybersecurity, but few say they can do it on their own," he said.

A 2019 Upstream report extrapolates a cost topping $1.1 billion for a breach that requires a large recall. The opportunity will certainly be there for criminal hackers. Juniper Research of Britain estimated in a 2018 report that by 2023 some 775 million cars would be connected to the web in some way (up from 330 million in 2018).

Tengler, of Kugler MaagCie, said it was easy to picture the danger that hackers posed to autonomous vehicles—potentially redirecting them as part of a theft. But the Jeep hack proved "it doesn't matter if someone is driving", he said. "If they can take control of the car, the vulnerable technology is already there."

Thieves have stolen cars by using fairly simple electronic technology, some of it freely available. A device that amplifies the signals from a car's remote can be used to unlock the target vehicle's doors. Kamkar said he had built such devices from off-the-shelf components for approximately $50. "It's a lot simpler than people think," he said.

Other devices include a radio transmitter that cycles through huge numbers of possible combinations until they "crack" the target car's key fob. In 2006, that was reportedly how soccer star David Beckham's armor-plated BMW X5 was stolen in Madrid. A second X5 belonging to Beckham was also stolen.

"Car thieves used to have crowbars; now they use laptops," said Plesco at KPMG. Jono Anderson, also a principal at KPMG, said the auto industry needed to learn from aerospace.

"They're very familiar with this kind of security," Anderson said, "but it's new to the auto industry. Maybe it's possible to hack the entertainment system in a plane and get free movies, but it's virtually impossible to hack the actual communications."

Words and Expressions

maliciously	[mə'lɪʃəsli]	adv.	in a way that is intended to cause harm, upset, or damage 恶意地
disgruntled	[dɪs'grʌntld]	a.	unhappy, annoyed, and disappointed about something 不满的
repossession	[ˌriːpə'zeʃn]	n.	the act of taking something back, or the thing that is taken back 恢复,取回
unscrupulous	[ʌn'skruːpjələs]	a.	behaving in a way that is dishonest or unfair in order to get what you want 肆无忌惮的
vulnerability	[ˌvʌlnərə'bɪləti]	n.	the quality of being vulnerable (= able to be easily hurt, influenced, or attacked), or something that is vulnerable 弱点,计算机安全隐患
ransom	['rænsəm]	v.	pay money in order to set someone free 勒索赎金
warranty	['wɒrənti]	n.	a written promise from a company to repair or replace a product that develops a fault within a particular period of time, or to do a piece of work again if it is not satisfactory 商品保用单
infotainment	[ˌɪnfəʊ'teɪnmənt]	n.	the reporting of news and facts in an entertaining and humorous way rather than providing real information; information that is provided on television, the Internet, etc. in an entertaining way 娱乐信息节目
academia	[ˌækə'diːmiə]	n.	the part of society, especially universities that is connected with studying and thinking, or the activity or job of studying 学术界
breach	[briːtʃ]	n.	an act of breaking a law, promise, agreement, or relationship (对法规等的)违背
incentive	[ɪn'sentɪv]	n.	something that encourages a person to do something 动机;刺激
extrapolate	[ɪk'stræpəleɪt]	v.	guess or think about what might happen using information that is already known 推断,推知

amplify	[ˈæmplɪfaɪ]	v.	increase the size or effect of something; make something louder 放大,扩大;增强
fob	[fɒb]	n.	a piece of leather or other material to which a group of keys is fastened, or a chain or piece of material used, especially in the past, to fasten a watch to a man's waistcoat 钥匙圈;怀表链
crowbar	[ˈkrəʊbɑːr]	n.	a heavy iron bar with a bent end that is used to help lift heavy objects off the ground or to force things open 撬棍

- **Multiple Choice**

Select the most appropriate answer for each of the following questions.

1. Who hacked a car in vicious intensions?

    A) An annoyed former employee at Texas Auto Center in Austin.

    B) A veteran hacker named Samy Kamkar.

    C) A hacker wearing a white hat.

    D) Chris Valasek, who could remotely control a car's brakes, etc.

2. Which of the following is NOT a digital threat included in the 2018 University of Michigan report?

    A) Hackers who would try to control a vehicle.

    B) Criminals who could ransom a vehicle.

    C) Hackers who would disable a vehicle and steal it.

    D) Thieves who would direct a car to relocate it.

3. Why is the Jeep Cherokee instance cited?

    A) To illustrate how a car can be hacked.

    B) To illustrate that protection will always be needed by automakers.

    C) To illustrate Fiat Chrysler is an irresponsible company.

    D) To illustrate Fiat Chrysler provides good service.

4. Why haven't we seen more major attacks on automobile cybersecurity?

    A) Because hackers are not well-educated to do it.

    B) Because automakers are now aware of the problem and have good protections.

    C) Because hackers consider it valueless to hack a car.

D) Because it's not easy to hack into a car's driver control.

5. Which of the following is NOT a tool thieves now use to steal a car?

A) A device which amplifies signals from a car's remote.

B) A radio transmitter.

C) A crowbar.

D) A laptop.

- **Sentence Completion**

Complete the sentences below with words taken from Text A. Use NO MORE THAN THREE WORDS for each answer.

1. Now vehicles carry more electronic equipment and _____ is on the horizon.

2. Doug Newcomb thinks that automakers added all the connectivity but don't think of ____ _____ that exist.

3. Hacking issues mean protection will most likely require _____.

4. There isn't much _____ for thieves today because there's limited identity information stored onboard the car.

5. It is said 2018 saw more than 60 documented _____, a sixfold increase in four years.

- **Matching**

Classify the following ideas as belonging to.

A. Samy Kamkar   B. Doug Newcomb

C. Faye Francy   D. Ron Plesco

E. Jono Anderson

1. The auto industry ought to learn from aerospace in terms of cybersecurity.

2. Automakers are not prepared for the threat of cyberattacks.

3. Hackers are clever and educated, and hacking a car is not impossible.

4. Despite the increasing security of cars, it takes time to install necessary new software and hardware.

5. The automobile is more like a computer and there will be more motivation to steal it.

 Discussion Questions

1. According to the article, Samy Kamkar is a "white hat". What is a "white hat" then? How much do you know about this group of persons? What role do you think they play in the information age?

2. It is said in the article that "Concern that cars could be seriously hacked ... has prompted a new round of security efforts on the part of the auto industry". What measures have the auto companies taken to secure their smart cars?
3. As cars become smarter, what can consumers do to prevent their cars from being hacked or stolen?

 Text B

The Internet Knows You Better than Your Spouse Does

By Frank Luerweg
March 14, 2019
Scientific American ①

A. It seems that our like clicks by themselves can be pretty good indicators of what makes us tick. In 2015 David Stillwell and Youyou Wu, both at the University of Cambridge, and Michal Kosinski of Stanford University demonstrated that algorithms can evaluate what psychologists call the Big Five dimensions of personality quite accurately just by examining a Facebook user's likes. These dimensions—openness to experience, conscientiousness, extroversion, agreeableness and neuroticism—are viewed as representing the basic dimensions of personality. The degree to which they are present in individuals describes who those people are.

B. Facebook activity is by no means the only data that can be used to assess your personality. In a 2018 study, computer scientist Sabrina Hoppe of the University of Stuttgart in Germany and her colleagues fitted students with eye trackers. The volunteers then walked around campus and went shopping. Based on their eye movements, the researchers were able to predict four of the Big Five dimensions correctly.

C. How we speak—our individual tone of voice—may also divulge clues about our personality. Precire Technologies, a company based in Aachen, Germany, specializes in analyzing spoken and written language. It has developed an automated job interview: job seekers speak with a computer by telephone, which then creates a detailed psychogram based on their responses. Among other things, Precire analyzes word selection and certain

---

① *Scientific American* is an American popular science magazine published monthly. Many famous scientists, including Albert Einstein, have contributed articles to it. It is the longest continuously published magazine in the US, and has been bringing its readers unique insights about developments in science and technology for more than 170 years.

word combinations, sentence structures, dialectal influences, errors, filler words, pronunciations and intonations. Its algorithm is based on data from more than 5,000 interviews with individuals whose personalities were analyzed.

D. Software that analyzes faces for clues to mood, personality or other psychological features is being explored as well. It highlights both what is possible and what to fear.

E. In early 2018 four programmers at a hacker conference, nwHacks ①, introduced an app that discerns mood by analyzing face-tracking data captured from the front camera of the iPhone X. The app, called Loki, recognizes emotions such as happiness, sadness, anger and surprise in real time as someone looks at a news feed, and it delivers content based on the person's emotional state. In an article about Loki, one of the developers said that he and his colleagues created the app to "illustrate the plausibility of social media platforms tracking user emotions to manipulate the content that gets shown to them". For instance, when a user engages with a news feed or other app, such software could secretly track the person's emotions and use this "emotion detector" as a guide for targeting advertising. Studies have shown that people tend to loosen their purse strings when they are in a good mood; advertisers might want to push ads to your phone when you are feeling particularly up.

F. Kosinski, too, has examined whether automated image-recognition technology can surreptitiously discern psychological traits from digital activity. In an experiment published in 2018, he and his Stanford colleague Yilun Wang fed hundreds of thousands of photographs from a dating portal into a computer, along with information on whether the person in question was gay or straight. They then presented the software with pairs of unknown faces: one of a homosexual person and another of a heterosexual individual of the same sex. The program correctly distinguished the sexual orientation of men 81 percent of the time and of women 71 percent of the time; human beings were much less accurate in their assessments.

G. Given that gay people continue to fear for their lives in many parts of the world, it is perhaps not surprising that the results elicited negative reactions. Indeed, Kosinski got death threats. "People didn't understand that my intention wasn't to show how cool it is to predict sexual orientation," Kosinski says. "The whole paper is actually a warning, a call for increasing privacy."

H. In late 2016 computer scientists at the Swiss Federal Institute of Technology Zurich

---

① nwHacks is a two-day event, dedicated to creating a thriving community of technology lovers in the Pacific Northwest region by bringing together the brightest minds.

demonstrated that the personalities of Facebook users can be pinned down more precisely if their likes are coupled with analyses of their profile photograph. Interestingly, the researchers, like many others who use machine-learning software, do not know exactly how the algorithm forms its judgment—for example, whether it relies on such features as a person's haircut or the formality of the individual's dress. They are in the dark because machine-learning programs do not reveal the rules they apply in drawing conclusions. The investigators know that the software finds correlations between features in the data and personality but not exactly how it concludes that a man in a photograph is attracted to other men or which characteristics in my e-mail might indicate that I am conscientious and somewhat introverted.

I. "The image we are often given is that predicting personality is a kind of magic," says Rasmus Rothe, who was involved in the Swiss study. "But in the final analysis, computer models do nothing other than find correlations."

J. The use of facial-recognition technology for analyzing psychology is not merely an object of research. It has been adopted by several commercial enterprises. Israeli company Faception, for example, says it can recognize whether a person has a high IQ or pedophilic tendencies or is a potential terrorist threat.

K. Even if a correlation is found with a trait, experts have their doubts about the usefulness of such analyses. "All that the algorithms give us are statistical probabilities," Rothe says. It simply is not possible to identify with certainty whether a person is Mensa material. "What the program can tell us is that someone who looks sort of like you is statistically more likely to have a high IQ. It could easily guess wrong four times out of 10."

L. With some applications, incorrect predictions are tolerable. Who cares if Apply Magic Sauce comes to comically erroneous conclusions? But the effect can be devastating in other circumstances. Notably, when the characteristic being analyzed is uncommon, more errors are likely to be made. Even if a company's computer algorithms were to finger terrorists correctly 99 percent of the time, the false positives found 1 percent of the time could bring harm to thousands of innocent people in populous places where terrorists are rare, such as in Germany or the US.

Words and Expressions

algorithm	[ˈælgərɪðəm]	n.	a set of mathematical instructions or rules that, especially if given to a computer, will help to calculate an answer to a problem 算法
dimension	[daɪˈmenʃn] [dɪˈmenʃn]	n.	a part or feature or way of considering something 方面，部分，维度
conscientiousness	[ˌkɒnʃɪˈenʃəsnəs]	n.	the trait of being painstaking and careful 尽责；责任心
extroversion	[ˌekstrəˈvɜːʒn]	n.	the quality of being energetic and not shy, and enjoying being with other people 外向性
neuroticism	[njʊəˈrɒtɪsɪzəm]	n.	the condition of often feeling worried and nervous, often because of a mental illness 神经质
divulge	[daɪˈvʌldʒ]	v.	make something secret known 泄露；暴露
plausibility	[ˌplɔːzəˈbɪləti]	n.	the quality of seeming likely to be true, or possible to believe 合理性
surreptitiously	[ˌsʌrəpˈtɪʃəsli]	adv.	secretly, without anyone seeing or knowing 偷偷地，秘密地
portal	[ˈpɔːtl]		a page on the Internet that allows people to get useful information, such as news and weather, and to find other websites 门户网站
elicit	[ɪˈlɪsɪt]	v.	get or produce something, especially information or a reaction 引出；诱出
correlation	[ˌkɒrəˈleɪʃn]	n.	connection or relationship between two or more facts, numbers, etc. 相关性
pedophilic	[ˌpiːdəˈfɪlɪk]	a.	being sexually interested in children 恋童的

- **True/False/Not Given**

Do the following statements agree with the information given in Text B?

In Blanks 1-5 write

True   if the statement is true

False   if the statement is false

_____ 1. Users' like clicks on Facebook are the only data to describe their personalities.

_____ 2. Precire Technologies is a Germany-based company specializing in analyzing spoken and written language.

_____ 3. The app Loki is created to manipulate the content to show to readers and to target advertising.

_____ 4. Up till now, researchers are still not sure how the algorithm forms its judgment.

_____ 5. Some experts are skeptical about whether the use of facial-recognition technology for analyzing psychology is useful.

- **Matching**

Match the number in front of each paragraph with the information it contains.

1. A German company has developed an automated job interview.
2. Kosinski was threatened to death because of the results of his experiment.
3. An experiment has found out that eye movement can be used to predict personality.
4. According to some studies, people are more likely to do shopping when they are in a good mood.
5. An Israeli company claims to be able to recognize whether a person has a high IQ.
6. Machine-learning software finds correlation between features in the data and personality.

- **Short Answer Questions**

1. What are the Big Five dimensions of personality?
2. What date can be used to assess one's personality besides Facebook activity?
3. What is Loki?
4. What is Kosinski's purpose in conducting the experiment in which a computer software can quite successfully distinguish sexual orientation?
5. Why do researchers not know how machine-learning programs form judgments?
6. In the last paragraph, why does the writer claim incorrect predictions can be devastating in certain circumstances?

- **Writing**

By reading the article, we find that big data collected online can be used to predict our personalities. How much do you know about this technology? What do you think of it? Will it bring us benefits or risks? Write a comment of no less than 300 words on these issues.

Academic Reading

Critical Thinking (1)

Learning Objective

In the section, you will learn to:
* Distinguish between critical thinking and random thinking.
* Discuss the benefits and uses of critical thinking.

Critical Thinking Versus Random Thinking

Take a few moments just to let some thoughts pass through your mind. What are you thinking about? Are you reflecting on what you did last night or what you intend to do this weekend? Are you worried about an assignment that is due or a test that is coming up? Maybe you are focusing on an important person in your life. Perhaps you are just thinking about how hungry or tired you are. The possibilities are endless.

What you just did was an example of random thinking, which is thinking without a clear purpose or objective in mind. We all do this kind of thinking countless times each day, often without even realizing it. Sometimes we are simply daydreaming, thinking about past experiences, or wondering or worrying about some future activity. Thoughts pop into mind and just as quickly out; they come and go without much effort on our part. Nothing is really accomplished as a result, except perhaps a rest or escape from whatever we may be doing at that particular time.

Random thinking is not critical thinking. How do they differ? Let's look at an example.

Suppose that you and a friend are considering whether to take a particular course next semester. The two of you approach another student who enrolled for that course last year, and she informs you that she dropped it after two weeks because it was so boring. On the basis of that conversation, your friend decides not to take the course. Although you are tempted to do the same thing, you decide instead to give the matter more thought because you do not think it wise to base your decision solely on the opinion of one student, who might have had a personal reason for not appreciating the course. For example, she could have had a problem at the time that interfered with her ability to fulfill the course requirements, or she could have been uncomfortable with the instructor's personality and teaching style. These may have been good reasons at the time for her not to stay in the course, but that does not mean that they should have an effect on your decision.

Consequently, rather than automatically accepting one person's opinion, you decide to spend more time and effort getting additional information before coming to a final decision.

You organize your efforts by first getting a class schedule for next semester in order to find out the days and times that the course is offered and which faculty teach it. You want to determine if you can fit the course into your schedule and whether you have a choice of instructor. Second, you check the college catalog so that you can read the course description to see what it is about in a general sense and whether it can be used as part of your program of study. Third, you obtain a copy of a recent course syllabus from the department, a counselor, the instructor, or a student so that you can get additional information on assignments and grading. Fourth, you ask around so that you can find and talk to more students who have taken the course. Fifth, you discuss the course with a faculty member and your counselor or academic adviser.

After considering carefully all the information you gathered, you now feel confident about coming to a conclusion regarding whether to enroll in the course. You know that it fits into your program of study and your schedule, and you have a better understanding of its content. Furthermore, you are aware of who teaches the course and can determine whether you are comfortable with his or her teaching style, grading policies, and personality. No matter what you ultimately decide to do, you have placed yourself in a much stronger position to make the right decision for you. However, you do continue to reconsider that decision right up until the time of registration, just in case you find out some additional information that changes your mind.

The process that you used in the example above involved critical thinking, which is best described as a very careful and thoughtful way of dealing with events, issues, problems, decisions, or situations. As you can see, critical thinking can be very helpful to you. Let's take a brief look at its many benefits and uses.

Benefits and Uses of Critical Thinking

Critical thinking is important because it makes you a much more careful decision maker who has the best chance of assessing situations accurately, making sense of issues and events, and coming up with solutions to problems. Because critical thinkers do not accept blindly everything they see, hear, or read, they place themselves in better positions to understand what is going on around them, to avoid costly mistakes, and to accomplish whatever they set out to do.

There are no limits to the uses of critical thinking. It can help you evaluate textbook material and other types of reading; uncover motivations and assess arguments; consider options, products, advertisements, and commercials; and judge policies and programs such as those offered by the various levels of government. The benefits of critical thinking for you are very real and substantial no matter what roles you play in life now and in the future, including those of student, professional, parent, and citizen. Make it a habit to think critically about everything.

Part 3　Learning After Class

Additional Reading 1

It's Complicated: Facebook Users' Fraught Relationship with Social Giant

Facebook has become such a ubiquitous presence that many users find it difficult to withdraw from the platform.

By Eoin O'Carroll

December 20, 2018

The Christian Science Monitor [①]

Ask Facebook users about their relationship with the social network, and many will pick "it's complicated".

That's because, even though Facebook helps people maintain vital social bonds, often providing the sole link for former classmates, colleagues, and distant friends, maintaining these connections on the social network comes at a steep price. A growing number of studies suggest that, on an individual level, Facebook is making people unreasonably sad, envious, and angry, and that excessive use can damage in-person relationships. On a societal level, the social network has been implicated in everything from spreading political propaganda in the United States to fueling a genocide in Myanmar.

In 2018, this relationship grew even more complicated. The year began amid unfolding revelations that the social network had facilitated the spread of Russian political

---

① The Christian Science Monitor is an international news organization that publishes daily articles in electronic format as well as a weekly print edition. It was founded in 1908 as a daily newspaper.

propaganda; the year closes with news that Facebook bartered users' personal data with some of Silicon Valley's biggest firms, including a scheme that gave companies like Netflix and Spotify the ability to read users' private messages. Along the way, users learned that the company handed the personal data of up to 87 million users over to a right-wing British political consulting firm, fell victim to a massive data breach that exposed the information of nearly 50 million users, and paid another consulting firm to push anti-Semitic conspiracy theories in the media.

Accompanying these scandals are increased calls to boycott Facebook. The NAACP ①, for example, launched its #LogOutFacebook campaign, "in response to the tech company's history of data hacks which unfairly target its users of color." Big names in tech, from Elon Musk to veteran technology columnist Walter Mossberg, have announced that they are leaving the platform.

For many users, it's clear that the time has come to quit, but Facebook has proven to be hard to break up with.

Ryan Schurtz says that he quit Facebook twice, the second time for good. A regular user for about 10 years before finally giving it up, the Stevenson University social psychologist found that the social network was making him sad. "It creates sort of a posting arms race where we're in this competition with our friends to get the most likes or have the largest group," says Professor Schurtz, who studies how people compare themselves to others.

He initially wanted to delete his account permanently in 2015, he says, but he noticed that doing so would have also disabled Pandora ②, so instead he simply stopped using Facebook while keeping his account open. Schurtz returned about nine months later, only to finally realize that he had been right to quit. "I came back to Facebook during the 2016 election," he says. "That was a mistake." This time, it stuck. "For me," writes Schurtz, "quitting Facebook was a little thing that I found made me a lot happier."

But giving up the social network didn't come without its costs. "It helps us stay connected," he says. "I wouldn't say I lost a lot of friends, but I'd say I lost touch with a

---

① The National Association for the Advancement of Colored People (NAACP) is a civil rights organization in the United States, formed in 1909 as a bi-racial endeavor to advance justice for African Americans by a group including W. E. B. Du Bois, Mary White Ovington and Moorfield Storey. Its mission is to secure the political, educational, social, and economic equality of rights in order to eliminate race-based discrimination and ensure the health and well-being of all persons.

② Pandora (also known as Pandora Media or Pandora Radio) is an American music streaming and automated music recommendation Internet radio service powered by the Music Genome Project.

lot of friends." Overall, Schurtz now says that he's happier, but somewhat lonelier, an experience consistent with at least one study that suggests Facebook nonusers tend to be lonelier than users.

Another reason Facebook is so hard to walk away from is that it has almost become a part of the plumbing of the Internet. An array of apps, including Spotify ① or Tinder ②, have at some point in the past required a Facebook login to be able to use them. That means that deleting your Facebook account could result in wiping out your playlists and Tinder matches.

Even if you don't use these apps, all kinds of basic social functions, from organizing a political protest to polling friends on a podcast recommendation, are often most easily achieved via the social network.

Those seeking to distance themselves from Facebook have many options. Like professor Schurtz, you can keep your account active and log into it rarely, or not at all. Alternatively, you can "deactivate" your account, which hides it but keeps it on Facebook's servers in case you ever want to re-activate it.

And then there's the nuclear option, which Larry Carvalho opted for in March. "It was a very difficult decision," says Mr. Carvalho, a research director at International Data Corporation in Mason, Ohio, on permanently deleting his account. "The thing I missed most were the local community groups. Somebody to fix your house or a handyman, references from a broader group who you could choose to trust."

But he says that his interactions with people have become more pleasant as a result. Online, he says, "Some people got argumentative with me. I'd rather sit down face to face with a person than argue on a digital forum ... I prefer to go and say, 'Mike let's go have a coffee.'"

Carvalho hasn't completely ruled out returning to Facebook someday, but only if the company is willing to make some changes. "They have to significantly change their attitude from just being a profit machine to more of doing a social benefit for society," he says. "They have to tighten their privacy laws and ... make money responsibly."

Jasmine McNealy agrees that Facebook, like many tech companies, ought to shift its ad-driven business model. "If your business model is 'We make money off of personal data and selling it or licensing it,'" says the assistant professor of telecommunications at

---

① Spotify is a digital music service that gives users access to millions of songs.

② Tinder is a location-based social search mobile app most often used as a dating site that allows users to like or dislike other users, and allows users to chat if both parties like each other. Information available to users is based on pictures, a short bio, and optionally, a linked Instagram, Facebook or Spotify account. Tinder was launched in 2012.

the University of Florida, "then that needs to change."

The company is actually seeing a decline of users in Europe, and user growth in North America remains flat, as younger users move to other platforms such as Snapchat ① or Instagram ② (which Facebook owns). But the company is continuing to see its revenue rise, as it squeezes more money from each user profile and as it makes inroads into the developing world.

"Facebook has moved itself internationally," says Professor McNealy. "Facebook has moved to fertile harvests other places." Those other places may soon start experiencing the privacy breaches and invasive targeting that users in the West have become so accustomed to. "The data practices that they're using that are really terrible here, they're exporting those same if not worse data practices to the continent of Africa, attempting places in Asia," she says.

Still, these practices are not enough to prompt McNealy to walk away from the site. The social bonds that the platform facilitates are just too strong. "I'm still on Facebook," she says. "It's community, my mom, my family."

 Words and Expressions

genocide	[ˈdʒenəsaɪd]	n.	the murder of a whole group of people, especially a whole nation, race, or religious group 种族灭绝, 种族屠杀
barter	[ˈbɑːtə]	v.	exchange goods for other things rather than for money 以物易物
boycott	[ˈbɔɪkɒt]	v.	refuse to buy a product or take part in an activity as a way of expressing strong disapproval 联合抵制
deactivate	[ˌdiˈæktɪveɪt]	v.	cause something to be no longer active or effective 使不活动; 停止使用账号

---

① Snapchat is a multimedia messaging app used globally, created by Evan Spiegel, Bobby Murphy and Reggie Brown, former students at Stanford University, and developed by Snap Inc., originally Snapchat Inc. One of the principal features of Snapchat is that pictures and messages are usually only available for a short time before they become inaccessible to their recipients.

② Instagram is a photo and video-sharing social networking service owned by Facebook, Inc. It was created by Kevin Systrom and Mike Krieger, and launched in October 2010 exclusively on IOS. A version for Android devices was released a year and half later, in April 2012, followed by a feature-limited website interface in November 2012, and apps for Windows 10 Mobile and Windows 10 in April 2016 and October 2016 respectively.

rule out			prevent something from happening 排除；取消
revenue	[ˈrevənjuː]	n.	the income that a government or company receives regularly 税收
make inroads			start to have a direct and noticeable effect on something 侵犯

Discussion Questions

1. What is this article mainly about?
2. Why is it difficult to totally quit Facebook, according to the article?
3. Have you encountered similar problems when you use social media such as WeChat? What do you think of the problems mentioned in the article?

Additional Reading 2

China, US Still Have Room to Cooperate in Science and Technology

By Zhang Zhihao

July 15, 2019

China Daily

The scientific communities of China and the United States still have room for exchanges and cooperation despite ongoing trade and technology disputes between the two countries, a senior science policy researcher said.

Stability, development, exchanges and global integration will remain China's top priorities in the coming decade. Hence, it is crucial for China and the US to respect, rationally perceive and adjust to each other's national needs, Pan Jiaofeng, president of the Chinese Academy of Sciences' Institutes of Science and Development ①, told *China Daily* in an interview.

The scientific communities should also enhance mutual exchanges and integration of standards to jointly tackle global issues including climate change, aging populations,

---

① The Chinese Academy of Sciences' Institutes of Science and Development (CASISD) is a research organization supporting the Academic Divisions of CAS (CASAD), pooling elite research forces in related fields both in and outside the Chinese Academy of Sciences (CAS). It plays its role as China's highest advisory body in science and technology, and a comprehensive integration platform for CAS to build a high-level national S & T think tank.

energy and resources, and natural disasters, he said.

In recent years, China has seen substantial development in science and technology due to strong government planning and support, bigger investments, greater efforts from tech enterprises and sweeping reforms tailored to the needs of researchers to unleash their full innovative potential.

China's budget for research and development increased to 2.18 percent of its GDP last year, reaching a record high of 1.96 trillion *yuan*, according to the National Bureau of Statistics ①. There also was a 16.9 percent year-on-year increase last year in patent applications from Chinese innovators, amounting to 4.32 million at home and abroad.

China broke into the world's top 20 most innovative economies, jumping from 22nd in 2017 to the 17th last year, according to the Global Innovation Index ② 2018, published by Cornell University, the World Intellectual Property Organization ③ and INSEAD ④, a global business graduate school.

Pan said these achievements are manifestations of China's growing technological capability, fueled by the desire to use innovations to push socioeconomic progress.

This, however, has led to some Western countries, such as the US, fearing that China's scientific and technological rise will challenge their global position. "This sentiment is understandable, but misguided," he said.

"China is still a developing country, lacking a base and accumulation of innovation capability compared with the US, as well as drastically different national conditions," Pan said. "This means we cannot follow the developmental path that the West expects us to take, and we have to forge our own path one step at a time."

"But now the US is treating China like a developed country capable of challenging its global dominance, it is holding China to standards that we cannot meet for the time

---

① The National Bureau of Statistics, abbreviated as NBS, is a deputy-cabinet level agency directly under the State Council of the People's Republic of China. It is responsible for collection, investigation, research and publication of statistics concerning the nation's economy, population and other aspects of the society.

② The Global Innovation Index (GII) provides detailed metrics about the innovation performance of 126 countries which represent 90.8% of the world's population and 96.3% of global GDP. GII aims to capture the multi-dimensional facets of innovation and provide the tools that can assist in tailoring policies to promote long-term output growth, improved productivity, and job growth.

③ The World Intellectual Property Organization, abbreviated as WIPO, is one of the 15 specialized agencies of the United Nations. WIPO was created in 1967 "to encourage creative activity, to promote the protection of intellectual property throughout the world". WIPO currently has 192 member states, administers 26 international treaties, and is headquartered in Geneva, Switzerland.

④ INSEAD is a graduate business school with campuses in Europe, Asia, and the Middle East. INSEAD is consistently ranked among the best business schools in the world.

being, and it makes accusations against us if we don't," he said.

As of late May, the US Department of Commerce had placed more than 140 entities from the Chinese mainland on its Entity List, a ledger of firms legally prohibited to trade with the US, on the basis of an alleged threat to US national security and interests.

In June, five entities were added to the list: Chinese supercomputer manufacturers and institutions including Sugon, Higon and the Wuxi Jiangnan Institute of Computing Technology, the chipmaker for China's most powerful supercomputer, Sunway TaihuLight, which also ranked as the third most powerful globally.

The United States also is targeting Chinese scholars and students by closing their labs or denying visas to visit the US over alleged spying dangers. In May, Emory University in Atlanta fired neuroscientists Li Xiaojiang and his wife, Li Shihua, both US citizens who had worked at Emory for more than two decades, accusing them of hiding funding and ties to institutions in China.

"These actions are antithetical to the US' immigrant roots and interests, and will impede global scientific exchange and progress," Pan said.

As for China, US seclusion means scientific fields that rely heavily on importation of advanced equipment will be affected the most. "The silver lining of US pressure is that China will be forced to innovate and be self-sufficient," Pan said. "The US cutting off exchanges will slow us down a little, but will not stop our strides for progress."

Given the uncertainty of the situation, scientists and scholars around the world fear that the world will be divided into two major blocs, like during the Cold War. "Splitting the world into two systems and hyping the clash of civilizations will be disastrous for all humanity," Pan said.

"The current international systems were mostly put in place after World War II, but this world order did not anticipate the astonishing rise of China," he said. "As a result, some norms within the current global systems must change in order to accommodate the new dynamics, a process in which China is willing to help."

China has been slowly and sincerely contributing its own standards and knowledge to global governance, especially in regard to the social impact and governance of artificial intelligence, biosciences and other emerging technologies, Pan said.

"China is not a disrupter, but a contributor to the current world order," he said.

Words and Expressions

tailor	[ˈteɪlə(r)]	v.	make or prepare something following particular instructions 调整
manifestation	[ˌmænɪfesˈteɪʃn]	n.	a sign of something existing or happening 表现
sentiment	[ˈsentɪmənt]	n.	a thought, opinion, or idea based on a feeling about a situation, or a way of thinking about sth. 情绪, 感情
accumulation	[əˌkjuːmjəˈleɪʃn]	n.	an amount of something that has been collected; the process of gradually increasing in amount, or the increased amount 堆积物; 积累
entity	[ˈentɪti]	n.	an organization or a business that has its own separate legal and financial existence 实体
ledger	[ˈledʒə(r)]	n.	a book in which things are regularly recorded, especially business activities and money received or paid 总账; 分类账
antithetical	[ˌæntɪˈθetɪkl]	a.	exactly the opposite of someone or something or of each other 相反的
impede	[ɪmˈpiːd]	v.	make it more difficult for something to happen or more difficult for someone to do something 阻碍, 妨碍
seclusion	[sɪˈkluːʒn]	n.	the state of being alone, away from other people 隔离, 闭塞
silver lining			advantage that comes from a difficult or unpleasant situation (不幸或失望中的) 一线希望
hype	[haɪp]	v.	repeatedly advertise and discuss something in newspapers, on television, etc. in order to attract everyone's interest 大肆宣传
norm	[nɔːm]	n.	an accepted standard or a way of behaving or doing things that most people agree with 规范
accommodate	[əˈkɒmədeɪt]	v.	provide with a place to live or to be stored in 容纳; 使适应

Discussion Questions

1. According to the writer, what are the developments in science and technology in China?
2. Can you give any examples of Chinese scientific and technological developments?
3. It's common sense that cooperation is better than confrontation. Can you predict what the future would be if China and the US cooperate in scientific and technological fields?

Additional Reading 3

CES 2019: The 4 Biggest Trends, Demystified

After the annual deluge, several themes emerge from CES that will impact 2019 and beyond.

BY Jason Hiner

January 15, 2019

CNET ①

After all the CES ② product blitzes are done, the multimillion dollar booths are packed up and the PR buzz has utterly spent itself, the real trends become a lot more clear.

Tech that adapts to you

By far, the most used tech term at CES 2019 was AI. The problem is that when most people hear "artificial intelligence", they still think of human-like machines that could one day eliminate humanity, like in *The Terminator*. While there were a few robots at CES 2019, most of them were barely functional and entirely harmless. The AI that took center stage at CES was something very different.

"AI pervades the show," said Gary Shapiro, CEO of the Consumer Technology

---

① CNET, formerly Computer Network, is an American media website that publishes reviews, news, articles, blogs, podcasts and videos on technology and consumer electronics globally. Founded in 1994 by Halsey Minor and Shelby Bonnie, it was the flagship brand of CNETN Networks and became a brand of CBS Interactive through CNET Networks' acquisition in 2008.

② CES, Consumer Electronics Show, is an annual trade show organized by the Consumer Technology Association. Held in January at the Las Vegas Convention Center in Las Vegas, Nevada, the United States, the event typically hosts presentations of new products and technologies in the consumer electronics industry.

Association ① that runs CES. "Almost every major company is showing AI and applications that are just truly jaw-dropping." The closest thing to jaw-dropping was probably self-driving cars, which have been at CES for the past several years but took another step forward this year.

The biggest battleground of CES 2019 intension—Amazon Alexa ② versus Google Home ③—is primarily an AI battle that plays out in voice-powered smart speakers that are the hottest new category in consumer electronics.

The rest of the AI on display at CES was more subtle. It's the software and algorithms that make phone cameras, 4K TVs, ovens, vacuum cleaners and other devices much smarter. It helps cameras take better photos based on the lighting conditions you're shooting in. It helps TVs adjust their color and sound settings based on what you're watching. It helps ovens identify foods in order to cook them properly. And, it helps robotic vacuums recognize socks and other objects in order to avoid running over them and getting clogged up.

These are just a few examples of the most common ways companies were talking about AI at CES 2019. It's important to note that this represents a fundamental shift in the technology world.

Up until now, most technologies centered around people having to learn and adapt to the tech, whether it was cars or computers, phones or TV remotes. That's why the user interface has always been a priority—the ones that were the easiest for people to learn were often the ones that made the biggest impact.

Now AI is turning that entire paradigm on its head. It's no longer about people adapting to technology. It's about technology adapting itself to each person and each scenario. And that new paradigm took a big step forward this week.

---

① The Consumer Technology Association (CTA) is a standards and trade organization representing more than 2,200 consumer technology companies in the United States. CTA works to influence public policy, holds events such as CES and CES Asia, conducts market research, and helps its members and regulators implement technical standards. CTA is led by President and CEO Gary Shapiro.

② Amazon Alexa, known simply as Alexa, is a virtual assistant developed by Amazon, first used in the Amazon Echo and the Amazon Echo Dot smart speakers developed by Amazon Lab126. It is capable of voice interaction, music playback, making to-do lists, setting alarms, streaming podcasts, playing audiobooks, and providing weather, traffic, sports, and other real-time information, such as news. Alexa can also control several smart devices using itself as a home automation system.

③ Google Home is a brand of smart speakers developed by Google. The devices enable users to speak voice commands to interact with services through Google Assistant, the company's virtual assistant. Both in-house and third-party services are integrated, allowing users to listen to music, control playback of videos or photos, or receive news updates entirely by voice. Google Home devices also have integrated support for home automation, letting users control smart home appliances with their voice. The first Google Home device was released in the United States in November 2016, with subsequent product releases globally from 2017 to 2019.

Tech that transforms mundane things

After AI, the next hottest buzzword at CES 2019 was 5G. For many, 5G simply means faster connections that will make it possible to download whole TV seasons in minutes, play games in real time and livestream events from a phone. But the larger effect of 5G is going to involve connecting a lot more things to the Internet.

While the Internet of things (IoT)① has been a leading topic of recent CES shows, it faded into the background as a topic in 2019—even though it was everywhere, if you were really looking. That's not surprising when you consider the nature of IoT itself.

Much technology has become like fashion—conspicuous stuff that people use to express themselves, whether that's a new phone, a flashy pair of headphones or a giant TV. But while the technologies of recent decades have become more and more conspicuous, the IoT is going in the opposite direction. It's about technology fading into the background and becoming part of everything. It's about quietly transforming mundane things with data. And 5G will unleash a tidal wave of new projects, likely to begin en masse at CES 2020.

Tech that helps you sleep better

On the show floor at CES 2019, health tech and sleep tech were among the busiest booths, and there were more of them than ever. While you could think of sleep tech as being part of health tech, sleep tech has had its own separate pavilion at CES since 2017. Meanwhile, sleep tech booths keep multiplying and expanding—it's emerged as one of the hottest new categories at CES, and for good reason.

Americans especially are getting less sleep than ever, with some even declaring a "great American sleep recession". New data from the US Centers of Disease Control and others have made Americans acutely aware of how bad their sleep habits are. Insufficient sleep has been linked to chronic diseases, including type 2 diabetes, cardiovascular disease, obesity and depression.

Sleep Number has been one of the most prominent sleep tech companies at CES for the last several years. Its beds have had basic tech in them for a long time—with remote controls for adjusting the hardness or softness of the mattress and sleep angle. But now they've turned into smart beds by adding sensors and using an app that can give you data on your sleep patterns. They can connect to other health tech such as your fitness tracker

---

① The Internet of things (IoT) is the extension of Internet connectivity into physical devices and everyday objects. Embedded with electronics, Internet connectivity, and other forms of hardware (such as sensors), these devices can communicate and interact with others over the Internet, and they can be remotely monitored and controlled.

and then give recommendations on how to adjust your daily patterns to improve sleep.

However, sleep tech at CES 2019 had far more to offer than just several brands of smart mattresses. One popular set of products was smart sleep masks and headbands, led by the Philips Smart Sleep. Philips also has a separate Snoring Relief Band. There were also special lighting and sound products to help you fall asleep and stay asleep, smart sensors that can slide under your existing mattress, smart pillows to control your temperature while you sleep, smart hepa filters to keep you breathing clearly as you sleep and more.

Tech that saves lives

With so many people concerned about the state of the world and the future of humanity, it wasn't a surprise that CES 2019 put a greater emphasis on technology that could make a larger impact on society.

The newest pavilion at CES 2019 focused on the topic of Resilience. As CES chief Shapiro explained: "Recent natural disasters and climate change make it clear that our future history must ensure innovation will focus on preparedness and recovery ... Resilience will [offer] a greater focus on how technology aids the localism and continuity of critical infrastructure and the ability to operationally bounce back or keep going during a crisis."

The Resilience pavilion is an outgrowth of the CES expansion into Smart Cities ① in recent years. This year put greater focus around technologies and innovations that can help communities better protect against and recover from natural disasters, resolve water crises, improve food security, support first responders and make communication networks strong enough to survive epic storms.

"This need for more robust products to create an impervious infrastructure is becoming apparent in all geographies, so we want to see innovations that are truly resilient, which should dramatically protect and improve the lives of human beings," said Carmichael Roberts, a board member of Zero Mass Water, a CES 2018 exhibitor that uses tech to pull water directly from the abundant oxygen in the air.

---

① A smart city is an urban area that uses different types of electronic Internet of things (IoT) sensors to collect data and then use these data to manage assets and resources efficiently. This includes data collected from citizens, devices, and assets that is processed and analyzed to monitor and manage traffic and transportation systems, power plants, water supply networks, waste management, crime detection, information systems, schools, libraries, hospitals, and other community services.

Words and Expressions

blitz	[blɪts]	n.	a lot of energetic activity 集中力量的行动
interface	[ˈɪntəfeɪs]	n.	connection between two pieces of electronic equipment, or between a person and a computer 界面,交界面
paradigm	[ˈpærədaɪm]	n.	a model of something, or a very clear and typical example of something 范式
scenario	[sɪˈnɑːriəʊ]	n.	description of possible actions or events in the future 情境,场景
mundane	[mʌnˈdeɪn]	a.	very ordinary and therefore not interesting 平凡的
unleash	[ʌnˈliːʃ]	v.	suddenly release a violent force that cannot be controlled 释放;(使)爆发
en masse	[ˌɒ̃ˈmæs]	adv.	all together and usually in large numbers 全体地,一同地
resilience	[rɪˈzɪliəns]	n.	the ability to be happy, successful, etc. again after something difficult or bad has happened; the ability of a substance to return to its usual shape after being bent, stretched, or pressed 弹力,恢复力
impervious	[ɪmˈpɜːviəs]	a.	not affected or influenced by 不受影响的

Discussion Questions

1. What are the new trends in this year's CES?
2. What does the writer mean by saying "... technology adapting itself to each person and each scenario? Can you give any examples of such technology?
3. In the part "Tech that transforms mundane things", the writer mentioned the Internet of things. What do you know about IoT? Will IoT bring dangers and risks to our life?
4. What do you know about Smart Cities?

Part 4　Topical Vocabulary

access 入口；接入
blog 博客
blue tooth 蓝牙
browser 浏览器
byte 字节
code 代码
connectivity 连通性
create a personal profile 注册一个个人信息
cyberspace 网络空间
database 数据库
default 默认值
distance learning 远程教育
firewall 防火墙
genetically modified (GM) food 转基因食品
hard drive 硬盘驱动器
home page 主页
icon 图标
information retrieval 信息检索
instant messaging 即时信息
light rail 轻轨
megabyte 兆字节
multi-tasking 多任务的
online community 网络社区
page view 浏览量/访问量
podcast 播客
screen saver 屏幕保护
server 服务器
spam 垃圾邮件
sophisticated technology 尖端科技
tablet (computer) 平板式电脑

account 账户
back up 备份
boot up 启动
bug 漏洞
click rate 点击量
compilation 编辑，编写
copyright 版权
cyberculture 网络文化
data 数据
decipher 解密
desktop 桌面
emerging industry 新兴产业
genetic engineering 基因工程
hacker 黑客
hardware 硬件
hypertext 超文本
infiltrate 渗入，渗透
information technology 信息技术
interface 界面
log in / log off 登录/退出
Maglev train 磁悬浮列车
navigate 导航
operating system 操作系统
password 密码
registry 注册表
search engine 搜索引擎
smart phone 智能手机
social networking 社交网络
system crashed 死机
technology property right 技术产权

technology-intensive product 技术密集产品　telecommunication 远程通信
terminal 终端　　　　　　　　　　　　　　visual conference 视频会议
virus 病毒　　　　　　　　　　　　　　　voice and video chat 语音视频
upload / download 上传/下载　　　　　　user-friendly 便于用户使用的（用户友好的）
zoom 缩放

• Unit 6 Environment •

Unit 6

Environment

Part 1   Learning Before Class

- **Listening**

Air Pollution Contributes to Childhood Asthma

Directions: *Listen to the news and answer the questions.*

1. How many premature deaths are caused by air pollution every year according to the World Health Organization?
2. What specific pollutant is pointed to as the leading cause of childhood asthma by a new study from George Washington University?
3. What's one of the most surprising findings concerning the World Health Organization guideline for annual average NO_2 pollution level according to the passage?

- **Watching and Thinking**

Global Warming—Is It Real?

Directions: *Watch the video and discuss the questions with your partner.*

1. How does greenhouse effect come into being?
2. What are the consequences of climate change?
3. What can humans do to combat climate change according to the video?
4. Brainstorm and make a list of human activities that involve burning fossil fuels. What

choices shall we make to lower greenhouse gas emissions in our daily life?

• Reading and Discussing

It's Not Entirely Up to School Students to Save the World

By Bill McKibben
May 24, 2019
The New Yorker ①

In the past several months, people around the world have watched in awe as school students, led by the Swedish teenager Greta Thunberg, have taken their concerns about the climate crisis to a new level, with a series of one-day strikes. The latest took place on Friday, and drew what is estimated as more than a million participants in 125 countries. The strikes have been the biggest boost yet for the global climate movement, galvanizing public attention by reminding people just who will have to deal with the mess that older generations have created.

Thunberg has spoken to the Pope and to the British and European parliaments—and this week she and her fellow student leaders are speaking to everyone else who's older than them. On Thursday, they issued an appeal to adults to take up the same tactic, and on Friday a number of them responded, with a letter pledging to organize the first of a series of all-ages, one-day climate strikes, on Friday, September 20th. The initial list of signees is composed of a wide array of, well, adults, from around the world. Some have spent their lives trying to make change from within the system, such as Christiana Figueres, the United Nations diplomat who served as the lead negotiator of the Paris climate accords. Others are writers, scientists, trade-union leaders, and indigenous leaders from Australia to America and the Arctic.

What all of these people have in common is a strong sense that business as usual has become the problem, and that it needs to be interrupted, if only for a day. The climate crisis is a perplexing one because, mostly, we just get up each day and do what we did the day before, as if an enormous emergency weren't unfolding around us. That hasn't been true of past crises: during the Second World War, oceans may have separated American civilians from the fighting, but every day they were aware of the need to change

---

① *The New Yorker* is an American magazine featuring journalism, commentary, criticism, essays, fiction, satire, cartoons, and poetry. Established as a weekly in 1925 by Harold Ross, the magazine is now well-known for its in-depth reporting, political and cultural commentary, fiction, poetry, and humor. In addition to the weekly print magazine, *The New Yorker* has become a daily digital destination for news and cultural coverage by its staff writers and other contributors.

their ways of life: to conserve resources, buy bonds, black out their windows at night if they lived on the coast.

The climate emergency, however, is deceptive. Unless it's your town that day that's being hit by wildfire or a flood, it's easy to let the day's more pressing news take precedence. It can be hard to remember that climate change underlies so many daily injustices, from the forced migration of refugees to the spread of disease. Indeed, the people who suffer the most are usually those on the periphery—the iron law of climate change is that the less you did to cause it, the more you suffer from it. So we focus on the latest Presidential tweet or trade war instead of on the latest incremental rise in carbon dioxide, even though that, in the end, is the far more critical news.

A one-day work stoppage—a decision to spend a day demanding action from governments or building a bike path—is a way to break out of that bad habit. It gives people a chance to do the hard but necessary work of talking about an issue of paramount importance with their co-workers and bosses. And here's my prediction: if you do, you'll be surprised how many of those co-workers and bosses are grateful for the chance to do something. The trouble with global warming is not that people don't care—indeed, polling shows that people care a great deal. But the crisis seems so big, and we seem so small, that it's hard to imagine that we can make a difference.

In previous social movements, other institutions have been key: the African-American church, for instance, was the heart and soul of the civil-rights movement. But we live in an age when work defines our lives, so work is a crucial place to organize. In the past few weeks, employees at Amazon have brought together thousands of their co-workers to demand that the company reduce its carbon footprint. That kind of organizing is daunting, because it means confronting the boss. A one-day climate strike may be easier—you just have to tell your boss that you'll be elsewhere that day. Or you could ask her to go along, too.

Obviously, it's not that simple for everyone: some bosses would fire you; too many people can't live without a day's wages; and firefighters can't very well take a day off. That just increases the urgency for people who can act. The strikes may take a while to catch on, just as the school students' strikes did. But, if the momentum builds, there's a chance that we can shift the Zeitgeist toward the quick and transformative kind of action that science demands. We need to try. There's something fundamentally undignified about leaving our troubles to school kids to resolve. It's time for the elders to act like elders.

Directions: *Read the passage and discuss the questions with your partner.*

1. What do you know about the Paris climate accords? Please search for information about the Paris Agreement and discuss with your partner about the significance of the agreement.

2. What does the author mean by saying climate emergency is deceptive? Do you agree with his opinion? Give your reasons.

3. A poll conducted by researchers from Yale and George Manson University between Nov. 28 and Dec. 11, 2018 showed that 72% of US adults regard climate change as personally important. Yet, according to the author, a number of people harbor the misconception that "the crisis seems so big, and (as individuals) we seem so small, that it's hard to imagine that we can make a difference". Please discuss with your partner: how to convince people that we can do something to make a big difference?

Part 2　Learning in Class

Warm Up

China and India Making Earth Greener, NASA Study Shows

By Ma Chi

February 14, 2019

China Daily

　　NASA satellite data reveals the Earth is greening, with China and India leading the increase in green leaf area. A study by NASA has revealed China and India, the world's two most populous countries, are primarily responsible for making the Earth greener over the past 2 decades.

　　The study, published on Feb. 11 in the journal *Natural Sustainability*, has found that since 2000 the Earth's green leaf area has increased by 5%, or over 5 million square kilometers. That's an area equivalent to the total of the Amazon rainforests. "China and India account for 1/3 of the greening, but contain only 9% of the planet's land area covered in vegetation—a surprising finding, considering the general notion of land degradation in populous countries from overexploitation," said Chen Chi of the Department of Earth and Environment at Boston University, lead author of the study.

　　The effect mainly stems from ambitious tree-planting programs in China and intensive agriculture in both countries, NASA said in a statement. China is the source of 1/4 of the planet's increase in forest area, despite having only 6.6% of the world's vegetated area, according to the study. Forest conservation and expansion programs account for 42% of the increase, and another 32% come from intensive agriculture of food crops, NASA said. While raising their green leaf areas, China and India have also greatly increased their food production through "multiple cropping" practices, where a field is replanted and crops are harvested several times each year. "Production of grains, vegetables, fruits and more have increased by about 35%-40% since 2000 to feed their large populations," NASA said. The study is based on high-resolution data gathered by a NASA sensor called Moderate Resolution Imaging Spectroradiometer (MODIS) of Earth's surface from 2000 to 2017.

Over the past decades, China has made great efforts to green the land. In 1978, the central government launched a national-level forestation project—the Three North Shelterbelt Forest Program. By the end of 2017, the forest coverage rate among the regions in the project reached 13.57%, compared to 5.05% 40 years ago. In an exemplary greening project, Kubuqi Desert, the 7th largest in the country, has seen 1/3 of its area covered by vegetation during the past 3 decades thanks to forestation efforts.

Nationwide, China has a forest cover of 21.6%, and it aims to increase the number to 23.04% by 2020 and 26% by 2050. To achieve this ambitious goal, China has taken a series of measures, from reforesting hillsides to creating protected grassland and nature reserves.

Directions: *Read the passage and discuss the questions with your partner.*

1. What endeavors did China and India make to not only save the two populous countries from land degradation but also lead the increase in the Earth's green leaf area?
2. What ambitious goal does China aim to achieve by 2020 and by 2050? What measures has China taken to achieve the goal?
3. Search for information about deforestation and discuss with your partner: What are the causes and consequences of deforestation? What can be done to make it up?

Text A

The False Choice Between Economic Growth and Combating Climate Change

By Carolyn Kormann
February 4, 2019
The New Yorker

In 1974, the economist William Nordhaus [1] described the transition from a "cowboy economy" to a "spaceship economy". [2] In the former, he wrote, "We could afford to use our resources **profligately**," and "the environment could be used as a sink without becoming fouled". But, in the spaceship economy, "great attention must be paid to the sources of life and to the dumps where our refuse is piled." He added, "Things which have traditionally been treated as free goods—air, water, quiet, natural beauty—must now be treated with the same care as other scarce goods." Toward the end of his landmark paper, "Resources as a Constraint on Growth," Nordhaus discussed the possible adverse effects of energy consumption, most notably the "greenhouse effect". From a "rough calculation", he found that the atmospheric concentration of carbon dioxide (CO_2) would increase by more than 40% in the next 60 years. "Although this is below the fateful doubling of CO_2 concentration," he wrote—scientists had already predicted that such a doubling could cause the polar ice caps to melt catastrophically—"it may well be too close for comfort". He was prescient. We are now dangerously on track to hit his estimate, 487 parts per million, by 2030.

In the United States, after 3 years of decline, CO_2 emissions increased by an estimated 3.4% in 2018, according to a report released earlier this month by the Rhodium Group, a private climate-research firm. The authors blame 2 main factors: a particularly

---

[1] William Nordhaus is an American economist and Sterling Professor of Economics at Yale University, best-known for his work in economic modeling and climate change. He is one of the laureates of the 2018 Nobel Memorial Prize in Economic Sciences. Nordhaus received the prize "for integrating climate change into long-run macroeconomic analysis".

[2] Kenneth Boulding, an English-born American economist, put forward the concepts of "cowboy economy" and "spaceship economy" in 1966. He delivered a lecture entitled "The Economics of the Coming Spaceship Earth", in which he contrasted an open ended economy and a closed economy. He called the open economy the "cowboy economy", the cowboy being symbolic of the illimitable plains and also associated with reckless, exploitative, romantic, and violent behavior, which is characteristic of open societies. The closed economy of the future might similarly be called the "spaceman economy". Here the earth has become a single spaceship, without unlimited reservoirs of anything, either for extraction or for pollution. Humans must find their place in a cyclical ecological system that is capable of continuous reproduction of material form even though it cannot escape having inputs of energy.

cold winter and fast economic growth. In the past 2 decades, the only greater annual gain in emissions was in 2010, when the economy was rebounding from the Great Recession ①. Historically, emissions have aligned with the ebb and flow of the economy. In 2018, economic growth was driven by a higher demand for energy, trucking and air travel, and industrial activity. Companies were manufacturing more stuff, including steel, cement, and chemicals. The carbon intensity of the power sector, meanwhile, did not decline fast enough to offset all those demand increases. As has been common since Nordhaus's 1974 paper, the report seems to pit controlling climate change against a growing global economy.

The picture could have been much different. Nordhaus went on to publish a series of foundational studies on the economics of climate change. In 1992, he created an integrated economic and scientific model that could be used to determine the most efficient ways to cut greenhouse-gas emissions. His work showed that a low tax on carbon, set to rise slowly over time, could be enough to keep emissions at reasonable levels, saving us from climate change at little, if any, cost. A "spaceship economy" could thrive if governments made sure that companies paid an appropriate price for the environmental damage they caused—what would come to be called the social cost of carbon. Companies that were most easily able to reduce their level of pollution would be incentivized to make the greatest reductions, and to invest in cheaper and better pollution-reduction systems. The dirtiest activities would be the most costly. The tax would promote innovations in new forms of power generation and, eventually, a widespread adoption of clean-energy technologies. The way to break the chain was to reimagine how we fuel the global economy. "It's absolutely the case that emissions and growth can be decoupled," said Marshall Burke, an assistant professor in Stanford University's Department of Earth System Science. He pointed to research plotting how 35 countries, including the United States, did, in fact, experience economic growth in the past 15 years while reducing their emissions—and not solely due to recessions. But the decline was not nearly enough. "The technology is available to have faster economic growth while reducing over-all emissions," said Trevor Houser, the head of Rhodium Group's energy and climate team, and one of the authors of the report. But the switch to nuclear and renewables needs to happen more rapidly. "It takes policy. It won't happen through markets alone," Houser

---

① The Great Recession was a period of general economic decline observed in world markets during the late 2000s and early 2010s. The scale and timing of the recession varied from country to country. The International Monetary Fund has concluded that it was the most severe economic and financial meltdown since the Great Depression and it is often regarded as the second worst downturn of all time.

said.

In October, Nordhaus and another economist, Paul Romer, won the Nobel Prize in Economic Sciences for, respectively, "integrating climate change" and "technological innovations" into "long-run macroeconomic analysis". The timing of the announcement from Sweden was painfully ironic. Hours earlier, the United Nations had released its dire report warning that, if climate change's worst impacts were to be avoided, the nations of the world had about a decade to revolutionize the energy economy. "The policies are lagging very, very far—miles, miles, miles behind the science and what needs to be done," Nordhaus said after receiving the prize. "It's hard to be optimistic ... We're actually going backward in the United States, with the disastrous policies of the Trump Administration." The Obama Administration had, in its final years, partially incorporated concepts that Nordhaus had helped to develop, such as putting a price on the economic harm that results from every additional ton of CO_2 emitted into the atmosphere. The price was set at \$45 a ton, and used in both regulatory cost-benefit analyses, which undergirded new fuel-efficiency standards, and the Clean Power Plan ①, which would have propelled a faster retirement of coal-powered electric plants and a broader transition to renewables. Just as such policies were "beginning to bear fruit", Houser said, "that whole framework was dismantled." Under Trump, the social cost of a ton of carbon is as little as \$1.

As emissions keep growing, and climate change advances, there is less and less time to make the necessary cuts. "The pace we needed to decline was already much larger than what was happening," Houser noted. "Now we have to go even faster to meet our Paris Agreement target by 2025"—on average, a 2.6-per-cent reduction in annual energy-related CO_2 emissions in the next 7 years.

A modest carbon tax of the sort Nordhaus proposed decades ago—one that was then **palatable** to conservatives—will therefore no longer bring us anywhere near the Paris Agreement targets. But it's one of many weapons in the arsenal that policy-makers need to employ. "The real challenge is finding ways to reduce emissions and maintain economic growth on the timeline demanded by the nature of climate change," Kenneth Gillingham, an associate professor of economics at Yale University, pointed out. But, as much as the

---

① The Clean Power Plan was an Obama administration policy aimed at combating anthropogenic climate change that was first proposed by the Environmental Protection Agency in June 2014. The final version of the plan was unveiled by President Obama on August 3, 2015. The 460-page rule titled "Carbon Pollution Emission Guidelines for Existing Stationary Sources: Electric Utility Generating Units" was published in the *Federal Register* on October 23, 2015. The Obama administration designed the plan to lower the CO_2 emitted by power generators.

costs of climate mitigation will undoubtedly increase, the question is whether the benefits of mitigation exceed those costs. "It's a straw man ① —and terrible economics—to just point out the costs while ignoring the benefits," Burke said. He and 2 co-authors published a paper in Nature last May that shows that the economic benefits of mitigation are going to be much larger than previously believed. Cooler temperatures would help maintain and grow productivity, and reducing carbon emissions means reducing air pollution—specifically particulate matter, or soot—which brings immediate health benefits. They found that keeping global warming to 1.5℃, as opposed to 2℃, would potentially save more than 20 trillion dollars around the world by the end of the century, and significantly reduce global inequality. Beyond 2℃, they wrote, "We find considerably greater reductions in global economic output." If nations met their commitments under the Paris Agreement, the world would still see the average global temperature rise by 2.5℃-3℃, which, according to Burke's paper, would result in a 15%-25% reduction in per capita output by 2100. "To just complain about the costs of this transition and ignore the benefits, as is common in the discussion from this Administration," Burke said, "is some pretty poor cost-benefit analysis from an Administration that prides itself on economic savvy."

As a small but growing coalition of congressional Democrats, led by Representative Alexandria Ocasio-Cortez, have outlined as part of their Green New Deal ②, transforming the energy sector will require some sort of carbon tax (preferably a "fee and dividend" approach, which distributes tax revenues as rebates directly to citizens), and also new regulations and huge investments. "We can decarbonize the electric sector at a fairly low cost," Gillingham revealed. Extensive government subsidies could hasten the spread of renewables—specifically, solar, wind, and batteries—and offset any rise in emissions elsewhere. As Gillingham said, "We might want to be careful about fighting climate change by preventing people from staying warm in the winter. If a winter is really cold enough, emissions increases are to be expected."

Economists and other market observers predict that over-all economic growth will be slower, and the full impact of recent cuts to coal-plant capacity has not yet been

---

① A straw man is a form of argument and an informal fallacy based on giving the impression of refuting an opponent's argument, while actually refuting an argument that was not presented by that opponent. One who engages in this fallacy is said to be "attacking a straw man".

② The Green New Deal is a package of policy proposals that aims to address global warming and financial crises. It echoes the New Deal, the social and economic programs launched by US President Franklin D. Roosevelt in the wake of the Wall Street Crash of 1929 and the onset of the Great Depression.

recorded. Still, in the absence of major policy changes—which is mostly dependent on a new President who makes climate policy a top and urgent priority—there is almost no chance that the US will achieve the average emissions cuts necessary to meet the Paris targets by 2025. Houser claimed that our only hope would be extremely favorable market and technological conditions. "If, over the next couple of years, no more nuclear power plants retired, wind, solar, and battery prices fall far faster than the currently most optimistic projections estimate, it is possible that we could come pretty close to meeting the Paris Agreement targets," he said. "Everything would really have to light up in the right direction".

 Words and Expressions

concentration	[ˌkɒnsn'treɪʃn]	n.	the amount of a substance in a liquid or in another substance 浓度
catastrophically	[ˌkætə'strɒfɪkli]	adv.	in a way that involves or causes sudden great damage or suffering 灾难性地
prescient	['presiənt]	a.	having or showing knowledge of events before they take place 有预知能力的；有先见之明的
align with			support, agree with, or form an alliance with a particular person or idea 与……保持一致；与……结盟
ebb and flow			the way in which the level of something regularly becomes higher or lower in a situation（有规律的）涨落；起伏
offset	[ˌɒf'set]	v.	balance one influence against an opposing influence, so that there is no great difference as a result 补偿；抵消；弥补
pit ... against			cause one person, group, or thing to fight against or be incompetition with another 使相斗；使竞争；使较量
thrive	[θraɪv]	v.	grow, develop, or be successful 茁壮成长；兴旺,繁荣
incentivize	[ɪn'sentɪvaɪz]	v.	make someone want to do something 刺激；激励
decouple	[diː'kʌpl]	v.	separate, disengage, or dissociate something from something else 使分离；拆开；隔断
available	[ə'veɪləbl]	a.	able to be obtained, used, or reached 可用的；可获得的

renewable	[rɪˈnjuːəbl]	a.	relating to forms of energy that are produced using the sun, wind, etc., or from crops, rather than those using fuels such as oil or coal 可再生能源的；可更新的；可继续的
dire	[daɪə(r)]	a.	very serious or extreme 极其严重的；危急的
undergird	[ˌʌndəˈɡɜːd]	v.	support something by forming a strong base for it 加强；从底层加固
propel	[prəˈpel]	v.	move, drive or push something forward or in a particular direction 推进；驱动；推动；驱策
dismantle	[dɪˈsmæntl]	v.	take apart or to come apart into separate pieces; get rid of a system or organization 拆除；解散；取消
arsenal	[ˈɑːsənl]	n.	a building where weapons and military equipment are stored 军火库；兵工厂
mitigation	[ˌmɪtɪˈɡeɪʃn]	n.	the act of reducing how harmful, unpleasant, or bad something is 缓解；减轻损失；减缓
dividend	[ˈdɪvɪdend]	n.	(a part of) the profit of a company that is paid to the people who own shares in it 红利；股息；股利
rebate	[ˈriːbeɪt]	n.	an amount of money that is returned to you, especially by the government, for example, when you have paid too much tax 退还（部分付款）；折扣；返利
subsidy	[ˈsʌbsədi]	n.	money given as part of the cost of something, to help or encourage it to happen 补贴；津贴；补助金

- **Multiple Choice**

Select the most appropriate answer for each of the following questions.

1. According to the context, the underlined word "profligately" in Paragraph 1 is close in meaning to the following words EXCEPT "_____".

   A) wastefully   B) dissolutely   C) improvidently   D) extravagantly

2. In 1992, Nordhaus created an integrated _____ model that could be used to

determine the most efficient ways to cut greenhouse-gas emissions.

   A) political and economic   B) mathematic and economic

   C) political and scientific   D) economic and scientific

3. Based on scientific research and the fact that 35 countries, including the US, experienced economic growth in the past 15 years while reducing their emissions, Marshall Burke concluded that _____.

   A) economic growth can result in emissions reduction

   B) emissions and growth can be decoupled

   C) economic recessions can cause emissions reduction

   D) economic recessions and emissions reduction can be decoupled

4. Trevor Houser, one of the authors of the report, pointed out that the switch to nuclear and renewables won't happen through _____ alone; the switch takes _____.

   A) science; economy   B) science; policy

   C) markets; policy   D) markets; science

5. In Oct., 2019, Nordhaus was rewarded the Nobel Prize in Economic Sciences as a co-recipient for _____.

   A) the concepts that Nordhaus had helped develop were incorporated in the Obama Administration

   B) the price on additional carbon dioxide emissions that Nordhaus helped to set was used in both regulatory cost-benefit analyses and the Clean Power Plan

   C) the policies that incorporated Nordhaus' concepts were beginning to bear fruit

   D) "integrating climate change" into "long-run macroeconomic analysis"

6. The underlined word "palatable" in Paragraph 6 is close in meaning to "_____".

   A) pleasant   B) tasty   C) acceptable   D) agreeable

- **True/False/Not Given**

Do the following statements agree with the information given in the text?

In Blanks 1-8 write:

True   if the statement is true

False   if the statement is false

Not Given   if the statement is not given in the text

_____ 1. According to a report released by the Rhodium Group, the 3.4% increase of CO_2 emissions in 2018 in the United States blame 2 factors: a particularly cold winter and the Great Recession.

_____ 2. In a series of foundational studies published on the economics of climate change, Nordhaus pit controlling climate change against a growing global economy.

Unit 6 Environment

_____ 3. Historically, the increase or decrease in CO_2 emissions has coincided with the fluctuations of the economy.

_____ 4. A "spaceship economy" could thrive if companies paid their share of "the social cost of carbon" for the environmental damage.

_____ 5. A modest carbon tax of the sort Nordhaus proposed decades ago is not sufficient to help decline the CO_2 emissions to meet the Paris Agreement target; hence it's not worth the effort.

_____ 6. To just point out the costs of climate mitigation while ignoring its economic benefits is a logical fallacy.

_____ 7. Fighting climate change by preventing people from staying warm in the winter might cause resistance from the public.

_____ 8. The "fee and dividend" approach means distributing tax revenues as rebates directly to citizens.

- **Sentence Completion**

Complete the sentence below with words taken from the text. USE NO MORE THAN THREE WORDS for each answer.

1. In his 1992 works, Nordhaus showed that a low _____ could be employed to keep emissions at reasonable levels. Companies would be incentivized to _____ in new forms of power generation, and eventually _____ of clean-energy technologies.

2. Marshall Burke, an assistant professor in Stanford University, holds that to just complain about _____ of the transition to renewables and ignore _____ _____ is some pretty poor _____ from an Administration that prides itself on economic savvy.

3. Extensive government subsidies could hasten the _____—specifically, solar, wind, and batteries—and offset any _____ elsewhere.

4. A new president who makes _____ a top and urgent priority might make it possible for the US to achieve the _____ necessary to meet _____ by 2025.

5. Trevor Houser believes that the only hope for the US to achieve the emissions cut target would be extremely _____ and _____, that is, if over the next couple of years, no more nuclear power plants _____, and the prices of renewables _____ than the currently most optimistic projections estimate.

Discussion Questions

1. What are the economic benefits of climate mitigation according to a paper published in *Nature* by Marshall Burke and 2 co-authors in May 2018? What do you think about his viewpoint that "It's a straw man—and terrible economics—to just point out the costs while ignoring the benefits"?
2. Do you think the benefits of climate mitigation would exceed the costs? Development and environment, which should come first?

Text B

Crude Awakening: ExxonMobil and the Oil Industry Are Making a Bet That Could End Up Wrecking the Climate

February 9, 2019

The Economist [1]

A. In America, the world's largest economy and its second biggest polluter, climate change is becoming hard to ignore. Extreme weather has grown more frequent. In November wildfires scorched California; last week Chicago was colder than parts of Mars. Scientists are sounding the alarm more urgently and people have noticed—73% of Americans polled by Yale University late last year said that climate change is real. The left of the Democratic Party wants to put a "Green New Deal" at the heart of the election in 2020. As expectations shift, the private sector is showing signs of adapting. Last year around 20 coal mines shut. Fund managers are prodding firms to become greener. Warren Buffett, no sucker for fads, is staking $30bn on clean energy and Elon Musk plans to fill America's highways with electric cars. Yet amid the clamour is a single, jarring truth. Demand for oil is rising and the energy industry, in America and globally, is planning multi-trillion-dollar investments to satisfy it. No firm embodies this strategy better

---

[1] *The Economist* is an English-language weekly news magazine owned by the Economist Group and edited in offices in London. Continuous publication began under its founder, James Wilson, in September 1843. In 2009 its average weekly circulation was reported to be over 1.6 million, about half of which were sold in North America and other English-speaking countries. *The Economist* takes an editorial stance of classical and economic liberalism which is supportive of free trade, globalisation, free immigration and cultural liberalism. It targets highly educated readers and claims an audience containing many influential executives and policy-makers.

Unit 6 Environment

than ExxonMobil ①, the giant that rivals admire and green activists love to hate. As our briefing explains, it plans to pump 25% more oil and gas in 2025 than in 2017. If the rest of the industry pursues even modest growth, the consequence for the climate could be disastrous.

B. ExxonMobil shows that the market cannot solve climate change by itself. Muscular government action is needed. Contrary to the fears of many Republicans (and hopes of some Democrats), that need not involve a bloated role for the state.

C. For much of the 20th century, the 5 oil majors ②—Chevron, ExxonMobil, Royal Dutch Shell, bp and Total—had more clout than some small countries. Although the majors' power has waned, they still account for 10% of global oil and gas output and 16% of upstream investment. They set the tone for smaller, privately owned energy firms. And millions of pensioners and other savers rely on their profits. Of the 20 firms paying the biggest dividends in Europe and America, four are majors.

D. In 2000 bp promised to go "beyond petroleum" and, on the face of it, the majors have indeed changed. All say that they support the Paris Agreement to limit climate change and all are investing in renewables such as solar. Shell recently said that it would curb emissions from its products. Yet ultimately you should judge companies by what they do, not what they say.

E. According to ExxonMobil, global oil and gas demand will rise by 13% by 2030. All of the majors, not just ExxonMobil, are expected to expand their output. Far from mothballing all their gas fields and gushers, the industry is investing in upstream projects from Texan shale to high-tech deep-water wells. Oil companies, directly and through trade groups, lobby against measures that would limit emissions. The trouble is that, according to an assessment by the IPCC, an intergovernmental climate-science body, oil and gas production needs to fall by about 20% by 2030 and by about 55% by 2050, in order to stop the Earth's temperature rising by more than 1.5℃ above its preindustrial level.

F. It would be wrong to conclude that the energy firms must therefore be evil. They

---

① Exxon Mobil Corporation, doing business as ExxonMobil, is an American multinational oil and gas corporation headquartered in Irving, Texas. It is the largest direct descendant of John D. Rockefeller's Standard Oil Company, and was formed on November 30, 1999 by the merger of Exxon and Mobil.

② Chevron Corporation (the United States), ExxonMobil Corporation (the United States), Royal Dutch Shell plc (the Netherlands and United Kingdom), BP plc (the United Kingdom), and Total SA (France) are world's largest publicly owned oil and gas companies, and are sometimes collectively referred to as the "oil majors". They control a majority of global oil and gas reserves and decide a majority of the crude oil tanker chartering business. The term "oil majors" emphasizes their economic power and perceived influence on politics, particularly in the United States; hence is often associated with the fossil fuels lobby.

are responding to incentives set by society. The financial returns from oil are higher than those from renewables. For now, worldwide demand for oil is growing by 1%-2% a year, similar to the average over the past 5 decades—and the typical major derives a minority of its stockmarket value from profits it will make after 2030. However much the majors are vilified by climate warriors, many of whom drive cars and take planes, it is not just legal for them to maximise profits, it is also a requirement that shareholders can enforce.

G. Some hope that the oil companies will gradually head in a new direction, but that looks optimistic. It would be rash to rely on brilliant innovations to save the day. Global investment in renewables, at $300bn a year, is dwarfed by what is being committed to fossil fuels. Even in the car industry, where scores of electric models are being launched, around 85% of vehicles are still expected to use internal-combustion engines in 2030.

H. So, too, the boom in ethical investing. Funds with $32trn of assets have joined to put pressure on the world's biggest emitters. Fund managers, facing a collapse in their traditional business, are glad to sell green products which, helpfully, come with higher fees. But few big investment groups have dumped the shares of big energy firms. Despite much publicity, oil companies' recent commitments to green investors remain modest.

I. And do not expect much from the courts. Lawyers are bringing waves of actions accusing oil firms of everything from misleading the public to being liable for rising sea levels. Some think oil firms will suffer the same fate as tobacco firms, which faced huge settlements in the 1990s. They forget that big tobacco is still in business. In June a federal judge in California ruled that climate change was a matter for Congress and diplomacy, not judges.

J. The next 15 years will be critical for climate change. If innovators, investors, the courts and corporate self-interest cannot curb fossil fuels, then the burden must fall on the political system. In 2017 America said it would withdraw from the Paris Agreement and the Trump administration has tried to resurrect the coal industry. Even so, climate could yet enter the political mainstream and win cross-party appeal. Polls suggest that moderate and younger Republicans care. A recent pledge by dozens of prominent economists spanned the partisan divide.

K. The key will be to show centrist voters that cutting emissions is practical and will not leave them much worse off. Although the Democrats' emerging Green New Deal raises awareness, it almost certainly fails this test as it is based on a massive expansion of government spending and central planning. The best policy, in America and beyond, is to tax carbon emissions, which ExxonMobil backs. The gilets jaunes in France ① show how hard that will be. Work will be needed on designing policies that can command popular support by giving the cash raised back to the public in the form of offsetting tax cuts. The fossil-fuel industry would get smaller, government would not get bigger and businesses would be free to adapt as they see fit—including, even, ExxonMobil.

Words and Expressions

prod	[prɒd]	v.	encourage someone to take action, especially when they are being slow or unwilling 刺激；督促；提醒
sucker (for)	[ˈsʌkər]	v.	if you are a sucker for something, you like it so much that you cannot refuse it 对……着迷；喜欢
fad	[fæd]	a.	style, activity, or interest that is very popular for a short period of time 时尚；一时的爱好；一时流行的狂热
stake (on)	[steɪk]	v.	risk harming or losing something important if an action, decision, or situation does not have the result you want or expect 拿……打赌；把赌注押在……上面
clamour	[ˈklæmə(r)]	n.	a loud complaint about something or a demand for something; loud noise, especially made by people's voices 强烈抗议；吵闹声
jarring	[ˈdʒɑːrɪŋ]	a.	different from surrounding or usual things, or disagreeing with others, or unexpected, and therefore unpleasant, disturbing, surprising or upsetting 不和谐的；刺耳的；产生不快影响的
bloated	[ˈbləʊtɪd]	a.	swollen and rounded because of containing too much air, liquid, or food; a bloated organization employs too many people in relation to the amount of work that there is and therefore costs too much money to run 膨胀的；过度渲染的

---

① The gilets jaunes in France is also referred to as the yellow vests movement, is a protest movement that started online in May 2018 and led to demonstrations that began in France on 17 November, 2018. The movement takes its name from the high-visibility jackets protesters have adopted as a symbol of their complaint. Protests sprang up spontaneously against hikes in car fuel taxes, with supporters donning the fluorescent safety vests that French law requires all motorists to carry.

clout	[klaʊt]	n.	power and influence over other people or events 影响力；势力
set the tone (for)			establish a particular mood or character for something 为……设定基调；定下……的风格
mothball	[ˈmɒθbɔːl]	v.	stop work on an idea, plan, or job, but leaving it in such a way that you can start on it again at some point in the future 封存；搁置
Texan shale			a kind of fissile rock usually formed from clay that breaks easily into thin layers 得克萨斯州页岩
lobby (against)	[ˈlɒbi]	v.	try to persuade a politician, the government, or an official group that a particular thing should or should not happen, or that a law should be changed 游说议员不通过（某议案）；游说反对议案通过
vilify	[ˈvɪlɪfaɪ]	v.	say or write unpleasant things about someone or something, in order to cause other people to have a bad opinion of them 诽谤；轻视；贬低
rash	[ræʃ]	a.	careless or unwise, without thought 轻率的；匆忙的
dwarf	[dwɔːf]	v.	if one thing dwarfs another, it makes it seem small by comparison 相形见绌
dump	[dʌmp]	v.	put down or drop something in a careless way; get rid of something unwanted, especially by leaving it in a place where it is not allowed to be; sell unwanted goods very cheaply, usually in other countries 抛售；倾倒；倾销
liable (for)	[ˈlaɪəbl]	a.	law specialized having (legal) responsibility for something or someone 有……责任；有……义务
settlement	[ˈsetlmənt]	n.	an arrangement, often with payment of money, to end a legal disagreement without taking it to court 庭外和解；协议解决纷争
rule	[ruːl]	v.	decide officially 裁决；规定
curb	[kɜːb]	v.	control or limit something that is not wanted 控制；抑制
resurrect	[ˌrezəˈrekt]	v.	bring someone back to life, or bring something back into use or existence after it disappeared 使复兴；恢复使用

| prominent | [ˈprɒmɪnənt] | a. | very well-known and important 突出的；杰出的；卓越的 |
| worse off | | | in a less satisfactory or less successful situation; poorer or in a more difficult situation 愈加贫穷的；每况愈下的 |

- **Matching**

The author argued from the opposite angle that muscular government action is needed to curb fossil fuels. Which paragraph contains the following information?

1. Higher profits from oil than renewables serve as incentives to energy firms.
2. Oil companies' commitments to green investors remain modest.
3. Climate change are ruled as a matter for congress and diplomacy, instead of judges.
4. Investment in energy innovations is dwarfed by that in fossil fuels.

- **Table Completion**

The author employs contrast to show that what the oil companies say do not consist with what they do. Complete the table with words taken from the text.

What the oil companies say	What the oil companies do
Bp promised to go ___(1)___ .	Global oil and gas demand will ___(2)___ by 2030.
All claim to support ___(3)___ to limit climate change.	Oil companies, directly and through trade groups, ___(4)___ measures that would limit emissions.
All say they are investing in ___(5)___ such as solar.	Far from ___(6)___ gasfields and gushers, the industry is investing in upstream projects from ___(7)___ to ___(8)___ .
Shell said it would ___(9)___ from its products.	All of the oil majors are expected to ___(10)___ their output.

- **Short Answer Questions**

1. What evidence shows that dramatic climate change is ongoing in America, and is becoming hard to ignore?
2. At what rate should the world reduce its oil and gas production in order to stop the Earth's temperature rising by more than 1.5℃ above its pre-industrial level according to the assessment by the IPCC?
3. Why does the author say that the energy firms are just responding to incentives set by

society by expanding their oil and gas output?

4. How do people win the support from centrist voters for emissions reduction according to the author?

5. What policy does the author suggest to adopt to curb emissions, and how do people command popular support for the policy?

- **Summary**

Complete the summary below; choose ONE WORD from the text for each answer.

America is undergoing dramatic climate change, the disastrous consequence for which makes it hard to ignore. Yet meanwhile, demand for oil is __(1)__ and the energy industry is planning huge __(2)__ to satisfy it.

The oil companies cannot solve climate change by itself, because the __(3)__ returns from oil are higher than those from renewables, and corporate self-interest determines how they are responding to market __(4)__. Innovators are unlikely to save the day, as global investment in renewables is __(5)__ by what is being committed to fossil fuels. Investors are not reliable to change the situation, for few big investment groups have dumped the shares of big energy firms, while oil companies' green investing remains __(6)__. The courts cannot be counted on either, since from their perspective, climate change is a matter for __(7)__ and diplomacy, not judges. Hence __(8)__ government action is needed to __(9)__ fossil fuels. The best policy is to __(10)__ carbon emissions and win public support through offsetting tax cuts.

Academic Reading

Critical Thinking (2)

Learning Objective

In the section, you will learn to list, explain and demonstrate the characteristics of critical thinking.

Characteristics of Critical Thinking

How do you know for sure when you are thinking critically? The answer to that question involves a discussion of its characteristics. Critical thinking requires:

- flexibility
- a clear purpose
- organization
- time and effort
- asking questions and finding answers

- research
- coming to logical conclusions

(1) Flexibility

Critical thinking is flexible thinking because it involves a willingness to consider various possibilities before coming to a conclusion. Critical thinkers do not jump to conclusions or automatically accept what they first see, hear, or read. They are willing to gather and consider additional information, even if it does not support what they initially think or want to do. In the course selection example, it would have been easy for you simply to accept the first student's opinion and your friend's decision regarding the course. Even though you may have been tempted to take the quick and easy way out, you delayed your decision until you had a chance to gather more information. Realizing that your first reaction to the course was negative, you still managed to keep an open mind and were willing to consider carefully other viewpoints.

Critical thinkers, then, are aware of their initial feelings about decisions, issues, problems, or situations yet willing to look at other possibilities before taking action. They are also willing to allow others the opportunity to voice their opinions, and they give careful consideration to those opinions before coming to their own conclusions. In the end, critical thinkers may stick with their initial feelings, but only after much investigation and thought.

(2) Clear Purpose

Critical thinking is deliberate thinking because it always involves a clear purpose, a specific goal. When you think critically, you are looking for reasons or explanations for events, considering various sides of an issue, attempting to solve a problem, coming to a decision, or making sense of a situation. For example, you may be trying to figure out how an event such as an automobile accident occurred, distinguish among the arguments on both sides of an issue such as abortion, come up with a solution to a problem such as a low grade in a course, decide where to go on vacation, or understand the reasons behind a political event such as a war or revolution. In the course example, the decision whether to register for the course was the purpose you, as a critical thinker, had in mind.

(3) Organization

Students often complain that lack of time makes it difficult for them to accomplish everything that they have to do. There is no doubt that their lives are very busy, with classes to attend, assignments to be completed, studying to be done, and tests to be taken. As a typical college student, there are occasions when you must feel under a great deal of time pressure. For that reason, you probably schedule your daily activities very carefully so that you are able to get everything done. You have certain hours that you devote to going to and preparing for classes, and you work your other personal responsibilities around them. In other words, you use organization, or careful planning, to make the most productive use of your limited time.

Critical thinkers also depend on organization to help them deal effectively with events, issues, problems, decisions, and situations. In the example, you certainly used an organized approach to help you to make a decision regarding whether you should take the course. You went through a series of specific steps in order to gather more information, which placed you in a much stronger position when deciding what to do. Critical thinking always involves that kind of organization.

(4) **Time and Effort**

At this point, it is probably obvious to you that critical thinking requires much time and effort. Furthermore, critical thinkers are willing to take time away from other activities so that they can concentrate on a specific event, issue, problem, decision, or situation. The examples you have read about and the activities that you have been asked to complete all involve not only setting aside time but also putting in extra effort. In the example, the easy road would have been for you to follow your first reaction, which was not to register for the course. You opted instead to take some additional time to gather information, because you felt that it would help you make the right decision. In short, you were taking the time and making the effort that critical thinking requires.

(5) **Asking Questions and Finding Answers**

Critical thinkers are aware of what is going on around them. They observe their surroundings carefully and put substantial effort into looking for causes, explanations, or reasons. In other words, critical thinkers ask questions continuously and are very patient and persistent when trying to find answers. They often use words that are found in questions, such as who, when, what, where, how, and why. For example, critical thinkers would wonder: Who is responsible for determining the price of an automobile? Where can I find information about a fair price for a particular automobile? Where can I find information about a fair loan rate for an automobile? When is the best time to study for a test? How do I decide what career to pursue? What are the requirements for the career that I want to pursue? What provides the pressure that forces water through a faucet? Where does electricity originate from? How is sewage carried through underground pipes without clogging them? Why do leaves turn different colors in many areas of the United States? Have you thought about answers to these questions and others like them? If you have, you have experience at being a critical thinker. Furthermore, if you are very persistent in trying to find answers before making a decision, you are being a critical thinker.

(6) **Research**

Critical thinking is a way of dealing with events, issues, problems, decisions, or situations in a very thoughtful, careful manner. For that reason, critical thinking often requires research, the process of looking for and gathering information to increase your knowledge and understanding of a given topic. In the example that we have been using, you did research to place yourself in a stronger position in deciding whether to take the course. You studied the class schedule, the catalog, and a syllabus and talked with students, faculty, and your counselor to gather as much information as possible concerning the course. In other words, all of the research that you did provided you with more information to help you make a decision.

The kind of research that critical thinkers do and the sources of information that they use vary with the matter at hand. In other words, research can involve using the Internet, going to libraries, reading official reports or documents, interviewing people, visiting various agencies and organizations, or some combination of these. For example, if a young man wants to find out more about the issue of gun control, he might go to the library or use the Internet to read about the topic in newspapers, magazines, books, or reports. In addition, he might talk with individuals who know something about the issue—perhaps police officials, gun owners, and members of various organizations that support and oppose gun control. By contrast, if he wants to investigate a traffic accident, he might study the police report, read newspaper accounts, talk with persons actually involved, and interview any witnesses who were present.

As these examples illustrate, critical thinkers are careful about using the sources that are most relevant, applicable, or appropriate and therefore most likely to provide useful, reliable information—information that is not only specific to the topic, but also accurate and trustworthy. Thus, our young researcher would probably not seek information about gun control from a mechanic, a physician, or an accountant unless the individual was somehow involved with the issue, nor would he read general magazines or books to find out about a particular traffic accident. You certainly used appropriate sources when doing research for the course decision. Each of the individuals you talked with was in a good position to provide useful information, and the written sources were all relevant to the matter under consideration.

Critical thinkers are not only aware of their own feelings and opinions; they also try to be aware of any prejudice or bias on the part of a given source. In other words, our researcher would determine if the source is providing information that supports a particular point of view instead of being impartial or evenhanded. For example, if he is discussing gun control with a representative of an organization that does not support it, such as the National Rifle Association, he would keep in mind that the information he is getting is probably slanted in one direction. Similarly, if our researcher is reading literature put out by that same organization, he realizes that it is likely to include only information supporting its viewpoint regarding the issue. This is not to say that he should necessarily ignore the information. However, at the very least, he would need to search for information from other sources that might offer opposing viewpoints. You were using critical thinking when you realized that the student who had dropped the course was only giving her personal point of view, which was not unbiased. That is precisely why you turned to additional sources of information before making a decision.

Words of Caution when Using the Internet for Research

As you know, the Internet consists of an enormous number of computers that are linked through a worldwide network. It is a very rapid means of sharing information, some of which is excellent and some of which is not very worthwhile. This results from the fact that, unlike books and articles in periodicals and newspapers, there is no review by others before publication on the Internet. Thus, anyone can publish personal views on a variety of topics without having the information evaluated first by editors, experts, or others who are knowledgeable about the subject matter. Therefore, in those instances, you as the researcher must be extra careful about determining not only the relevance and impartiality of the information presented but its reliability as well. How should you go about doing that?

First, as with all sources, use common sense to make sure that the information offered is useful or appropriate for your research needs. Ask yourself whether a particular source focuses on the subject matter that is of interest to you and whether it does so in a fair and thorough manner. For instance, if you are investigating the issue of capital punishment, a source that devotes several pages to a discussion of the opposing viewpoints would probably be more useful than one that devotes a few paragraphs to life on death row.

Second, try to use material published by educational institutions, such as Harvard (with Web addresses that end in .edu), or posted on governmental (.gov) sites. The information these sites provide is quite likely to be reliable. Sites maintained by professional organizations (.org), such as the American Medical Association, can usually be relied on for accurate information, but keep in mind that some organizations simply want to persuade you to accept their points of view. The National Rifle Association is a good example of such an organization. Commercial sources (sites that end in .com), such as Philip Morris USA, are more questionable because they are often trying to sell you their products or influence your thinking so that they can continue to make profits. Thus, if you were looking into the effects of cigarette advertising on young people, Philip Morris would probably not be a good source of information to use because of its obvious bias, whereas a report put out by the US Office of the Surgeon General would be much more reliable.

Third, when possible, try to find the professional affiliation of the author in the credits or e-mail address so that you can determine his or her expertise on a given topic. For example, if you were investigating an issue involving medical ethics, a medical doctor who is also on the faculty of the University of Pennsylvania Medical School would probably be a more reliable source than an individual complaining about the high cost of medical treatment on a personal home page.

Fourth, check whether the author lists a bibliography of the sources used so that you can gauge whether the sources are reputable and scholarly. Publications such as *The New York Times*, *Newsweek*, *New England Journal of Medicine*, and textbooks in general are usually recognized by most people as providers of accurate, well-researched, and well-documented information. Thus, if sources like those are listed, you can feel a bit more secure about using the author's material.

Finally, there are online databases on the Internet, such as EBSCO, ProQuest, and LEXIS-NEXIS, which provide access to full-text articles from scholarly and popular periodicals such as the *New England Journal of Medicine*, *Columbia Journalism Review*, *The New York Times*, and *Newsweek*. Libraries have databases for references in their own collection and other tools, such as Research Quickstart, to acquire further Web site links by subject area. Furthermore, there are online encyclopedias, such as *World Book*, *Britannica*, and *Encarta*, that are good starting points for research. All of these sources can generally be relied upon for relevance, reliability, and impartiality. Remember that the Internet can be a very helpful source of information, but you must exercise great care when using it for research purposes.

(7) **Coming to Logical Conclusions**

After completing research, critical thinkers try to come to logical conclusions about the events, issues, problems, decisions, or situations they are considering. Conclusions are logical or reasonable if they are based solidly on the information or evidence gathered.

Let us look at an example about whether you should enroll for a particular course.

Suppose, while doing the research, you found that the course fits both your schedule and program of study, that you are interested in at least some of its content, that you are comfortable with the instructor, assignments, and grading, and that most of the people you talk with like the course. Under those circumstances, it would be logical to conclude that it is good for you to take the course because most of the information supports that conclusion.

On the other hand, if you found that the course does not seem very interesting, that it is taught by only one instructor whom you are not too crazy about, and that only half the students you talked with liked it, a logical conclusion is that the course is not for you because most of the information points in that direction. Of course, the evidence could be approximately evenly divided, making it logical to conclude that it may or may not be the right course for you. In that instance, you would have to determine which factors—perhaps the content of the course, the instructor, or the requirements—are the most important to you and then decide accordingly. It is also important to emphasize that the information gathered could change in the future, thereby altering any one of those three possible conclusions. For instance, there could be a change of instructor, which could in turn affect course content, assignments, grading, and opinions regarding the course. That is why critical thinkers always reconsider their conclusions to make sure that the evidence on which they are based has not changed or that no new information has been uncovered.

Let's look at another example. Suppose that, in your investigation of a traffic accident, the police report, newspaper accounts, and several witnesses all state that one person went through a red light. A logical conclusion would be that this driver was responsible for the accident—certainly, most of the information points in that direction. But if none of the evidence is clear as to who actually caused the collision, then the only reasonable conclusion is that no one person can be held responsible, at least at this particular time. However, that conclusion could change if additional evidence comes to light that points to one person as the culprit. Again, it is always necessary for critical thinkers to reconsider their conclusions from time to time.

Unit 6　Environment

Part 3　Learning After Class

Additional Reading 1

These Bacteria Eat Plastic

By Morgan Vagu
May 29, 2019
https://www.ted.com ①

　　Plastics: you know about them, you may not love them, but chances are you use them every single day. By 2050, researchers estimate that there will be more plastic in the ocean than fish.

　　Despite our best efforts, only 9% of all plastic we use winds up being recycled. And even worse, plastic is incredibly tough and durable and researchers estimate that it can take anywhere from 500 to 5,000 years to fully break down. It leaches harmful chemical contaminants into our oceans, our soil, our food, our water, and into us.

　　So how did we wind up with so much plastic waste? Well, it's simple. Plastic is cheap, durable, adaptable, and it's everywhere. But the good news is there's something else that's cheap, durable, adaptable and everywhere. And my research shows it may even be able to help us with our plastic pollution problem.

　　I'm talking about bacteria. Bacteria are microscopic living beings invisible to the naked eye that live everywhere, in all sorts of diverse and extreme environments, from the human gut, to soil, to skin, to vents in the ocean floor, reaching temperatures of 700 °F. Bacteria live everywhere, in all sorts of diverse and extreme environments. And as such, they have to get pretty creative with their food sources. There's also a lot of them. Researchers estimate that there are roughly 5 million trillion trillion—that's a 5 with 30 zeros after it—bacteria on the planet. Now, considering that we humans produce 300

---

　　① TED is a nonpartisan nonprofit devoted to spreading ideas, usually in the form of short, powerful talks. It began in 1984 as a conference where Technology, Entertainment and Design converged, and today covers almost all topics—from science to business to global issues—in more than 110 languages. Meanwhile, independently run TEDx events help share ideas in communities around the world.

million tons of new plastic each year, I'd say that our plastic numbers are looking pretty comparable to bacteria's.

So, after noticing this and after learning about all of the creative ways that bacteria find food, I started to think: could bacteria in plastic-polluted environments have figured out how to use plastic for food? Well, this is the question that I decided to pursue a couple of years ago. Now, fortunately for me, I'm from one of the most polluted cities in America, Houston, Texas.

In my hometown alone, there are 7 EPA-designated Superfund sites. These are sites that are so polluted, that the government has deemed their cleanup a national priority. So I decided to trek around to these sites and collect soil samples teeming with bacteria. I started toying with a protocol, which is fancy science talk for a recipe. And what I was trying to cook up was a carbon-free media, or a food-free environment. An environment without the usual carbons, or food, that bacteria, like us humans, need to live.

Now, in this environment, I would provide my bacteria with a sole carbon, or food, source. I would feed my bacteria polyethylene terephthalate, or PET plastic. PET plastic is the most widely produced plastic in the world. It's used in all sorts of food and drink containers, with the most notorious example being plastic water bottles, of which we humans currently go through at a rate of 1 million per minute. So, what I would be doing, is essentially putting my bacteria on a forced diet of PET plastic and seeing which, if any, might survive or, hopefully, thrive.

See, this type of experiment would act as a screen for bacteria that had adapted to their plastic-polluted environment and evolved the incredibly cool ability to eat PET plastic. And using this screen, I was able to find some bacteria that had done just that. These bacteria had figured out how to eat PET plastic.

So how do these bacteria do this? Well, it's actually pretty simple. Just as we humans digest carbon or food into chunks of sugar that we then use for energy, so too do my bacteria. My bacteria, however, have figured out how to do this digestion process to big, tough, durable PET plastic.

Now, to do this, my bacteria use a special version of what's called an enzyme. Now, enzymes are simply compounds that exist in all living things. There are many different types of enzymes, but basically, they make processes go forward, such as the digestion of food into energy. For instance, we humans have an enzyme called an amylase that helps us digest complex starches, such as bread, into small chunks of sugar that we can then use for energy. Now, my bacteria have a special enzyme called a lipase that binds to big, tough, durable PET plastic and helps break it into small chunks of sugar that my bacteria can then use for energy. So basically, PET plastic goes from being a big, tough, long-lasting pollutant to a tasty meal for my bacteria. Sounds pretty cool, right?

And I think, given the current scope of our plastic pollution problem, I think it sounds pretty useful. The statistics I shared with you on just how much plastic waste has accumulated on our planet are daunting. They're scary. And I think they highlight that while reducing, reusing and recycling are important, they alone are not going to be enough to solve this problem. And this is where I think bacteria might be able to help us out.

But I do understand why the concept of bacterial help might make some people a little nervous. After all, if plastic is everywhere and these bacteria eat plastic, isn't there a risk of these bacteria getting out in the environment and wreaking havoc? Well, the short answer is no, and I'll tell you why. These bacteria are already in the environment. The bacteria in my research are not genetically modified frankenbugs. These are naturally occurring bacteria that have simply adapted to their plastic-polluted environment and evolved the incredibly gnarly ability to eat PET plastic.

So the process of bacteria eating plastic is actually a natural one. But it's an incredibly slow process. And there remains a lot of work to be done to figure out how to speed up this process to a useful pace. My research is currently looking at ways of doing this through a series of UV, or ultraviolet, pretreatments, which basically means we blast PET plastic with sunlight. We do this because sunlight acts a bit like tenderizer on a steak, turning the big, tough, durable bonds in PET plastic a bit softer and a bit easier for my bacteria to chew on.

Ultimately, what my research hopes to do is create an industrial-scale contained carbon-free system, similar to a compost heap, where these bacteria can thrive in a contained system, where their sole food source is PET plastic waste. Imagine one day being able to dispose of all of your plastic waste in a bin at the curb that you knew was bound for a dedicated bacteria-powered plastic waste facility. I think with some hard work this is an achievable reality.

Plastic-eating bacteria is not a cure-all. But given the current statistics, it's clear that we humans, we could use a little help with this problem. Because people, we possess a pressing problem of plastic pollution. And bacteria might be a really important part of the solution.

Words and Expressions

wind (up)	[ˈwaɪnd]	v.	end up, come to a conclusion, bring to an end 结束
leach	[liːtʃ]	v.	come out of or be removed from another substance, esp. dirt, by passing water through（被）过滤；萃取
microscopic	[ˌmaɪkrəˈskɒpɪk]	a.	very small and only able to be seen with a microscope 微观的；用显微镜可见的
teem (with)	[tiːm]	v.	contain large numbers of animals or people 大量出现；充满
toy (with)	[tɔɪ]	v.	consider something or do something, but not in a very serious way 不太认真地考虑
protocol	[ˈprəʊtəkɒl]	n.	a set of rules that are followed when doing a scientific experiment or giving someone medical treatment technical 科学实验计划；治疗方案
recipe	[ˈresəpi]	n.	a set of instructions telling you how to prepare and cook food, including a list of what food is needed for this 食谱；处方；秘诀
polyethylene	[ˌpɒliˈeθəliːn]	n.	a light, usually thin, soft plastic, often used for making bags or for keeping things dry or fresh 聚乙烯（PE）
notorious	[nəʊˈtɔːriəs]	a.	famous for something immoral or bad 声名狼藉的；臭名昭著的
chunk	[tʃʌŋk]	n.	a roughly cut thick solid piece, a part of something, especially a large part 厚块；厚片；大块
enzyme	[ˈenzaɪm]	n.	any of a group of chemical substances that are produced by living cells and cause particular chemical reactions to happen while not being changed themselves 酶
amylase	[ˈæmɪleɪz]	n.	a chemical substance made by living cells in saliva, plants, and in the pancreas 淀粉酶；淀粉酵素

starch	[stɑːtʃ]	n.	a white substance that exists in large amounts in potatoes and particular grains such as rice 淀粉
lipase	[ˈlaɪpeɪz]	n.	a substance that is produced mainly in the pancreas and that helps the body to digest lipids 脂肪酶;脂肪分解酵素
daunting	[ˈdɔːntɪŋ]	a.	making you feel slightly frightened or worried about your ability to achieve something 使人畏缩的;使人气馁的
havoc	[ˈhævək]	a.	confusion and lack of order, especially causing damage or trouble 严重破坏;浩劫
gnarly	[ˈnɑːli]	a.	very good or excellent, used by young people 很好的,顶呱呱的
tenderizer	[ˈtendəraɪzə]	n.	substance that is put onto raw meat to make it softer and easier to eat after it has been cooked 嫩肉剂

Discussion Questions

1. What does frankenbugs refer to? Why are some people nervous about the plastic-eating bacteria?
2. People come up with various creative ways to combat plastic pollution, but the most efficient way is to throw away less plastic waste. Discuss with your partner, and design a campaign persuading your fellow students to buy reusable products despite the higher price and inconveniences.

Additional Reading 2

Australia's Biodiversity at Breaking Point

Land clearing, deforestation, emissions, drought and warming oceans are all worsening the attack on Australia's threatened species.

By Alexandra Spring & Carly Earl

May 15, 2019

The Guardian

Australia's biodiversity is in trouble. The UN global assessment report painted a stark picture: the decline of the world's natural support systems means that human society is in danger. According to the report, nature is being destroyed at a rate tens to hundreds of times higher than the average over the past 10 million years. More than a million species are at risk of extinction, natural ecosystems have declined by about 47% and the biomass of wild mammals has fallen by 82%. All of this is largely because of human activity. And the resulting impacts are likely to worsen unless we take action immediately.

As *Guardian Australia* has reported, Australia's natural support systems are at breaking point. Increased land-clearing, warming oceans and a drought exacerbated by climate change are taking their toll on our biodiversity. The country is already experiencing rising oceans, marine heatwaves, longer fire seasons and extreme heat patterns. These are consistent with a changing climate.

However, there has been a lack of leadership from state and federal governments in this area, protections and funding have been slashed and emissions continue to rise unabated. Without drastic action, the future of Australia's biodiversity looks bleak.

Threatened species

There is a "extinction crisis unfolding in plain sight" in Australia. More than 50 animal and 60 plant species have been lost, with Australia recording the highest rate of mammalian extinction in the world over the last 200 years. There's more to come. Conservative estimates put more than 1,800 plant and animal species and woodlands, forests and wetlands at risk of extinction due to the intertwined pressures of climate change, land use practices, habitat loss and invasive species. The downward trend could be stopped, say conservationists, but only if there is meaningful government intervention. The Australian Conservation Foundation's James Trezise told *Guardian Australia*: "From a conservation standpoint we know what needs to happen, but it seems there isn't the political will to get us there."

The lack of political engagement in these issues is staggering. In February 2018, it was revealed that less than 40% of Australia's nationally listed threatened species have recovery plans in place and, for the 10% of listed threatened species that require plans, supporting documentation was unfinished, according to the environment and energy department's own data. There hasn't been any critical habitat listed on the federal critical habitat register for threatened species since 2005. And the Coalition has been accused of spending the $255m in threatened species funding on unrelated projects. Then in March, the federal environment department was forced to admit that it didn't know whether recovery plans to prevent extinctions are actually being implemented.

Land-clearing and deforestation

One of the main threats to Australia's biodiversity is habitat loss, and land-clearing is happening at a staggering rate. Projections suggest that 3m hectares of untouched forest will have been bulldozed in eastern Australia by 2030, thanks to a thriving livestock industry and governments that refuse to step in.

Funding for national parks, often a sanctuary for threatened species, has been slashed at both the state and federal levels and the creation of new national parks has stalled.

Regional forestry agreements have also not helped to protect many forest-dwelling species facing extinction. The Wilderness Society found that 48 federally-listed threatened species of forest-dwelling vertebrate fauna live in areas subject to state-run logging operations.

The disregard for the protection of these areas was made clear when Liberal senator Anne Ruston, the federal minister responsible for forests, said in February during a Senate debate: "I'm sure that trees were put on this earth in the very first instance because they were able to be cut down, because they would grow again and because they would provide a resource for myriad different things."

Emissions

Climate change is increasing the pressure on our biodiversity—yet Australia's emissions rise unabated. National emissions are the highest they have ever been, with the increased production of LNG the major contributor. *Guardian Australia* reported that emissions growth between 2015 and 2020 from the rapidly growing natural gas industry will effectively wipe out any gains already made.

Questions have been raised about the government's $2.5bn emissions reduction fund and whether it provided value for money with funding wasted on projects that would have gone ahead regardless. Emissions from land and forest clearing are also negating any gains made under the ERF. According to government data, forest-clearing has released more than 160m tones of CO_2 since the emissions reduction fund began in 2015, with an estimated 60.3m tones to be emitted in the next year.

Drought

Climate change is making Australia's droughts worse, according to climate scientist Andrew King. "In general climate change is exacerbating drought, mainly because in a warmer world we experience more evaporation from the surface, and we project for that to continue in the future." "So when it does rain, more of that water is likely to be lost to the atmosphere through evaporation than before human-caused climate change."

Although there has long been rainfall variability in Australia, King said other measures of drought including temperatures effects and evaporation changes pointed to a changed climate, with these patterns set to continue into the future.

Murray-Darling

The UN report identified agriculture as one of the primary causes of the deterioration of biodiversity around the world. The deterioration of the Murray-Darling, the so-called food bowl of Australia, is a case in point. Some of Australia's most eminent environmental scientists have warned that the Murray-Darling basin plan, the strategy set up to save Australia's largest river system, is not delivering the environmental outcomes promised. They point to watered down rules, state and federal governments shy of delivering reform, over-extraction and a lack of compliance by irrigators and no allowances for climate change.

The South Australian royal commission set up to investigate the issues found that the government and MDBA officials were "guilty of maladministration, negligence and unlawful actions". The commissioner, Bret Walker SC, also warned the Murray-Darling basin plan's failure to take account of climate change was "potentially catastrophic". Scientists have already reported that the climate in the region is changing, with temperatures rising and rainfall decreasing.

The federal government and the authority, who had refused to take part in the royal commission, dismissed the findings.

Oceans

The UN report found the accelerating factors of climate change, pollution and invasive species were impacting the biodiversity of the world's oceans.

Australia's oceans are already suffering. The 2016-2018 climate change-induced mass bleaching of the Great Barrier Reef caused an "unprecedented" decline of coral according to a report by the Australian Institute of Marine Science—with more damage to come. "More intense disturbances mean greater damage to reefs, so recovery must take longer if the growth rate remains the same. At the same time, the intervals between acute disturbance events are decreasing and chronic stresses such as high turbidity and high ocean temperatures can slow rates of recovery." Since the mass bleaching, the number of new corals on the Great Barrier Reef has crashed by 89%.

Climate change is also causing marine heatwaves to happen more frequently and with more intensity, which have a devastating impact on the ocean's ecosystems. In our region, the extreme intense marine heatwave of 2017-2018 caused major disruption including kelp habitat loss, new species invasions and fisheries season changes. It's a stark warning of things to come.

Words and Expressions

stark	[stɑːk]	a.	obvious; unpleasant; real, and impossible to avoid 明显的;鲜明的;真实而无法回避的
extinction	[ɪkˈstɪŋkʃn]	n.	a situation in which a plant, an animal, a way of life, etc. stops existing 灭绝;消亡
biomass	[ˈbaɪəʊmæs]	n.	the total quantity or weight of plants and animals in a particular area; dead plant and animal material suitable for using as fuel(单位面积或体积内的)生物量;生物质能
exacerbate	[ɪɡˈzæsəbeɪt]	v.	make something that is already bad even worse 使加剧;使恶化
take a toll			cause harm or suffering 造成损失;造成伤亡
biodiversity	[ˌbaɪəʊdaɪˈvɜːsəti]	n.	the number and types of plants and animals that exist in a particular area 生物多样性
unabated	[ˌʌnəˈbeɪtɪd]	a.	without becoming weaker in strength or force; continuing without becoming any weaker or less violent 不减弱的;不衰退的
bleak	[bliːk]	a.	not encouraging or giving any reason to have hope 不乐观的;无望的
staggering	[ˈstæɡərɪŋ]	a.	so great, shocking or surprising that it is difficult to believe 令人震惊的;令人难以相信的
coalition	[ˌkəʊəˈlɪʃn]	n.	the joining together of different political parties or groups for a particular purpose, usually temporarily, to achieve something, or a government that is formed in this way 联合;联合政府
bulldoze	[ˈbʊldəʊz]	v.	destroy buildings trees, etc., and make an area flat with a bulldozer(用推土机) 推倒;推平
sanctuary	[ˈsæŋktʃuəri]	n.	a place where birds or animals can live and be protected, especially from being hunted or dangerous conditions 鸟兽保护区;禁猎区;避难所

stall	[stɔːl]	v.	delay taking action or avoid giving an answer in order to have more time to make a decision or get an advantage; stop making progress 拖延（以赢得时间）；暂缓；搪塞
vertebrate	[ˈvɜːtɪbrət]	n.	having a spine 脊椎动物
fauna	[ˈfɔːnə]	n.	all the animals that live wild in a particular area or period in history（某个地区或时期的）动物群；动物区系
myriad	[ˈmɪriəd]	a.	a very large number of something 无数的；种种的
wipe (out)	[waɪp]	v.	destroy a group of people or animals completely 摧毁；使灭绝
negate	[nɪˈɡeɪt]	v.	state that something does not exist or is untrue; cause something to have no effect 否定；取消；使无效
evaporation	[ɪˌvæpəˈreɪʃn]	n.	the process of changing from a liquid to a gas, or a change from a liquid to a gas 蒸发；汽化；消失
project	[prəˈdʒekt]	v.	calculate an amount or number expected in the future from information already known 预测；计划
deterioration	[dɪˌtɪəriəˈreɪʃn]	n.	the process or fact of becoming worse 恶化；退化；堕落
waterdown	[ˌwɔːtəˈdaʊn]	v.	deliberately make an idea or opinion less extreme, usually so that other people will accept it 淡化；稀释
shy (of)	[ʃaɪ]	v.	try to avoid something 对……有顾虑；对……畏缩；迟疑
over-extraction	[ˈəʊvəˌɪkˈstrækʃn]	n.	the process of removing or taking out too much of something 过度开采
compliance	[kəmˈplaɪəns]	n.	the act of obeying an order, a rule, agreement, or demand 服从；遵守
irrigator	[ˈɪrɪɡeɪtə]	n.	something used to supply land or crops with water 灌溉车；灌溉设备
allowance	[əˈlaʊəns]	n.	an amount of money that you are given regularly or for a special purpose 一笔钱；津贴；补助
unprecedented	[ʌnˈpresɪdentɪd]	a.	never having happened or existed in the past 空前的；前所未有的

Discussion Questions

1. Why should we worry about the loss of biodiversity?
2. What influence human beings have had on biodiversity?
3. What are the options that would help to reduce biodiversity loss while still improving the quality of human life?

 Additional Reading 3

Inspired Life: In a World Drowning in Trash, These Cities Have Slashed Waste by 80%

By Terrence McCoy

February 13, 2019

The Washington Post

Little Kamikatsu was facing a big problem. The rural Japanese town of 1,500 residents didn't know what it was going to do with its trash. Residents had always burned it, first in front of their homes or on the farms, then in a large community pit, then in an incinerator the government quickly banned out of fear of pollutants. The town didn't have money for a newer, safer incinerator. It had to find a new way.

"They had to look into zero waste," said Akira Sakano, chair of the board of directors of the Zero Waste Academy, an educational institution in Kamikatsu, explaining the discussions of those days in the early 2000s.

That research introduced the town to what was then a virtual unknown but has since grown into one of the most widespread and successful recycling efforts in history, bringing cities the world over to the precipice of what once seemed fantastical: the elimination of waste. Today, places in rural Japan to metropolitan Sweden send very little of their trash to the landfill. Many more—including the District—have a "Zero Waste" plan. In the United States, San Francisco leads the way, diverting more than 80% of its waste—two and a half times more than the national average. It has become a lifestyle, with millions of images flooding Instagram touting a zero-waste existence, and generating new businesses.

The concept calls on people to think differently about waste. It starts with the creation of categories. There are recyclables, like aluminum cans and glass bottles. Reusables such as clothing. Compostables such as uneaten food. And then those that shouldn't be used at all such as plastic bags, which are very difficult to recycle. The number of categories might expand or contract depending on the location, but the goal behind the zero waste philosophy is the same: to vastly reduce the amount of trash going to the landfill—"diverting" it, in the parlance of waste experts, away from landfills and incinerators.

Debbie Raphael, director of the San Francisco Department of the Environment, who oversees the city's zero-waste initiative, said it's top-down and bottom-up. In San Francisco, there are three bins, one for recycling, one for compost and one for the landfill. The categorization is left to residents, and the sorting is left to the city contractor, Recology. "It takes policy," Raphael said of the zero-waste philosophy, which has purportedly cut the city's waste in half. "It takes financial incentives. It takes consequences for not participating. And it takes an ethic … of a sense of responsibility for the health of our planet."

It is a planet drowning in trash. Every year, the world is making more of it. In 2016 alone, the world's cities produced more than 2 billion tons of solid waste. Americans produce a disproportionate amount, throwing away the equivalent of their own body weight every month. And as the planet's population grows, the problems are poised to become significantly worse. Large landfills, according to a Washington Post project on trash, get as many as 10,000 tons of waste every day and are filling quickly. Within 3 decades, trash will outweigh fish in the ocean, according to the World Economic Forum.

If zero waste has an origin story, it would wind back more than 40 years to a man in Berkeley, Calif., named Dan Knapp. A former college professor with a PhD in sociology, he rode his bike to the Berkeley landfill nearly every day and scavenged—hands going through refuse for valuable metals, mind going through big questions. Where does all of this stuff come from? In the chaos of a landfill, could order be found? Patterns began to emerge, and from those patterns, categories. Here were the textiles. And the glass piles. And rotting food. And soil hauled from construction sites. This wasn't at all what he'd expected. He'd thought he'd find a bunch of unusable stuff. But it was an untapped resource.

Recycling, he realized, could go way beyond what was then a lofty goal of 35%, beyond aluminum cans and paper. Our trash just needed to be categorized appropriately, he said. Recycling shouldn't be made simple. It should be made complex. The thought ultimately led to a taxology of trash—called the "12 master categories of recyclable materials"—laying some of the initial groundwork for the "zero waste" concept.

But few people were listening. Knapp was just another Berkeley environmentalist—long hair, beard, the works. It took a city on the other side of the world, working on a plan that seemed stripped from the pages of the hippie manual. "In a natural ecosystem there is a balance," began "No Waste by 2010", a plan that Canberra, Australia, initiated in 1996. "The wastes from one process become the resources for other processes. Nothing is wasted. In a consumer society waste is an accepted part of life. A strategy is needed to reverse this trend."

Knapp, the owner of Urban Ore, which salvages Berkeley's waste, said he was flown in as a consultant to advise the city. He brought back the town's plan and soon was passing it around. He'd been calling his idea "total recycling". But here was something much catchier, right there on the plan's cover: No Waste, which quickly transformed to "zero waste", according to interviews with environmentalists. "Dan was very instrumental in bringing [the plan] over," said Neil Seldman, an official with the Institute of Local Self-Reliance in Washington.

But Canberra's plan accomplished more than that, said Paul Connett, a retired professor at St. Lawrence University who wrote, "*The Zero Waste Solution: Untrashing the Planet One Community at a Time*". People took the idea seriously for the first time. "It wasn't an activist talking about zero waste," he said. "It was a government law. All of a sudden, it became a topic of conversation."

One town in the early 2000s where it had become a topic of conversation was Kamikatsu, on the island of Shikoku, where the categories had been taken to an almost absurd level. The town had created 34 categories of waste disposal, possibly more than anywhere in the world. It asked people to differentiate between metal caps and aluminum cans, between milk cartons and paper cups—hewing as close as possible to the notion that the enemy of recycling is bad recycling. When a piece of plastic gets mixed with paper, or some metal mixes with glass—or, worse, something not recyclable is tossed in—it can lower the quality of the recycled product.

Sakano, of the Zero Waste Academy, said it may sound counterintuitive, but making recycling more complicated made it easier. "This is an aluminum can," she said. "This is a glass bottle. Clear color. Other colors. Newspaper. Cardboard. Paper tubes … It's all about putting the right product in the right places because mixture and contamination is the biggest challenge of waste recycling."

The town's residents compost in their homes, then haul their own trash to the town's collection center for additional sorting. Here, they also find a "kuru-kuru" factory—"circular" in Japanese—where bags and clothes are made from discarded clothing, and a kuru-kuru shop, where residents can drop off and pick up unwanted items. In fiscal year 2016, nearly 90% of the 15 tons of items brought in were taken by someone else.

Still, Kamikatsu is stuck. So is San Francisco. There are still too many items that aren't recyclable in the waste stream, like used diapers, to finally do away with all waste. "As a community, we can only do so much," Sakano said. "The businesses need to change their product design."

Is it enough to be proud of slashing the waste total? "Yes. We've already shown that we can do this," Sakano said.

But is it enough to stop? "Everyone needs to start," she said. "Otherwise we don't see the future."

 Words and Expressions

incinerator	[ɪnˈsɪnəreɪtə(r)]	n.	a device for burning things that are no longer wanted 焚烧炉；垃圾焚化炉
precipice	[ˈpresɪpɪs]	n.	a dangerous situation in which something very bad could happen 危局；险境
elimination	[ɪˌlɪmɪˈneɪʃn]	n.	the removal or destruction of something 消除；根除
tout	[taʊt]	v.	praise something or someone in order to persuade people that they are important or worth a lot 赞扬；吹捧
aluminum	[əˈlumənəm]	n.	silver-white metal that is very light and is used to make cans, cooking pans, window frames, etc. 铝
compostable	[kɒmˈpɒstəbl]	n.	something that can be used as compost when it decays 可堆肥物；可堆肥垃圾
parlance	[ˈpɑːləns]	n.	a group of words or style of speaking used by a particular group of people 说法；语调；发言
contractor	[kənˈtræktə(r)]	n.	a person or company that arranges to supply materials or workers for building or for moving goods 承包人；立契约者
purportedly	[pəˈpɔːtɪdli]	adv.	in a way that is stated to be true, although this may not be the case 据称，据称地
disproportionate	[ˌdɪsprəˈpɔːʃənət]	a.	too large or too small in comparison to something else, or not deserving its importance or influence 不均衡的；不成比例的

238

equivalent	[ɪˈkwɪvələnt]	a.	having the same amount, value, purpose, qualities, etc. 相等的；等价的；等量的；同意义的
poised (to)	[pɔɪzd]	a.	not moving, but ready to move or do something at any moment 准备行动的
scavenge	[ˈskævɪndʒ]	v.	look for or get food or other objects in other people's rubbish(从废弃物中)觅食；从废弃物中拾捡(有用的东西)
untapped	[ʌnˈtæpt]	a.	available but not yet used 未开发的，未利用的
taxology	[tækˈsɒlədʒi]	n.	a system for naming and organizing things, especially plants and animals into groups that share similar qualities(动植物等的)分类学
salvage	[ˈsælvɪdʒ]	v.	save something from an accident or bad situation in which other things have already been damaged, destroyed, or lost(从事故或糟糕情形中)抢救出(某物)；救助；挽救
transform	[trænsˈfɔːm]	v.	completely change the appearance, form, or character of something or someone, especially in a way that improves it 使变形；使转化；使改变
be instrumental in (doing) sth.			be important in making something happen 对(做)某事起重要作用；有帮助的
differentiate	[ˌdɪfəˈrenʃieɪt]	v.	show, recognize or express the difference between things or people that are compared 辨别；区别
hew	[hjuː]	v.	obey or behave according to rules, principles, or expectations 遵循；坚持
counter-intuitive	[ˌkaʊntə(r)mˈtʃuːɪtɪv]	a.	seemingly contrary to common sense 违反常理的；违反直觉的
contamination	[kənˌtæmɪˈneɪʃn]	n.	a substance that contaminates 污染；污染物

 Discussion Questions

1. Why is the categorization of waste so important?
2. What does Debbie Raphale mean by saying San Francisco's zero-waste initiative is

"top-down and bottom-up"? Can you add anything more to the list he made about the factors involving in zero-waste initiative?

3. In the 2019 World Economic Forum, British naturalist Sir David Attenborough delivered a speech, in which he pointed out that human beings had left the Holocene epoch, and entered a new geological age, the Anthropocene—the Age of Humans. He warned that human-driven climate change would risk destroying our planet, but there was also a vast potential for what we might do. Work with your partner and write a speech calling on people to take actions to protect our earthly home.

Part 4　Topical Vocabulary

sustainable development 可持续发展
carbon footprint 碳足迹
ozone layer 臭氧层
solar radiation 太阳辐射
El Nino phenomenon 厄尔尼诺现象
weather modification 人工影响天气
humidity 湿度
smog 烟雾；雾霾
arid and semi-arid area 干旱和半干旱地区
vegetation 植被
afforestation 植树造林
ecosystem 生态系统
sandstorm 沙尘暴
wind breaks 防风林
drought 干旱
land restoration 土地恢复
soil degradation 土壤退化
natural drainage system 自然排水系统
natural habitat 自然栖息地
poaching 非法打猎；盗猎
pollutant 污染物
disposable 可丢弃的

low-carbon economy 低碳经济
atmosphere 大气层
ultraviolet ray 紫外线
adverse weather condition 恶劣的天气状况
precipitation 降雨或降雪量
desertification 沙漠化
sandstorm 沙尘暴
visibility 能见度
soil erosion 土壤侵蚀
revegetation 植被恢复
landslide 山体滑坡
greenbelt 绿化带
forest coverage 森林覆盖率
sand breaks 防沙林
land reclamation 土地开垦
soil conservation 土壤保持
freshwater resources 淡水资源
sewage treatment plants 污水处理厂
nature reserve 自然保护区
endangered species 濒危物种
biodegradable packaging 可降解包装
erode 腐蚀

acid rain 酸雨	deterioration 恶化
environmental degradation 环境恶化	glacier 冰川
permafrost 永冻层；永冻土	sea level rise 海平面上升
coastal erosion 海岸侵蚀	coral reefs 珊瑚礁
conservation of genetic resources 基因资源保护	gene banks 基因库
biosafety 生物安全	cloning 无性繁殖
bioethics 生物伦理学	net resource depletion 资源净损耗
ecotourism 生态旅游	environmental risk assessment 环境风险评估

Unit 7

Social Security and Crime Prevention

Part 1 Learning Before Class

- **Listening**

Who Listens to Google Assistant Recordings?

Directions: *Listen to the news and answer the questions.*

1. Have you ever used any artificial intelligence system such as Google Assistant? What do you think of those systems?
2. Do you know that someone might listen to recordings of what people say to artificial intelligence system? What do you think we should do in response?
3. What would be a better way to balance the convenience and our privacy?

- **Watching and Thinking**

Saving Them, Saving Us

Directions: *Watch the video and discuss the questions with your partner.*

1. How did Niakomba find the stray elephant?
2. What did the United Nations adopt to fight smuggling of wild animals on July 30, 2015?
3. Why does the author say "saving wildlife is saving ourselves"?

- **Reading and Discussing**

Zhang Yingying Murder Case:
Jury Deliberations Begin After Lengthy Closing Arguments

July 18, 2019
CGTN

Following more than a month of testimony at trial and sentencing, jurors began deliberating Brendt Christensen's appropriate sentence following closing statements on Wednesday in Illinois' federal court. The jurors, this time, have to choose between life in prison without parole and the death penalty.

The closing arguments of the sentencing phase for Christensen took place around 9 a.m. at a federal court of Peoria, in the US state of Illinois. Jurors were dismissed for the night before 5 pm after a first day of deliberations without a decision.

The 30-year-old man was convicted by the same jury who took less than two hours last month to convict Christensen of kidnapping and killing 28-year-old Chinese scholar Zhang Yingying in 2017.

The jury received Christensen's capital case at about 1:40 p.m. after the closing arguments from both sides who deliberated differing portraits of Christensen. The defense described him as a whole man mired in pain, and the prosecution called him a depraved and brutal killer.

Federal defender Elisabeth Pollock asked the 12-person jury to show mercy and spare her client, claiming he struggled with alcoholism, suffered from the family's history of mental illness and sought help for his homicidal thoughts in the weeks and months before he killed Zhang.

On the other hand, the prosecution presented a much darker side with assistant attorney James Nelson stating that Christensen premeditated the crime and tortured Zhang before "destroying" her body, acting in a "heinous, cruel or depraved" manner.

"He disposed of her remains in a way in which they'll never be recovered," Nelson said. He also described how Christensen cleaned his car and home to cover up the crime and continued to use the mattress where Zhang's DNA was found as if nothing happened.

Prosecutors argued Christensen has expressed no remorse for killing Zhang and he never told investigators what he did to the body and where it could be found. They again appealed to the jury to sentence Christensen to death.

The death penalty was abolished in Illinois in 2011, but it remains legal at the federal level, where Christensen's case was prosecuted. A death sentence would require the unanimous agreement of all jurors. If Christensen is executed, he would be the first Illinois resident to receive the death penalty since it was abolished.

The deliberations will resume Thursday morning and can last hours or weeks.

Directions: *Read the passage and discuss the questions with your partner.*

1. After a month of testimony at trial and sentencing, what is the jurors' choice so far as Brendt Christensen's sentence is concerned?
2. What was Christensen convicted of?
3. According to the prosecution, what did Christensen do to Zhang Yingying?

Part 2　Learning in Class

To This Day

Directions: *Watch the video and discuss the questions with your partner.*

1. How did the speaker get his first nickname: Porkchop?
2. Why did the girl get called "Ugly"?
3. Why did the speaker say "all of this is just debris left over when we finally decide to smash all the things we thought we used to be"?

Text A

This Viral Schwarzenegger Deepfake Isn't Just Entertaining. It's a Warning.

The emergence of fake videos has become a sort of test run and public service announcement, heightening public awareness of deepfake technology.

By Ben Collins

June 13, 2019

NBC News Digital ①

The video starts like dozens of others on YouTube—with former "Saturday Night Live" star Bill Hader offering up a celebrity impression, this time of Arnold Schwarzenegger.

The impression is spot-on, but that's not why the video has almost 6 million views in the last month. About ten seconds into the video, Hader's face slowly, almost imperceptibly starts to morph into Schwarzenegger's face. The full transformation takes about six seconds, but the changes are so subtle that it seems like magic. Suddenly, it looks like Schwarzenegger, albeit a skinnier version, is doing an impression of himself.

The video quickly became one of YouTube's most watched deepfake videos, a burgeoning genre of content on the Internet that uses powerful—and often free—software to create extremely lifelike videos of people saying just about anything.

The emergence of these videos has led to growing concern that they could be used to spread a new, powerful form of misinformation ahead of the 2020 elections. Videos of politicians could be easily **manipulated** to portray them as saying things they never really said. But the Hader-Schwarzenegger video, along with other celebrity-based videos, have become a sort of test run and public service announcement, heightening public awareness of deepfake technology and also making sure some deepfakes have trouble getting monetized.

"With the Bill Hader video, half of the people who comment don't know it's modified," said Tom, a graphic illustrator from the Czech Republic who created the video, and who asked that NBC News not use his last name out of privacy concerns. Tom was the first to post the video to Reddit and YouTube and sent over examples of his data set and process for making deepfakes. "We need for people to know what's possible, and to think before they believe," he said.

On Thursday, the House Intelligence Committee will hold a hearing to examine what it calls "the national security threats posed by AI-enabled fake content, what can be done to detect and combat it, and what role the public sector, the private sector, and society as a whole should play to counter a potentially grim, 'post-truth' future."

Despite a rocky start that prominently featured illicit use of deepfakes, the

---

① NBC News Digital is a collection of innovative and powerful news brands that deliver compelling, diverse and visually engaging stories on your platform of choice. NBC News Digital features world-class brands including NBCNews.com, MSNBC.com, TODAY.com, Nightly News, Meet the Press, Dateline, and the existing apps and digital extensions of these respective properties. We provide something for every news consumer with our comprehensive offerings that deliver the best in breaking news, segments from your favorite NBC News shows, live video coverage, original journalism, lifestyle features, commentary and local updates.

communities supporting the videos and how to make them have flourished in the last year on YouTube and Reddit. Users on Reddit's deepfake forum used the community to post and solicit requests for fake pornography, with celebrity and even private citizens' faces superimposed without permission into graphic sex scenes. Reddit swiftly banned the community in February of last year because of the requests. A replacement community called GIFFakes, which bans deepfakes used in pornography, is now thriving instead, and Tom posts his latest videos there.

Still, researchers say nefarious applications of deepfake technology pose a significant threat to both democracy and the day-to-day lives of average citizens targeted by fake revenge porn. Danielle Citron, a law professor at the University of Maryland and author of *Hate Crimes in Cyberspace*, is scheduled to testify before the House Intel Committee's deepfake panel to talk about potential ways—including legislation—to stop deepfakes that could affect elections, personal lives and businesses.

"Deepfakes can cause real, concrete harm. Whether that's a deepfake sex video, or a fake porn video targeting political enemies, or a well-timed deepfake, maybe used to cause harm to an IPO①," Citron said. "And in unrest, if you time it just right, you can incite violence." A deepfake video of Gabon's President Ali Bongo deepened tensions in the African nation last year, and was released by the government one week before an unsuccessful coup.

Citron said there has "definitely been thinking going on" among researchers and lawmakers, who "could craft a narrow enough statue, a provision that has to do with elections and disclosure law" that could limit the spread of manipulated videos.

Citron admitted, however, that legislation might not be able to provide a full solution to deepfakes created and distributed from overseas. "There's no recourse with those kinds of bad actors. The law is really limited in a whole number of spaces," said Citron. "There's a lot of hurdles here. I love the law. I'm a law professor. But we have to be modest."

Tom said he is aware he could be one of those foreign individuals with a certain set of skills prized by someone looking to do a lot of political harm. That's why he said he's sworn off creating political deepfakes or working for someone who wants them. That doesn't mean he hasn't received offers. He said someone in China reached out to see if he could edit a TV series and superimpose faces. (He turned them down, saying the task

---

① IPO stands for Initial Public Offering, which is the first sale of the stock by a private or any government company that opens to the general public.

was too complicated.)

While the software to make deepfakes is not hard to acquire, Tom said there are other barriers for creation of fake videos, including the need for powerful computer rigs and a deep dataset of pictures for each celebrity, shot from all angles. "It's a good thing that not everyone can do it," Tom said. "People on the Internet are animals, and they might use it for not very good stuff."

In the meantime, Tom has been happily surprised with the millions of views his YouTube channel has accrued over the last month. But he can't make any money off of his Schwarzennegger video. YouTube's copyright algorithm was still able to detect that his video was taken from Conan O'Brien's show, despite the subtle alterations to Hader's face, and didn't allow Tom to make ad money off of it.

That's why Tom says he's hopeful deepfakes can be used more for art and less for political disruption and revenge porn, because the people and machines who are making deepfakes are now focused on detecting them.

The creator of the YouTube channel that helped Tom learn how to make deepfakes, a computer graphics and algorithms professor named Károly Zsolnai-Fehér, is particularly focused on it. He has already made a video on his channel, Two Minute Papers, talking up an AI that can detect deepfakes by itself.

But Tom added that he hopes deepfakes aren't entirely banned. "When you take photography, Photoshop existed for over a decade," he said. "We didn't ban Photoshop because you can do malicious stuff with it. It's mostly used positively. What's important is that people are more cautious, just like with some sensationalistic photos that have been in the news."

 Words and Expressions

viral	[ˈvaɪrəl]	a.	like a virus 像病毒一样流行的
celebrity	[səˈlebrəti]	n.	a famous person 名人;名流
impression	[ɪmˈpreʃn]	n.	an amusing copy of the way a person acts or speaks 滑稽模仿
spot-on	[ˌspɒtˈɒn]	a.	exactly correct 准确无误的
imperceptibly	[ˌɪmpəˈseptəbli]	adv.	hard to be noticed 难以察觉地
morph	[mɔːf]	v.	change smoothly from one image to another using computer animation (利用电脑动画使图像)平稳变换

albeit	[ˌɔːlˈbiːɪt]	conj.	although 尽管；虽然
burgeon	[ˈbɜːdʒən]	v.	begin to develop rapidly 激增；迅速发展
genre	[ˈʒɒ̃rə]	n.	a particular style of literature, art, film or music with its special features（文学、艺术、电影或音乐的）体裁，类型
manipulate	[məˈnɪpjuleɪt]	v.	control or influence sb./sth., often in a dishonest way so that they do not realize it（暗中）控制，操纵
portray	[pɔːˈtreɪ]	v.	describe sb./sth. in a particular way, esp. when this does not give a complete or accurate impression of what they are like 将……描写成；给人以某种印象
monetize	[ˈmʌnɪtaɪz]	v.	coin into money 赚钱；变现
grim	[grɪm]	a.	looking very serious 严肃的
rocky	[ˈrɒki]	a.	difficult and not certain to continue or to be successful 困难的；难以维持的；不稳定的
illicit	[ɪˈlɪsɪt]	a.	not allowed by the law 非法的
solicit	[səˈlɪsɪt]	v.	ask sb. for sth., such as support, money, or information 索求，请求……给予（援助、钱或信息）
fake	[feɪk]	a.	made to look like something else 伪造的
pornography	[pɔːˈnɒgrəfi]	n.	books, videos, etc. that describe or show naked people and sexual acts 淫秽作品；色情书刊（或音像制品等）
superimpose	[ˌsuːpərɪmˈpəʊz]	v.	put one image on top of another so that the two can be seen combined 使（图像甲）叠映在（图像乙）上
ban	[bæn]	v.	decide officially that something is not allowed 明令禁止；取缔
nefarious	[nɪˈfeəriəs]	a.	criminal; immoral 罪恶的；不道德的
testify	[ˈtestɪfaɪ]	v.	make a statement that sth. happened or that sth. is true, especially as a witness in court（尤指出庭）作证
panel	[ˈpænl]	n.	a small group of people who are chosen to do something, for example, to discuss something in public or to make a decision（进行公开讨论或做决策的）专门小组

incite	[ɪnˈsaɪt]	v.	encourage sb. to do sth. violent, illegal or unpleasant, esp. by making them angry or excited 煽动；鼓动
coup	[kuː]	n.	a sudden, illegal and often violent, change of government 政变
craft	[krɑːft]	v.	make sth. using special skills, esp. with your hands (尤指用手工) 精心制作
disclosure	[dɪsˈkləʊzə(r)]	n.	the act of making sth. known or public that was previously secret or private 揭露；透露；公开
recourse	[rɪˈkɔːs]	n.	the right to demand payment from the maker or endorser of a negotiable instrument 追索权
hurdle	[ˈhɜːdl]	n.	a problem or difficulty that must be solved or dealt with before you can achieve sth. 难关；障碍
swear off			promise to abstain from 放弃
rig	[rɪg]	n.	an equipment that is used for a special purpose 有专门用途的设备
shot	[ʃɒt]	n.	a scene in a film/movie that is filmed continuously by one camera (电影中的) 镜头
accrue	[əˈkruː]	v.	increase over a period of time 增长，增加
algorithm	[ˈælgərɪðəm]	n.	a set of rules that must be followed when solving a particular problem 算法；计算程序
disruption	[dɪsˈrʌpʃn]	n.	an act of delaying or interrupting the continuity 中断；扰乱
malicious	[məˈlɪʃəs]	a.	having or showing hatred and a desire to harm sb. or hurt their feelings 怀有恶意的；恶毒的
sensationalistic	[senˈseɪʃənəlɪstɪk]	a.	producing or designed to produce startling or thrilling impressions or to excite and please vulgar taste 耸人听闻的

- **Multiple Choice**

Select the most appropriate answer for each of the following questions.

1. What has led to growing concern that they could be used to spread a new, powerful form of misinformation ahead of the 2020 elections?

    A) Cyber attacks.　　　　　　　　B) Terrorist attacks.

    C) Deepfake videos.　　　　　　　D) A rash of mass shootings.

2. The underlined word "manipulate" in Paragraph 4 is the closest in meaning to "_____".

    A) play　　　　　　　　　　　　B) edit

    C) hide　　　　　　　　　　　　D) control or influence

3. Why did Reddit swiftly ban the community in February of last year?

    A) Because it cannot manage the Internet traffic.

    B) Because of the unexpected blackout.

    C) Because of the fierce competition.

    D) Because of the users' requests of illicit use of deepfakes.

4. According to Tom, what are NOT barriers for creation of fake videos?

    A) Shot from all angles.

    B) The difficulty of obtaining the software to make deepfakes.

    C) The need for powerful computer rigs.

    D) A deep dataset of pictures for each celebrity.

5. Why does Tom hope that deepfakes aren't entirely banned?

    A) Because he still needs them in his work.

    B) Because other people still need them in their work.

    C) Because technologically they can never be entirely banned.

    D) Because it is people who do malicious stuff with them and they should not be to blame.

- **Sentence Completion**

Complete the sentences below with words taken from Text A. Use ONLY ONE WORD for each answer.

1. The Hader-Schwarzenegger video, along with other celebrity-based videos, has become a sort of _____ run and public service announcement.

2. On Thursday, the House Intelligence Committee will hold a hearing to examine what it calls "… society as a whole should play to counter a potentially grim, '_____-

truth' future".

3. "Deepfakes can cause real, concrete harm ..." Citron said. "And in unrest, if you time it just right, you can _____ violence."

4. Tom can't make any money off of his Schwarzennegger video because YouTube's _____ _____ algorithm detected that his video was taken from Conan O'Brien's show.

5. Tom says he's hopeful deepfakes can be used more for art and less for political _____ _____.

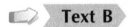

As the old saying goes, "Seeing is believing." However, after reading the passage above, you may find that this may not be true. What you have seen may not be so reliable as you thought, so are many other elements. In this case, what else do you think we should rely on when we are in the pursuit of the truth? Please discuss with your partners and come up with some solutions.

Based on the discussions above, please write a composition of no less than 300 words, commenting on what we should cherish most and resort to in this world.

Text B

Why China Can Guarantee Food Safety

September 4, 2019
CGTN

Gutter oil, cadmium rice, dyed fruits and water-injected meat ... these are just some of the well-publicized food safety scandals that shocked China in recent memory.

For years, grocery shoppers in the country would check food packaging for sketchy ingredients, wonder how much pesticide is left on vegetables and know exactly which imported brands to reach for through word of mouth. On other occasions, consumers might suspect whether something being sold as food is even edible.

National outrage over food safety erupted in 2008, when it was revealed that infant formula produced by a Chinese dairy brand had been contaminated with melamine, a toxic industrial chemical that resulted in tens of thousands of sick children and several deaths. The scandal single-handedly devastated China's domestic dairy industry. Nearly a decade later in 2017, a report found 53 percent of people surveyed in 44 Chinese cities preferred foreign brands of baby formula. That's despite domestically made products passing quality inspection at a rate of 99.9 percent. But no one wants to take chances with their children.

With fears and distrust came widespread misinformation. Rumors about unsafe food often caught on quickly on Chinese social media. Shocking stories about "fake eggs" and pork floss made from cotton are still driving Internet traffic long after they were dismissed by officials. When it comes to the food industry, one bad incident can decimate an entire sector, expert says.

"In fact, in this situation, 100 minus one is equal to zero," said Dr. Samuel Godefroy, a professor of Food Risk Analysis and Regulatory Policies at Laval University in Canada. "Today with social media … the mission of government authorities becomes very difficult, because you are one voice among many voices out there."

With the largest population in the world to feed, China takes food safety very seriously, having elevated the issue to a national strategy. From 2015 to 2018, the Chinese government adopted new laws and regulations related to food safety every year to address new areas such as Internet catering services. In 2017, a food safety plan was officially included in the country's 13th Five-Year Plan (2016 – 2020).

In addition to laws and regulations, concrete actions have been taken to encourage more supervision and transparency. China has initiated the "Open Kitchen" and "Clean Kitchen" campaigns which let customers watch their food being cooked in restaurants' kitchens. Food producers are required to list all ingredients on product packaging.

Public satisfaction has improved considerably in the past few years. Disqualification rates in random food safety inspections dropped from 5.3 percent in 2014 to 2.4 percent in 2018.

However, ensuring food safety and quality and rebuilding consumer confidence is a continuous work and a shared responsibility, Godefroy said, adding that there are common challenges, including man-made ones.

"We have many small farms. The farmers don't know how to use pesticides or attend drugs rightly. They don't know what food safety standards are, so they just use pesticides as they want," said Dr. Fang Yongxiang, director of the Center for Food Safety Standards under the China National Center for Food Safety Risk Assessment.

China uses 47 percent of all pesticides in the world, the majority of which are chemical. While developed countries have switched to greener and healthier biological options, only eight percent of all pesticides used in China are biological ones, and the average use of pesticides in unit farmland space is four times of that used in the United States.

The Chinese government is actively developing pesticide residue standards to improve the safety of agricultural products from the source. By 2035, China aims to become a world leader in food safety control.

There have been signs of progress. Currently, China is a host for a number of international standard setting committees, and has already adopted many international standards as the basis of its own regulatory requirements, noted Godefroy.

Misinformation is another challenge. There can be commercial interests associated with spreading rumors about food safety in order to undermine a competitor, an offense punishable by Chinese law, Godefroy said.

According to the State Administration for Market Regulation, more than 6,500 cases of food safety frauds were busted and more than 11,000 people arrested on fraud offenses in the first half of 2018.

More work needs to be done with capacity building, because food safety is an issue requiring continuous vigilance, said Fang. "Food safety is a very professional field, and you need to have enough scientific knowledge, or some background to know how to regulate and produce food," he said.

China proposes adopting the strictest criteria, supervision, punishment, and **accountability** for food safety control, and the food industry is directly responsible for consumers' well-being from the farmland to the dining table. On the other hand, Fang said that consumers also need to educate themselves about food, so that they become more informed and eat better.

Words and Expressions

gutter	[ˈgʌtə(r)]	n.	a channel at the edge of a road where water collects and is carried away to drains 路旁排水沟；阴沟
cadmium	[ˈkædmiəm]	n.	a soft poisonous bluish-white metal that is used in batteries and nuclear reactors 镉
sketchy	[ˈsketʃi]	a.	not complete or detailed 粗略的；不完备的
edible	[ˈedəbl]	a.	fit to be eaten; not poisonous 适宜食用的；(无毒而)可以吃的
outrage	[ˈaʊtreɪdʒ]	n.	a strong feeling of shock and anger 义愤；愤慨
erupt	[ɪˈrʌpt]	v.	start happening, suddenly and violently 突然发生；爆发

formula	[ˈfɔːmjələ]	n.	a type of liquid food for babies, given instead of breast milk 配方奶
contaminate	[kənˈtæmɪneɪt]	v.	make sth. dirty or harmful 污染；弄脏
melamine	[ˈmeləmiːn]	n.	a strong hard plastic material, used esp. for covering surfaces such as the tops of tables, and for making cups, etc. 三聚氰胺
scandal	[ˈskændl]	n.	a behaviour or an event that people think is morally or legally wrong and causes public feelings of shock or anger 使人震惊的丑事；丑闻
devastate	[ˈdevəsteɪt]	v.	completely destroy a place or an area 彻底破坏；摧毁；毁灭
misinformation	[ˌmɪsɪnfəˈmeɪʃn]	n.	wrong information which is given to someone, often in a deliberate attempt to make them believe something is not true（常指有意提供的）假消息，错误消息
catch on			become popular 时兴；流行
decimate	[ˈdesɪmeɪt]	v.	severely damage sth. or make sth. weaker 严重破坏；大大削弱
elevate	[ˈelɪveɪt]	v.	increase the level of sth. 提高；使升高
catering	[ˈkeɪtərɪŋ]	n.	the work of providing food and drinks for meetings or social events 饮食服务，酒席承办
supervision	[ˌsuːpəˈvɪʒn]	n.	the supervising of people, activities, or places 监督；管理
transparency	[trænsˈpærənsi]	n.	the quality of sth., such as an excuse or a lie that allows sb. to see the truth easily 显而易见；一目了然
initiate	[ɪˈnɪʃieɪt]	v.	make sth. begin 开始；发起
disqualification	[dɪsˌkwɒlɪfɪˈkeɪʃn]	n.	the state of being officially stopped from taking part in a particular event, activity, or competition（通常因做错事而）使无资格，取消……的资格
residue	[ˈrezɪdjuː]	n.	a small amount of sth. that remains at the end of a process 剩余物；残留物；残渣
undermine	[ˌʌndəˈmaɪn]	v.	make sth., esp. sb.'s confidence or authority, gradually weaker or less effective 逐渐削弱（信心、权威等）

bust	[bʌst]	v.	suddenly enter a place and search it or arrest sb. 突击搜查（或搜捕）
fraud	[frɔːd]	n.	sth. that is not as good, useful, etc. as people claim it is 伪劣品；冒牌货
vigilance	[ˈvɪdʒɪləns]	n.	more careful attention, especially in order to notice possible danger 小心戒备，小心谨慎
accountability	[əˌkaʊntəˈbɪləti]	n.	responsibility to someone or for some activity 责任

- **Multiple Choice**

Select the most appropriate answer for each of the following questions.

1. What aroused the national outrage over food safety in 2008?

    A) Gutter oil and cadmium rice.

    B) Dyed fruit and water-injected meat.

    C) Pesticide left on vegetables.

    D) Infant formula contaminated with a toxic industrial chemical resulting in tens of thousands of sick children and several deaths.

2. Which of the following is NOT the concrete actions that have been taken to encourage more supervision and transparency in food safety?

    A) The "Open Kitchen" campaign.

    B) The "Clean Kitchen" campaign.

    C) Consumers participate in the process of food production.

    D) Food producers are required to list all ingredients on product packaging.

3. According to Dr. Fang Yongxiang, what is the first man-made challenge so far as food security is concerned?

    A) It is very difficult to convince the public to have confidence in food safety.

    B) Food producers fail to abide strictly by the laws.

    C) The public is dissatisfied with the food security.

    D) Small farmers don't know what food safety standards are and just use pesticides as they want.

4. What is another man-made challenge?

    A) The public distrust in food security.

B) The authorities' negligence of the food safety frauds.

C) Rumors about food safety in order to undermine a competitor.

D) The unfair play from the competitors.

5. Which of the following is the closest in meaning to the underlined word "accountability" in the last paragraph?

A) The ability of an accountant.

B) Consequence.

C) Accommodation.

D) An obligation or willingness to accept responsibility for one's actions.

- **True/False/Not Given**

Do the following statements agree with the information given in Text B?

In Blanks 1-5 write

True   if the statement is true

False   if the statement is false

Not Given   if the information is not given in Text B

_____ 1. Food safety is an issue that has shocked China only in recent years.

_____ 2. Consumers have never suspected whether something being sold as food is safe to eat.

_____ 3. In 2007, a report found 53 percent of people surveyed in 44 Chinese cities preferred foreign brands of baby formula.

_____ 4. Today with social media … the mission of governments becomes very easy, because they are the authorities among many voices out there.

_____ 5. Ensuring food safety and quality and rebuilding consumer confidence is a continuous work and a shared responsibility.

- **Topic for Debate**

Which factor do you think is more crucial in dealing with the problem of food safety: the public continuous vigilance, or the strict enforcement of laws and regulations? Form two groups to debate. Discuss with your group members and defend your views.

- **Comments**

Based on the debate above, please write a composition of no less than 300 words, commenting on the statement that you can never be too careful on such matters as food safety. You can analyze the causes of some cases of food safety and then talk about what we can do to deal with the problem.

Unit 7 Social Security and Crime Prevention

 Academic Reading

Using Inference

Learning Objective

In the section, you will learn to use knowledge experience, and clues to draw inferences in problem situations.

What Is Critical Reading?

Critical reading can be defined as very high-level comprehension of written material requiring interpretation and evaluation skills that enable the reader to separate important from unimportant information, distinguish between facts and opinions, and determine a writer's purpose and tone. Critical reading also entails using inference to go beyond what is stated explicitly, filling in informational gaps, and coming to logical conclusions. These various skills require much thought, and that is why critical reading is dependent on critical thinking. Indeed, all of the characteristics of critical thinking can be applied to critical reading. The following diagram illustrates the relationship between critical thinking and critical reading skills.

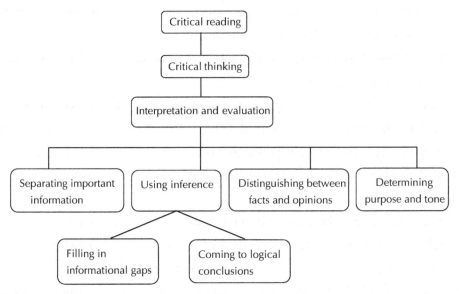

Drawing Inferences

Inferences are a part of communication in everyday life—in listening, speaking, reading, and writing. The receiver of information gains a better understanding of a topic or idea through this interactive process that involves what is known and what is learned.

Applied to reading, an inference is a reasonable or educated guess about what the author does not say based on what he or she does say. Inferences must be made when an author suggests an idea but does not directly state it. These ideas are implied, or inferred.

Inferring, or drawing conclusions, makes you think in depth about stated and unstated information. You often use your personal experience to comprehend what is inferred. Inferring requires background information and abstract thinking in order to think as the writer wishes you to think. The clues the writer gives you steer your thinking. A valid inference is one that has a sufficient amount of supportable and verifiable information.

When you read the material associated with your college courses, you frequently need to make inferences. Writers do not always present their ideas directly. There are several reasons why textbook authors and other writers require you to make inferences. Information is left out because it would make the message too long or would divert the reader from the central point.

- An author assumes readers know enough to fill in the omitted ideas.
- The writer believes the reader will get more meaning or enjoyment by making an inference.
- Some writers leave out pertinent information in order to make it easier to influence the reader to draw a desired conclusion, especially if he or she might have challenged the details had they been included.

Use Knowledge, Experience, and Clues to Draw Inferences in Problem Situations

(1) Using Knowledge to Infer

Knowledge of different subjects or topics varies from person to person: It comes down to what we have learned and experienced through the years. In that sense, knowledge really cannot be separated from experience because the latter adds to our knowledge base. On the other hand, our knowledge helps shape the way we interpret our experiences.

It follows, then, that the more we know and the more we have experienced, the easier it will be to draw inferences, depending of course on the circumstances. There will be occasions when we are in a much better position to make educated guesses and other occasions when we will not be able to do so with any degree of confidence. For example, look at the photograph on the following page.

Certainly, most of us have enough knowledge to realize that this is a picture of a bus that is used for sightseeing purposes. However, what if I asked you to infer where the photograph was taken? There is one clue, and that is the name "Beantown". If you know the name of the city that is called "Beantown", you would feel very secure answering that the photograph was probably taken in the city of Boston. Thus your knowledge helped you use the clue to answer the question. People without that knowledge would be forced either to do some research or to take a wild guess. If they took a wild guess, the chances are fairly high that they would be wrong. Following are examples of how knowledge can play a significant part when it comes to drawing inferences.

Examples:

1. Fact: All of the people with a certain disease know one another and are not necessarily related. In order to make an inference, you would need to know something about diseases and how they are spread. You could then infer that the disease is probably not diabetes or heart failure but something that is passed on such as a cold or the flu.

Inference: The disease is contagious.

2. Fact: Certain states have a significantly higher death rate than others. Which states are they? In order to make this inference, you would need to know that a large number of older people live in these states, possibly because they tend to retire there. Therefore, the death rate is higher in these states than other states.

Inference: The states are Arizona and Florida.

3. Fact: The flowers we planted come up and bloom every year. What type of flowers are they? In order to make this inference, you would need to know that some flowers—annuals—need to be planted every year and that others—perennials—grow back every growing season.

Inference: The flowers are perennials.

We all need to accept the fact that we do not know everything, and no two people will possess the same degree of knowledge on every matter. In other words, we should not be embarrassed if we do not have enough knowledge in certain situations to draw inferences, and in those instances, it is probably better not to draw inferences because there is a greater chance of being wrong. Keep in mind that there will be other situations in which we will find ourselves in better positions to come to logical conclusions. Furthermore, knowledge is not a constant but increases as we go through life.

(2) **Using Experience to Infer**

Our experiences add to our knowledge base and place us in a better position to come to logical conclusions about our surroundings. Once again, our experiences vary from person to person and therefore with regard to how much they help us draw inferences in different situations.

Examples from Personal Experience:

Listening: The fire siren in town goes off. What can you infer?

- You may infer that there is a fire or an emergency somewhere.
- If it goes off around lunchtime, you may infer that it is the 12:00 noon siren instead of a fire or emergency.

Speaking: You tell someone that an umbrella is needed today.
- The listener may infer that it is raining.
- The listener may infer that you need protection from the sun.

Reading: You see the headline in the newspaper, "Ethiopia on the Brink of Famine Again: World Must Act."
- You may infer that Ethiopia is a poor country that has encountered vast and extreme famine before.
- You may infer that this article is encouraging the world to help Ethiopia in some way to solve a crisis.

Writing: You just received a present. Before you unwrap the gift, you are asked to write down your guesses as to its contents.
- You write what you think it might be based on the size of the box.
- You write what you think it might be based on the occasion for the present such as a specific holiday or birthday.
- You write what you suspect it might be after shaking the box.

(3) **Using Clues to Infer**

As you have seen, in addition to knowledge and experience, we all depend on clues to help us draw inferences. The clues or facts presented in a given situation interact with our knowledge and experiences, thus enabling us to make sense of our surroundings.

For example, you saw a messy office with a messy desk. Although you do not know for sure, you can conclude reasonably that this person is disorganized or just has lots of tasks going on at the same time. It would appear that this person might work through lunch break or late at night because of the banana peel, coffee cups, and snacks strewn around. He or she has to meet deadlines. There is a "To Do List" on the computer and a journal or calendar propped open on the desk. There are files labeled "images or pictures". This might mean that this person works for a newspaper or television station or in another job in which writing, photographs, and deadlines are important.

As you can see, by using the clues in combination with your knowledge and experiences, you were able to infer some things about the person who uses this office. Much like a detective, you pieced together some important information that gave meaning to what you were observing. We all do this kind of exercise very often without even realizing it, and much of the time, our inferences are correct. Obviously, the more clues or facts available in a given situation, the better the chances of our inferences being accurate.

Part 3 Learning After Class

Additional Reading 1

Hong Kong: A Story of Self-harm

By Adam Garrie [1]
August 11, 2019
CGTN

  This summer, protests in the Hong Kong Special Administrative Region of the People's Republic of China began as a response to the so-called judicial fugitive bill that Hong Kong's legislative authorities were in the process of deliberating.

  The proposals were designed to close a loophole in which criminals from other parts of China could evade justice by illegally sheltering in Hong Kong and abusing the "One Country, Two Systems" political model.

  To give one perspective, such a bill would allow for the kind of inter-jurisdictional justice that occurs on a daily basis in the United States when a criminal flees from one US state to another. Likewise, the EU's controversial European Arrest Warrant (EAW) allows for the extradition of suspects between sovereign states without any significant judicial review available. The Hong Kong bill was to be far more reduced in its scope in comparison to the realities in the United States and European Union. Transferring a criminal taking refuge in Hong Kong after committing a criminal act elsewhere in China would only have taken place if the offence in question was considered a crime in Hong Kong.

  Secondly, a thorough process of judicial review was to be available and the provisions were to be highly limited in their overall scope.

---

 [1] Adam Garrie is director of the UK-based global policy and analysis think tank Eurasia Future and co-host of a talk show "The History Boys".

In spite of the rather anodyne nature of the bill when compared with the realities in major Western countries, protesters successfully convinced the legislative authorities to suspend the bill.

Under normal circumstances, this would have been the end of the protests but self-evidently sinister elements sought not to achieve a goal but instead they sought to sow supreme chaos.

Since the protesters ostensibly got what they wanted after the fugitive bill was shelved, the demonstrations have metamorphosed into overt provocations against ordinary people, against businesses and against lawful authorities. A video of young thugs assaulting a very elderly man at a train station like rabid gangsters is now emblematic of the brutal atmosphere caused by the provocateurs. Equally emblematic is the extreme vandalism of Hong Kong's legislative chamber, the defacing of national symbols and the erection of a colonial flag on modern Chinese soil.

Many have called such acts treasonous. Certainly, if violent thugs broke into the US Congress and erected a foreign flag before a defaced symbol of the US government, most Americans would correctly label this as treason.

At a human level, the events are sad and infuriating. At a legal level, it is curious as to why the police have used so little force against the provocateurs whilst in countries like France, protesters are dealt with in an extremely brutal fashion even if the protests remain non-destructive.

But the most important development in the medium and perhaps in the long term is that the provocations have changed the international image of Hong Kong.

Hong Kong has traditionally been known as a prosperous, open, business and trade oriented and cosmopolitan Chinese region. Now, Hong Kong looks dangerous; it looks tense, chaotic and as such, the international business community will take notice.

The authorities themselves must be aware of this, which is why a minimal amount of force has been used against the provocateurs when compared, for example, with the French response to the "yellow vest" protesters.

And yet the other side of this equation is that far from exercising reason and taking to their senses, the provocateurs continue their war against their own region. It is not the rest of China that is suffering this summer. China as a whole remains a totally peaceful and prosperous country.

But Hong Kong which has maintained unique characteristics under the "One Country, Two Systems" model has descended to a level of hitherto unknown chaos that could potentially affect the future of all Hong Kong people.

The protests themselves are therefore totally self-destructive. Whilst the authorities have dropped proposals for the so-called fugitive bill and whilst normal democratic institutions continue to function according to the rule of law, the streets are rejecting law and order, the streets are rejecting the overwhelming will of ordinary people for peace and order and the streets are sending negative messages to the international business community as well as to tourists.

When the history books record the story of Hong Kong's 2019 summer of despair, they may not be kind to the young and violent elements who have transformed Hong Kong from a place of tranquility and robust commerce to one of violence, thuggery, banditry and gangsterism. This is a mark of shame that will forever taint those responsible for these self-harming crimes.

 Words and Expressions

think tank			a group of experts who provide advice and ideas on political, social or economic issues 智囊团；智库
judicial	[dʒuˈdɪʃl]	a.	relating to the legal system and to judgments made in a court of law 司法的；法庭的；审判的
fugitive	[ˈfjuːdʒətɪv]	n.	someone who is running away or hiding, usu. in order to avoid being caught by the police 逃亡者；(通常指)逃犯
legislative	[ˈledʒɪslətɪv]	a.	involving or relating to the process of making and passing laws 立法的；有关立法的
deliberate	[dɪˈlɪbəreɪt]	v.	think about something carefully, esp. before making a very important decision 慎重考虑；仔细思考
loophole	[ˈluːphəʊl]	n.	a small mistake which allows people to do something that would otherwise be illegal (法律上的)漏洞，空子
allow for			include some extra time or money in planning so that they can be dealt with if they occur 考虑到；将……计算在内；为……酌留余地
inter-jurisdictional	[ˌɪntəˌdʒʊərɪsˈdɪkʃən(ə)l]	a.	跨司法管辖权的

anodyne	[ˈænədaɪn]	a.	unlikely to cause disagreement or offend anyone 不得罪人的；温和的
sinister	[ˈsɪnɪstə(r)]	a.	evil or harmful 邪恶的；不祥的
ostensibly	[ɒˈstensəbli]	adv.	seemingly to be true or is officially stated to be true, but about which people have doubts 表面上的；貌似真实的；宣称的
metamorphose	[ˌmetəˈmɔːfəʊz]	v.	develop and change into sth. completely different（使）完全变形；（使）彻底改变
overt	[əʊˈvɜːt]	a.	done or shown in an open and obvious way 公开的；明显的
thug	[θʌg]	n.	a violent person or criminal 恶棍；凶手；罪犯
rabid	[ˈræbɪd]	a.	having very strong and unreasonable opinions or beliefs about a subject, esp. in politics（政治上）偏激的，固执的
emblematic	[ˌembləˈmætɪk]	a.	symbolically representing the quality or idea 象征(性)的；标志(性)的
vandalism	[ˈvændəlɪzəm]	n.	the deliberate damaging of things, esp. public property（对公共财产的）故意破坏，捣毁
deface	[dɪˈfeɪs]	v.	spoil sth. by writing or drawing things on it 损伤……的外观；在……上乱涂乱画
erection	[ɪˈrekʃn]	n.	the act of building sth. in an upright position 建造；竖起
treasonous	[ˈtriːzənəs]	a.	having the character of, or characteristic of a traitor 谋反的；犯叛国罪的
infuriating	[ɪnˈfjʊərieɪtɪŋ]	a.	annoying very much 使人大怒的
cosmopolitan	[ˌkɒzməˈpɒlɪtən]	n.	(a place or society) full of people from many different countries and cultures 世界性的, 国际化的; 受各国文化影响的
hitherto	[ˌhɪðəˈtuː]	adv.	up to this time 到目前为止
banditry	[ˈbændɪtri]	n.	acts of robbery and violence in areas where the rule of law has broken down 强盗行为；匪盗行径
taint	[teɪnt]	v.	damage or spoil the quality of sth. 毁坏；损害，败坏

Unit 7 Social Security and Crime Prevention

Discussion Questions

1. What were the initial cause of the chaos in Hong Kong?
2. What happened after the legislative authorities suspended the fugitive bill?
3. What does the author think of the story of Hong Kong's 2019 summer of despair?

Additional Reading 2

Missing 9-year-old Girl, Whose Disappearance Gripped China, Found Dead

By Steven Jiang
July 15, 2019
CNN

Beijing (CNN) A 9-year-old Chinese girl's mysterious weeklong disappearance came to a tragic end Sunday after authorities confirmed her lifeless body had been found in the East China Sea.

In a statement released Sunday, Zhejiang Provincial Police confirmed that missing girl Zhang Zixin had drowned in waters off Xiangshan County. They said that her body showed no signs of violence but ruled out her death as an accident.

Millions of people across China had been gripped by the case, closely following the developments as search crews had spent days trying to find the bespectacled second-grader with a long pony tail in waters and caves along the shoreline.

The girl's government services identity card was found in a pavilion near the coast last Wednesday night. Zhang was last seen just over a week ago, when a witness saw her traveling with a middle-aged couple on a road not far from the search area around 8 p.m. on July 7.

The couple had been renting rooms at her family's house in rural Chun'an County, some 150 kilometers away, according to police. When the two adults were seen again on surveillance cameras two hours later, the girl wasn't with them. Police said the man and woman, both hailing from the southern province of Guangdong, drowned themselves in a nearby lake later that night.

In their latest statement, police said the 43-year-old man, surnamed Liang, and the 45-year-old woman, surnamed Xie, had been swindling money from family and friends for years, and ran out of cash after traveling extensively across China. Police said the couple had been increasingly discarding their personal belongings in recent months and an analysis of their social media posts pointed to a desire to commit suicide together with Zhang as their symbolic goddaughter.

In an interview with the mass-circulating *Dushi Kuaibao* newspaper Wednesday, a Zhejiang-based state-run publication, the girl's father Zhang Jun said the couple had tricked his elderly farmer parents, who were Zixin's primary caretakers, into letting them take the girl away while he was working in a northern Chinese city hundreds of miles away. In the interview, Zhang Jun said the nightmare began when Liang and Xie told him on July 3 that they wanted to make Zixin a flower girl at a wedding in Shanghai. Despite his objections, Zhang said the couple took the girl with them the next morning.

For three days, Zhang Jun said he was able to stay in touch with Liang via WeChat, China's most popular social media platform. Liang promised to bring the girl home by the end of July 6 and sent frequent updates, according to the father, who said everything seemed "normal" initially. In footage that Liang sent to Zhang Jun, who later shared with state-run media outlet Beijing News, Zixin can be seen visiting tourist sites with the two suspects and watching videos on a phone on a train. The girl appeared relaxed, answering Liang's questions with a smile. Her voice in audio messages also sounded relaxed.

But Zhang was worried that none of the locations were anywhere near Shanghai. After being increasingly suspicious, Zhang Jun finally took an overnight train home on July 6. He said he spoke to Zixin for the last time midday on July 7, saying she sounded calm and told him she was in northern Xiangshan, a county just south of Shanghai.

By the time night fell on July 7, things had started to look more ominous. Liang had refused the father's offer to drive to their location to pick Zixin up, but agreed to have him pay for a taxi to drive them back to Zixin's home, according to Zhang Jun. Shortly afterward, Liang switched off his phone.

Zhang's family reported her missing to local police on Monday morning, and posted the girl's and Liang's information online the next day. After police confirmed the death of the two adults, Zixin's fate became a nationwide fixation.

Conspiracy theories abounded across Chinese cyberspace, with some commentators wondering aloud if Liang and Xie were members of a cult—based on certain images and seemingly odd content posted by Liang.

Dismissing the speculation, Zhejiang police said Sunday that the two suspects didn't have criminal records and weren't found to have engaged in cult activities. Neither of them had used alcohol or drugs prior to killing themselves.

CNN has reached out to Zhang Jun for comment. His brother-in-law told the Beijing

News on Sunday that the family would like to "have some quiet time" and would not field any interview requests for now. "Although this result isn't the miracle we had hoped for, it's better than not finding the girl's body," he was quoted as saying.

Words and Expressions

grip	[grɪp]	v.	hold the interest of sb. strongly 吸引住(某人)的注意
rule out			exclude 排除
bespectacled	[bɪˈspektəkld]	a.	wearing an eyeglass 戴眼镜的
pavilion	[pəˈvɪlɪən]	n.	an ornamental building in a garden or park 亭，阁
hail from			be or have been native to or a resident of 来自
swindle	[ˈswɪndl]	v.	cheat sth. in order to get sth., esp. money, from them 诈骗；骗取
discard	[dɪˈskɑːd]	v.	get rid of sth. 丢弃；抛弃
circulate	[ˈsɜːkjəleɪt]	v.	pass from person to person or place to place to become widespread 传递；传阅
ominous	[ˈɒmɪnəs]	a.	presaging ill fortune 恶兆的；不吉利的
abound	[əˈbaʊnd]	v.	exist in great numbers or quantities 大量存在；有许多
cult	[kʌlt]	n.	a small group of people who have extreme religious beliefs and who are not part of any established religion 异教团体
speculation	[ˌspekjuˈleɪʃn]	n.	the act of forming opinions about what has happened or what might happen without knowing all the facts 推测；推断

Discussion Questions

1. Who do you think should be accountable for the death of the child? Explain your viewpoint?
2. According to her father, how did the girl go missing?
3. What do you think we should do to protect children, especially those who do not live with their parents?

Additional Reading 3

Driver Protection to Improve After Fatal Bus Plunge

By Li Hongyang
November 14, 2018
China Daily

Expert: Partitions can help prevent accidents

Experts and industry insiders are working on ways to better protect transit workers after 13 people died when a bus driver was attacked by a passenger and his vehicle plunged from a bridge into the Yangtze River in Chongqing last month.

Two people are still missing after the bus smashed through a guard rail on the bridge. Footage from the vehicle shows the driver being hit on the head by a female passenger who had missed her stop and was refused permission to get off. The driver retaliated with one hand, but lost control of the bus.

Chen Yuefeng, an associate professor of transportation law at East China University of Political Science and Law in Shanghai, said such accidents could be avoided by using simple but effective measures such as installing a partition to separate drivers from passengers. "Both airplanes and trains have cabins, but I rarely see cabins on buses. It is now time for the government and companies to consider providing them, along with protective doors, for drivers," he said.

Since 2013, the Judgments Online website of the Supreme People's Court has recorded more than 67 criminal cases in which passengers were accused of endangering public safety by attacking bus drivers. Most of the defendants were sent to prison for more than three years. These incidents all involved fighting between passengers and bus drivers and led to traffic accidents.

In 2015, in Longnan, Gansu Province, a bus driver was attacked by a passenger, and lost control of the vehicle, which mounted a sidewalk. One pedestrian was killed and two others were injured.

A week after the accident, cities nationwide announced that safety partitions would be set up or upgraded for bus drivers. They include Xi'an, capital of Shaanxi Province; Wuhan, capital of Hubei Province; Changsha, capital of Hunan Province; Nanjing, capital of Jiangsu Province; and Chongqing.

Beijing is playing a leading role in upgrading its buses. Li Qingyuan, deputy head of the security department at Beijing Public Transport Group, said drivers' partitions had been phased in since 2011, and installation work had been completed on 70 percent of the 26,363 buses in the city. The remainder will be upgraded in the next few years.

"Beijing is the country's political center. Terrorists and other extremists have posed threats on buses, so bus drivers in the city are vulnerable and need more protection.

"The municipal government has invested a lot of money on buying new buses fitted with safety partitions, which ensure that passengers are unable to commit any acts of violence," Li said.

In June, the Bus Operator and Pedestrian Protection Act was introduced in the United States. The act requires transportation agencies to install barriers for drivers and to report the number of incidents targeting them to the Department of Transportation.

However, Li has concerns that while a partition can protect drivers it could also lead to passengers feeling that they have been isolated, perhaps triggering conflict.

Of all the cases on the China Judgments Online website, 46 percent involved fighting caused by passengers who had been refused permission to get off at places where there were no bus stops. Twenty percent were caused by disputes over fares. In 30 percent of the cases, passengers not only hit the driver but also tried to grab the steering wheel.

"Bus security guards can prevent fighting by communicating with passengers and tackling a problem promptly. If a problem occurs, the guard can stop it immediately," Li said. Beijing now has at least one security guard on each bus. Li considers installing partitions to be a "trend" but said security systems are more effective than partitions in deterring violence.

Yang Bin, head of the service department at Beijing Public Transport Group, said, "Physically separating drivers and passengers is not the best solution. What if a passenger insults the driver outside the partition? That is also disturbing and dangerous. It's more effective to solve the problem through communication," he said.

Li said security guards hired by the group must have a license issued by the public security department and also a certificate from the group after they pass an exam. The group employs 43,842 guards, and each earns 4,300 *yuan* a month, involving an outlay of about 2.2 billion *yuan* annually for the municipal government.

However, this is a significant amount to invest on safety. Large cities such as Beijing and Shanghai have a strong demand for security guards and vast financial resources, but others are unable to afford to introduce safety measures immediately. Unlike Beijing's state-owned transport group, such companies in many other cities are privately run. Bus routes are contracted to different individuals.

Zhang Yong, who owns the franchise for 25 of the 3,284 buses running in Changchun, said he is unable to make any large investments now.

"The ticket price has remained at 1 *yuan* for 10 years, as it is set by the city transportation authority, but other costs have risen three or even 10 times in this period, such as repairs and drivers' salaries.

"If an accident happens, I will have to spend money dealing with it. I am now trying not to incur any losses, let alone upgrade buses or even hire security guards. This is impossible for me now," Zhang said.

"To avoid accidents, we have rules for bus drivers, the most important being 'Never fight back, never shout back'. But our drivers are sometimes too tired to be polite to trouble-makers.

"I have encountered about 10 accidents caused by conflict between passengers and drivers since 2008. We called the police, but each time the incidents only resulted in fines being imposed. No one was detained or imprisoned. I think stricter laws or enforcement are needed to educate and warn passengers, therefore keeping drivers and buses safe," Zhang added.

In Canada, people who assault public transit operators can find themselves facing harsher penalties under a new amendment to the Criminal Code made in 2015.

However, Chen, the law professor, said there are no such laws to categorize assaults on bus drivers in China because only a small number of accidents are caused by violence. "The current law is governed by the results of accidents, not preventing them. Detailed laws against disturbing bus drivers who are working should be introduced in the future. In this way, sentencing will be easier and people will be more aware of what constitutes illegal behavior," he said.

 Words and Expressions

partition	[pɑːˈtɪʃn]	n.	a wall or screen that separates one part of a room or vehicle from another 隔断；隔板
transit	[ˈtrænzɪt]	n.	a system for moving people or goods from one place to another 交通运输系统
smash	[smæʃ]	v.	move with a lot of force against sth. solid; make sth. do this (使)猛烈撞击；猛烈碰撞
footage	[ˈfʊtɪdʒ]	n.	a film of a particular event or the part of a film which shows this event (影片中)连续镜头，片段

retaliate	[rɪˈtælieɪt]	v.	make a counter-attack and return like for like, esp. evil for evil 报复；反击
defendant	[dɪˈfendənt]	n.	a person who has been accused of breaking the law and is being tried in court 被告
sidewalk	[ˈsaɪdwɔːk]	n.	a path with a hard surface by the side of a road 人行道
pedestrian	[pəˈdestriən]	n.	a person who is walking, esp. in a town or city 步行者，行人
upgrade	[ˌʌpˈgreɪd, ˈʌpgreɪd]	v.	make a piece of machinery, computer system, etc. more powerful and efficient 使（机器、计算机系统等）升级；提高
deputy	[ˈdepjuti]	n.	the second most important person in an organization such as a business or government department 副职；副主管
pose	[pəʊz]	v.	cause a problem or some kind of danger 产生（问题）；造成（威胁、危险）
vulnerable	[ˈvʌlnərəbl]	a.	weak and without protection, easily hurt physically or emotionally 脆弱的；易受伤害的
municipal	[mjuːˈnɪsɪpl]	a.	associated with or belonging to a city or town 城市的；市政的
trigger	[ˈtrɪgə(r)]	v.	cause an event or situation to begin to happen or exist 引起；发动；促使
tackle	[ˈtækl]	v.	deal with a difficult problem or task in a very determined or efficient way（果断或高效地）应对；处理；解决
deter	[dɪˈtɜː(r)]	v.	make someone not want to do it or continue doing it 威慑住；阻止；制止
outlay	[ˈaʊtleɪ]	n.	the amount of money used to buy something or start a project 费用；开支
franchise	[ˈfræntʃaɪz]	n.	an authority that is given by an organization to sb. allowing them to sell its goods or services or to take part in an activity which the organization controls 特许经营权；专卖权
incur	[ɪnˈkɜː(r)]	v.	make oneself subject to; bring upon oneself 招致；带来；遭受
detain	[dɪˈteɪn]	v.	keep people in a place under control 拘留；扣押

assault	[əˈsɔːlt]	v.	physically attack 袭击;殴打
penalty	[ˈpenəlti]	n.	a punishment that sb. is given for doing sth. against a law or rule 刑罚;处罚
amendment	[əˈmendmənt]	n.	a section that is added to a law or rule in order to change it(法令或法规的)修正条款;修正案
categorize	[ˈkætəɡəraɪz]	v.	divide people or things into sets 对……进行分类;把……归类
constitute	[ˈkɒnstɪtjuːt]	v.	form or compose 被视为;可算作

Discussion Questions

1. What do you think have caused so many accidents involving passengers and bus drivers?
2. Do you think partitions can really solve the problem? Why or why not?
3. What do you think is the best way to maintain peace on buses?

Part 4 Topical Vocabulary

acceptance 受理
alibi 不在现场证明
defamation 诽谤
indictment 控告
jury 陪审团
perjury 伪证
recess 休庭
ruling 裁决
sue 起诉
void 不具有法律效力的
breach of contract 不履行合同
capital punishment 极刑
chief justice 首席大法官
clear up a criminal case 破案

accused 被告
creditor 债权人
identification 鉴定
juror 陪审员
misconduct 失职行为
plaintiff 原告
reconciliation 和解
seize 缴获
summon 传票,传唤
administrative proceedings 行政诉讼
burden of proof 举证责任
chief judge of a tribunal 法庭庭长
chief procurator 首席检察官
confession to justice 自首

contempt of court 藐视法庭罪
crack down on counterfeit goods 打假
interference with public administration 妨害公务
deprivation of political right 剥夺政治权利
dismiss a motion 驳回请求
exemption from criminal penalty 免于刑事处分
false imprisonment 非法禁锢
incompetent for civil conduct 无民事行为能力
institute a public prosecution 提起公诉
joint property of the spouses 夫妻共同所有财产
legal guardian 法定监护人
life imprisonment 无期徒刑
losing party 败诉方
material evidence 物证
unlawful detention 非法拘禁
proclamation of a person as missing 宣告失踪
public security bureau 公安局
reckless driving 鲁莽驾驶
revoke a case placed on file 撤销立案
seal up 查封
security regulations 治安条例
spousal relationship 夫妻关系
sustain the original judgement 维持原判
termination of contract 解除合同
the Supreme People's Court 最高人民法院
trial in public 公开审理
the bail pending trial with restricted liberty of moving 取保候审
the Supreme People's Procuratorate 最高人民检察院
abducting and trafficking human beings 拐卖人口
disrupting the order of social administration 妨害社会管理秩序

court of final appeal 终审法院
intentional homicide 故意杀人
selling bogus medicines 贩卖假药
detention house 拘留所
driving while intoxicated 酒醉后驾驶
extort bribe 索取贿赂
fixed-term imprisonment 有期徒刑
initiate legal proceeding 打官司
intellectual property rights 知识产权
juvenile delinquency 青少年犯罪
legal representative 法人代表
liquidated damages 违约金
winning party 胜诉方
natural child 亲生子女
presiding judge 审判长
property of ownerless 无主财产
pyramid selling 传销
residential surveillance 监视居住
right in succession 继承权
security administration 治安管理
special pardon 特赦
suspended sentence 缓刑
term in custody 羁押期限
voluntary surrender to justice 自动投案
time limit provided by law 法定期限
unjustifiable self-defense 防卫过当

Unit 8

Health

Part 1　Learning Before Class

• **Listening**

What's So Bad About Processed Foods?

Directions: *Listen to the news and answer the questions.*

1. What have scientists already linked to rising obesity rates around the world?
2. What are mostly made of industrialized materials and additives?
3. What did the researchers in France find?
4. Who can it be hard for to avoid processed foods?

• **Watching and Thinking**

How Stress Affects Your Body

Directions: *Watch the video and discuss the questions with your partner.*

1. What does the video mainly talk about?
2. When do we experience the feeling of stress?
3. Why may stress affect our digestive and overall health?
4. What shall we do if we want to live longer according to the video?

• Reading and Discussing

Why China Can Provide 1.4 Billion People with Healthcare Coverage?

June 14, 2019
CGTN

Health care is a very complicated issue that all governments are struggling with. And for China, the world's largest developing country with 1.4 billion citizens, the challenge is even bigger.

In 2017, the average life expectancy of the Chinese people reached 76.4, rising to the 40th place globally to become one of the fastest-ascending countries.

The Lancet, an internationally renowned medical journal, has ranked China among the top five countries in the world with the greatest medical advancement, which is largely attributed to the country's medical reform.

How does the country make it possible?

China has rebuilt its health care system, especially for the rural area. Every person is covered by basic health insurance. In addition to covering the employed urban population, it also takes care of the urban unemployed and rural population, effectively safeguarding the health of the Chinese people.

Despite the rising health spending as a share of GDP in China and the falling personal health spending in the total health expenditure each year, China still lags behind.

Compared to the US in 2017, China's total health expenditure amounted to 6.2 percent of its GDP and about 560 US dollars per capita, whereas that of the US amounted to 16.2 percent of its GDP and about 9,500 US dollars per capita.

China's health spending per capita equates to only about one seventeenth that of the US globally, in 2014, the average world health spending as a share of GDP already reached 9.9 percent, whereas China has yet to reach this figure even today.

As part of its medical reform efforts, the country has been taking action to solve some of the most troublesome problems for its citizens. For example, certain drugs for major and serious diseases are rather pricey in China, which often drives patients and their families into poverty.

Statistics show that the five-year survival rate of cancer patients in China is about 30 percent, whereas in developed countries in Europe and the United States the rate is about 70 percent to 80 percent. And a key reason behind the disparity is the affordability of cancer drugs.

From May 1, 2018, most of the imported drugs, particularly anticancer drugs, have become tariff-free in China, which reduce the prices of anticancer drugs by up to 20 percent. On October 10, 2018, the medical insurance began to cover 17 additional anticancer drugs. The newly negotiated drug prices are on average more than 50 percent lower. With these efforts, China is aiming to give its citizens affordable treatments for not only minor complaints but also major diseases.

Other than the universal medical insurance, China is also taking other measures key to improve the health conditions of the Chinese people and prevent the occurrence of diseases. The "toilet revolution" is a case in point.

In 1993, the first rural environment-health investigation revealed that only 7.5 percent of the rural areas in China have toilets. By the end of 2016, the figure had gone up to 80.3 percent. China's target is to reach 85 percent by 2020.

The introduction of the toilet revolution harmlessly processes excrement, which effectively kills bacteria and parasites in the excrement, and reduces the breeding of flies and mosquitoes. Consequently, epidemic-prone diseases are prevented and controlled right from the start, and the overall medical expenses reduced.

2019 marks the 10th anniversary of a new round of intensified health and medical care reform. The Chinese government is still working to provide higher level of public medical insurance that will allow the 1.4 billion people enjoy equal medical resources of high quality. More than that, China will ensure the delivery of comprehensive lifecycle health services for its people, which is known as the "Healthy China Strategy".

Directions: *Read the passage and discuss the questions with your partner.*

1. Why has China been ranked among the top five countries in the world with the greatest medical advancement?
2. What efforts did China make to give its citizens affordable treatments?
3. What are the outcomes of the toilet revolution in China?

• Unit 8 Health •

Part 2 Learning in Class

Why Is It So Hard to Cure ALS?

Directions: *Watch the video and discuss the questions with your partner.*

1. What did Hawking retain after his diagnosis with ALS?
2. When do the symptoms of ALS typically first appear?
3. What is disrupted when motor neurons degenerate in ALS?
4. Why is there currently no single test that can determine whether someone has ALS?

Text A

What Mental Health Statistics Can Tell Us

By Elaine K. Howley

June 26, 2019

U. S. News & World Report [①]

A. Most of us know someone who's struggled with mental health issues. Whether it's depression, anxiety, bipolar disorder, post-traumatic stress disorder or another problem, mental health issues are common. The Centers for Disease Control and Prevention reports that 3.9% of adults aged 18 and older have experienced serious psychological distress in the past 30 days; 7.6% of persons aged 12 and older have depression in any two-week period; 8.4% of children aged 6 to 17 have been diagnosed with anxiety and/or depression; suicide is the second leading cause of death in 10 to 34 years old.

B. Access to care is improving, but most Americans still have no access to care. The report states that 12.2% adults with a mental illness remain uninsured, and 56.4% of

---

① *U. S. News & World Report* is an American news magazine published from Washington, D. C. Along with *Time and Newsweek*, it was for many years a leading news weekly, focusing more than its counterparts on political, economic, health and education stories. In recent years, it has become particularly known for its ranking system and annual reports on American colleges, graduate schools and hospitals.

adults with a mental illness received no treatment. A severe shortage of mental health clinicians is adding to the problem.

What do all those numbers actually mean?

C. Moe Gelbart, a psychologist in private practice and founder of the Thelma McMillen Center for Alcohol and Drug Treatment at Torrance Memorial Medical Center in Torrance, California, says that based on the epidemiological or population-based data, we know that "clearly the most prevalent mental health disorders are anxiety and then depression closely following it". Bipolar disorder and schizophrenia trail behind, but are still fairly prevalent conditions.

D. "Probably 20% of people in the country have some form of mental health issue at some point in their lives, with less than 5% having severe problems with mental health issues, such as bipolar disorder, schizophrenia or another less common, severe mental health issue," Gelbart says. What this shows us is that "mental health problems are on a continuum from very little to very severe", he says. And it's important to talk about these issues so that people know what they are and how to access help.

E. Mary A. Fristad, professor of psychiatry and behavioral health, psychology and nutrition at the Ohio State University Wexner Medical Center, agrees that the most common forms of mental health problems in America are "depression and anxiety", but adds that another issue that takes a big toll is substance abuse and alcohol use disorders.

F. When it comes to children, the statistics and current trends in mental health are especially worrying, says Dr. David A. Axelson, chief of the Department of Psychiatry and Behavioral Health at Nationwide Children's Hospital in Columbus, Ohio. "A very recent article just came out talking about the rates of major depression increasing among teenagers aged 12 to 17 by about 52% over the time period from 2009 to 2017."

G. Even more concerning, he says, is that suicide rates among 10 to 19-year-olds has increased. "We're very worried about that," he says. "There's been an 86% increase in the rate of death by suicide for kids 10 to 19 over the past decade, that would be from 2007 to 2017. It's now the second leading cause of death in that age group. And in particular, there's been a very large increase in the rate among younger kids in the 10 to 14 range, where the rate has increased by 190% in that 10-year period. So we're very concerned about the increased rates of depression, increased rates of death by suicide and also increased rates of diagnosis of autism spectrum disorders."

H. Determining what's causing these sharp increases is a complicated undertaking. Axelson says "there's a lot of hypotheses, but there's no definitive answer". Still, the quick rise and pervasiveness of social media that's been concurrent with these upticks in mental health disorders may play a role. At the same time, the amount of exercise most kids are getting daily has been steadily declining as physical education curriculums have been cut across the country. An increase in environmental toxins may also play a role.

I. Axelson says the mental health trends reflected in the data have been showing up in the emergency room, putting strain on the system. "More and more kids are presenting to emergency rooms in crisis, and we're noticing that trend at our hospital to the point we really needed to design a facility that was specialized." Nationwide will open a new hospital dedicated to pediatric behavioral and mental health disorders in early 2020 called the Big Lots Behavioral Health Pavilion at Nationwide Children's Hospital.

J. Among both adults and children, the statistics paint a bleak picture. But when you look beyond the basic statics, you see an even bigger scope of problem, Gelbart says. While the statistics note that some 20% of people are dealing with a mental health issue, "that impact is multiplied by three or four when you're thinking about the impact on society. For example, if dad is depressed, he might not be going to work. His wife is feeling the effects of that. And so on. It spreads beyond" the person with the mental health problem, so it's important to think about these figures in context of how they impact society at large.

K. Fristad says, "We're not alone in this; the World Health Organization reports that globally, more than 300 million people are affected by depression, making it the leading cause of disability worldwide and a major contributor to the overall global burden of disease."

Why is it important to track mental health statistics?

L. Keeping track of health statistics—which illnesses are most prevalent and how many people they impact—is important for understanding how diseases move through and affect populations. Tracking trends over time is an important component of public health. With mental illness, this information can help researchers and doctors understand how the mental health of America is changing over time and which issues need the most attention.

M. The hope is that firm data can improve treatment options, says Theresa Nguyen, vice president of policy and programs for Mental Health America. "We launched the State of Mental Health in America report back in 2014 because parity legislation," which puts mental health on the same level in terms of insurance reimbursement as physical health, "had just passed and we wanted to start tracking longitudinal data across the country to see if we could identify trends in the data". They were looking to see whether putting mental health issues on the same plane as physical health concerns would alter how many people were accessing care and in what areas. "We wanted to do that nationwide because at that point, some states were expanding Medicare and some were not." They wanted to see how increased coverage might improve access figures, and they needed hard data to tell the story. "If there's no data, then all we have are anecdotal findings," she says.

N. What they've found is that when access to mental health services is increased, people do take advantage of that, but that shortages of mental health workers remain a big problem. "People can't get care if they can't find a child psychiatrist or a team, for example. If they're struggling with a problem and you can't find that care," it almost doesn't matter whether insurance will cover it. "I think that people think it's fine. People are getting care since we passed the Parity Act, but that's not the case. Even in the best states, you have a 50-50 chance of getting care if you need it. That's horrible," she says, and the numbers highlight a real problem. Maine ranked the best in this measure, but still, 41.5% of adults in the state are not being treated for mental illness. Hawaii ranked the worst with 67.5% of adults going untreated.

O. To this end, Nguyen says the data could potentially help push more people to go into the field of mental health and help address a need that's clearly been demonstrated. It can also help direct policy-makers on where money should be spent to develop new programs, treatments or to study certain conditions in more depth. "We have to invest in the mental health workforce," and find ways to make mental health care more affordable and accessible in underserved communities. "We need to invest in early identification and intervention. We can't wait until people are in jail or homeless and disconnected from their family," she says.

P. Axelson adds that that although the situation looks dire, "we can't be overwhelmed. We've got to be willing to keep working on this problem and develop resources. We can have a wonderful impact to help kids and families, and we've been able to help save lives and turn lives around. You can't lose hope even though the problem is pretty massive." Data can help direct those efforts.

What to do about mental health issues?

Q. If you or someone you know is struggling with mental health issues, Fristad says it's important to "take steps to maximize physical and mental health", such as: getting enough sleep; exercising regularly; eating healthy foods; avoiding excessive alcohol consumption; making time for friends, family and loves ones; spending time in nature; maintaining a sense of humor; volunteering to help others in need; seeking professional help if mood, behavior or thinking patterns are interfering with life.

R. Gelbart says that cognitive behavioral therapy (CBT)—also known as talk therapy or counseling—can work wonders for people struggling with anxiety, depression and other forms of mental illness. Sometimes offered in conjunction with medications, CBT helps patients understand the issues at play and develop strategies for coping with them. "The most important thing is CBT. To me all forms of counseling and therapy are CBT," Gelbart says. While we might not be able to change the stressors that are leading to anxiety and depression, we can change how we respond to them, and CBT equips people with the tools to make those changes in how they react by offering them a safe place to "look at how you think and you recognize that how you think affects how you feel". He says if you want to change how you feel, you should examine how you're thinking and work to eliminate distortions of perception or incorrect information that could be causing you to feel bad. "That's the core of counseling and psychotherapy—to understand where your feelings come from and your ability to change that."

S. In addition to CBT, many patients find relief from mindfulness and meditation practices. By taking a step back and giving yourself room to think and breathe, you can teach yourself to relax and let go of some of the stress, tension, anxiety and depression that's plaguing you, Gelbart says.

T. The bottom line, he says, is that you "don't have to suffer silently". If you're dealing with a mental health concern, talk to someone—whether it's a specialized mental health provider, your primary care doctor or a school counselor. Ask for help getting connected with help when you're struggling.

Words and Expressions

bipolar disorder			a mental disorder characterized by episodes of mania and depression 躁郁症
post-traumatic	[ˌpəʊst-trɔːmæˈtɪk]	a.	after trauma 受到创伤后的
uninsured	[ˌʌnɪnˈʃʊəd]	a.	not covered by insurance 未投过保险的
clinician	[klɪˈnɪʃn]	n.	a practitioner (of medicine or psychology) who does clinical work 临床医生
epidemiological	[ˌepɪˌdiːmɪəˈlɒdʒɪkl]	a.	of or relating to epidemiology 流行病学的
schizophrenia	[ˌskɪtsəˈfriːnɪə]	n.	any of several psychotic disorders characterized by distortions of reality and disturbances of thought and language and withdrawal from social contact 精神分裂症
psychiatry	[saɪˈkaɪətri]	n.	the branch of medicine dealing with the diagnosis and treatment of mental disorders 精神病学

substance abuse			excessive use of drugs 滥用药品
autism	[ˈɔːtɪzəm]	n.	a severe mental disorder that makes someone unable to respond to other people 自闭症
hypothesis	[haɪˈpɒθəsɪs]	n.	(pl. hypotheses) a proposal intended to explain certain facts or observations 假设
pervasiveness	[pəˈveɪsɪvnəs]	n.	the quality of filling or spreading throughout 遍布；普遍蔓延
concurrent	[kənˈkʌrənt]	a.	occurring or operating at the same time 同时发生的；并存的
uptick	[ˈʌptɪk]	n.	a rise or increase 上升；增长
toxin	[ˈtɒksɪn]	n.	a poisonous substance produced by bacteria, animals, or plants 毒素
pediatric	[ˌpiːdɪˈætrɪk]	a.	of or relating to the medical care of children 儿科的
scope	[skəʊp]	n.	a range of matters being dealt with, studied; opportunity to do or achieve sth. 范围；机会
parity	[ˈpærəti]	n.	the state or quality of being equal 同等；平等
reimbursement	[ˌriːɪmˈbɜːsmənt]	n.	compensation paid (to someone) for damages or losses or money already spent 偿还；赔偿
longitudinal	[ˌlɒŋgɪˈtjuːdɪnl]	a.	going from one end of an object to the other rather than across it from side to side 纵向的
identification	[aɪˌdentɪfɪˈkeɪʃn]	n.	the act of designating or identifying sth. 鉴定，识别
intervention	[ˌɪntəˈvenʃn]	n.	the act of intervening (as to mediate a dispute) 干涉，干预
overwhelm	[ˌəʊvəˈwelm]	v.	defeat or make powerless 打败；压倒
distortion	[dɪˈstɔːʃn]	n.	the changing of something into something that is not true or not acceptable 扭曲；曲解
perception	[pəˈsepʃn]	n.	a way of seeing or understanding sth. 观念；看法
mindfulness	[ˈmaɪndfʊlnɪs]	n.	the trait of staying aware of your responsibilities 注意；留心
meditation	[ˌmedɪˈteɪʃn]	n.	deep thinking 冥想；沉思
plague	[pleɪg]	v.	annoy; cause trouble or difficult to sb./sth. 折磨；烦扰；造成麻烦

Exercises

- **Multiple Choice**

Select the most appropriate answer for each of the following questions.

1. The following are common mental health issues EXCEPT _____.
   A) anxiety   B) bipolar disorder
   C) suicide   D) depression

2. According to Moe Gelbart, bipolar disorder and schizophrenia _____.
   A) are the most prevalent mental health disorders
   B) are more pervasive than other mental health disorders
   C) are severer mental health issues
   D) trail behind, but are still fairly prevalent conditions

3. It's important to talk about mental health issues so that people _____.
   A) can receive treatment
   B) know what they are and how to access help
   C) know the most common forms of mental health problems are depression and anxiety
   D) know they are on a continuum from very little to very severe

4. Dr. David A. Axelson indicates that experts are very concerned about all of the following EXCEPT _____.
   A) the increased rates of anxiety
   B) the increased rates of death by suicide
   C) the increased rates of diagnosis of autism spectrum disorders
   D) the increased rates of depression

5. According to the passage, _____ may be the cause of the sharp increases in the rate of death by suicide for kids.
   A) the amount of exercise most kids are getting daily
   B) the quick rise and pervasiveness of social media
   C) an increase in environmental toxins
   D) all of the above

6. The information about mental illness can help researchers and doctors understand how the mental health of America is changing over time and _____.
   A) which illnesses are the most severe
   B) what is important for public health
   C) which issues need the most attention

D) how diseases move through and affect populations

7. When access to mental health services is increased, people do take advantage of that, but _____ remain a big problem.

   A) many adults going untreated

   B) that shortages of mental health workers

   C) physical health concerns

   D) that shortages of longitudinal data across the country

8. Maintaining a sense of humor and volunteering to help others in need are important to _____.

   A) help save lives and turn lives around

   B) push more people to go into the field of mental health

   C) help people cope with all mental issues

   D) promote physical and mental health

- **Matching**

Which paragraph contains the following information?

1. Moe Gelbart points out that the most prevalent mental health disorders are anxiety and then depression closely following it.

2. The rates of major depression were increasing among teenagers aged 12 to 17 by about 52% over the time period from 2009 to 2017.

3. Axelson says the mental health trends reflected in the data have been showing up in the emergency room.

4. According to the World Health Organization reports, more than 300 million people are affected by depression, making it the leading cause of disability worldwide.

5. We need to invest in early identification and intervention. We can't wait until people are in jail or homeless and disconnected from their family.

6. Gelbart holds that cognitive behavioral therapy can work wonders for people struggling with anxiety, depression and other forms of mental illness.

7. In addition to the cognitive behavioral therapy, many patients find relief from mindfulness and meditation practices.

8. If you're dealing with a mental health concern, you need at least to talk to someone.

- **Sentence Completion**

Complete the sentences below with words taken from Text A. Use NO MORE THAN THREE WORDS for each answer.

1. It is reported that 3.9% of adults aged 18 and older have experienced serious _____ _____ in the past 30 days.

2. Most Americans have no access to care. A severe shortage of mental health _____ _____ is adding to the problem.
3. Mary A. Fristad points out that another issue that takes a big toll is _____ and alcohol use disorders.
4. Determining what is causing the sharp increases in the rate of death by suicide for kids is _____.
5. Nationwide will open a new hospital _____ pediatric behavioral and mental health disorders in early 2020.
6. They wanted to see how _____ might improve access figures, and they needed hard data to tell the story.
7. We have to invest in the mental health workforce and find ways to make mental health care more affordable and _____ in underserved communities.
8. If you want to change how you feel, you should examine how you're thinking and work to _____ of perception that could be causing you to feel bad.

- Writing

Based on the above passage, write a minimum 200-word summary about mental health issues in America.

Text B

The Global Efforts to Boost Childhood Cancer Care

U. S. News & World Report traveled to four parts of the world to examine the barriers to treating children with cancer, and successful strategies that are offering pathways for hope.

By Kevin Drew and Steve Sternberg

September 5, 2019

U. S. News & World Report

Although pediatric cancers are rare, treatment increases five-year survival from 0% to more than 80%. Childhood cancer survivors have years of productive life ahead of them. Yet childhood cancer is not a top health priority in many countries, especially those with scarce resources and competing health problems. *U. S. News* correspondents journeyed to countries where health workers are defying these norms and saving thousands of young lives.

U. S. News staff reporter Gaby Galvin and photojournalist Jessica Pons traveled to

Yakima, Washington, where they spoke with farm workers and their children who are battling cancer, as well as with local health care workers reaching out to the families. They also traveled to Seattle, a leading center in the United States for cancer treatment, where people at Seattle Children's Hospital are helping migrant families navigate the U. S. health care system.

Hong Kong-based journalist Ting Shi reports from Shanghai, a locus of a new national effort in China to reverse years of neglect and provide care for kids with cancer based on new evidence that treats childhood cancer saves lives and is cost-effective. Shi also reports from Hong Kong, where a recently opened children's hospital is providing centralized care for kids with cancer and other afflictions. Photographer Yue Wu illustrated both stories.

Prue Clarke, a veteran journalist who for years has reported from across sub-Saharan Africa, files dispatches from both Liberia and Rwanda to show the scale of the challenge to improve cancer care in developing countries that have few resources, as well as the inspiring possibilities to dramatically improve treatment. Photojournalist Carielle Doe chronicled the cancer-care landscape in Liberia, while photographer Jacques Nkinzingabo illustrated the amazing work being done in Rwanda.

Beirut-based writer Abby Sewell reports from both Lebanon and Jordan on the efforts to treat young refugees who have fled war only to be faced with the challenge of battling cancer. Photojournalist Natalie Naccache illustrated the work being done in Lebanon and photographer Nadia Bseiso chronicled treatment efforts in Jordan.

The decision to undertake this project comes from new research that challenges long-held assumptions, work that has the potential to reshape policy and improve childhood cancer care.

For years, perhaps decades, medical experts, health care researchers and government policy-makers around the world have considered childhood cancer through the lens of a firmly held set of beliefs. Chief among those is the conviction that the number of children fighting cancer, tragic as it may be, is smaller than other illnesses striking youth. Health care experts have also believed that the burden cancer imposes on children is a fraction of what adults face.

Those beliefs were wrong.

The number of children suffering from cancer around the world—including in wealthy countries such as the United States—is far greater than previously believed. The research, carried out by Drs. Lisa Force, Nickhill Bhakta and Christina Fitzmaurice and published in *Lancet Oncology* in July, estimates that more than 400,000 new cases of children with cancer annually occur around the world, a figure roughly twice the amount of cases that are diagnosed.

Their research also quantifies for the first time the global scale of the burden cancer imposes on children, their families and even governments. They do so by calculating the number of years children lose because of ill health, disability or early death. That measure, called disability-adjusted life-years (DALYs), helps public health care experts assess the health of countries' populations and in turn develop strategies to treat patients.

Force and Bhakta, who work at St. Jude Children's Research Hospital in Memphis, Tennessee, and Fitzmaurice, who works at the University of Washington's Institute for Health Metrics and Evaluation in Seattle, estimate that childhood cancer resulted in 11.5 million DALYs around the world in 2017, ranking second among all cancers, after those of the lung and respiratory tract, and fifth among other childhood diseases.

But they also say that figure is likely an underestimation because of a variety of factors, such as a lack of data and the use of diagnosis techniques that work well for adults but not for children.

Their research also shows that the burden of cancer disproportionately affects people in poor- and middle-income countries, where resources to treat the disease are scarce. This information is especially powerful in those settings, Bhakta says. "Though it pains me as a physician to think in these terms, you have to choose which interventions are going to carry the biggest bang for the buck."

Health care officials in China found the evidence so compelling that it launched a national childhood cancer program from scratch. "China is an incredible success story," Bhakta says. "You're talking about thousands of children who are getting treatment who didn't before."

These efforts are the latest expression of an international movement to improve childhood cancer treatment in all countries, especially in the developing world where local resources and knowledge are inadequate for the challenge. Individuals, organizations, institutions and governments are increasingly working together to establish global networks to improve diagnosis and care.

U.S. News' reporting shows both similar and unique challenges as health care communities in countries tackle improving childhood cancer treatment. In the United States, China, Africa and the Middle East, many families lack basic literacy about cancer: what it is, its deadly threat and how to recognize it.

Just reaching treatment poses immense challenges. In Lebanon, for example, refugee families must pass through a gauntlet of checkpoints to travel from their assigned camps to clinics and hospitals in the country's cities. In China, families living in rural provinces know that the best cancer care is available in a very few cities, such as Beijing, Shanghai and Guangzhou—and that it will cost them much more to be treated there.

In the Yakima Valley, rural parents face painful choices if their children are sick. For some, deciding to seek medical help can carry the risk of deportation, given the current political climate in the U.S. over undocumented workers. Once their child is diagnosed with cancer, farm worker parents must decide whether to give up badly needed cash earned from working in the agricultural fields to travel to Seattle for the best care, and even risk losing their job.

Paying for cancer treatment is a major hurdle in all countries. As Prue Clarke reports, "In Africa, where few people have access to affordable health care, children with cancer face a terrifying lottery, where survival depends on luck: either you find a doctor and someone able to pay for treatment, or you die."

Maintaining follow-up care is also a challenge. Migrant workers in the US must move from state to state to find work, a life that makes maintaining regular treatments for their children extremely difficult.

Yet progress is being made. In Rwanda, government officials are working with local health care workers and visiting international experts to develop a health care system that is being seen as a regional model that can offer a possible blueprint for poor, developing countries. In Lebanon and Jordan, local doctors, international organizations and civil society are working together to reach and treat young refugees, an approach that may work for others living near conflict zones.

In China, years of work to improve a database of children with cancer is paying off, increasing the number of young patients diagnosed and treated. And in Washington's Yakima Valley, local care organizations and clinics are working with cancer treatment centers in Seattle and elsewhere to provide care.

The common theme for successfully treating childhood cancer is collaboration at the local, regional and international level. As Dr. Douglas Lowy, acting director of the US National Cancer Institute, writes for *U.S. News*, collaboration with national and international partners is key to improving population-based cancer registries, particularly in low- and middle-income countries.

And as Dr. Carlos Rodriguez-Galindo writes in a commentary for *U.S. News*, that collaboration is taking place on an international scale with new urgency. Rodriguez-Galindo is executive vice president and chair of St. Jude's Department of Global Pediatric Medicine, as well as director of St. Jude Global. In December 2018 more than 160 people from 52 countries met in Memphis to form the St. Jude Global Alliance, an international collaboration intended to improve health care around the world.

"With our global partners, bringing quality care and cures to children with cancer everywhere in the world is now possible," Rodriguez-Galindo tells *U. S. News*. "We realize this won't happen overnight; it's a long process that will require the best of us."

 Words and Expressions

correspondent	[ˌkɒrəˈspɒndənt]	n.	a person who contributes news or comments regularly to a newspaper, radio station 通讯记者
defy	[dɪˈfaɪ]	v.	resist or confront with resistance 公然反抗；违抗
norm	[nɔːm]	n.	a standard or model or pattern regarded as typical 规范；标准
navigate	[ˈnævɪgeɪt]	v.	cope with 成功应对
locus	[ˈləʊkəs]	n.	a position or place, esp. where something happens or can be found 地点，所在地
reverse	[rɪˈvɜːs]	v.	change to the contrary 改变；逆转
affliction	[əˈflɪkʃn]	n.	(something that causes) suffering or unhappiness 痛苦；疾患；苦恼
veteran	[ˈvetərən]	a.	rendered competent through trial and experience 经验丰富的，资深的
file	[faɪl]	v.	place in a file; place on record 把……归档
dispatch	[dɪˈspætʃ]	n.	an official report (usually sent in haste)(由身在外地的记者发给报纸的)新闻报道
chronicle	[ˈkrɒnɪkl]	n.	a record or narrative description of past events 编年史；记录
		v.	record in chronological order; make a historical record 记录；把……载入编年史
assumption	[əˈsʌmpʃn]	n.	sth. that is taken as a fact or believed to be true without proof 假定；设想
a fraction of			a very small piece or amount 小部分；少量
quantify	[ˈkwɒntɪfaɪ]	v.	express or measure the quantity of 量化；确定数量
respiratory tract			the passages through which air enters and leaves the body 呼吸道
disproportionately	[ˌdɪsprəˈpɔːʃənətli]	adv.	out of proportion 不成比例地

gauntlet	[ˈɡɔːntlət]	n.	accepting a challenge; a harsh test 挑战;严酷考验
deportation	[ˌdiːpɔːˈteɪʃn]	n.	the act of expelling a person from their native land 驱逐出境
undocumented	[ˌɪnˈdɒkjumentɪd]	a.	lacking necessary documents (as for permission to live or work in a country) 无事实证明的;无正式文件的
pay off			get success or profit after a period of time 取得成功;带来好结果
registry	[ˈredʒɪstri]	n.	an official written record of names or events or transactions 注册;记录

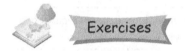

Exercises

- **True / False / Not Given**

Do the following statements agree with the information given in Text B?

In Blanks 1-10 write

True   if the statement is true

False   if the statement is false

Not Given   if the information is not given in Text B

_____ 1. Childhood cancer is a top health priority in many countries.

_____ 2. Seattle Children's Hospital is the only center in the United States for cancer treatment.

_____ 3. A recently opened children's hospital in Hong Kong is providing centralized care for kids with cancer.

_____ 4. Health care experts have believed for years that the burden cancer imposes on children is a fraction of what adults face.

_____ 5. The number of children suffering from cancer around the world is far greater than previously believed.

_____ 6. Force, Bhakta and Fitzmaurice estimate that childhood cancer resulted in 11.5 million DALYs around the world in 2017, ranking second among all childhood diseases.

_____ 7. The vast majority of people in Africa lack basic literacy about cancer.

_____ 8. Paying for cancer treatment is a major hurdle in all countries.

- **Matching**

Match the following information as referring to.

A. Prue Clarke

B. Drs. Lisa Force, Nickhill Bhakta and Christina Fitzmaurice

C. Abby Sewell

D. Douglas Lowy

E. Carlos Rodriguez-Galindo

1. Their research shows that the burden of cancer disproportionately affects people in poor- and middle-income countries.
2. She files dispatches from both Liberia and Rwanda to show the scale of the challenge to improve cancer care in developing countries.
3. Collaboration with national and international partners is key to improving population-based cancer registries.
4. She reports from both Lebanon and Jordan on the efforts to treat young refugees who have fled war only to be faced with the challenge of battling cancer.
5. With our global partners, bringing quality care and cures to children with cancer everywhere in the world is now possible.
6. They do so by calculating the number of years children lose because of ill health, disability or early death.
7. Collaboration is taking place on an international scale with new urgency.
8. Their research quantifies for the first time the global scale of the burden cancer imposes on children, their families and even governments.

- **Short Answer Questions**

1. What did Gaby Galvin and Jessica Pons do when they traveled to Yakima, Washington?
2. How many new cases of children with cancer annually occur around the world based on the research of Drs. Lisa Force, Nickhill Bhakta and Christina Fitzmaurice?
3. What is the measure DALYs used for?
4. Why do children with cancer face a terrifying lottery in Africa according to Prue Clarke's reports?
5. What is achieved in China after years of work to improve a database of children with cancer?

- **Writing**

What do you think is the most urgent childhood issue which needs global efforts to cope with in addition to the childhood cancer issue? Write a composition of no less than 300 words to state your opinions.

Academic Reading

Distinguishing Between Facts and Opinions

Learning Objective

In the section, you will learn to distinguish between facts and opinions.

What Is a Fact?

A fact is something that can be proved true through objective evidence. Facts are accurate, verified, or confirmed in an unbiased manner. As you know, unbiased means "evenhanded", "objective", "impartial" or "without prejudice". You can prove, verify, or confirm a fact by personal observation, by using the observations of others or by checking with reliable sources—such as studies that have been conducted, reputable books that have been written, or noted experts in a given field.

Personal observation simply involves checking something for ourselves, such as going to a person's home to verify that the person lives there. However, for practical reasons, we sometimes have to rely on the observations of others who serve as witnesses when we are unable to be there ourselves. For information about an event that occurred in the past or one that is happening in a far-off place that we cannot get to—such as the taking down of the Berlin Wall in Germany—we must rely on the eyewitness accounts of others. Finally, sometimes we must rely on written materials or other people who have more expertise than we do in a particular subject to determine if something is indeed factual. For instance, most people would rely on what they have read in medical literature, including the results of studies conducted by prominent physicians, to conclude a statement dealing with heart disease is factually accurate.

One of the keys to uncovering facts, then, is our determination that they have been or can be proved in an unbiased way. In other words, we have to be reasonably certain that the observations, experts, and any additional sources that we use or that are presented to us by others are as evenhanded as possible and not clouded by personal opinion.

Also, keep in mind that facts can change over time as conditions change, resulting in the elimination of some facts and the addition of others. For example, it was once a fact that there were 48 states in the United States, but that was no longer a fact after the addition of the states of Alaska and Hawaii in 1959, thereby bringing the total to 50. Thus, one fact was replaced by another. In short, determining whether something is a fact is an ongoing process that involves careful evaluation and continuous reevaluation, both of which are important characteristics of critical thinking.

What Is an Opinion?

An opinion is something that cannot be objectively proven and is subjective in nature. Opinions are beliefs, personal judgments, or viewpoints about something that has not been proved, verified, or confirmed in an unbiased manner. Many times opinions are easy to detect by certain clue words or value words that emphasize a value, judgment, or tone that the individual has about the subject. Emotive words such as great, relaxing, or improving express a feeling about a subject. The words strict, liberal, or informational express a value judgment. Words that express a certain tone about a subject could be nostalgic, angry, or humorous. In obvious cases, words such as good, bad, right, or wrong are often used with opinions. However, sometimes people are more subtle when offering their opinions, which makes their opinions more difficult to recognize. For example, the statements "He was a bad president" and "He, as president, left something to be desired" both express negative opinions, but the first is stronger and more obvious than the second. They are both opinions, or subjective statements.

Also, be on the lookout for opinions that are couched in factual terms, such as "The fact of the matter is that smoking is wrong!" Just because the word fact is used does not make the statement a fact.

Finally, opinions can sometimes turn into facts after they have been proved, verified, or confirmed in an unbiased manner. For instance, a week before your birthday, you can claim that it is going to rain on that day, which is your opinion. However, if it does rain on that day, your original claim has become a fact, which can now be proved. Thus, opinions like facts, can change over time and should therefore be reevaluated.

Distinguishing Between Facts and Opinions

Read the list of ten statements below; place an O next to the statements that you think are opinions and an F next to those that you think are facts.

1. Washington, D. C., which is the capital of the United States, is a beautiful city.
2. World War II was the last major war to be fought in the twentieth century.
3. The winters in Canada are really horrible because they are usually very cold.
4. Ronald Reagan, who was the fortieth president of the United States, was a wonderful leader.
5. The Berlin Wall, which separated East from West Berlin, has been taken down.
6. There are 50 states in the United States, and it is a widely accepted fact that Puerto Rico will become the fifty-first.

7. Experts tell us that the Mercedes-Benz is the best automobile on the market today.
8. Carbon monoxide is a poisonous gas that can be extremely deadly.
9. The United States is the most powerful country in the world.
10. Heart disease, which strikes people of all ages, can be caused by high blood pressure, smoking, and lack of exercise.

Now let's examine the responses:

Statement 1 combines both fact and opinion because Washington is the capital of the United States, but whether it is a beautiful city is a matter of opinion. Certainly, some people would agree that it is beautiful while others may not. It could depend on both the definition of the word beautiful and the other cities to which Washington is being compared.

Statement 2 is an opinion because it could be argued convincingly that there have been other major wars fought since World War II, including the one in Vietnam, which caused the loss of many American and Vietnamese lives. Furthermore, it really depends on one's definition of the word major. For example, does it mean many casualties, number of countries involved, or something else?

Statement 3 is a combination of fact and opinion because, although it is true that the winters in Canada are usually very cold, some people would argue that cold does not necessarily make them horrible. For instance, many Canadians like cold weather because it enables them to earn a living or do things that they enjoy doing, such as skiing, skating, and playing hockey. It is a fact that Ronald Reagan was the fortieth President of the United States, but not everyone is of the opinion that he was a wonderful leader. Thus, Statement 4 is also a combination of a fact and an opinion.

Statements 5, 8, and 10 are all facts that can be supported by checking various sources. They can be proved and are generally accepted by everyone.

Statement 6 is a combination of a fact and an opinion. Whereas the first part of the statement is obviously a fact, the second part is an opinion because it is a prediction and a matter of conjecture that Puerto Rico will become the fifty-first state. Also, the use of the word fact in the sentence does not necessarily prove that the information is indeed factual.

Statement 7 is an opinion for two reasons: First, the "experts" are not identified, so we do not know if they are reliable, and second, no data is presented that would indicate how the word best is being used in the sentence. For example, does it refer to economical gas mileage, reliability, extensive safety equipment, exceptional good looks, or all of those pluses taken together?

Finally, Statement 9 is also an opinion because the meaning of the word powerful as used in the sentence is not clear. If it refers to military power, a strong case can be made for the accuracy of the statement, although some people would argue that as long as other countries possess nuclear weapons, no single country, including the United States, is all-powerful. By contrast, if it refers to economic power, more people might argue that the United States is indeed not the most powerful country in the world.

As you can see, it is sometimes not simple to distinguish between opinions and facts, yet if you think and read critically, you will be able to separate fact from opinion as part of evaluating what you see, hear, and read. In other words, you should not automatically accept information without first considering its accuracy, its source, and the motivations of whoever is presenting it. Otherwise, you are in danger of accepting opinions as facts, and that could have a negative effect on the decisions you make in life. For example, you could end up taking the wrong course, choosing the wrong solution to a problem, accepting the wrong version of a story, buying the wrong product, dating the wrong person, or voting for the wrong candidate. Thus, the cost of confusing facts and opinions can be quite substantial.

Facts and Opinions in Combination

As you just saw, facts and opinions are often used in combination, which makes it more difficult to distinguish between them. Sometimes this is done inadvertently when we are trying to express ourselves orally or in writing, but it can also be an intentional device to influence or persuade others. Commercials that influence our decisions as to what to purchase or whom to vote for and propaganda that attempts to persuade people to think in a certain way or support a certain course of action come to mind as examples of how this technique can be used effectively.

For instance, a political commercial that states "Inflation is rising dramatically. But don't worry—our candidate has the answer! Remember that when you vote next Tuesday!" is probably a combination of fact and opinion. A rising inflation rate can be proved by published statistics, but whether or not the candidate has the answer to the problem is not so simple to prove, at least not at this time. Of course, the whole purpose of the commercial is to get you to vote for that candidate. If indeed the official does eventually solve the inflation problem after the election, the latter part of the original commercial has become a fact. Remember, if you can identify a clue or value word that emphasizes a judgment about a subject, it is probably an opinion or partially an opinion. Once again, you must carefully evaluate and continuously reevaluate what you see, hear, and read.

Part 3　Learning After Class

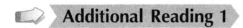 **Additional Reading 1**

Healing Hands

August 19 marks World Humanitarian Day and also Medical Workers' Day in China. CGTN looks at China's medical teams who have been providing humanitarian assistance for other developing countries since 1963.

August 19, 2019

CGTN

South Sudan is the world's youngest nation. Merely eight years old, it lacks certain basic necessities. Poor medical services, inadequate water supply and power cuts are commonplace.

In May 2017, Dr. Zhu Xingguo became the head of the fifth Chinese medical team to South Sudan. He was in charge of a 15-member team assigned to work with South Sudanese medical workers at the Juba Teaching Hospital, the only referral hospital in the entire country. One of the team's tasks was to help lift the medical standards at the facility, but what Zhu encountered surprised him.

"The medical condition was worse than we had imagined," Zhu said. "The wards were dirty and messy with flies everywhere. Many patients suffered from wound infections."

The situation was so bad that sometimes doctors would reject patients for fear of spreading further infections into the hospital. This was the case with a young woman, whose first name is Assia. "She had a parotid tumor and visited the hospital several times before, but no one dared to give her any treatment," Zhu told CGTN.

Zhu decided to operate on Assia as soon as possible. But the quality of local medical services meant greater uncertainties during the operation, and the surgery itself proved to be far more complicated than estimated.

"If her facial nerve was damaged, she might have ended up with facial paralysis," Zhu said. "I was under huge pressure at the time." Zhu even consulted specialists in China for their advice. Fortunately, the operation was successful, and the patient

Unit 8 Health

recovered perfectly afterward.

"It was such a huge relief for me," Zhu said. "I feel happy, and I don't know what I can do to thank the doctor," Assia said. Assia was lucky. For many of her South Sudanese peers, timely access to medical treatment and recovery remains a faraway dream.

A history of sending medical teams

Africa is the second-largest and second most populated continent on earth. It had an estimated population of 1.2 billion people in 2016. By the end of the century, it will host 4 billion people, more than one-third of the global population.

The World Health Organization's (WHO) African Regional Health Report 2014 found that 19 of the 20 countries with the highest maternal mortality ratios worldwide were in Africa. The African region had some of the highest neonatal death rates in the world, the WHO report said. It also found that noncommunicable diseases, such as hypertension, heart disease and diabetes were on the rise, and injuries remained among the top causes of death in the region. The report also offered ways to address the health challenges over time, given sufficient international support.

China is one of the countries that has stepped forward to lend humanitarian support to countries in the African region. Its history of sending medical teams overseas dates back to the early 1960s. China sent its very first medical team to Algeria in April 1963 at the invitation of the Algerian government.

According to the National Health Commission, as of July 2018, China has dispatched 26,000 medical staff to 71 countries and helped 280 million patients in Asia, Africa, Latin America, Europe and Australasia.

"In the past, the medical aid China offered to other developing countries came mainly in the form of clinical service," said Feng Yong, deputy director of the International Cooperation Department under the National Health Commission. "Now, it has reached a higher level, combining both clinical and public health services, with a focus on improving their healthcare capabilities."

Skills sharing efforts

Besides sending medical teams, China also offers training programs for medical personnel from other developing countries, especially from Africa. For instance, the Chinese government has committed to strengthening health cooperation between China and Africa under the framework of the Forum on China-Africa Cooperation (FOCAC).

One example is a cardiovascular program that was jointly launched by China and Ghana in 2014, under which 13 Ghanaian medical staff received training in southern

China's Guangdong Province, enabling Ghana to build its own team of cardiologists upon their return home. Chinese medical staff also conducted 30 cardiovascular surgeries free of charge in Ghana and helped carry out the country's first epidemiological survey on heart health among local residents, which provided critical information that would inform the government's decision-making.

The United Nations 2030 Agenda for Sustainable Development focuses on "ensuring healthy lives and promoting well-being for all at all ages" because healthy people are the basis for a country to improve its comprehensive national strengths and sustainable development abilities.

More importantly, nothing would stop China's endeavors in lending a helping hand to countries in need, as the country bears one vision in mind: building a community with a shared future for humanity.

"As a healthcare worker, it is my duty to save lives. We hope more healthcare workers would join us so that we could beat diseases together," Zhu told CGTN.

Words and Expressions

referral	[rɪˈfɜːrəl]	n.	the act of referring (as forwarding an applicant for employment or referring a matter to an appropriate agency) 转诊; 转交
infection	[ɪnˈfekʃn]	n.	the act or progress of causing or getting a disease; disease caused by a micro-organism 传染; 传染病
parotid	[pəˈrɒtɪd]	a.	relating to or located near the parotid gland 腮腺的
paralysis	[pəˈræləsɪs]	n.	loss of the ability to move a body part 瘫痪; 麻痹
mortality ratio			死亡率
neonatal	[ˌniːəʊˈneɪtl]	a.	relating to or affecting the infant during the first month after birth 新生(儿)的
noncommunicable	[ˈnɒnkəˈmjuːnɪkəbl]	a.	(of disease) not capable of being passed on 不会传染的
diabetes	[ˌdaɪəˈbiːtiːz]	n.	any of several metabolic disorders marked by excessive urination and persistent thirst 糖尿病
cardiovascular	[ˌkɑːdɪəʊˈvæskjələ]	a.	involving the heart and blood vessels 心脏血管的

cardiologist	[ˌkɑːdɪˈɒlədʒɪst]	n.	a specialist in the structure and function and disorders of the heart 心脏病学家
epidemiological	[ˌepɪˌdiːmɪəˈlɒdʒɪkl]	a.	relating to epidemiology 流行病学的

Discussion Questions

1. What medical aids have been offered by China to other developing countries since the early 1960s according to the passage?
2. China remains a developing country with a low per-capita income and a large poverty-stricken population. In spite of this, China has provided a significant amount of humanitarian aid to developing countries. What do you think about China's humanitarian aid to developing countries?

Additional Reading 2

How Job Stress Can Age Us

By Dhruv Khullar, M. D.①
July 25, 2019
The New York Times

I noticed my first gray hair during my medical residency. It sneaked up on me at the end of a long, frenzied shift—one of those nights when Murphy's Law seems stronger than the law of gravity. Two of my patients did slip and fall, though, so Newton made a strong showing too.

The next day, I found another gray. Then another and another, until I stopped counting. I was in my mid-20s, and it was the first time I'd noticed my body aging—not getting stronger or faster or wiser, but starting its decline. The human body performs so many impressive functions, I thought: It heals wounds, clears waste, digests Doritos. Can't it find a little pigment to keep my hair colored?

This month, a new cohort of medical school graduates began their residencies. It's no secret that medical training is an intense, sometimes grueling, process. But a new study,

---

① Dhruv Khullar, M. D. is a physician and assistant professor of health care policy at Weill Cornell Medicine, and director of policy dissemination at the Physicians Foundation Center for Physician Practice and Leadership.

one of the first of its kind, shows how long hours, disrupted sleep and constant stress can take a biological toll on newly minted doctors.

Researchers at the University of Michigan tested the DNA of 250 first-year medical residents around the country. They took samples of their saliva to examine the length of their telomeres—the protective caps at the ends of chromosomes that prevent DNA damage—before and after the first year of residency.

Telomeres shorten every time our cells replicate, acting as a kind of fuse at the end of DNA. Once they become too short, cells know that it's time to retire or self-destruct. Telomere attrition also plays a role in the aging process and is linked to many age-related diseases, including diabetes, cancer and heart disease.

Researchers found that the DNA of first-year residents aged six times faster than normal. Telomeres usually shrink at a rate of about 25 DNA base-pairs per year, but first-year medical residents experienced a decline of more than 140 base-pairs on average. Residents who worked longer shifts or more hours over all were at even higher risk: Telomere shrinkage increased steadily with the number of hours worked, but skyrocketed for those working more than 75 hours per week to over 700 base-pairs.

"Most prior research on residency well-being has used self-reported questionnaires," said Dr. Srijan Sen, the study's senior author and an associate professor of psychiatry at the University of Michigan. "We hope that showing measurable physiological effects at the cellular level will help catalyze residency reforms that really move the needle."

How long and how hard trainees should work is a subject of perennial debate in medicine. But it has new urgency amid growing recognition of widespread anxiety, depression and burnout among medical trainees and physicians.

This study comes on the heels of other research showing that doctors in training lose three to seven hours of sleep per week and are much less physically active compared to their pre-residency lives. For some, a vicious cycle emerges: short sleep leads to worse mood the next day, which in turn makes it harder to sleep at night, culminating in a chronic depressive state.

The solution is not simply to reduce work hours—though avoiding extremely long workweeks would help. Becoming a doctor requires intense, repeated, constant immersion, such that diagnosis and treatment enter a kind of muscle memory. Most residents, some of whom are approaching 40 when they finish training, would probably balk at an offer to trade shorter hours for more years of training—even if it does cost them a little telomere.

But there are opportunities to improve well-being in medical training—many of which are commonplace in other industries. Consider something as basic as healthy food, which can be surprisingly scarce for doctors working evening or weekend shifts in the hospital. While the 20-somethings at Google and Facebook enjoy sparkling water and organic vegetables, most medical residents scrounge for greasy pizza, leftover Thai food and sugary soda—something close to the opposite of what they recommend for their patients.

It also matters how residents work all those hours. Training programs should reduce the number of day-to-night transitions residents have to make, as these can lead to circadian rhythm disruptions and mood problems. All residencies incorporate lectures and educational conferences, but doctors in training are often too busy juggling pagers, paperwork or other demands to attend. Ensuring residents can actually participate in these educational activities would create a sense that learning is a real priority. And having more flexibility and autonomy over one's work schedule is critical. Long hours are tough, but having to miss a close friend's wedding is what really hurts.

Finally, structured wellness programs are emerging. Stanford's Balance in Life program, started in 2011 after the suicide of a surgical residency graduate, provides trainees with a comprehensive set of resources to support professional and personal well-being. A mentorship program allows junior residents to meet regularly with senior trainees and faculty members to discuss their concerns and goals.

Every six weeks, residents also meet with a clinical psychologist to share challenging experiences and discuss personal issues. While on call, they have access to a dedicated refrigerator stocked with healthful snacks and beverages. And all residents are encouraged to have regular checkups with their own doctor and dentist—ironically, an elusive luxury during medical training.

Medical training is—and needs to be—intense. Developing the skills and intuition needed to care for patients independently requires a certain exhaustive immersion. But too often our current system strains, instead of supports, trainees along their journey. That's not good for doctors or for patients.

Words and Expressions

residency	[ˈrezɪdənsi]	n.	the period of specialized training in a hospital 住院医生实习期
sneak up			advance stealthily or unnoticed 悄悄地靠近
frenzied	[ˈfrenzid]	a.	wild, excited and uncontrolled 疯狂的

pigment	[ˈpɪgmənt]	n.	a substance that gives something a particular colour 颜料；色素
cohort	[ˈkəʊhɔːt]	n.	any group of people who share some common quality, esp. those of the same age 一群人；同龄人
grueling	[ˈgruːəlɪŋ]	a.	characterized by toilsome effort to the point of exhaustion, especially physical effort 使人筋疲力尽的
minted	[ˈmɪntɪd]	a.	new; newly produced or completed 新的；刚完成的；刚制作的
saliva	[səˈlaɪvə]	n.	the watery liquid that forms in your mouth and helps you to chew and digest food 唾液
telomere	[ˈteləmɪə]	n.	either of the ends of a chromosome 染色体终端；端粒
chromosome	[ˈkrʊɪməsəʊm]	n.	a threadlike body in the cell nucleus that carries the genes in a linear order 染色体
replicate	[ˈreplɪkeɪt]	v.	do or make again so as to get the same result or make an exact copy 复制；重复
attrition	[əˈtrɪʃn]	n.	a wearing down to weaken or destroy 消耗；削弱
skyrocket	[ˈskaɪrɒkɪt]	v.	suddenly increase by a very large amount 飞涨，猛涨
physiological	[ˌfɪziəˈlɒdʒɪkl]	a.	of or concerning the bodily functions 生理的
catalyze	[ˈkætəlaɪz]	v.	change by catalysis; stimulate; promote 催化；刺激，促进
perennial	[pəˈreniəl]	a.	lasting forever or for a long time 反复的；持久不断的
on the heels of			紧随……之后；接踵而来
vicious	[ˈvɪʃəs]	a.	deliberately harmful 恶性的；恶意的
culminate (in)	[ˈkʌlmɪneɪt]	v.	reach the highest point, degree or stage of development in; end in 达到顶点；以……告终
chronic	[ˈkrɒnɪk]	a.	being long-lasting 长期的
depressive	[dɪˈpresɪv]	a.	causing or suggestive of sorrow or gloom 抑郁的；压抑的
immersion	[ɪˈmɜːʃn]	n.	complete attention; intense mental effort 专心；潜心钻研

balk	[bɔːk]	v.	refuse to comply 退缩；拒绝
scrounge	[skraʊndʒ]	v.	collect or look around for (food) 四处搜寻；索要
circadian	[sɜːˈkeɪdiən]	a.	of or relating to biological processes occurring at 24-hour intervals 昼夜节律的；生理节奏的
autonomy	[ɔːˈtɒnəmi]	n.	the ability to act and make decisions without being controlled by anyone else 自主；自主权
clinical	[ˈklɪnɪkl]	a.	involving or relating to the direct medical treatment or testing of patients 临床的
psychologist	[ˌsaɪˈkɒlədʒɪst]	n.	a person who studies the human mind and tries to explain why people behave in the way that they do 心理学家
elusive	[ɪˈluːsɪv]	a.	difficult to find, describe, remember, or achieve 难找的；难以描述的；难以记起的；难以达到的

 Discussion Questions

1. Doctors have to be subjected to long working hours, disrupted sleep, constant stress and even anxiety, depression and burnout. Now more than ever, doctors have to gear up for many challenges. What do you think is the greatest challenge doctors have to face up to?
2. Doctors' lack of communication with patients can often cause frustration and confusion for patients. Meanwhile, patients have greater expectations for service from doctors and are increasingly demanding. What do you think are good solutions to improve communication and avoid malpractice lawsuits?

 # Additional Reading 3

Food Insecurity in America Tied to Prices, Poverty

By Gaby Galvin

May 1, 2019

U. S. News & World Report

  Highfood prices have contributed to a stubborn food-insecurity rate across the more than 3,100 counties in the US during the last decade, a new report shows. But exactly who is at risk of going hungry varies across the country.

"If we want to look at the health and well-being of America, one of the best ways to look at it is through food insecurity," says Craig Gundersen, lead researcher for hunger relief organization Feeding America's Map the Meal Gap project, which explores hunger and related trends in local communities.

According to the US Department of Agriculture, some 40 million people in the US were food-insecure in 2017, meaning they lacked consistent access to enough food for an active and healthy life. And although the national food-insecurity rate among individuals fell between 2016 and 2017—from 12.9% to 12.5%—it remained above what it was before the Great Recession that began in 2007.

The latest annual Map the Meal Gap report, published Wednesday, shows the food-insecurity rate across US counties was a similar 13.3% in 2017, down from 13.7% the year before. Rates ranged from a top mark of nearly 36% in Jefferson County, Mississippi, to just 3% in North Dakota's Steele County, yet researchers say no place is immune from the problem.

"Although we see pockets of high need across the country, like areas in the South and in rural parts of the country, the fact remains that individuals and families are at risk of hunger in every community," says Adam Dewey, a researcher with Feeding America.

For example, in Los Angeles County, an estimated 11% of people were food-insecure in 2017, but that amounts to roughly 1.1 million people, including more than 410,000 children, according to the report. Yet even communities with relatively few people in need—such as Schleicher County, Texas, where an estimated 260 people were food-insecure—can benefit from a more targeted focus on reducing hunger, researchers say.

The implications for health

Food insecurity has serious implications for health, the report notes. Among the 10% of counties with the highest estimated rates of food insecurity in 2017, 1 in 8 residents had diabetes, 1 in 3 were obese and 1 in 5 had some form of disability.

A separate analysis from the Centers for Disease Control and Prevention indicates that on average, food insecurity added about 11% to the health care costs of older adults in recent years—whether they had a chronic health condition or not.

"Food insecurity is a national health care crisis," says Gundersen, also a professor of agricultural and consumer economics at the University of Illinois at Urbana-Champaign.

Food-insecurity rates also are tied to higher unemployment and poverty: In 2017, two-thirds of counties with the highest food insecurity rates experienced "persistent poverty", where at least 20% of the population had lived in poverty for more than 30 years, the Feeding America research shows.

But the tie between health and food insecurity may be even closer than the link between health and income, homeownership or other financial challenges, Gundersen says, "Economic hardship is closely related to food insecurity, but they are not one and the same."

Many who need help don't qualify for it

Roughly 60% of low-income households are food-secure, he says. Yet 29% of individuals estimated to be food-insecure likely do not qualify for federal aid through initiatives such as the Women, Infants and Children program or the Supplemental Nutrition Assistance Program.

Households that earn too much to qualify for SNAP can find themselves caught in a hunger gap, especially if they live in more expensive areas. Nationally, the average cost of a meal was $3.02 in 2017, for example, but counties in the Northeast saw an average meal cost of $3.32, while those in the West saw an average meal cost of $3.27, according to the report.

"Most counties with the highest meal costs (56%) are part of populous metropolitan areas," the report says. "While these urban counties with high meal costs tend to have lower rates of food insecurity, they are home to large numbers of people who are food insecure."

Adjusting for inflation, researchers estimated that the annual food budget shortfall for the nation's 40 million food insecure families reached nearly $21 billion in 2017.

SNAP addresses the problem

Expanding SNAP benefits to more people and addressing barriers to accessing the program—such as complex application and recertification processes—are key to reducing food insecurity in the US, Gundersen says. Those measures could be particularly important for food-insecure families living in wealthier areas because they also may not know they're eligible or face stigma for relying on federal aid.

"SNAP gives these low-income individuals the ability to go to food stores, purchase food that's correct for their families, and then engage in the civic culture of being able to shop at these stores alongside everybody else," Gundersen says.

Health care organizations also can leverage their partnerships with local food banks and other community groups to target food insecurity, Dewey says. Local food banks have hosted SNAP nutrition education programs to address diabetes and other health issues, while primary care providers can screen patients for food insecurity and refer them to Feeding America's services.

"There is need every county, and we're striving to meet that need in every community," Dewey says. "SNAP is hugely important and the first line of defense against hunger, while connecting people to healthier foods and different resources is a huge component of addressing this through our partnerships."

 Words and Expressions

contribute to			conduce to; result in 促成;导致
consistent	[kən'sɪstənt]	a.	always keeping to the same pattern or style; unchanging 持续的;一致的
immune	[ɪ'mju:n]	a.	not affected by a given influence 不受影响的
roughly	['rʌfli]	adv.	imprecisely but fairly close to correct; approximately 大约;粗略地
target	['tɑ:gɪt]	v.	intend (something) to move towards a certain goal 把……作为目标;针对
implication	[ˌɪmplɪ'keɪʃn]	n.	a possible later effect of an action, decision, etc. (行动、决定等可能产生的)影响
initiative	[ɪ'nɪʃətɪv]	n.	the first movement or action which starts sth. happening 倡议
metropolitan	[ˌmetrə'pɒlɪtən]	a.	belonging to a large, busy city 大都市的
recertification	['ri:sɜ:tɪfɪ'keɪʃn]	n.	重新认证;换发新证
eligible	['elɪdʒəbl]	a.	qualified for or allowed or worthy of being chosen 符合条件的;有资格当选的
stigma	['stɪgmə]	n.	a symbol of disgrace 耻辱;污名
leverage	['li:vərɪdʒ]	v.	exert influence on 对……施加影响
strive	[straɪv]	v.	make a great effort to gain sth. 努力;力求

 Discussion Questions

1. In 2017, an estimated 1 in 8 Americans were food insecure, equating to 40 million Americans including more than 12 million children. What is food insecurity according to the US Department of Agriculture?

2. The causes of food insecurity may include poverty, war and civil conflict, environmental degradation, barriers to trade, insufficient agricultural development, population growth,

poor health status, and natural disasters. What are the causes of food insecurity in America according to the passage?

3. What measures have been taken to reduce food insecurity in America?

Part 4　Topical Vocabulary

stress-related disease 和压力有关的疾病
improve blood circulation 改进血液循环
increase flexibility 提高灵活性
cross infection 交叉感染
symptom 症状
out-patient department 门诊部
general hospital 综合医院
medical aid fund 医疗救助基金
psychological obstacle; mental obstacle 心理障碍
anti-aging 抗衰老
genetic engineering 基因工程
Intensive Care Unit (ICU) 重症监护室
suspected case 疑似病例
coughing fit 咳嗽发作
euthanasia / mercy killing 安乐死
genetically modified food 转基因食品
four properties of medicinal herb 中药四性
heart failure 心力衰竭
(Chinese) cupping therapy 拔火罐疗法
human genome 人类基因图谱
mental disorder 精神紊乱
mutual generation and restriction 相生相克
I Ching; *Book of Change*《易经》
Shennong's Herbal Classic《神农本草经》
Compendium of Materia Medica《本草纲目》
healing the sick and saving the dying 救死扶伤
mutually opposing and constraining 对立制约

aerobic exercises 有氧运动
immune system 免疫系统
incurable disease 绝症
epidemic 流行病
registration office 挂号处
in-patient department 住院部
doctor in charge 主治医师
medical ethics 医德
high tempo of life 快节奏的生活
gene pool 基因库
heart attack 心力衰竭，心脏病发作
organ transplanting 器官移植
congenital defect 先天性缺陷
eating disorder 食欲紊乱
balanced diet 均衡的饮食
health care product 保健品
heart attack 心脏病发作
hypertension 高血压
hypotension 低血压
irregular pulse 脉律不齐
metabolism 新陈代谢
traditional Chinese medicine 中医
physical therapy 理疗
feeling the pulse 切脉
folk prescription 偏方
morbidity rate 发病率
herbal medicine 草药

five tastes of medicinal herb 中药五味

safety first, precaution crucial 安全第一，预防为主

Huang Di's Classic of Internal Medicine / *Yellow Emperor's Canon of Traditional Chinese Medicine*《黄帝内经》

yin-yang, the two opposing and complementary principles in nature 阴阳

skin scraping therapy with water, liquor or vegetable oil 刮痧疗法

secret prescription (normally of excellent curative effect) 秘方

secret prescription handed down from one's ancestors 祖传秘方

main and collateral channels inside human body 经络

maintain good health through the intake of nourishing food 食补保健

Unit 9

Arts and Youth

Part 1 Learning Before Class

● **Listening**

Summer Camp Uses Dance to Teach Students Life Skills

Directions: Listen to the news and answer the questions.

1. As a summer dance program, what does AileyCamp aim at and for what purpose?
2. When Espinoza said that she had the power to choose the right thing, what does it imply?
3. Why did Kameron Davis choose AileyCamp?

● **Watching and Thinking**

Art Explores African Americans' Past and Present

Directions: Watch the video and discuss the questions with your partner.

1. What do you think of the pictures made by the Terrells?
2. Do they remind you of any art in your own culture?
3. Many people liked to play with color when they were young. Have you ever painted any objects with colors reflecting that you see yourself in the works?
4. James Terrell's style is abstract. How do you interpret abstract artworks? Does it show the time and space you live in and work with?

- **Reading and Discussing**

An Old New World

By Claire Adam
January 5, 2019
The Economist

  Live-action remakes of classic cartoons are one of the most lucrative innovations in cinema. In January 1991 Jeffrey Katzenberg, then chairman of Walt Disney Studios, sent a 28-page memo to his colleagues. Entitled "The World is Changing: Some Thoughts on Our Business", it lamented that the studio had lost its way. The finances were sound. Disney had outdone its competitors at the box office the year before—but Mr Katzenberg felt the company was unduly focused on blockbusters. It should be less fixated on big budgets, big names and whizzy effects, he urged, and concentrate on developing original ideas and executing them well. "People don't want to see what they've already seen," he said. "Our job is not to count on recycled formulas, but to create and develop fresh, new stories."

  His advice now seems quaint. Of the ten most expensive films ever made, Disney is responsible for six. In 2012 the studio hired Alan Horn as its chairman after a successful stint at Warner Brothers, where he had devoted a hefty share of the budget to a handful of "event films", such as the *Harry Potter* series. If the average American only sees around five movies a year, he reasoned, they are most likely to opt for "something of high production value, be it because of the story, or the stars involved, or the special visual effects".

  Producers and directors can now draw on astoundingly sophisticated computer-generated effects. Except for the actor who played Mowgli, *The Jungle Book* was entirely digital; the authentically lush rain forest and convincing animals earned an Oscar. Jon Favreau, the director, will apply the same techniques to *The Lion King*. "We can put any animal next to a real one and not be able to tell the difference," claims Richard Stammers, the visual effects supervisor on "Dumbo". The animators size up muscle, the wrinkles of skin and the movement of fur. Lacking an airborne elephant to copy, researchers studied the physics of large birds. For imaginary creatures such as the Beast, animators use the latest motion-capture technology, which tracks actors' movements and facial expressions and then transposes them onto digital figures. The uncanny realism instills a sense of wonder of its own.

On Rotten Tomatoes, a review-aggregator site, audiences give *The Jungle Book* an 86% approval rating—a similar score to the original's, as is that of the new *Cinderella*. Still, Mr. Katzenberg's insistence on "fresh, new stories" has not been wholly discredited. There are only so many venerable cartoons to revisit, and the exciting novelty of seeing real actors and realistic animals breathe life into fantastical yarns may fade. Franchise apathy has already struck: *Solo: A Star Wars Story* (2018) received decent reviews but failed to break even. The circle of live-action films may yet turn out to be a wheel of fortune.

Directions: *Read the passage and discuss the questions with your partner.*

1. What should Walt Disney Studios innovate and focus on in order to make the live-action remakes of cartoons the most lucrative innovations in cinema?
2. Which action stories mentioned here are probably the animated backlist that generations of children might grow up on?
3. What latest technology has been used so as to draw on astoundingly sophisticated computer-generated effects? What is the precondition to transpose onto digital figures?

Part 2 Learning in Class

Warm Up

Architect I. M. Pei Dies at 102

Directions: *Watch the video and discuss the questions with your partner.*

1. What was I. M. Pei's major when he studied at the Massachusetts Institute of Technology and Harvard University? What materials are built in Pei's works?
2. What are Pei's well-known architectural designs in the world?
3. Why did Pei say his pyramids of Louvre Museum in Paris was the most difficult job of his career?

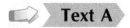

Text A

Exploring Unknown: What's So Fascinating About Sci-fi Films?

April 10, 2019
CGTN

Chinese fans of sci-fi films were excited after organizers of the 2019 Beijing International Film Festival (BJIFF) unveiled a list of its special screenings this year, among which included screening the classic sci-fi film *2001: A Space Odyssey* in IMAX theaters. Directed by Stanley Kubrick, one of the most influential figures in cinematic history, *2001: A Space Odyssey* is canonized among space exploration films.

It is hard to believe that the film was produced in 1968. Even five decades later, one is awestruck by the geometric forms of the spacecrafts in the film, the exquisite yet concise designs inside the capsule, and the imagination of artificial technology. This is not to mention the bold application of lavish colors and the language of the lens, which created a hallucinating vision of a higher-dimensional journey that is beyond the daily experience of human cognition, especially for the audience back in 1968. No wonder many A-listers today still call Kubrick the top of the pantheon, such as Christopher Nolan and Ang Lee.

And it seems to be a good time to bring the legendary film back onto the big screen, with China's first hard-core sci-fi film *The Wandering Earth* arousing a new round of enthusiasm in the genre and garnering a box office of over 4.6 billion *yuan*, the second highest in Chinese cinematic history.

But why are people so fascinated with sci-fi films? What about the genre is so appealing?

Cutting-edge technology & Dazzling visual effects

Themes for sci-fi films could be diverse, such as superheroes fighting again alien villains, exploration of extraterrestrial space and intelligence, doomsday escaping and salvation, artificial intelligence with cyborgs and robots walking down the streets … But whatever the film's theme, they all have one thing in common—to present to audiences what only exists in the imagination, with the most advanced technology in the industry. Ever since computer-generated-imagery (CGI) was first used in film making to bring a dinosaur back to life in *Jurassic Park* in 1993, it has gradually reshaped the industry. From animations to live-action films, and from motion captures to facial expressions, CGI has created movie making magic.

In the latest cyberpunk film *Alita: Battle Angel*, audiences could almost read all possible emotions from those pair of CG eyes, such as happiness, melancholy, angry, alertness and so on. It has only been 10 years since the release of James Cameron's *Avatar*, but CGI technology has leaped forward beyond expectation. In Netflix's newly released sci-fi animation series *Love, Death & Robots*, the hyper-realism of the CG characters could even deceive the audiences, and make them guess whether they are new Hollywood stars or pixels.

But of course, sci-fi films could bring far more stunning scenes than those, like the destruction of cities, doomsday for humans, alien worlds, depicting the vastness of the universe, much like what we have seen in the *Avengers*, *Star Wars*, *2012*, *Avatar*, *Interstellar* and *The Martian*.

Most of the audiences go to cinema seeking hours of recreation and a short gap to escape from their daily pressures and chaos. Sci-fi films, which provide constant sensory and spiritual stimulation, are among the best choices.

Break through limitations & Seek the unknown

America's supernatural horror fiction writer H. P. Lovecraft once said, "The oldest and strongest emotion of mankind is fear, and the oldest and strongest kind of fear is fear of the unknown." However, in the unknown, there also lies deadly temptations, which mankind could never resist. Curiosity lies in human nature. Therefore, in the sci-fi films, we saw that the fear of the unknown never stops mankind from going deeper into outer space, seeking extraterrestrial intelligence, or exploring the deeper psychological and physical boundaries of their own lives.

Christopher Nolan is a master in exploring the unknown. In *Interstellar*, human beings are risking their lives to penetrate the mysteries of gravity, time and space, black hole and dimensions, trying to decipher the puzzles that have not yet been solved by science. In *Inception*, Nolan dives into dreams, seeking the secrets and possibilities within the sub-consciousness.

Matt Damon, who starred as astronaut Mark Watney in *The Martian*, successfully grew potatoes on Mars in the film and therefore colonized the Red Planet. In *Arrival*, linguist Louise Banks has managed to penetrate through time and see the future, after successfully interpreting an alien language. In *The Wandering Earth*, human beings even try to push their mother planet out of the solar system and find another sun for it.

What's more attractive about sci-fi films is that the magnificent scenes on the big screen are not groundless at all. Most of them have solid basis in science. And to the surprise of many, an increasing number of technologies depicted only in film decades ago have now appeared in our daily lives. To some extent, the imaginary worlds have inspired technological developments, and vice versa. Thinking beyond human cognition, and who knows, maybe the worlds of higher-dimensions spacecrafts, wormholes and black holes, cyberpunk ... and a more convenient future society are not that far away from us.

Reflection & Alert, before it's too late

Of course, there is a "but" here. Things are not always optimistic, especially with the increasing threat to the environment on Earth. UN Secretary-General Antonio Guterres released a flagship report on global warming on March 28 this year, calling for world leaders to come to a September summit with concrete plans to deal with climate change. And according to the United Nations' weather agency, extreme weather hit 62 million people worldwide in 2018, and forced two million to relocate, as global warming worsened. The World Meteorological Organization predicted that the planet may see temperatures increase three to five degrees Celsius by the end of the century.

Doomsday caused by human behaviors are quite common in sci-fi films. In the 2004 film, *The Day After Tomorrow*, the world and all species are almost wiped out due to the extreme weather caused by the climate change. In *Interstellar*, sandstorms almost devoured every living thing on Earth, and forced humans to drift in space while seeking a new planet.

Philosophical and ethnics studies are the eternal themes in sci-fi films of mankind and artificial intelligence. While it is impossible to see in real life how mankind's destiny would end up, sci-fi films have offered various possibilities and at the same time mirrors that could trigger human reflection. Even though the strength of sci-fi films in changing the reality is quite limited, the shocking scenes would serve as an alert to everyone who watched them to show more respect to nature and be modest.

After all, as Chinese novelist Liu Cixin writes in his "Three-Body Problem" trilogy, "Weakness and ignorance are not barriers to survival, but arrogance is."

Words and Expressions

sci-fi film			a science fiction movie based on or characterized by the methods and principles of science 科幻电影
unveil	[ʌnˈveɪl]	v.	uncover (a new monument or work of art) as part of a public ceremony 揭开;公布

Unit 9 Arts and Youth

Odyssey	[ˈɒdəsi]	n.	a Greek epic poem traditionally ascribed to Homer 奥德赛
canonize	[ˈkænənaɪz]	v.	(in the Roman Catholic Church) officially declare (a dead person) to be a saint 追封为圣徒
awestruck	[ˈɔːstrʌk]	a.	filled with or revealing awe 肃然起敬的
capsule	[ˈkæpsjuːl]	n.	a small case or container, especially a round or cylindrical one 胶囊
hallucinating	[həˈluːsɪneɪtɪŋ]	n.	conducting an experience involving the apparent perception of something not present 幻觉
pantheon	[ˈpænθiən]	n.	all the gods of a people or religion collectively 万神殿
extraterrestrial	[ˌekstrətəˈrestriəl]	n.	a hypothetical or fictional being from outer space, especially an intelligent one 外星人
temptation	[tempˈteɪʃn]	n.	a desire to do something, especially something wrong or unwise 诱惑
doomsday	[ˈduːmzdeɪ]	n.	the last day of the world's existence 末日
cyborg	[ˈsaɪbɔːg]	n.	a fictional or hypothetical person whose physical abilities are extended beyond normal human limitations by mechanical elements built into the body 半机器人
penetrate	[ˈpenɪtreɪt]	v.	succeed in forcing a way into or through (a thing) 穿透
decipher	[dɪˈsaɪfə]	v.	convert (a text written in code, or a coded signal) into normal language 解码；破译
cyberpunk	[ˈsaɪbəpʌŋk]	n.	a genre of science fiction set in a lawless subculture 庞克
trilogy	[ˈtrɪlədʒi]	n.	a group of three related novels, plays, films, operas, or albums 三部曲
arrogance	[ˈærəgəns]	n.	the quality of being arrogant 傲慢

• Multiple Choice

Select the most appropriate answer for each of the following questions.

1. The organizers of the 2019 Beijing International Film Festival unveiled a list of its special screenings which included China's first hard-core sci-fi film _____.

A) *2001: A Space Odyssey* B) *The Wandering Earth*
   C) *Avatar* and *Interstellar* D) *The Day After Tomorrow*
2. *2001: A Space Odyssey* was awestruck owing to _____.
   A) the geometric forms of the spacecrafts
   B) the exquisite yet concise designs inside the capsule
   C) the imagination of artificial technology
   D) all of the above
3. Most of the audiences go to cinema seeking hours of recreation and a short gap to _____.
   A) read all possible emotions from those pairs of CG eyes
   B) appreciate far more stunning scenes
   C) escape from their daily pressures and chaos
   D) enjoy the constant sensory and spiritual stimulation by sci-fi film
4. What makes sci-fi films more attractive is that the magnificent scenes on the big screen are _____.
   A) not groundless at all
   B) of solid basis in science
   C) reflecting the oldest and strongest emotion of mankind
   D) filled with the secrets and possibilities within the sub-consciousness
5. Why did the author quote H. P. Lovecraft's remark that the oldest and strongest kind of fear is fear of the unknown?
   A) He implies the fear of the unknown lies in temptations mankind never resists.
   B) Curiosity in human nature is the driving force to go deeper into out space.
   C) The fear of the unknown never stops mankind from going deeper into outer space.
   D) The fear of the unknown is the barrier of the deeper psychological and physical boundaries of their own lives.

- **Matching**

Match the following information as referring to.

1. Mark Watney in *The Martian*
2. Linguist Louise Banks in *Arrival*
3. Human beings in *The Wandering Earth*
4. Secretary-General Antonio Guterres
5. Sandstorms in *Interstellar*

A. almost devoured every living thing on Earth
B. grew potatoes on Mars

C. has successfully interpreted an alien language

D. called for world leaders to put forward concrete plans to deal with climate change

E. try to push their mother planet out of the solar system

- **Short Answer Questions**

1. Why are people so fascinated with sci-fi films and its genre is so appealing?
2. Why did H. P. Lovecraft say that the oldest and strongest kind of fear is fear of the unknown?
3. What are the common ground between the sci-fic film *Interstellar* and *Inception*?
4. Can you exemplify that the worlds of wormholes and black holes are not that far away from us?
5. Is there any connection between human behaviors and the sci-fi film making?

- **Writing**

Architecture is used as a communication tool through which directors and film makers send certain messages. Write a composition of no less than 300 words commenting on the statement that future architecture in sci-fi films acts as architectural symbols used by the directors to convey their personal ideas and visions.

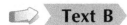

Arts for Youth Development

By Adam Fletcher

June 25, 2019

The Guardian

Art, social change, and young people have always walked hand-in-hand. Engaging youth in the Arts can promote positive, powerful social change in countless art forms, including dance, music, graffiti art, and more. Young people can change the world in a lot of ways through the arts.

"We are all creative, but by the time we are three of four years old, someone has knocked the creativity out of us. Some people shut up the kids who start to tell stories. Kids dance in their cribs, but someone will insist they sit still. By the time the creative people are ten or twelve, they want to be like everyone else," Maya Angelou said.

It is more than a number. The arts plays an important tole in youth development programs. Elpus, K. launched a study examining the influence of adolescent participation in the arts on cognitive, behavioral, and social outcomes. Data were collected from two major longitudinal studies of American high school students and statistical analyses were performed in order to investigate differences between arts and non-arts students throughout adolescence and into adulthood.

This study controlled for per-existing systematic differences between students who choose to study the arts in high school and those who do not in order to produce unbiased results. The researcher found that arts participation had a wide range of positive effects. Most notable were the findings that arts students were more likely than their non-arts peers to find school engaging, to attend a post-secondary school, and to earn a four-year college degree.

He found that arts participation in high school was found to have a positive effect on: (1) Academic outcomes and behaviors including the likelihood of being suspended, optimism about college attendance, school attachment and engagement, scores on a standardized test of vocabulary, and attendance of post-secondary schooling and subsequent degree attainment. (2) Personal outcomes and behaviors including alcohol consumption and illicit substance abuse (except for visual arts students, who were slightly more likely to have used drugs), delinquent behaviors and motivation to be sexually active in adolescence, optimism, and involvement with the criminal justice system.

The significance of the findings shows that the findings provide much evidence for wide-ranging and long-lasting positive impacts of arts participation on adolescents and adults. Importantly, unlike many studies that focus only on academic outcomes, this study provides a more well-rounded picture of positive youth development that includes personal, social, and behavioral factors outside of standardized test scores. That these benefits were seen to extend into adulthood further illustrates the importance of providing children with opportunities for arts participation in school as the children are driven force to change the world.

When it comes to the ways youth can change the world, May Angelou said that focusing on the arts is the effective way. She mentioned the best doings for youth are as follows:

Get Active. When young people interact with art in sustained ways that acknowledge its social impact and meaning, they are critically engaging with art. Whether happening in theaters, on screens, in galleries, at school, on the streets, online, or anywhere else, young people can change the world through critical engagement with the arts.

Make Art. Studying, practicing, performing, creating, deconstructing, writing poems, obliterating and recreating art is a skill and ability all young people are endowed with from the youngest of ages, and all people are capable of throughout their entire lives.

Engaging youth as artists can happen in countless ways for countless purposes, and as long as they are positive, powerful and purposeful, youth can change the world.

Do Things with Adults. Working together to co-create artistic works can allow young people and adults to work across age barriers and divisions to create unity, community and empowerment for everyone involved. Youth adult partnerships can empower everyone to make and share what's in their hearts and on their minds, especially when they're focused on the arts.

Arts education is positive with youth development: cognitive, behavioral, and social outcomes of adolescents who study the arts. So for youth who holds the burden to change the world through the arts, there are at least three things to do.

Opportunities. Young people need many opportunities to interact with art in a lot of different ways throughout their lives. Schools shouldn't be seen as the only source of art in the lives of young people; television, the Internet, cell phones, stores, ally walls and public art all provide opportunities. Children and youth should have different people around them when they interact with art, too, including their families, educators, other young people, strangers, different social classes, different educational levels, and all types of diversities.

Education. As children and youth, young people can learn how to create art, how to critique art, how to observe art, and how to engage with art. They can also teach others how to do the same, interacting with art in yet another way. Creating art is a way to learn, and providing the tools, spaces, educators and activities for young people can change the world.

Inspiration. Feeling the drive and motivation can lead to the courage and inner-strength needed to create and share art. Sharing stories, ideas and other inspirations with young people can drive children and youth to change the world through the arts.

 Words and Expressions

graffiti	[grəˈfiːti]	n.	writings or drawings scribbled, scratched or sprayed illicitly on a wall or other surface in a public place 涂鸦
cognitive	[ˈkɒgnətɪv]	a.	connected with thinking or conscious mental processes 认知的
longitudinal	[ˌlɒŋgɪˈtjuːdɪnl]	a.	used to refer to lines or distances east or west of an imaginary line between the North Pole and the South Pole 纵向的

unbiased	[ʌnˈbaɪəst]	a.	showing no prejudice for or against something; impartial 公正的；无偏见的
suspend	[səˈspend]	v.	temporarily prevent from continuing or being in force or effect 暂停
subsequent	[ˈsʌbsɪkwənt]	a.	happening after something else 随后的
illicit	[ɪˈlɪsɪt]	a.	forbidden by law, rules or custom 非法的
delinquent	[dɪˈlɪŋkwənt]	a.	showing or characterized by a tendency to commit crime, particularly minor crime 违法的
adolescent	[ˌædəˈlesənt]	n.	a young person who is developing into an adult 青少年
endow	[ɪnˈdaʊ]	v.	give a large amount of money to pay for creating a college, hospital, etc. or to provide an income for it 赋予
critique	[krɪˈtiːk]	n.	a detailed analysis and assessment of sth., especially a literary, philosophical or political theory 批评；评论

- **True/False/Not Given**

Do you think the following statements is in accordance with the information given in Text B?

In Blanks 1-8 you write：

T   if the statement is true

F   if the statement is false

Not Given if the information is not given in Text B

_____ 1. When Maya Angelou was young, she was creative.

_____ 2. Engaging young people in arts can promote positive, powerful world change in a lot of ways.

_____ 3. According to Elpus' study, only the arts on cognitive, behavioral and social outcomes play an important role in youth development.

_____ 4. Arts students were more likely to earn a four-year college degree than their non-arts peers.

_____ 5. Arts participation in high school was found to have a positive effect on academic outcomes and behaviors.

_____ 6. May Angelou thought the effective ways to change the world is through critical engagement with the arts.

_____ 7. Young people are critically engaging with art when they interact with art in sustained ways that has less social meaning.

_____ 8. Working together with adults to co-create artistic works can allow young people to go across age barriers and divisions to build united community and empowerment for everyone involved.

- **Short Answer Questions**

1. Do you agree the statement that the arts plays an important role in youth development program?
2. Why do you think engaging youth in arts can enable them to change the world?
3. What do you comment on the kids in American elementary school being taught to learn how to create poetry?
4. Do you think it is necessary to teach the kids in Chinese classroom how to write poetry besides reciting Tang Poems and Song Lyrics?
5. How many ways are there to make art in university?

Discussion Questions

1. If we want our kids to grow up to be thoughtful and engaged citizens, we should help them be part of social change now. Discuss with your partners and tell how to help them to be part of social change.
2. Some people believe that the high school students should be taught music and art. Some people think that providing music and art education for high school students is not necessary. What is your opinion and why?

Write an argumentative essay titled "Creativity Is the Key to a Bright Future". To make your argumentative essay strong, you have to present relevant evidences that support the argument and convince your readers. The essay should be no less than 300 words.

Academic Reading

Recognizing Purpose and Tone (1)

Learning Objective

In the section, you will learn to recognize the various kinds of purpose.

The Importance of Recognizing Purpose

When reading, part of the evaluation process involves recognizing the writer's purpose, or reasons for writing. That, in turn, can help you distinguish between facts and opinions, uncover bias, and assess the overall reliability of information.

Although writers always have a purpose for writing, they usually do not come right out and say what it is. Consequently, it is up to the reader to make an inference or an educated guess regarding their motivations, based on:

- Author's background or affiliation
- Publication in which the writing appears
- The information itself
- How the information is presented

For example, a physician who is a member of the American Medical Association may write a piece in a popular magazine dealing with the high cost of malpractice insurance in order to persuade readers to be sympathetic to rising medical fees. In doing so, she may not state that purpose explicitly but instead present convincing information that supports that point of view without providing any contradictory information. Thus, the reader could infer her purpose by taking into consideration the fact that she is a physician who is affiliated with a major medical association representing doctors, by keeping in mind that the article appears in a magazine that is read widely by the general public, and by recognizing that the information provided appears to be one-sided.

Generally speaking, a writer's purpose for writing is usually **to inform, to persuade, to entertain, or some combination of the three**. The ease with which you will be able to recognize these purposes will often depend on how obvious a particular writer chooses to present the material. As noted, it will sometimes be necessary for you to use your inference skills. Let us look more closely at each of the three purposes.

(1) **To Inform**

When the purpose is to inform, a writer simply provides facts, data, or information about a given subject so that you can learn more about it. Textbook writers generally have this as their overall purpose. For example, read the following passage from a Biology textbook.

Biology Is Connected to Our Lives in Many Ways

Endangered species, genetically modified crops, global warming, air and water pollution, the cloning of embryos, nutrition controversies, emerging diseases, medical advances—is there ever a day that we don't see several of these issues featured in the news? These topics and many more have biological underpinnings. Biology, the science of life, has an enormous impact on our everyday life.

Most of these issues of science and society also involve technology. Science and technology are interdependent, but their basic goals differ. The goal of science is to understand natural phenomena. In contrast, the goal of technology is generally to apply scientific knowledge for some specific purpose. Biologists and other scientists often speak of "discoveries", while engineers and other technologists more often speak of "inventions". The beneficiaries of those inventions also include scientists, who put new technology to work in their research. And scientific discoveries often lead to new technologies.

The potent combination of science and technology has dramatic effects on society. For example, discovery of the structure of DNA by James D. Watson and Francis Crick some 50 years ago and subsequent achievements in DNA science have led to the many technologies of DNA engineering that are transforming many fields, including medicine, agriculture, and forensics (DNA fingerprinting, for example). Perhaps Watson and Crick envisioned their discovery as someday leading to important applications, but it is unlikely that they could have predicted exactly what those applications would be.

Technology has improved our standard of living in many ways, but not without consequences. Technology that keeps people healthier has enabled the Earth's population to grow more than tenfold in the past three centuries, to double to over 6 billion in just the past 40 years. The environmental effects of this growth can be devastating. Global warming, toxic wastes, acid rain, deforestation, nuclear accidents, and extinction of species are just some of the repercussions of more and more people wielding more and more technology. Science can help us identify such problems and provide insight into what course of action may prevent further damage. But solutions to these problems have as much to do with politics, economics, and cultural values as with science and technology. Now that science and technology have become such powerful aspects of society, every thoughtful citizen has a responsibility to develop a reasonable amount of scientific literacy. The crucial science-technology-society relationship is a theme that adds to the significance of any biology course.

Biology—from the molecular level to the level of the biosphere—is directly connected to our everyday lives. Biology offers us a deeper understanding of ourselves and our planet and a chance to more fully appreciate life in all its diversity.

The writer's purpose here is to **inform** the reader about the many important connections that the subject of biology has to our everyday lives, including its contributions to technology and medicine and its help in finding solutions to environmental problems. Several examples are provided for support and clarification.

(2) **To Persuade**

When a writer's purpose is to persuade, the writer is trying to get the reader to think in a certain way or take a particular action. Although some facts may be presented, the writer's real intention is to get others to agree with the opinion being expressed or to engage in some activity in support of that point of view. For instance, as you read the following passage, think about the author's purpose.

The Littlest Killers

By Brent Staples

Imagine the terror of a 5-year-old child, dangling 14 stories above the pavement, as his brother tries fruitlessly to save him from two other boys, aged 10 and 11, who are determined to see him drop.

The image of Eric Morse, hurled to his death in Chicago in 1994, has been a recurrent one in both local and national politics. Newt Gingrich cited it in speeches. Henry Cisneros, the Secretary of Housing and Urban Development, called it a clinching fact in the Government's decision to take over the Chicago Housing Authority, deemed by federal authorities the most dangerous and ill managed in the country. The Illinois Legislature easily passed a bill permitting 10-year-old children to be charged with murder and—as "super predators"—sent to maximum-security jails. The rush to jail young children is catching on elsewhere as well. Nationwide last year, 700 pieces of legislation were introduced aimed at prosecuting minors as adults.

The judge who last week sent Eric Morse's killers to jails for juveniles came near to rending her robes as she described Eric's plunge and asked how the boys who caused his death had become so indifferent to human life. No one who has spent time in, or even near, Chicago public housing projects should need to ask such a question. Eric's fall—and the world he lived in—bears a disturbing resemblance to Lord of the Flies, William Golding's novel about a band of British schoolboys marooned on a jungle island. Without adults to keep them in check, the boys turn to blood lust and murder. A boy who tries to reason gets his skull split open when he is thrown from a cliff.

Eric was killed for refusing to steal candy for his tormentors. The public housing complex where he died qualifies as an "island" in Golding's sense—an island of poverty and pathology, cut off from the city proper. Of the 15 poorest census tracts in America, 11 are Chicago public housing communities. The city designed and treated them as pariah states, even while they were bright, shining steppingstones for the black middle class. Public housing was far too densely built, walled off with freeways and railroad lines used as ghetto walls. As the poverty deepened, there was simply no way to dilute it.

Chicago's Ida B. Wells housing development has few adult men. The women are disproportionately teenagers. At the time of Eric's death, a third of the complex's 2,800 apartments were abandoned, used primarily by drug dealers who hawked heroin from the windows. In a survey at a nearby high school, half the students said they had been shot at; 45 percent said they had seen someone killed. The boys who dropped Eric from the window did not originate the act. The gangs, which both boys knew well, occasionally used such punishment on members who tried to quit. Bear in mind that this environment is sustained with federal dollars.

The conduct of the two young killers was all the more understandable given that they have IQ's of 60 and 76, with perhaps less emotional maturity than 5-year-old Eric. The judge in the case has ordered psychiatric treatment and follow-up care. But in light of what experts describe as Illinois' poor record with treatment—and its high failure rate with juveniles—the prospects for treatment seem poor. In Massachusetts or Missouri, the two would have been sent to facilities with fewer than two dozen beds and extensive psychiatric help. In Illinois, the boys could go to lockdowns with hundreds of others—many of them gangsters who will recreate the projects behind bars.

Few things are more horrifying than the murder of a child. But in view of the antecedents, Eric Morse's death was almost a naturally occurring event. The projects have become factories for crime and killers, with homicide taking younger and younger victims each year. The judge who sentenced Eric's killers called it "essential to find out how these two young boys turned out to be killers, to have no respect for human life and no empathy for their victim". We know quite well what made them killers. What we need is the political will to do something about it.

The passage above does present facts regarding the murder of Eric Morse by two other boys and the very poor conditions in the Chicago public housing projects that have led to crimes like that. However, the writer concludes by stating "We know quite well what made them killers. What we need is the political will to do something about it" (Paragraph 7). We can infer from those statements that the writer is urging readers to support measures that will help correct the conditions in the housing projects or politicians who favor such measures. In short, he is trying to get us to agree with his point of view regarding the causes of crimes like the murder of Eric Morse and asking us to take action to eliminate them.

(3) **To Entertain**

A writer whose purpose is to entertain must try to bring enjoyment to readers by treating a topic in a light, cheerful, funny, or laughable manner. For example, as you read the passage that follows, think about its purpose.

However, to entertain does not always mean something is funny. An entertaining passage can captivate a reader with suspense rather than humor. It can engage the audience by stirring their emotions or imagination. The reaction can be one of fear, sympathy, and/or laughter.

Fork Manufacturer Introduces Fifth Tine to Accomodate Growing American Mouthfuls

In an effort to keep pace with the rapid growth of American mouthfuls, flatware manufacturer Kitchen Master announced yesterday the addition of a fifth tine to its line of dinner forks. "These days, a traditional four-tined fork is just not enough to handle the quantities of food people shove down their throats," said company spokesman Ken Krimstein, holding up a fork supporting six separate tortellini, two turkey sausages, and some mashed potatoes. "To stay relevant to our customer base and bring back some of those who have given up on using utensils entirely, this was an adjustment we just had to make." Krimstein added that the augmented forks would soon be followed by 25 percent deeper spoons and 3-gallon gravy boats.

The passage above is from *The Onion*, a satirical newspaper that is read by many college students and can be found on most campuses. Notice that the humor is through irony or satire. The writer uses a contemporary issue in the news and makes fun of it by writing an article that is fictitious. The purpose is to entertain readers by making them laugh.

(4) **Combination of Purposes**

Sometimes a writer has more than one purpose, as illustrated in the passage dealing with Eric Morse in the article "The Littlest Killers". As you recall, the writer provided factual information but also tried to persuade readers to accept his viewpoint and take action. The previous passage about dinner forks was designed to entertain. These examples are not at all unusual, especially when you are reading material that deals with controversial contemporary topics.

When there is a combination of purposes, try to uncover and concentrate on the writer's overall or main purpose by focusing on the most important messages and the information that lends direct support to them. Remember that recognizing the purpose (or purposes) helps you evaluate the reliability and objectivity of reading material. This is very important when dealing with issues that involve conflicting, debatable, and sometimes emotional viewpoints.

Part 3　Learning After Class

Additional Reading 1

Chinese Film Industry Joins "Space Race"

By Alice Yang
February 14, 2019
The New York Times

China's first blockbuster of science fiction movie has set in space recently. *The Wandering Earth* ①, opens Tuesday amid grandiose expectations that it will represent the dawning of a new era in Chinese film making.

It is one in a series of ambitious, big-budget films tackling a genre that, until now, has been beyond the reach of most filmmakers here—technically and financially. Those movies include *Shanghai Fortress*, about an alien attack on Earth, and *Pathfinder*, about a spaceship that crashes on a desert planet. "Filmmakers in China see science fiction as a holy grail," said Raymond Zhou, an independent critic, who noted that Hollywood had set the technological standards, and thus audience expectations, very high.

The Wandering Earth shown in 3-D takes place in a distant future in which the sun is

---

① *The Wandering Earth* is a renowned sci-fi movie, written by Liu Cixin and directed by Frant Gwo. It is much-anticipated sci-fi movie telling about the sun is about to die out, humanity sets a plan in motion to launch planet Earth out of orbit and to find a new home in space.

about to expand into a red giant and devour the Earth. The impending peril forces the world's engineers to devise a plan to move the planet to a new solar system using giant thruster. Things go very badly when Earth has to pass Jupiter, setting off a desperate scramble to save humanity from annihilation.

The special effects—like the apocalyptic climatic changes that would occur if Earth suddenly moved out of its cozy orbit—are certain to be measured against Hollywood's, as ever here. And the preliminary reviews have been positive. "It's like the coming-of-age of the industry," Zhou said. *The Wandering Earth* opens with the Lunar New Year, the beginning of an official, week-long holiday that is traditionally a peak box-office period in China. It has a limited release in the United States, Canada, Australia and New Zealand.

At home, it will compete with *Crazy Alien*, a comedy inspired by *E.T. the Extra-Terrestrial* about two brothers hoping to capitalize on the arrival of a visitor from outer space. Both *The Wandering Earth* and *Crazy Alien* are adapted from works by Liu Cixin, the writer who has led a renaissance in science fiction here, becoming the first Chinese winner of the Hugo Award for the genre in 2015.

His novels are sprawling epics and deeply researched. That makes them plausible fantasies about humanity's encounters with a dangerous universe. Translating them into movies would challenge any filmmaker, as the director of *The Wandering Earth*, Guo Fan, acknowledged during a screening in Beijing last week. That has made the film, produced by Beijing Jingxi Culture & Tourism Co., Ltd and the state-owned China Film Group Corp., a test for the industry.

Guo, who uses the name Frant Gwo in English, noted that Chinese audiences have responded coolly to many of Hollywood's previous sci-fi blockbusters. Studios, therefore, have been wary of investing the resources required to make convincing sci-fi. The film's budget reportedly reached nearly $50 million, modest by Hollywood standards but still significant here in China. More than 7,000 people were involved in the production. Much of it was filmed in the new Oriental Movie Metropolis, an $8 billion studio in the coast city of Qingdao, built by the real estate and entertainment giant Dalian Wanda.

"I really hope that this movie will not lose money at least," said Guo, whose previous film, *My Old Classmate*, was a romantic comedy. "As long as this one does not lose money, we can continue to make science-fiction films." The popularity of Liu's novels could help. So could two recent Hollywood films, *Gravity* and *The Martian*. Both included important plot twists that, not incidentally, cast China's space program in a positive light, and both were huge hits here.

The openings also come as China reached a milestone in space: the landing of a probe on the far side of the moon in January. Although decades behind Russia and the United States, China has now put astronauts in orbit and has ambitious plans to join—or even lead—a new age of space exploration. "I think there is a very close connection between Chinese cinema and the nation's fortunes," said Sha Dan, a curator at the China Film Archive, who moderated a discussion with Guo. He cited the most popular film in China last year: *Operation Red Sea*, an action drama loosely based on the Chinese rescue of several hundred civilians from Yemen when war erupted there in 2015.

"When we have the ability to go to war, we can make movies like *Operation Red Sea*," he said, alluding to China's military modernization in recent years. "Only when China can enter the space era can we make works like *The Wandering Earth*." Unlike *Operation Red Sea* movie, which featured a hero battling Western villains, *The Wandering Earth* is not stupid, though it does star Wu Jing, the hero of the *Wolf Warrior* films, who put up his own investment in the project. He plays an astronaut aboard an international space station who has to contend with a HAL-like computer.

Guo said he consciously avoided making Wu's character a do-it-alone superhero. The fight to save Earth is fought instead by an ensemble, including an affable Russian cosmonaut who explains why his country prohibited alcohol in space, at least officially.

The Wandering Earth takes for granted China's central role in future space exploration, but it also has a vision of the international collaboration necessary to cope with the threats facing the planet, a theme that runs deeply through Liu's fiction. Liu, who attended a screening last week, noted that science-fiction films in China dated as far back as the 1930s, when the director Yang Xiaozhong made ones like *Exchanged* and *Visiting Shanghai After 60 Years*, but those were largely forgotten.

A 1980 movie, *Death Ray on Coral Island*, was a campy. There have been few attempts since. "This is mainly because Chinese society is relatively closed and conservative," Liu said in a written response to questions. "There were not the conditions for science-fiction movies to have an impact."

A film project based on Liu's best-known work, the trilogy that began with *The Three-Body Problem*, was optioned and even filmed in 2015 but has since languished in post-production, reportedly because of technical challenges and costs. The conditions now seem ripe. Seeing the *The Wandering Earth* on the screen, Liu said, was "soul shaking".

Words and Expressions

blockbuster	[ˈblɒkbʌstə]	n.	a thing of great power or size, in particular a movie, book or other product that is a great commercial success 一鸣惊人的事物
grandiose	[ˈɡrændiəus]	a.	impressive because of unnecessary largeness or grandeur 不切实际的；华而不实的
devour	[dɪˈvauə]	v.	eat (food or prey) hungrily or quickly 吞食
impending	[ɪmˈpendɪŋ]	a.	being about to happen 即将发生的
thruster	[θrʌstə]	n.	推进器
scramble	[ˈskræmbl]	v.	rush about hastily in an undignified way 争夺；抢夺
apocalyptic	[ˌəpɒkəˈlɪptɪk]	a.	describing or prophesying the complete destruction of the world 世界末日的
terrestrial	[təˈrestriəl]	a.	of, on, or relating to the earth 陆生的
capitalize	[ˈkæpɪtəlaɪz]	v.	take the chance to gain advantage from 利用
fantasy	[ˈfæntəsi]	n.	the faculty or activity of imagining things, especially things that are impossible or improbable 幻想
erupt	[ɪˈrʌpt]	v.	(of a volcano) become active and eject lava, ash and gases 爆发
allude	[əˈluːd]	v.	mention sb. or sth. in an indirect way 暗指；暗示
affable	[ˈæfəbl]	a.	friendly, good-natured or easy to talk to 和蔼可亲的

Discussion Questions

1. As a big-budget film, *The Wandering Earth* is beyond the reach of most film-makers. What is the main idea of this film?
2. Why did Liu Cixin, the writer who has led a renaissance in science fiction here, become the first Chinese winner of the Hugo Award for the genre?
3. How do you comprehend the statement "I think there is a very close connection between Chinese cinema and the nation's fortunes"?

Additional Reading 2

Veteran Author Still Young at Art

By Fang Aiqing
July 29, 2019
China Daily

Veteran writer Wang Meng, at the age of 85, has just published an anthology of four of his recent works—and three of them deal with love, a theme that is often regarded as a preserve of the younger generation. "I don't necessarily have to write about love. These love stories just come to me," he says. Wang Meng has retained a youthful passion for writing over his six-decade career, and his unconventional style has charted a new course for Chinese literature, Fang Aiqing reports.

As a former cultural minister who began writing in 1953, he is adept at embedding China's social changes over the past six decades and changes in people's way of thinking into family histories and romantic stories. Most of the anthology is taken up by a novella, which shares its name with the book: *Love Through Life and Death*.

While the cliché title may prevent many readers from associating the work with Wang, the story is certainly his—and the writing is by no means conventional. In fact, one of his editors has jokingly suggested that Wang should join the list of "young writers who are pioneering new realms".

The novella features two families who have shared a *hutong* (alleyway) residence since the 1950s, and how their lives, spanning two generations, become increasingly entangled over the course of the next six decades. Dun Yongshun is the housekeeper for an expert on Germany, Lyu Fengde, and his wife Su Juechen. Divorced twice due to infidelity, Dun lives with his son Dun Kaimao.

Lyu is wrongly sent to jail in the mid-1950s, and Su gives birth to her son Su Erbao about 10 months later as gossip circulates about the identity of the father. But just as the truth is about to emerge, the author stops short of unmasking the man.

Speaking at a recent launch event for the book in Beijing, Wang says he has seldom created a villain in his decades' long writing career, which has seen him pen some 18 million Chinese characters that extend to more than 50 volumes. "You have to understand everyone, including the people you don't like. They too have their own ethics and a contribution to make," Wang says of the complexity of human nature, adding that his works are "love letters to the world".

The novella unfolds from Dun Kaimao's perspective, who, born in 1946, marries a journalist and later becomes a university lecturer. He witnesses the transformations in the lives of Su Erbao and his wife Shan Lihong, sometimes trying to intervene in one way or another, in the hope of preventing them from being led astray. Shan was convinced that Su Erbao would be her partner from the age of 11. She helps with the family chores and takes care of his ailing parents, before finally marrying him at the age of 27.

Dun Kaimao looks on Su Erbao's gradual rise from an irascible overseas student to becoming a successful entrepreneur. Dun Kaimao plots the milestones in Su's life: from becoming the father of twins to embarking on an affair, from his divorce and his failure to marrying his lover—to his eventual suicide. Before he takes his own life, Su Erbao struggles to find meaning in his existence. Swept along by the tumultuous times, he fails to find spiritual release or face up to his conflicting issues about intimacy. While some readers may doubt the rationale behind Su Erbao's death as seen from a modern societal perspective, Wang says he used the real events that unfolded around him and employed artistic license to present them from an altogether different perspective.

Wang himself appears in the novella as an omniscient figure, frankly justifying his reasons for writing in this way and his perceptions of literature gained over a lifetime of reading and writing. The names of almost every one of the characters in the novella indicate their personalities and destinies. And Wang's "explosive language", as Wu Shulin, executive vice-president of the Publishers Association of China, has described it, is full of enthusiasm and contrast, and stands out for its rhythmic forms and use of sublimation.

Wu says the novella, and the nonfiction work *Postal Anecdotes*, which is also included in the book, present both the positive, progressive side and the darker side of Chinese society over the past century. The latter work revolves around the author's interactions with China Post and the Postal Savings Bank of China over decades of seemingly trivial remittance matters. The sounds of old steam locomotives described in the novella, as well as the images of postal workers dressed in green carrying bags of letters slung over their bicycles, so deeply touches the collective memory of Chinese people that the details immediately draw readers back to the old days where strong bonds between people were commonplace.

More than 65 years have passed since he first picked up his pen, and Wang says while he is still enthralled by writing, he is also keen on swimming, and watching movies. And his "six-pack abs" are still a source of TV talk show quips. His achievements in fiction, poetry and prose, and his research into comparative and classical literature are

Unit 9 Arts and Youth

widely recognized. And as critic Wang Gan has pointed out, Wang Meng has been a key innovator in Chinese literature, who pioneered the use of stream of consciousness techniques, broke down the boundaries between literary creation and criticism, and experimented with a new form of what he calls the "nonfictional novel" with *Postal Anecdotes*.

Keen to support the next generation of young Chinese writers, Wang Meng set up a literary prize to encourage authors below the age of 30 between 2000 and 2005. Many of the winners, including Zhang Yueran, Xu Zechen and Li Xiuwen, remain in the spotlight today.

"You have to understand everyone, including the people you don't like. They too have their own ethics …" Wang Meng writes.

 Words and Expressions

veteran	[ˈvetərən]	a.	rendered competent through trial and experience 老练的；资深的
embed	[ɪmˈbed]	v.	fix (an object) firmly and deeply in a surrounding mass 嵌入
novella	[nəʊˈvelə]	n.	a short novel or long short story 中篇小说
cliché	[ˈkliːʃeɪ]	n.	a phrase or opinion that is overused and betrays a lack of original thought 陈词滥调
irascible	[ɪˈræsəbl]	a.	having or showing a tendency to be easily angered 暴躁的
tumultuous	[tjuːˈmʌltʃuəs]	a.	making a loud, confused noise; uproarious 汹涌的
omniscient	[ɒmˈnɪsiənt]	a.	knowing everything 无所不知的
enthrall	[ɪnˈθrɔːl]	v.	keep someone completely interested 迷住，迷惑；吸引住

 Discussion Questions

1. Why did one of his editors suggest that Wang should join the list of "young writers who are pioneering new realms"?
2. The novella *Through Life and Death* deals with love that features two families who have shared a *hutong* (alleyway) residence. What is the main plot about this story?

333

3. Why did Wang Meng set up a literary prize?

Additional Reading 3

My Life as a Work of Art

By Daniel Lismore
July, 2019
TED

My day starts just like yours. When I wake up in the morning, I check my phone, and then I have a cup of coffee. But then my day truly starts. It may not be like yours, because I live my life as an artwork. Picture yourself in a giant jewelry box with all the beautiful things that you have ever seen in your life. Then imagine that your body is a canvas. And on that canvas, you have a mission to create a masterpiece using the contents of your giant jewelry box. Once you've created your masterpiece, you might think, "Wow, I created that. This is who I am today." Then you would pick up your house keys, walk out the door into the real world, maybe take public transport to the center of the town ... Possibly walk along the streets or even go shopping.

That's my everyday life. When I walk out the door, these artworks are me. I am art. I have lived as art my entire adult life. Living as art is how I became myself. I was brought up in a small village called Fillongley, in England, and it was last mentioned in the "Domesday Book", so that's the mentality.

I was raised by my grandparents, and they were antiques dealers, so I grew up surrounded by history and beautiful things. I had the most amazing dress-up box. So as you can imagine, it started then. I moved to London when I was 17 to become a model. And then I went to study photography. I wasn't really happy with myself at the time, so I was always looking for escapism. I studied the works of David La Chapelle and Steven Arnold, photographers who both curated and created worlds that were mind-blowing to me. So I decided one day to cross over from the superficial fashion world to the superficial art world.

I decided to live my life as a work of art. I spend hours, sometimes months, making things. My go-to tool is a safety pin, like this—they're never big enough. And I use my fabrics time and time again, so I recycle everything that I use. When I get dressed, I'm guided by color, texture and shape. I rarely have a theme. I find beautiful objects from all over the world, and I curate them into 3-D tapestries over a base layer that covers my whole-body shape ... because I'm not very happy with my body.

I ask myself, "Should I take something off or should I put something on? 100 pieces, maybe?" And sometimes, I do that. I promise you it's not too uncomfortable—well, just a little—I might have a safety pin poking at me sometimes when I'm having a conversation with you, so I'll kind of go off. It usually takes me about 20 minutes to get ready, which nobody ever believes. It's true—sometimes. So, it's my version of a T-shirt and jeans.

When I get dressed, I build like an architect. I carefully place things till I feel they belong. Then, I get a lot of my ideas from lucid dreaming. I actually go to sleep to come up with my ideas, and I've taught myself to wake up to write them down. I wear things till they fall apart, and then, I give them a new life. The gold outfit, for example—it was the outfit that I wore to the Houses of Parliament in London. It's made of armor, sequins and broken jewelry, and I was the first person to wear armor to Parliament since Oliver Cromwell banned it in the 17th century. Things don't need to be expensive to be beautiful. Try making outfits out of bin liners or trash you found out on the streets. You never know, they might end up on the pages of *Vogue*.

There's over 6,000 pieces in my collection, ranging from 2,000-year-old Roman rings to ancient Buddhist artifacts. I believe in sharing what I do and what I have with others, so I decided to create an art exhibition, which is currently traveling to museums around the world. It contains an army of me—life-size sculptures as you can see behind me, they're here—they are my life, really. They're kind of like 3-D tapestries of my existence as living as art. They contain plastic crystals mixed with diamonds, beer cans and royal silks all in one look. I like the fact that the viewer can never make the assumption about what's real and what's fake. I find it important to explore and share cultures through my works. I use clothing as a means to investigate and appreciate people from all over the world.

Sometimes, people think I'm a performer or a drag queen. I'm not. Although my life appears to be a performance, it's not. It's very real. People respond to me as they would any other type of artwork. Many people are fascinated and engaged. Some people walk around me, staring, shy at first. Then they come up to me and they say they love or absolutely hate what I do. I sometimes respond, and other times I let the art talk for itself. The most annoying thing in the world is when people want to touch the artwork. But I understand. But like a lot of contemporary art, many people are dismissive. Some people are critical, and others are abusive. I think it comes from the fear of the different—the unknown. There are so many reactions to what I do, and I've just learned not to take them personally.

I've never lived as Daniel Lismore, the person. I've lived as Daniel Lismore, the artwork. And I've faced every obstacle as an artwork. It can be hard … especially if your wardrobe takes up a 40-foot container, three storage units and 30 boxes from IKEA—and sometimes, it can be very difficult, getting into cars, and sometimes—well, this morning I didn't fit through my bathroom door, so that was a problem. What does it mean to be yourself? People say it all the time, but what does it truly mean, and why does it matter? How does life change when you choose to be unapologetic yourself?

I've had to face struggles and triumphs whilst living my life as art. I've been put on private jets and flown around the world. My work's been displayed in prestigious museums, and I've had the opportunity—that is my grandparents, by the way, they're the people that raised me, and there I am. So I've been put on private jets, flown around the world, and yet, it's not been that easy because at times, I've been homeless, I've been spat at, I've been abused, sometimes daily, bullied my entire life, rejected by countless individuals, and I've been stabbed. But what hurt the most was being put on the "Worst Dressed" list.

It can be hard, being yourself, but I've found it's the best way. There's the "Worst Dressed". As the quote goes, "Everyone else is already taken." I've come to realize that confidence is a concept you can choose. I've come to realize that authenticity is necessary, and it's powerful. I've tried to spend time being like other people. It didn't work. It's a lot of hard work, not being yourself. I have a few questions for you all. Who are you? How many versions of you are there? And I have one final question: Are you using them all to your advantage?

In reality, everyone is capable of creating their own masterpiece. You should try it sometime. It's quite fun. Thank you.

 Words and Expressions

mentality	[menˈtæləti]	n.	the characteristic attitude of mind or way of thinking of a person or group 心理
escapism	[ɪˈskeɪpɪzəm]	n.	the tendency to seek distraction and relief from unpleasant realities 空想；逃避现实
curate	[ˈkjʊərət]	v.	select, organize and look after the items in (a collection or exhibition) 策划；组织
superficial	[ˌsuːpəˈfɪʃl]	a.	existing or occurring at or on the surface 浅的；肤浅的

tapestry	[ˈtæpɪstri]	n.	a large piece of heavy cloth with a picture woven into it using coloured threads 挂毯；织锦
lucid	[ˈluːsɪd]	a.	expressed clearly; easy to understand 清楚易懂的；表达清楚的
artifact	[ˈɑːtɪfækt]	n.	an object made by a human being, typically an item of cultural or historical interest 文物
dismissive	[dɪˈsmɪsɪv]	a.	feeling or showing that something is unworthy of consideration 不屑一顾的
abusive	[əˈbjuːsɪv]	a.	extremely offensive and insulting 滥用的

 Discussion Questions

1. How does the narrator live his regular life as art?
2. How does the narrator make his version of a T-shirt and jeans?
3. Why does the narrator use clothing as a means to investigate and appreciate people from all over the world?
4. What qualifications are needed for the best way to be yourself?

Part 4 Topical Vocabulary

typical viewer 典型的观众
trilogy 三部曲
graffiti art 涂鸦艺术
folk art 民间艺术
graphic arts 形象艺术
elegant / refined / high art 高雅艺术
artistic quality 艺术性
art circles / world 艺术界
Realism 现实主义
Neoclassicism 新古典主义

science fiction movies 科幻电影
digital art 数字艺术
graffiti artist 涂鸦艺术家
plastic arts 造型艺术
stage art 舞台艺术
artistic value 艺术价值
artistic attraction 艺术魅力
art troupe / ensemble 艺术团体
classicism 古典主义,古典风格
Romanticism 浪漫主义

Symbolism 象征主义
Art Nouveau 新艺术主义
Cubism 立体派,立体主义
Naturalism 自然主义
Futurism 未来主义
Chinese painting 国画
painting in fresco 壁画
wash 水墨画
drawing from nature 写生画
classical literature 古典文学
popular literature 大众文学
folklore 民间文学

Impressionism 印象主义
Expressionism 表现主义
Surrealism 超现实主义
Existentialism 存在主义
brush drawing 毛笔画
oil painting 油画
pastel drawing 蜡笔画
engraving 版画
tracing 临摹
contemporary literature 现代文学
light literature 通俗文学

Unit 10

Sports

Part 1 Learning Before Class

• **Listening**

Copenhagen Turns Mountain of Waste into Sport

Directions: *Listen to the news and answer the questions.*

1. What might be your worries about skiing on a waste-mountain?
2. Do you support that the snowless waste-mountain shall be used for professional athletes' training? Why or why not?
3. How would you combine any other sports with environment protection?

• **Watching and Thinking**

The Woman Leading the Global Promotion of F1

Directions: *Watch the video and discuss the questions with your partner.*

1. What do you know about the F1 market in China?
2. What is the role of working females in F1 according to the interview?
3. Which Chinese city holds the new F1 race possibly and what might be the reasons?

• Reading and Discussing

"A Huge Step Forward": British Breakers Hail Olympic Proposal

By Aamna Mohdin
Feb. 23, 2019
The Guardian

It was the early 1970s and dancers couldn't get enough of the instrumental "breaks" on a record. DJ Kool Herc, now widely hailed the father of hip-hop, was just a teen DJing at his sister's parties in the Bronx when he extended these breaks and mixed them between different tracks. Some filled these instrumental breaks with raps, birthing a new form of music, while others, so-called B-boys and B-girls, began breaking, now better known as breakdancing.

More than four decades on from those hot, unassuming summer block parties in New York City, breaking could reach new heights: it has been put forward as a possible future official Olympic sport. The proposal has been warmly welcomed by British breaking crews.

Karam Singh was just 10 when he burst on to the World Championship stage, becoming the youngest breaker ever to compete. Now aged 20, he's keen to represent Britain if the sport is included in the Olympics. "I think it's amazing. It's a huge step forward on what we do," he said.

Singh trains in breaking twice a day then heads to the gym; he also runs long-distance during the week and swims. "I compete in some of the biggest events of the world, but I also have to work part-time in a call centre," he says. "Going into the Olympics will give that recognition and a sense of direction that would benefit us and the generations to come."

Paco Box, 35, runs British Breaking League, a competition for 6-to-17-year-olds. "A lot of the public see breaking as spinning on your head in a club or doing the worm, but it's much more than that," he said.

The league has hundreds of children across the country competing against each other. "They're battling, but also showing respect for each other," Box said. "They're humble and driven. A few kids in the league struggle in the school, but through dance they get the drive to say 'I am good enough to progress in life'."

A British Olympic Association spokesperson said: "We look forward to welcoming all new sports into the Olympic Games and will work with the relevant bodies to develop our relationships at the appropriate time."

Marso Riviere, a manager of the breaking group Mad Dope Kru, based in Birmingham, admitted there was some concern across the community that having the sport included in the Olympics could take away the spontaneity that defined the early years of breaking: "Some people are worried of it becoming too much of a sport. It's still a dance and people are worried of the actual rawness of the dance being stripped off."

It's easy to prevent that from happening, Riviere said, "So long as you preserve good music, bring the funk and the original flavours".

Directions: *Read the passage and discuss the questions with your partner.*

1. Do you agree with the inclusion of breaking in the Olympics? Why or why not?
2. Someone worried that making breaking an Olympic sport might strip off its rawness and spontaneity. Please argue against this opinion.
3. What might be people's impression on breaking if they are teenagers, adults or senior citizens?

Part 2 Learning in Class

Warm Up

The Surprising Reason Our Muscles Get Tired

Directions: *Watch the video and discuss the questions with your partner.*

1. What are the major factors accounting for our muscle fatigue?
2. Try to explain how a muscle contracts in response to signals from the brain in your own words.
3. How do we reduce muscle fatigue? And how do we refresh ourselves if our muscles are tired?

Text A

Fixing College Sports Is Vital to Increasing Public Support for Colleges

By W. Taylor Reveley, IV ①

January 6, 2019

FOX News ②

America's greatness in higher education stands in real danger. Frustrations over the cost, purpose and value of college are symptomatic of a crucial and more basic issue: the fraying bond of trust between our universities and the broad American public. According to the Pew Research Center, 61 percent of Americans feel higher education is moving in the wrong direction. One place to start repairing their bond with higher education is by fixing what ails one of its underappreciated elements: college sports.

I am in the uncommon position of being a former college football player who now leads a university—Longwood University in Virginia. Both those experiences have shown me, from all sides, why sports are so important to the academic cause.

As the son and grandson of college presidents, I'm one of the very few third-generation college presidents in America. This perspective has also helped me realize that athletic competition has historically served as a vital link between the public and higher education.

In the late 19th century, America's colleges were a struggling patchwork. Their emergence in the century that followed as the world's first mass-scale and dominant higher education system was almost unforeseeable.

Many institutions enrolled just a few dozen students in the late 1800s, and—despite the emphasis America's founding generation had put on college—higher education had relatively little hold on popular culture.

But this formative period had some important ingredients that spurred competition, including weak central government and deep religiosity. College athletics—especially

---

① W. Taylor Reveley, IV is the president of Longwood University in Virginia.

② FOX News Channel (FNC) is a 24-hour all-encompassing news service delivering breaking news as well as political and business news. The number one network in cable, FNC has been the most watched television news channel for 17 consecutive years. According to a 2019 Suffolk University poll, FOX News is the most trusted source for television news or commentary in America while a 2019 Brand Keys Emotion Engagement Brand Analysis survey found that FOX News was the most trusted cable news brand. Owned by FOX Corporation, FNC is available in nearly 90 million homes and dominates the cable news landscape, routinely notching the top ten programs in the genre.

football and later basketball—have often been thought of as an aside in the history of American higher education. But at this critical and highly competitive juncture they were a central catalyst.

It's notable that Frederick Rudolph's magisterial 1962 book *The American College & University: A History* devotes an entire chapter to college football's critical role during the late 19th and early 20th centuries, when American college enrollment expanded more than ten-fold.

Recruiting of athletes democratized student bodies and social life. Supporting athletics galvanized alumni and—as institutions grew and students no longer uniformly followed a single, common curriculum—also forged bonds of institutional loyalty that even extended beyond students and alumni.

Athletics created a range of college and university supporters "for whom the idea of going to college was out of the question but for whom the idea of supporting the team was a matter of course", Rudolph writes.

The political impact soon followed. "Land-grant colleges and state universities discovered that athletic victories often were more important than anything else in convincing reluctant legislators to open the public purse," Rudolph writes.

Stanford sociologist David Labaree advances that story considerably in his recent book *A Perfect Mess: The Unlikely Ascendancy of American Higher Education.* He also gives athletics—along with the assorted traditions of homecoming, school colors, fight songs and other aspects of campus life and institutional loyalty—great credit for the globally unique bond between the broad American public and higher education.

Only one-third of American adults hold a college degree, but many without a degree cheer for college teams and aspire for their children and grandchildren to have the experience of college and become graduates.

And Frederick Rudolph would be amazed today by how many more college students there are and by how proportionally few Americans think of college as "out of the question". Participation in college athletics is part of that story, too.

A half-million student-athletes compete in the NCAA [1]—the vast majority in sports attracting less attention than football and basketball. The stories of these student-athletes show their home communities that there are pathways—rooted in hardwork—into institutions of higher learning. And student-athletes overwhelmingly make the most of the opportunity, graduating overall at much higher rates than non-student athletes.

---

[1] NCAA, the National Collegiate Athletic Association.

Athletics forge a crucial connection with the public, and so it should be no surprise that as new scandals emerge in college sports with dispiriting routine, Americans are also simultaneously losing faith in higher education as a whole.

Today, the NCAA and other bodies are serious in their resolve to improve. Whether sports fans or not, we should support these efforts and demand more. Beyond technical and regulatory changes, reforming college athletics calls for robust energy and far-sighted attention similar to the actions of President Roosevelt in scope—acts of political boldness in higher education.

A national commission to restore faith in college athletics could propose recommendations to improve student-athlete safety and well-being, rationalize recruiting, and ensure the lion's share of money in big-time college sports serves as a catalyst to the academic enterprise.

It may be difficult to imagine political leadership for such a project in this day and age, but it can be done. The Rice Commission Report made meaningful recommendations in recent months that focused on college basketball—including NCAA governance changes, stricter penalties for violations, and greater freedom and flexibility for student-athletes to make decisions about pursuing professional opportunities. Unfortunately, those recommendations were drowned out in the public debate by critics upset the report didn't take the much more dramatic step of professionalizing college basketball.

But that decision was the right one. In 2006, a University of California report on accountability in higher education also concluded: "Public trust is the single most important asset of higher education in this nation." Were this trust to falter, "institutions will find decreasing support from public funds, donors will not give, policy-makers will be increasingly adversarial and resources and institutional autonomy will be replaced by increased governmental intervention."

In reality, athletics lie at the heart of the uniquely American bond between the public and higher education. That bond is essential if higher education is to play the role the founders envisioned in maintaining a democratic republic. To preserve that bond, we of course must keep college affordable and accessible to the full range of Americans, of all backgrounds and viewpoints. But we can also help by fixing what ails big-time college athletics—and appreciating all that remains so deeply valuable and inspiring.

Words and Expressions

enroll	[ɪnˈrəʊl]	v.	register formally as a participant or member 登记；招收
religiosity	[rɪˌlɪdʒiˈɒsəti]	n.	exaggerated or affected piety and religious zeal 虔诚
catalyst	[ˈkætəlɪst]	n.	a substance that makes a chemical reaction happen more quickly without being changed itself 催化剂
galvanize	[ˈɡælvənaɪz]	v.	make somebody take action by shocking them or by making them excited 激励，刺激
curriculum	[kəˈrɪkjələm]	n.	the subjects that are included in a course of study or taught in a school, college, etc. 课程
ascendancy	[əˈsendənsi]	n.	the position of having power or influence over sb./sth. 优势
recruit	[rɪˈkruːt]	v.	find new people to join a company, an organization, the armed forces, etc. 吸收（新成员）；征募（新兵）
governance	[ˈɡʌvənəns]	n.	the activity of governing a country or controlling a company or an organization 治理；管理
penalty	[ˈpenəlti]	n.	(in sports) a disadvantage given to a player or a team when breaking a rule 判罚
violation	[ˌvaɪəˈleɪʃn]	n.	an action that breaks a law, agreement, principle, etc. 违背，违反
flexibility	[ˌfleksəˈbɪləti]	n.	the ability to change or be changed easily to suit a different situation 灵活性
instill	[ɪnˈstɪl]	v.	slowly but firmly establish something 逐渐灌输
revive	[rɪˈvaɪv]	v.	become healthy and strong again, or to bring something back after it has not been used or has not existed for a period of time （使）复兴
envision	[ɪnˈvɪʒn]	v.	imagine what a situation will be like in the future, especially a situation you intend to work towards 展望；想象

| ail | [eɪl] | v. | cause problems for sb./sth. 困扰 |
| big-time | [ˈbɪgtaɪm] | a. | the highest level of an occupation (especially in entertainment) 一流的 |

- **True/False/Not Given**

Do the following statements agree with the information given in Text A?

In Blanks 1-6 write

True   if the statement is true

False   if the statement is false

Not Given   if the statement is not given in the text

_____ 1. According to Frederick Rudolph, American colleges and universities could only convince the public with their athletic victories.

_____ 2. Stanford sociologist David Lavaree gives athletics great credit for the bond between the broad American public and higher education.

_____ 3. College sports offer student-athletes easy pathways into institutions of higher education.

_____ 4. Americans lose faith in colleges when scandals emerge in college sports.

_____ 5. American student-athlete competition in the NCAA attracts more attention than football.

_____ 6. College sports scandals shake Americans' faith in higher education as a whole.

- **Short Answer Questions**

1. Why do 61% of Americans feel higher education is moving in the wrong direction?

2. According to the passage, what's the starting place to repair the bond between American public and higher education?

3. What role did college athletics play in the history of American colleges and universities?

4. What are the recommendations about college basketball made by the Rice Commission Report?

5. What might happen if the American public lost trust in their higher education?

- **Summary**

Complete the summary below with words taken from the text. Use ONLY ONE WORD for each answer.

Frederick Rudolph ____1____ in his book *The American College & University: A History* an entire chapter to college football's __2__ role during the late 19th and early 20th centuries. According to him, __3__ of athletes __4__ student bodies and social life. Athletics __5__ a range of college and university supporters "for whom the idea of going to college was out of the __6__ but for whom the idea of __7__ the team was a matter of course", Rudolph writes. He also claims "Land-grant colleges and state universities discovered that athletic __8__ often were more important than anything else in __9__ reluctant legislators to open the __10__ purse".

W. Taylor Reveley strongly assumes that college sports forge a crucial connection between American public and their higher education. Can you describe this bond? And what are the possible measures you can take to restore American faith in college athletics?

Text B

Sport and Safety: Knocking Heads Together

Few sports are doing enough to protect athletes from brain damage.
January 26, 2019
The Economist

Fans of large men colliding with one another are in luck. Next weekend the Super Bowl ① kicks off in Atlanta. Some 115 cameras will beam the final of the National Football League (NFL) to fans around the world, along with advertisements urging viewers to drink beer and eat nachos. It is not a time for healthy living. Yet there is growing awareness that it is not just gluttonous fans who suffer. Contact sports can lead to serious health problems for the players, too.

An occasional broken limb is an accepted, if unfortunate, part of such games. The big worry is about what they do to the brain. In 2017-2018 some 291 concussions were reported in the NFL, the highest number since records began six years ago. The same year English rugby union recorded 18 concussions per 1,000 hours of play, almost one a match, and three times as many as five years earlier. In December last year, Nicolas Chauvin, an 18-year-old rugby player for Stade Francais' youth team, was killed when a

---

① The Super Bowl is the annual championship game of the National Football League, the highest level of professional football in America.

tackle went wrong. He was one of at least four rugby players to die from head injuries in 2018. *L'Equipe*, a French newspaper, reached a simple conclusion: "Rugby kills."

Even when contact sports do not kill, they can still do grave damage. A study in 2017 of 111 deceased NFL players found that 110 had chronic traumatic encephalopathy (CTE ①), a degenerative disease that may cause erratic behaviour, memory loss and depression, and can be diagnosed definitively only after death. The study was self-selecting because families nominated deceased relatives with symptoms of the disease. But evidence from it and from analysis of collisions in the NFL suggests that 20%-45% of professional American footballers may sustain CTE during their careers, a far higher proportion than among the general population, says Thomas Talavage of Purdue University. Last year a study found that retired rugby-league players aged 40 to 65 had significantly worse reaction times and overall cognitive performance than others their age. Suffering a severe concussion also increases an individual's chance of getting dementia later in life.

Nevertheless, the rise in reported concussions is not all bad news. Since 2001, when medics ironed out the injury's definition, there have been improvements in how potential concussions are dealt with. Rather than stoically carrying on, players are more willing to admit to concerns about their heads. Michael Turner of the International Concussion and Head Injury Research Foundation says this is crucial because concussion is far harder to diagnose than most physical injuries, and second impacts—when a player is hit on the head while playing with an undiagnosed concussion—are more likely to lead to lasting damage and even death. "Now that we're better at diagnosing [concussion] we're going to see more of it," he says.

But there are less reassuring explanations for why concussions are being reported. Paradoxically, one reason for the trend may be improvements in technology designed to keep players safe. In American football better helmets have reduced the risk of skull fractures. They have also changed playing styles, making players more comfortable using their heads as weapons with which to dislodge the ball, notes Dr Talavage. Similarly, an increasingly professional approach to physical conditioning has made collisions more dangerous, as players are stronger, faster and heavier than they used to be. Three decades ago the average rugby player in the New Zealand national team weighed 92kg. Today he weighs 106kg.

Collisions are not only more explosive, they also happen more often. Modern sports

---

① CTE, chronic traumatic encephalopathy.

schedules are relentless. A new rugby-union calendar, to be introduced next year, means elite players will compete for 11 months of the year. More women are also playing contact sports, and are twice as likely as men to suffer concussion when doing so, says Dr Turner.

Growing numbers of youth-sport organisationsare therefore reconsidering their rules. In America soccer's governing body has abolished heading for players younger than 11 and ice-hockey leagues have banned body-checkingfor those younger than 13. Meanwhile, the Ivy League American-football competition has moved the kickoff and touchback lines to encourage players to avoid collisions with one another. As a result, the rate of concussions per 1,000 kickoff plays has decreased from 11 to 2.

Few other sports teams, or associations, can say the same. The NFL has limited contactin training sessions and moved the kickoff line, but lags behind the Ivy League. Soccer does not permit special substitutions for players with concussion at any level, thus encouraging players to continue with head injuries.

Moreover, a lack of funding means that many basic questions about head injuries remain unanswered. It is, for instance, unknown whether CTE is caused by a series of blows to the head or a single powerful one. Few sports associations have stepped in to help. In 2017-2018 England's Professional Footballers Association, a representative group, spent £125,000 on research into head injuries. The same year the organisation's chief executive took home £2.3m.

Some experts are pessimistic. Dr Talavage worries that the slow pace of change reflects a belief among those in charge of sports that most fans do not care much about the players' safety. So far, viewers have not switched off from dangerous sports as awareness of concussion has grown. And there is no strong movement to ban even the most dangerous spectacles, such as boxing and mixed martial arts.

Yet sports that fail to grapple with the problem may expose themselves to legal peril. In 2015 some 5,000 former players successfully sued the NFL, winning payouts that are expected to come to around $1bn. The money will go to former players suffering from medical conditions related to head trauma, as well as the families of those who have already died from such conditions. Another lawsuit is being brought against the governing body of Australian rules football. Some experts wonder if sports may now be vulnerable even if they do change the rules, as they may still be sued for not having done so sooner.

And then there is the next generation. The number of children playing high-school American football in America has fallen by 6% in the past decade. In England the proportion of children aged 11-15 playing rugby has dropped by a third since 2011. Fewer enthusiastic young players could eventually lead to fewer lifelong fans. Although contact sports will never be able to completely eliminate on-field tragedies, it is clear that changes to the rules can reduce risk. There would be a small measure of justice if sports that are slow to adapt suffer as a result.

Words and Expressions

collide (with)	[kəˈlaɪd]	v.	hit something or someone that is moving in a different direction from you 碰撞, 相撞
gluttonous	[ˈɡlʌt(ə)nəs]	a.	given to excess in consumption of especially food or drink 贪吃的, 暴食的
contact sports			the sports that emphasize or require physical contact between players 身体接触性运动
concussion	[kənˈkʌʃn]	n.	a temporary loss of consciousness caused by a blow to the head 脑震荡
tackle	[ˈtækl]	n.	the act of knocking someone to the ground in a game such as American football or rugby 擒抱摔倒
deceased	[dɪˈsiːst]	a.	dead 亡故的
erratic	[ɪˈrætɪk]	a.	(often disapproving) not happening at regular times; not following any plan or regular pattern 不规则的; 不稳定的
diagnose	[ˈdaɪəɡnəʊz]	v.	say exactly what an illness or the cause of a problem 诊断; 判断
cognitive	[ˈkɒɡnətɪv]	a.	connected with mental processes of understanding 认知的; 感知的
dementia	[dɪˈmenʃə]	n.	a serious mental disorder caused by brain disease or injury that affects the ability to think, remember and behave normally 痴呆
stoically	[ˈstəʊɪkli]	a.	not showing emotion or not complaining when bad things happen 坚忍的
paradoxical	[ˌpærəˈdɒksɪkl]	a.	seemingly contradictory but nonetheless possibly true 矛盾的; 似非而是的
fracture	[ˈfræktʃə(r)]	n.	a break in a bone or other hard material 骨折; 断裂

dislodge	[dɪsˈlɒdʒ]	v.	force or knock sth. out of its position 用力移动
abolish	[əˈbɒlɪʃ]	v.	officially end a law, a system or an institution 废除，废止
kickoff	[ˈkɪkɒf]	n.	the time when a football game starts, or the first kick of the game（足球比赛的）开始时间；开球
touchback	[ˈtʌtʃbæk]	n.	(American football) a play in which the opposing team has kicked the dead ball into your end zone 回阵
substitution	[ˌsʌbstɪˈtjuːʃn]	n.	the act of putting one thing or person in the place of another 换人
spectacle	[ˈspektəkl]	n.	a performance or an event that is very impressive and exciting to look at 精彩的表演；壮观的场面
grapple	[ˈɡræpl]	v.	(with sth.) try hard to find a solution to a problem 努力解决
vulnerable	[ˈvʌlnərəbl]	a.	weak and easily hurt physically or emotionally 脆弱的
eliminate	[ɪˈlɪmɪneɪt]	v.	remove or get rid of sb./sth. 消除；排除

 Exercises

- **True/False/Not Given**

Do the following statements agree with the information given in Text B?

In Blanks 1-6 write

    True   if the statement is true

    False   if the statement is false

    Not Given if the statement is not given in the text

_____ 1. Contact sports do little harm to the players.

_____ 2. Brain damage and even death can be caused by concussions of rugby players.

_____ 3. CTE can be diagnosed immediately after the injury.

_____ 4. According to the NFL, 60% of their players sustain CTE during their careers.

_____ 5. CTE is often caused by a series of blows on the head.

_____ 6. Fans continue to enjoy dangerous sports although they become aware of concussion risks for the players.

- **Sentence Completion**

Complete the sentences below with words taken from Text B. Use ONLY ONE WORD for each answer.

1. A study in 2017 of _____ 111 NFL players found that 110 had CTE.
2. Chronic traumatic encephalopathy is a _____ disease that may cause erratic behavior, memory loss and depression.
3. Retired rugby-league players aged 40 to 65 had significantly worse reaction times and overall _____ performance than others their age.
4. Since 2011, there have been improvements in how potential _____ are dealt with.
5. There is no strong movement to ban even the most dangerous _____, such as boxing and mixed martial arts.

- **Comments**

The mission of the NFL is "to provide our fans, communities and partners the highest quality sports and entertainment in the world". Make your comments in no less than 300 words on this statement and the reality on American football fields according to the information in Text B.

- **Topic for Debate**

Form two groups to debate about the following proposition:

Dangerous sports shall/shall NOT be banned to completely eliminate on-field tragedies.

Academic Reading

Recognizing Purpose and Tone (2)

Learning Objective

In the section, you will learn to recognize the various kinds of tone.

The Importance of Recognizing Tone

A writer's tone or mood is a reflection of the writer's attitude or feelings toward a given topic or issue. Tone is expressed by the words and phrases used in the information presented. As with purpose, it is important for you to recognize the tone because it helps you determine a writer's motivations or reasons for writing, which can in turn make it easier to recognize bias and distinguish between facts and opinions. Furthermore, it is part of the whole evaluation process that you should use when considering not only what you read but also what you see and hear.

Thus, tone is an important consideration when you deal with contemporary issues and also when you gather information from people and written sources for problem-solving purposes. When interacting face-to-face, a person's tone of voice and body language will sometimes reveal the person's feelings on a given matter, so you may find yourself in a better position to assess the quality of the information the person is giving you. This, in turn, may help you solve a problem more efficiently. The same benefit applies when dealing with written sources for problem solving, when you want to weigh their objectivity.

As with purpose, writers don't always come right out and say what they are feeling about a particular topic or issue. In those instances, it becomes necessary to "read between the lines" and use inference skills to help determine tone. Thus, the words and phrases a writer uses will serve as the clues to the writer's attitude. As you will recall, it is often necessary to use those same clues to infer a writer's purpose when it is not explicit. In fact, tone and purpose are related, and therefore each can be used sometimes to help figure out the other. For example, if a writer's tone is humorous, it would probably indicate that the writer's purpose is to entertain and vice versa. On the other hand, if the tone is matter-of-fact, the purpose is likely to be informational.

When trying to recognize the tone, there are several possibilities to be considered. This is certainly the case when dealing with contemporary issues, where writers sometimes have more than one purpose. In addition, they may also express more than one attitude toward the subject matter. On those occasions, follow the same procedure that you used when dealing with a combination of purposes. Concentrate on the most important messages and the information that lends direct support to them. This should help you uncover the overall tone.

We will focus on five common tones or moods that are often expressed by writers: **matter-of-fact, humorous, angry, sad, and ironic.** Each one represents an overall feeling or attitude by a given writer toward a particular subject. Let us look at each of these.

(1) **Matter-of-Fact Tone**

When adopting a matter-of-fact tone, which is common in textbooks, the writer sticks to the facts and presents them in a straightforward, unemotional manner. In other words, there is a concerted attempt to be evenhanded and objective. The purpose is informational. For example, read this paragraph:

> Although progress has been made with regard to women's rights in the United States, it appears that there is room for improvement. There are still jobs not open to them, and they are sometimes paid less than men occupying the same or similar positions. Furthermore, some women have been the victims of out-and-out sexual harassment on the job. In short, it will take a while longer before we can safely say that there is equality between men and women.

The paragraph expresses little emotion as the author attempts to present the information in a straightforward and unbiased way. For the most part, the words used are not extreme or slanted.

(2) **Humorous Tone**

A humorous tone is one in which a writer presents information in a lighthearted manner designed to entertain or make the reader laugh. For instance, read the following paragraph, which deals with the same subject matter as the previous one:

> If you believe that there has been much progress with regard to women's rights in the United States, you probably also believe in the Tooth Fairy. Wake up and smell the aftershave lotion! Women are still excluded from some jobs as if they were suffering from some weird contagious disease. And just compare their pay scales to those of men in certain positions—you could die laughing. Not to mention that some males turn into cavemen when they are around women on the job. Equality between the sexes? Give me a break!

Although the paragraph makes basically the same points as the previous matter-of-fact one, it does so in a much more lighthearted way. The use of expressions such as "Tooth Fairy", "weird contagious disease", "you could die laughing" and "turn into cavemen" and the various exclamations are an attempt to be funny and make the reader laugh.

(3) **Sad Tone**

A sad tone presents information in a gloomy, melancholy, or sorrowful way. For instance, read the following paragraph, which is on the same topic as the previous ones:

> Although some slight progress has been made with regard to women's rights in the United States, there is, regrettably, ample room for improvement. It is discouraging to realize that some jobs are still not open to women and that women are too often paid less than men occupying the same or similar positions. Furthermore, some women are still the unfortunate victims of sexual harassment on the job. In short, equality between the sexes at this point remains far beyond our grasp. What a sad state of affairs!

Once again, the points that are made in the paragraph are similar to those found in the others, but this time the points are presented in a downcast manner. The use of "regrettably", "discouraging", "unfortunate" and "sad state of affairs" and the generally negative approach to the material indicate that the writer is pessimistic about the situation.

(4) **Ironic Tone**

The dictionary defines irony as "a method of humorous or sarcastic expression in which the intended meaning of the words used is the direct opposite of their usual sense" or "a combination of circumstances or a result that is the opposite of what might be expected or considered appropriate". Thus, an ironic message conveys its meaning by using words to mean the opposite of what they usually mean, and an ironic event is an occurrence that is the opposite or reverse of what is normally expected. We might describe a bad day in a sarcastic manner by saying "What a wonderful day I've had!" We also might observe the irony in the fact that the first ship specifically designed to be unsinkable, the Titanic, sank on its very first voyage. A writer generally uses irony to present messages in a catchy, unusual way so that readers will take notice and remember them. For instance, read the following paragraph, which deals once again with women's rights:

> Now that women are in business suits, why don't we just assume that no further progress needs to be made with regard to women's rights in the United States? We can simply ignore the fact that some jobs are still not open to them and that they are sometimes paid less than men occupying the same or similar positions. It really doesn't even matter that some women are still being subjected to sexual harassment on the job. Let's just proclaim equality between the sexes a *fait accompli* and get the whole issue behind us.

Notice how the writer takes what is essentially the same information but this time uses expressions that mean the opposite of the points he really wants to convey. By using this somewhat unusual technique, he hopes that the reader will be jolted into taking note of and remembering the intended messages.

Part 3　Learning After Class

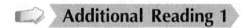 Additional Reading 1

Shanghai Pressing All the Right Buttons

By Shi Futian
January 15, 2019
China Daily

　　The value of China's fast-growing e-sports industry is attracting the favor of the nation's local governments, with many embracing gaming with open arms.

　　Now Shanghai, already a tournament hub and home to numerous e-sports organizations, is leveling up as it establishes itself as a major center for the sector.

　　Typical of Shanghai's expansion is a new deal announced on Saturday that makes the city's Oriental Sports Center the primary host stadium for Tencent E-sports tournaments.

　　Kicking off the partnership in style, Tencent's homegrown hit Honor of Kings held the final of its Champion Cup winter season at the venue on Sunday, watched by about 15,000 spectators.

　　"The e-sports industry now has a great development opportunity in China, and Shanghai has a very specific aim of becoming an international e-sports center," said Fan Jianlin, chairman of Shanghai Juss Sports Development (Group) Co. Ltd, which owns the stadium.

　　"We are experienced in organizing traditional sports events such as tennis' ATP Shanghai Masters and Formula One's Chinese Grand Prix. We are also China's leader in athletics arenas. The cooperation with Tencent is a milestone for China's e-sports development. The center was built a decade ago, and we have to upgrade its Internet and broadband infrastructure to meet the extremely high requirements of e-sports tournaments. It's a great chance for us to upgrade to a smart stadium."

　　Tencent hopes the Oriental Sports Center can set the standard for the industry. "We have been organizing e-sports tournaments for over a decade and we have been to many stadiums in China," said Mars Hou, general manager of Tencent's interactive entertainment marketing department.

"It's necessary to set a standard in the industry. As Shanghai aims to become China's e-sports center, the city boasts great infrastructure. The city and the industry both need a flagship e-sports stadium that can be an example to others that want to welcome e-sports." Last year, Tencent E-sports unveiled plans to nurture ties with local governments to help establish e-sports as a calling card for their areas.

Central to the plan are Honor of Kings, a title that boasts around 200 million registered users, and the King Pro League (KPL), China's largest mobile e-sports competition. Although broadcasts of KPL tournaments rack up billions of views online each season, Shanghai has been the only place to go to watch the action live and up close.

Last year the league split into eastern and western conferences, with a view to visiting more cities. Chengdu in Sichuan Province was the first new stop, and more are in the pipeline.

"The first requirement to select a new host city for our competitions is that it should have a big population of Honor of Kings gamers," said Zhang Yijia, president of the KPL.

"Secondly, we have to consider the local economy, including the city's infrastructure and the local government's preferential policies. Finally, we require clubs to have a deep bond with a city and local fans."

Honor of Kings has also shown its potential to go global after its international version was included as a demonstration event in last summer's Asian Games in Jakarta, where the Chinese squad won gold. Tencent marketing supremo Mars said there were many teething problems in Indonesia, so the company is keen to learn from Juss Sports' logistical expertise.

"Problems such as the players' urine tests, accommodation and especially their commute from the hotel to the stadium were very new to us in the e-sports sector. The cooperation with Juss presents a great chance for us to learn about event organization from traditional sports," said Mars.

Honor of King's international version differs greatly from the original, which has a much larger user base and more pronounced Chinese cultural elements. In a bid to expand the league further, Tencent is pushing the domestic version of the game more strongly in foreign markets.

Last year, the KPL established a South Korean league called KRKPL, whose most recent winner, KZ, competed in Shanghai. "E-sports can be a bridge of cultural communication and we want Honor of Kings to promote Chinese culture and history," said Zhang.

"We built the first foreign league, the KRKPL, which now has eight teams. We established the Champion Cup, an international tournament, based on the domestic version to allow foreigners to compete with China's KPL teams. Now we are working on increasing the competitiveness of our foreign league."

Words and Expressions

tournament	[ˈtʊənəmənt]	n.	a competition in which players compete against each other in a series of games until there is one winner 锦标赛
venue	[ˈvenjuː]	n.	a place where people meet for an organized event, for example, a concert, sporting event or conference 会场；场地
infrastructure	[ˈɪnfrəstrʌktʃə]	n.	the basic systems and services that are necessary for a country or an organization to run smoothly, for example, buildings, transport, and water and power supplies 基础设施，基础建设
unveil	[ˌʌnˈveɪl]	v.	show or introduce a new plan, product, etc. to the public for the first time (首次)展示；将……公之于众
rack up			collect sth., such as profits or losses in a business, or points in a competition 累计
in the pipeline			in the process 在进行中；在准备中
version	[ˈvɜːʃn]	n.	a form of sth. that is slightly different from an earlier form or from other forms of the same thing 型式；版本
demonstration	[ˌdemənˈstreɪʃn]	n.	an act of showing or explaining how sth. works or is done 演示
supremo	[suːˈpriːməʊ]	n.	(BrE, informal) a person who has the most power or authority in a particular business or activity 最高领导人；总管
teething problem			(phr.) a minor problem that a new company, project, product, etc. may have in the beginning 初期的困难
logistical	[ləˈdʒɪstɪkl]	a.	relating to the logistics of doing sth. 后勤的；安排协调方面的

urine	[ˈjʊərɪn]	n.	the waste liquid that collects in the bladder and that you pass from your body 尿；小便
accommodation	[əˌkɒməˈdeɪʃn]	n.	somewhere to live or stay, often also providing food or other services 住宿；膳宿
league	[liːg]	n.	a group of sports teams who all play each other to earn points and find which team is best(体育运动队的)联合会，联赛

Discussion Questions

1. Are e-sports games or sports? What's your opinion and how would you defend that?
2. Being a professional e-sports player means the athlete has to train at least 14 hours a day sitting in front of a computer to maintain ideal condition. However, addiction is an unfortunate side effect of the booming e-sports industry in China. How could we sustain the development of e-sports and simultaneously prevent children's addiction to gaming?
3. What are the requirements to select a host city for KPL tournaments?

Additional Reading 2

The NBA Three-point Contest Has Grown Stale. Here's How to Make It Fun.

By Ben Golliver

January 27, 2019

The Washington Post

The names of next month's all-star three-point contest participants are starting to leak, and it's shaping up to be a dreamy field. Two-time MVP Stephen Curry and his younger brother, Seth, will reportedly serve as hometown headliners Feb. 16 in Charlotte, with Dirk Nowitzki and Damian Lillard providing added star power.

Unfortunately, Stephen Curry's presence is a reminder that the event's anachronistic and unfulfilling format no longer highlights the best that NBA shooters have to offer. While the league has run into trouble by tinkering too often with the slam dunk contest, it has refused to significantly alter the three-point contest, which sees contestants shoot racks of five balls from five different spots around the arc, with the final "money ball" in each rack counting double. The only major format change in recent years saw the addition of a "money ball rack", in which all five shots from one spot count double.

Larry Bird won the inaugural contest in 1986 by scoring an impressive 22 out of 30 points at a time when the league didn't have multiple weekly showcase games, League Pass or social media. That event was the best opportunity for basketball fans to see Bird's elite skills on display, and watching him take 25 catch-and-shoot jumpers in quick succession was enthralling given that he never attempted more than seven threes in a game that season.

More than 30 years later, the proliferation of the three-point shot, the increased distribution of NBA games and advancements in video sharing have made this event obsolete. Consider: The 1986 Dallas Mavericks led the NBA with 141 three-pointers, a total that Curry surpassed by himself in fewer than 30 games this season. But players aren't just shooting way more three-pointers and making way more difficult three-pointers, they're doing it in an environment where a global fan base has constant access to their exploits.

Before every Golden State Warriors ① game, Curry puts on a better show than the three-point contest. He shoots off his left leg, then off his right leg. He heads the ball to himself like a soccer player and then spins into turnarounds. He slides around taking off-the-dribble step-backs. He tosses in bombs from the center-court logo and famously closes with a shot from the tunnel, all while media outlets live-stream the proceedings from the Bay Area to Beijing.

Asking Curry to compete in the traditional contest format is like asking a world-class driver to race a Toyota Prius ② at the Indy 500 ③. The three-point contest allows no room to display a shooter's personality, favorite spots or ability to execute high degree-of-difficulty attempts. Imagine how much less popular Olympic figure skating would be if the contestants were judged solely by how many single axels they could perform in a minute.

With that in mind, the NBA must follow three steps to redesign the three-point contest so that it rewards creative shot-making rather than mechanical repetition.

1. The shooting space must be expanded, adding zones for three-point shots, four-point shots and five-point shots so Curry, Lillard and others can showcase their well-honed long balls.
2. Players should be allowed to place their ball racks anywhere they like so that they can play to their strengths and craft individual strategies to maximize their points.

---

① Golden State Warriors (NBA) 金州勇士队
② Toyota Prius 丰田普锐斯油电混合车
③ the Indy 500 印第 500 赛车大奖赛

High-level shooters are obsessive and competitive, and watching their strategies unfold would be entertaining in and of itself.

3. Players should be awarded a bonus point for dribbling to set up a shot, thereby highlighting the added intrigue of the current step-back phenomenon led by James Harden and others. This would require loosening the time allotment, a small sacrifice given that the goal should be to celebrate innovation, not conformity.

Last year, Devin Booker won the three-point contest by scoring a record 28 out of a possible 34 points. It's not hard to imagine one of this year's shooters raising the bar or possibly even making a run at a never-before-seen perfect score.

But NBA organizers should ponder what would generate more hype, more viral clipsand a greater appreciation for shooting mastery: Curry hitting all 25 threes in the traditional format or Curry digging deep into his full bag of tricks, zigzagging from spot to spot as he buries off-the-dribble four-pointers and drains three straight moon balls from the logo?

It seems clear that the current format's best possible outcome pales in comparison to what could be awaiting fans if the three-point contest were to finally undergo a proper makeover.

 Words and Expressions

anachronistic	[əˌnækrəˈnɪstɪk]	a.	out-of-date or inappropriate at the time in question 落伍的;不合时宜的
slam dunk			in basketball, a shot in which a player jumps up and jams or slams the ball forcefully down into the basket 强力灌篮;扣篮
inaugural	[ɪˈnɔːgjərəl]	a.	first, and marking the beginning of sth. important 首次的;开始的
succession	[səkˈseʃn]	n.	a number of people or things that follow each other in time or order 一连串;一系列
proliferation	[prəˌlɪfəˈreɪʃn]	n.	the sudden increase in the number or amount of sth. 激增
off-the-dribble		a.	moving the ball along with you by short kicks, bounces or hits in a game of football, basketball, etc. 运球的

tunnel	[ˈtʌnl]	n.	a passage in a sports stadium by which players enter or leave the field 运动场运动员通道
axel	[ˈæksl]	n.	a jump in skating in which you jump from the front outside edge of one foot, turn in the air, and land on the outside edge of your other foot 前外一周半跳
in and of itself			with respect to its inherent nature 本身
intrigue	[ˈɪntriːg]	n.	the activity of making sb. very interested in knowing more about sth., especially sth. that seems mysterious 激发好奇；着迷
raise the bar			set a higher standard of quality or performance 提高标准
moon ball			高吊球

 Discussion Questions

1. Why did the traditional three-point contest become obsolete?
2. What do you know about Stephen Curry's shooting skills?
3. What might be your suggestions to improve the contest and find out the best three-point shooter?

 Additional Reading 3

Going It Alone: What Drives Solo Endurance Athletes?

From transatlantic rowers to cross-continental runners, solo adventurers rely as much on their mental strength as their physical attributes.

By Allison Torres Burtka

February 22, 2019

The Guardian

Few people have the will and the stamina needed to run across a continent or row across an ocean—and even fewer opt to do so alone and unsupported. What makes these endurance athletes different from others who pursue similar challenges as part of a team, or while competing against fellow athletes? Are they simply made of tougher stuff?

In August, Bryce Carlson broke the world record for the fastest west-to-east unsupported row across the North Atlantic Ocean. The previous record belonged to a boat of four people. Carlson set off solo from Newfoundland in a custom-made boat and landed at the Isles of Scilly a little more than 38 days later. He's the first American to row this route solo and unsupported.

Endurance sports are not new to Carlson, who rowed at the University of Michigan, ran ultramarathons and then ran across the US, from California to Maryland, with 11 other runners. On that run, Carlson always had other runners and support staff around.

Carlson, a high school biology teacher who holds a doctorate in biological anthropology, explained that "I felt I did not really have the opportunity to sit with my own thoughts as much as I would have liked", and he looked forward to that in his trans-Atlantic row. "It became a challenge, as well as an opportunity to explore myself and my psyche in ways that previous challenges of mine have not."

Carlson's boat capsized about a dozen times, and he got caught in bad weather and currents that took him in the wrong direction. He learned "to remain patient with things I couldn't change, and to remain focused on things I had control over", he said. He was able to avoid getting upset, which he attributes to a decade of ultra-running.

Kevin Alschuler, PhD, is a psychologist at the University of Washington School of Medicine who led the psychology portion of a study that followed Carlson's team's run across the US, and he also gathered data from Carlson on his row. He had Carlson complete a daily questionnaire while on the Atlantic, along with a brief diary response asking him to describe the biggest challenge he faced that day and how he responded to it. The 15 questions asked about effort, physical symptoms (pain, fatigue) and psychological variables (confidence, anxiety, frustration).

Alschuler and his team followed along in real time. "We were looking at things that we think are positive and helpful, as well as those that we think are negative or hurtful. In general, he was higher on the positive or helpful factors consistently, and he was lower on the negative or unhelpful," he said. They also asked Carlson to rate these factors, and his ratings showed "he really had the full range of experiences", even though he exhibited more positive than negative variables. From a psychologist's perspective, Alschuler said, "We're really interested in athletes' abilities to be mindful or fully present in the moment—what's happening in their competition or their event."

Carlson said staying in the moment and getting the most out of that moment had been a big challenge. On some days, he was less focused and more easily distracted.

"Modern sport psychology thought is that you want athletes who are driven by these goals and these outcomes" but who can set the goals aside and "really immerse themselves in whatever step they're on", Alschuler said. "Carlson wanted to get across as quickly and as safely as he could, and there was a record out there that he might be able to break, but each day was a day of rowing," Alschuler explained. "He focused on what could he do to make the most of that day."

When Carlson was positioning himself to avoid the worst of a hurricane, he landed in an adverse current that pulled him in the wrong direction. To cope, Carlson explained in his diary response, "I focused on what was near at hand and controllable, navigated my boat as best I could. Hope the current will weaken overnight, nothing else I can do." Alschuler said this response "shows that ability to be fully aware of what's going on, fully present with the challenge that's there, and yet then redirect his response to what's in his control and let go of what's out of his control".

The Ocean Rowing Society keeps records of ocean crossings, and it has documented nearly 500 successful attempts and more than 250 unsuccessful ones. Coordinator Tatiana Rezvaya-Crutchlow said many rowers quit on the first day, when they lose sight of the land, and "you have 360 degrees of just horizon". Some people celebrate their "freedom at last," but for others, fear sets in. "It's willpower over willpower," she said.

From a sport psychology standpoint, goal-setting is important, said Kristin Hoffner, principal lecturer in Arizona State's College of Health Solutions. Goals need to be attainable and achievable—but that's a matter of perspective, she said. If someone thinks they can achieve a goal, "that can be a very motivating thing for them, whether you think—from an outside perspective—it's attainable or not".

Athletes taking on such daunting challenges also may deal with their emotions differently when they're alone. "Endurance sports frequently involve ugly crying, swearing and moments of hysteria that might be better done in privacy," Carlson noted. "When I sign up for a race, I don't know if I can do it. It's something I'm not capable of doing in that moment, and I have to put together a plan to become the kind of person who can complete that challenge. It's good to get out of our comfort bubbles and know what we're capable of. That's part of the fun for me."

Words and Expressions

stamina	[ˈstæmɪnə]	n.	the physical or mental strength that enables you to do sth. difficult for long periods of time 毅力；耐力
endurance	[ɪnˈdjʊərəns]	n.	the ability to continue doing sth. painful or difficult for a long period of time without complaining 耐力
route	[ruːt]	n.	a way that you follow to get from one place to another 路线
solo	[ˈsəʊləʊ]	n.	any activity that is performed alone without assistance 单飞；独行
capsize	[kæpˈsaɪz]	v.	(a boat) turn over in the water (船)翻，倾覆
current	[ˈkʌrənt]	n.	the movement of water in the sea or a river 水流，潮流
symptom	[ˈsɪmptəm]	n.	a change in your body or mind that show that you are not healthy 症状
variable	[ˈveəriəbl]	n.	a situation, number or quantity that can vary or be varied 变量
immerse	[ɪˈmɜː(r)s]	v.	become or make sb. completely involved in sth. 沉浸在
hurricane	[ˈhʌrɪkeɪn]	n.	a violent storm with very strong winds, especially in the western Atlantic Ocean 飓风
attainable	[əˈteɪnəbl]	a.	that you can achieve 可达到的；可获得的
perspective	[pəˈspektɪv]	n.	a particular attitude towards sth.; a way of thinking about sth. 态度；观点
hysteria	[hɪˈstɪəriə]	n.	a state of extreme excitement, fear or anger in which a person loses control of his emotions and starts to cry, laugh, etc. 歇斯底里

Discussion Questions

1. What might enable solo athletes to accomplish their endurance adventures?
2. How did Alschuler collect data of Carlson's trans-Atlantic row for his psychological research?
3. What mental strengths did Carlson show when he was rowing across the ocean solo and unsupported?

Part 4　Topical Vocabulary

acrobatics 杂技
athletics/track and field 田径运动
backstroke 仰泳
birdie（高尔夫）低于标准杆的一击
breaststroke 蛙泳
clinch（格斗中双方的）互相扭抱
counterpunch（拳击）反击
dribbling（篮球）运球
foul 犯规
ice hockey 冰球
marathon 马拉松
medley 混合泳
parry（拳击）闪避
pole-vault 撑竿跳高
smash 扣球，杀球
springboard（跳水或体操中的）跳板
squash 壁球
striker 前锋
trampoline 蹦床
eagle（高尔夫）比标准杆少两杆的分数
the Summer/Winter Olympic Games 夏/冬季奥林匹克运动会
the Summer/Winter Paralympic Games 夏/冬季残奥会

archery 射箭
bare-knuckled 不戴拳击手套的
biathlon 现代冬季两项（越野滑雪和步枪射击）
bogey（高尔夫）高出标准杆一杆
bunker（高尔夫）沙坑
conversion（橄榄球）附加得分
decathlon 十项全能
deuce（网球）局末平分
field hockey 曲棍球
love（网球）零分
martial arts 武术
MVP（most valuable player）最有价值的球员
possession 控球
rebound 篮板球
somersault 空翻
southpaw（尤指拳击等运动中的）左撇子
steeplechase 障碍跑；越野赛马
taekwondo 跆拳道
heptathlon（尤指女子）七项全能（运动）
X-sports/extreme sports 极限运动

aquatic sports (swimming, diving, water polo) 水上运动(游泳、跳水、水球)
canoeing (slalom and sprint) 皮划艇(激流回旋赛和短途赛)
cycling (road, track, mountain, BMX) 自行车运动(公路、赛车场、山地、越野)
gymnastics (artistic, rhythmic, trampoline) 体操(艺术体操、韵律操、蹦床)
hot-dogging (冲浪、滑雪运动中的)特技动作
modern pentathlon 现代五项(包括跑步、游泳、马术、击剑和射击)
triathlon 三项全能运动(铁人三项,包括赛跑、游泳和骑自行车)
wrestling (freestyle and Greco-Roman) 摔跤(自由式和古典式)

Appendix 1

英美报刊常用缩略语

AA	Automobile Association	汽车协会
ABA	American Bankers Association	美国银行家协会
ABC	American Broadcasting Company	美国广播公司
ABU	Asian Broadcasting Union	亚洲广播联盟
A/C	Current Account	账户
ADB	Asian Development Bank	亚洲开发银行
ADF	Asian Development Fund	亚洲开发基金
ADSL	Asymmetrical Digital Subscriber Line	非对称数字用户线路
ADR	Asset Depreciation Range	资产折旧幅度
AEA	American Economic Association	美国经济协会
AFP	Agence France-Presse	法新社
AGM	Annual General Meeting	年会
AID	Agency for International Development	（美）国际开发署
AIDS	Acquired Immune Deficiency Syndrome	艾滋病
AMA	American Marketing Association	美国销售协会
AMEX	American Stock Exchange	美国股票交易所
AMTRK	American Track	美国国家铁路客运公司
A/N	Account Number	账号
ANS	American National Standards	美国国家标准
ANSA	Agenzia Nazionale Stampa Associata	（意大利）安莎通讯社

AP	Associated Press	(美国)美联社
APEC	Asia Pacific Economic Cooperation	亚太经济合作组织
ATM	Automated Teller Machine	自动取款机
AQL	Acceptable Quality Level	合格质量标准
ASEAN	Association of South East Asian Nations	东南亚国家联盟
A/T	Air Transportation	空运
A/W	Actual Weight	实际重量
AWT	Actual Work Time	实际工作时间

BA	Bachelor of Arts	文科学士
BBA	Bachelor of Business Administration	商贸管理学士
BBC	British Broadcasting Corporation	英国广播公司
BBS	Bulletin Board Service	公告牌系统；论坛
BIS	Bank for International Settlement	国际结算银行
BRITRAIL-PASS	British Travel Pass	英国铁路游览卡
B/S	Bill of Sale	销货清单
BS	Bachelor of Science	理科学士
BSI	Business Survey Index	企业调查索引
BTA	British Tourist Authority	美国旅游管理局

C/A	Capital Account	资本账户
CAA	Civil Aviation Authority	英国民航管理局
CAB	Civil Aeronautics Board	美国民用航空局
CACM	Central American Common Market	中美洲共同市场
CATV	Cable Television	有线电视
CBD	Central Business District	中央商贸区
CEAC	Commission Européenne de l'Aviation Civile	欧洲民航委员会
CEC	Commission of the European Communities	欧洲共同体委员会
CECF	Chinese Export Commodities Fair	中国出口商品交易会
CEO	Chief Executive Officer	首席行政官
CFO	Chief Finance Officer	首席财务官
CG	Consul General	总领事

CIA	Central Intelligence Agency	美国中央情报局
CITS	China International Travel Service	中国国际旅行社
CNN	Cable News Network	美国有线新闻电视网
CP	Communist Party	中国共产党
CPA	Certified Public Accountant	会计师
CPI	Consumer Price Index	消费品物价指数
CPU	Central Processing Unit	（计算机）中央处理机
C. R.	Conversion Rate/Ratio	兑换率
CRC	Cambridge Research Center	剑桥研究中心
CST	Central Standard Time	中部标准时间
C/T	Cable Transfer	电汇
CV	Curriculum Vitae	个人简历

DBS	Direct Broadcasting Satellite	卫星直播
D. Eng.	Doctor of Engineering	工程博士
Dept.	Department	部门
DG	Dangerous Goods	危险品
DI	Disposable Income	可支配收入
Diss.	Dissertation	论文
Dist.	District	街区；地区
Divd.	Dividend	股息；红利
DJI	Dow Jones Index	道琼斯指数
DNA	Deoxyribonucleic Acid	脱氧核糖核酸；基因
Doc	Document	文档
DP	Data Processing	数据处理
D. R.	Daily Report	每日报表
DVD	Digital Video Disc	数字化视频光盘

EAC	European Advisory Commission	欧洲咨询委员会
EC	European Community	欧洲共同体
ECM	European Common Market	欧洲共同市场
ECO	Economic Cooperation Organization	经济合作组织

EDP	Electronic Data Processing	电子数据处理
EEC	European Economic Community	欧洲经济共同体
EL	Export License	出口许可证
EMF	European Monetary Fund	欧洲货币基金
EPS	Earnings Per Share	每股盈利额
ERP	Enterprise Resource Planning	企业资源计划
ETV	Education Television	教育电视
EU	European Union	欧盟
EXPO	(World) Exposition	世界贸易博览会

FAO	Food and Agricultural Organization	(联合国)粮食及农业组织
Fed	Federal Reserve	美联储
FM	For Majeure	不可抗力
FOC	Free of Charges	免费
Fut.	Futures	期货
FWH	Flexible Working Hours	弹性工时
FYI	For Your Information	供参考

GA	General Agent	总代理
GAP	Gross Agricultural Product	农业总产量
Gas.	Gasoline	汽油
GDP	Gross Domestic Product	国内生产总值
GHQ	General Headquarter	总部
GM	General Manager	总经理
GMT	Greenwich Mean Time	格林尼治时间
GND	General National Demand	国民总需求
GNE	Gross National Expenditures	国民支出总额
GNP	Gross National Product	国民生产总值
GP	General Practitioner	普通医师
GPO	General Post Office	邮政总局
GSA	General Sales Agent	销售总代理

HAC	Hague Arbitration Convention	海牙仲裁公约
HO	Home/Head Office	总公司
HR	House of Representatives	众议院

IAA	International Advertising Association	国际广告协会
IAAA	Inter-American Accounting Association	泛美会计学会
IAEA	International Atomic Energy Agency	国际原子能代理机构
IBEC	International Bank of Economic Cooperation	国际经济合作银行
IBM	International Business Machine Corporation	国际商用机器公司
IBP	International Balance of Payments	国际收支
IBR	International Bank for Reconstruction and Development	国际复兴开发银行(世界银行)
ICA	International Cooperation Administration	国际合作总署
ICC	International Chamber of Commerce	国际商会
ICF	International Compensation Fund	国际赔偿基金
ICJ	International Court of Justice	(联合国)国际法院
ICM	International Currency Market	国际货币市场
ICRC	International Committee of Red Cross	红十字国际委员会
ICU	Intensive Care Unit	加护病房
ID	Identity Card	身份证
IDA	International Development Association	国际开发协会
IDD	International Direct Dialing	国际直播电话
IDL	International Date Line	国际换日线；日界线
IDP	International Driving Permit	国际驾驶执照
IE	Industrial Engineering	工业工程
IFAC	International Federation of Accountants	国际会计师联合会
IFC	International Finance Corporation	国际金融公司
IFJ	International Federation of Journalists	国际新闻工作者联合会
IIB	International Investment Bank	国际投资银行
I/L	Import License	进口许可证
ILA	International Law Association	国际法协会
ILO	International Labor Organization	国际劳工组织
IMF	International Monetary Fund	国际货币基金会

INS	International News Service	(美)国际新闻社
INTELSAT	International Telecommunications Satellite Consortium	国际通信卫星组织
INTERTEL	International Television Federation	国际电视联合会
INTERNET	International Network	国际网络
Inv.	Invoice	发票
I/O	Input/Output	输入/输出
IOC	International Olympic Committee	国家奥林匹克委员会
IPI	International Press Institute	国际新闻学会
IRB	International Resources Bank	国际资源银行
IRO	International Refugee Organization	国际难民组织
IPR	Intellectual Property Rights	知识产权
ISBN	International Standard Book Number	国际标准书号
ISIC	International Standard Industrial Classification	国际工业标准分类
ISSN	International Standard Serial Number	国家标准连续出版物编号
ISO	International Standard Organization	国际标准化组织
ITC	International Trade Center	(联合国)国际贸易中心
ITC	International Trade Charter	国际贸易宪章
ITPC	International Television Program Center	国际电视节目中心
ITU	International Telecommunication Union	国际电讯联盟

JE	*Journal of Economics*	《经济学》杂志
JV	Joint Venture	合资企业

Lab.	Laboratory	实验室
LACM	Latin American Common Market	拉美共同市场
LAFTA	Latin American Free Trade Association	拉美自由贸易协会
L/C	Letter of Credit	信用证
LDC	Less Developed Countries	较不发达国家
Lic.	License	许可证;执照
LIFFE	London International Finance Futures Exchange	伦敦国际金融期货交易所
LLDC	Least Less Developed Country	最不发达国家
LSE	London Stock Exchange	伦敦证券交易所

| LZT | Local Zone Time | 地区时间 |

MB	Memorandum Book	备忘录
MBA	Master of Business Administration	工商管理硕士
MBF	Medical Benefits Fund	医疗福利基金
MBO	Management by Objectives	目标管理
MC	Member of Congress	(美)国会议员
MC	Member of Council	(英)议会议员
ME	Middle East	中东
MFN	Most Favored Nation	最惠国
ML	Machine Language	计算机语言
MM	Maintenance Manual	维修手册
MMA	Merchandise Marks Act	(英)商标法
MNCS	Multinational Companies	跨国公司
MOL	Member of Parliament	(英)议员
MPR	Monthly Progress Report	月进度报告
MR	Market Research	市场调研
MS	Master of Science	科学硕士
MTV	Music Television	音乐电视
MV	Market Value	市面价值

NA	North America	北美
NASA	National Aeronautics and Space Administration	美国航空航天局
NATO	North Atlantic Treaty Organization	北大西洋公约组织
NCI	New Capital Issue	新发行股票
NCV	No Commercial Value	无商业价值
ND	Non Delivery	未交付
ND	National Debt	国债
NDP	Net Domestic Product	国内净产值
NIEO	New International Economic Order	国际经济新秩序
NNP	Net National Product	国内生产净值
NP	Nobel Prize	诺贝尔奖

NSF	National Science Federation	(美)国家科学基金会
NTO	Not Taken Out	禁止带出
NYSE	New York Stock Exchange	纽约股票交易所
NYFE	New York Futures Exchange	纽约期货交易所

OAU	Organization of African Unity	非洲统一组织
OEEC	Organization for European Economic Cooperation	欧洲经济合作组织
OEO	Office of Economic Opportunity	(美)经济机会就业局
OIRT	Organization of International Radio and Television	国际广播电视组织
OPEC	Organization of Petroleum Exporting Countries	欧佩克石油输出国组织
OPM	Output Per Man	人均产量
OTC	Organization of Trade Cooperation	贸易合作组织

PAR	Program Analysis and Review	项目分析与审查
PBS	Public Broadcasting Service	公共广播服务中心
PC	Payment Center	付款中心
PC	Personal Computer	个人电脑
PCT	Patent Cooperation Treaty	专利合作条约
PD	Preferential Duties	特惠关税
PGR	Population Growth Rate	人口增长率
PhD	Doctor of Philosophy	哲学博士;博士
PHS	Public Health Service	公共健康服务中心
PICA	Private Investment Company for Asia	亚洲私人投资公司
PICC	The People's Insurance Company of China	中国人民保险公司
PIN	Personal Identification Number	个人识别号码
PIR	Production Inspection Record	生产检查记录
PMA	Personal Management Analysis	人事管理分析
PO	Patent Office	专利局
P.O.B.	Post-Office Box	邮政信箱
POS	Point of Sale	销售点
PR	Public Relations	公共关系
PS	Public Sale	公卖;拍卖

PTO	Patent and Trademark Office	专利商标局
PTV	Public Television	公共电视
PU	Public Utilities	公共事业
PUC	Public Utilities Commission	公共事业委员会
PW	Public Welfare	公共福利

QC	Quality Control	质量控制
QV	Quod Vide	参阅

R & D	Research and Development	研究与发展
RB	Regular Budget	常规预算
RC	Red Cross	红十字会
RC	Release Clause	豁免条款
Rept.	Receipt	收据
Regd.	Registered	已注册
R. R.	Railroad	铁路
RWT	Round the World Tour	环球旅行

S. B.	Savings Bank	储蓄银行
SBN	Standard Book Number	标准书号
S. C.	Supreme Court	最高法院
SC	Security Council (of the United Nations)	（联合国）安理会
SCI	Science Citation Index	科学引文索引
SEATO	South East Asia Treaty Organization	东南亚条约组织
S/H	Stockholder	股东
SPC	State Planning Commission	国家计划委员会
SSA	Social Security Administration	（美）社会安全总署

TAB	Technical Assistance Board (United Nations)	（联合国）技术援助委员会
TC	Traveler's Check	旅行支票
TM	Trademark	商标
TNC	Transnational Company	跨国公司

TOT	Terms of Trade	贸易条件
TR	Technical Report	技术报告
TU	Trade Union	工会
TV	Television	电视
TW	Total Weight	总重量

UCC	Universal Copyright Convention	世界著作权公约
UCC	Uniform Commercial Code	（美）统一商法法典
UDC	Universal Decimal Classification	国际十进位分类法
UEA	Universal Esperanto Association	国际世界语协会
UFO	Unidentified Flying Object	不明飞行物；飞碟
UN	United Nations	联合国
UNCDF	United Nations Capital Development Fund	联合国资本开发资金
UNCHE	United Nations Conference on the Human Environment	联合国人类环境会议
UNCTAD	United Nations Conference on Trade and Development	联合国贸易和发展会议
UNDC	United Nations Disarmament Commission	联合国裁军委员会
UNDP	United Nations Development Program	联合国开发计划署
UNEF	United Nations Emergency Force	联合国紧急部队
UNEP	United Nations Environment Program	联合国环境规划署
UNESCO	United Nations Educational, Scientific, and Cultural Organization	联合国教科文组织
UNFAO	United Nations Food and Agriculture Organization	联合国粮农组织
UNEPA	United Nations Fund for Population Activities	联合国人口活动基金会
UNGA	United Nations General Assembly	联合国大会
UNHCR	United Nations High Commissioner for Refugees	联合国难民高级官员
UNICEF	United Nations Children's (Emergency) Fund	联合国儿童基金会
UNIDO	United Nations Industrial Development Organization	联合国工业发展组织
UNO	United Nations Organization	联合国组织
UPI	United Press International	合众国际社

VIP	Very Important Person	贵宾
VOA	Voice of America	美国之音（广播电台）

VOLAR	Volunteer Army	志愿军
VP	Vice President	副总统；副总裁

WB	World Bank	世界银行
WC	Without Charge	免费
WFC	World Finance Corporation	世界金融公司
WHO	World Health Organization	世界卫生组织
Wkly	Weekly	周报；周刊
WPA	World Patents Abstracts	世界专利文摘
WPI	World Patent Index	世界专利索引
WTO	World Trade Organization	世界贸易组织

XB	Extra-Budgetary	预算外
Xm；X'mas	Christmas	圣诞节
Xtry.	Extraordinary	非常的

YB	Year Book	年鉴
YHA	Youth Hostels Association	青年招待所协会
YO	Year Output	年产量
YOB	Year of Birth	出生年

ZEF	Zollfrei	免税
ZL	Zero Line	基准线
ZPG	Zero Population Growth	人口零增长

Appendix 2

英美著名媒体简介

一、美国的著名日报

英文名称	中文名称	网站地址
The New York Times	《纽约时报》	http://www.nytimes.com/
Los Angeles Time	《洛杉矶时报》	http://www.latimes.com/
Washington Post	《华盛顿邮报》	http://www.washingtonpost.com/
The Wall Street Journal	《华尔街日报》	http://www.wsj.com/
USA Today	《今日美国报》	http://www.usatoday.com/
International Herald Tribune	《国际先驱论坛报》	http://www.iht.com
Miami Gerald	《迈阿密先驱报》	http://www.miamiherald.com/
Baltimore Sun	《巴尔的摩太阳报》	http://www.baltimoresun.com/
Chicago Tribune	《芝加哥论坛报》	http://www.chicagotribune.com/
The New York Daily News	《纽约每日新闻》	http://www.nydailynews.com/
New York Post	《纽约邮报》	http://www.nypost.com/

二、美国的著名期刊

英文名称	中文名称	网站地址
TIME	《时代》	http://www.time.com/
News Weekly	《新闻周刊》	http://www.newsweekly.com.au/
New Yorker	《纽约客》	Http://www.newyorker.com/
Business Week	《商业周刊》	http://www.businessweek.com/
U.S. News & World Report	《美国新闻与世界报道》	http://www.usnews.com/

(To be continued)

英文名称	中文名称	网站地址
Fortune (biweekly)	《财富》(双周刊)	http://www.fortune.com/
Forbes (biweekly)	《福布斯》(双周刊)	http://www.forbes.com/
Reader's Digest	《读者文摘》	http://www.rd.com/
National Geographic	《国家地理》杂志	http://www.nationalgeographic.com/
Smithsonian	《史密森》	http://www.smithsonianmag.com/
Vanity Fair	《名利场》	http://www.vanityfair.com/
Atlantic Monthly	《大西洋月刊》	http://www.theatlantic.com/
Harper's Magazine	《哈珀斯杂志》	http://http://harpers.chadwyck.com/

三、美国的广播公司

英文名称	中文名称	简称	网站地址
National Broadcasting Company	全国广播公司	NBC	http://www.nbc.com/
American Broadcasting Company	美国广播公司	ABC	http://www.abc.com/
Associated Press	美联社	AP	http://www.ap.org/
United Press-International News Service	合众国际社	UPI	http://www.upi.com/
Voice of America	美国之音	VOA	http://www.voa.gov/
Columbia Broadcasting System	哥伦比亚广播公司	CBS	http://www.cbs.com/

四、英国的著名日报

英文名称	中文名称	网站地址
The Times	《泰晤士报》	http://www.thetimes.co.uk/
The Guardian	《卫报》	http://www.guardian.co.uk/
The Daily Mirror	《每日镜报》	http://www.mirror.co.uk/
The Sun	《太阳报》	http://www.thesun.co.uk/
Daily Mail	《每日邮报》	http://www.dailymail.co.uk/
Daily Star	《每日星报》	http://www.dailymail.co.uk/
Financial Times	《金融时报》	http://www.ft.com/home/uk
The Independent	《独立报》	http://www.independent.co.uk/
Daily Express	《每日快报》	http://www.express.co.uk/
The Daily Telegraph	《每日电讯报》	http://www.dailytelegraph.co.uk/
News of the World	《世界新闻报》	http://www.newsoftheworld.co.uk/
The Observer	《观察家报》	http://www.observer.co.uk/

五、英国的著名期刊

英文名称	中文名称	网站地址
The Economist	《经济学家》	http://www.economist.com/
Discovery	《发现》	http://www.discovery.com/
Nature	《自然》	http://www.nature.com/
The Spectator	《旁观者》	http://www.spectator.co.uk/
The New Statesman	《新政治家》	http://www.newstatesman.co.uk/
Now	《现在》	http://www.nowmagazine.co.uk/
The Listener	《听众》	http://www.listener.co.nz/
The New Society	《新社会》	http://www.newsociety.com/
The Geographical Magazine	《地理杂志》	http://www.geographical.co.uk/
Scientific World	《科学世界》	http://www.thescientificworld.com/

Appendix 3

美国行政州及其简称

美国各州州名	中文州名	缩写	首府名	中文首府名
Alabama	亚拉巴马州	AL	Montgomery	蒙哥马利
Alaska	阿拉斯加州	AK	Juneau	朱诺
Arizona	亚利桑那州	AZ	Phoenix	菲尼克斯
Arkansas	阿肯色州	AR	Little Rock	小石城
California	加利福尼亚州	CA	Sacramento	萨克拉门托
Colorado	科罗拉多州	CO	Denver	丹佛
Connecticut	康涅狄格州	CT	Hartford	哈特福德
Delaware	特拉华州	DE	Dover	多佛
Florida	佛罗里达州	FL	Tallahassee	塔拉哈西
Georgia	佐治亚州	GA	Atlanta	亚特兰大
Hawaii	夏威夷州	HI	Honolulu	火奴鲁鲁
Idaho	爱达荷州	ID	Boise	博伊西
Illinois	伊利诺伊州	IL	Springfield	斯普林菲尔德
Indiana	印第安纳州	IN	Indianapolis	印第安纳波利斯
Iowa	艾奥瓦州	IA	Des Moines	得梅因
Kansas	堪萨斯州	KS	Topeka	托皮卡
Kentucky	肯塔基州	KY	Frankfort	法兰克福
Louisiana	路易斯安那州	LA	Baton Rouge	巴吞鲁日
Maine	缅因州	ME	Augusta	奥古斯塔

(To be continued)

美国各州州名	中文州名	缩写	首府名	中文首府名
Maryland	马里兰州	MD	Annapolis	安纳波利斯
Massachusetts	马萨诸塞州	MA	Boston	波士顿
Michigan	密歇根州	MI	Lansing	兰辛
Minnesota	明尼苏达州	MN	St. Paul	圣保罗
Mississippi	密西西比州	MS	Jackson	杰克逊
Missouri	密苏里州	MO	Jefferson City	杰斐逊城
Montana	蒙大拿州	MT	Helena	海伦娜
Nebraska	内布拉斯加州	NE	Lincoln	林肯
Nevada	内华达州	NV	Carson City	卡森城
New Hampshire	新罕布什尔州	NH	Concord	康科德
New Jersey	新泽西州	NJ	Trenton	特伦顿
New Mexico	新墨西哥州	NM	Santa Fe	圣菲
New York	纽约州	NY	Albany	奥尔巴尼
North Carolina	北卡罗来纳州	NC	Raleigh	纳罗利
North Dakota	北达科他州	ND	Bismarck	俾斯麦
Ohio	俄亥俄州	OH	Columbus	哥伦布
Oklahoma	俄克拉何马州	OK	Oklahoma City	俄克拉何马城
Oregon	俄勒冈州	OR	Salem	塞勒姆
Pennsylvania	宾夕法尼亚州	PA	Harrisburg	哈里斯堡
Rhode Island	罗得岛州	RL	Providence	普罗维登斯
South Carolina	南卡罗来纳州	SC	Columbia	哥伦比亚
South Dakota	南达科他州	SD	Pierre	皮尔
Tennessee	田纳西州	TN	Nashville	纳什维尔
Texas	得克萨斯州	TX	Austin	奥斯汀
Utah	犹他州	UT	Salt Lake City	盐湖城
Vermont	佛蒙特州	VT	Montpelier	蒙彼利埃
Virginia	弗吉尼亚州	VA	Richmond	里士满
Washington	华盛顿州	WA	Olympia	奥林匹亚
West Virginia	西弗吉尼亚州	WV	Charleston	查尔斯顿
Wisconsin	威斯康星州	WI	Madison	麦迪逊
Wyoming	怀俄明州	WY	Cheyenne	夏延

Appendix 4

Keys

Unit 1 Education

Part 1 Learning Before Class

• **Listening**

1. How hard it can be to meet the academic expectations of their professors.
2. They strengthen their own understanding of their field of study.
3. They expect students to be able to write about subjects at much greater length, and present complex arguments supported with lots of research.
4. The first step is to recognize they are having some difficulties.

• **Watching and Thinking**

1. The US, South Korea, Israel, Japan and Canada.
2. The societal pressure to get into the best colleges.
3. Most Israelis are required to serve in the military, following their primary education.
4. They're being overeducated and underemployed after graduating.

• **Reading and Discussing**

1. There are modernizing education and becoming a strong educational power by 2035.
2. It has produced a more knowledgeable populace, sustaining economic development in the past two decades.
3. It has integrated technology to schools lacking sufficient resources.
4. It has focused on fostering the students' innovative thinking and practical abilities while boosting their holistic development in ethics, intelligence and sports.

Part 2 Learning in Class

Warm Up

1. Acquiring knowledge.
2. Strengthening critical and analytical skills.

3. Those who are well-read, well-spoken and knowledgeable on a variety of topics.

4. Because reading can increase connectivity between brain cells.

Text A

- **Multiple Choices**

1. C 2. B 3. A 4. D 5. B 6. D

- **Matching**

1. C 2. B 3. A 4. B 5. D 6. A 7. D 8. A

- **Sentence Completion**

1. value orientations 2. a prestigious university 3. advanced facilities 4. meditation and exercises

5. risk of automation 6. cultivation of entrepreneurship

Text B

- **True/False/Not Given**

1. False 2. True 3. False 4. False 5. False 6. True 7. False 8. True 9. True 10. False

- **Matching**

1. B 2. C 3. F 4. I 5. J 6. K 7. R 8. S

- **Short Answer Questions**

1. It can shape our thinking, political preferences, even our cognitive ability.

2. It emerges from interactions between biological dispositions, nutrition and health, parenting behaviors, formal and informal educational opportunities, and culture.

3. It shows that *Sesame Street* has similar effects around the world.

4. They attribute the decline to access to cable television.

5. By comparing siblings with greater or less exposure to cable television based on their age when cable infrastructure was put in.

Unit 2   Culture and Society

Part 1   Learning Before Class

- **Listening**

1. The traditional dragon and lion dances.

2. 16 years.

3. On the first new moon of the lunar calendar.

4. Middle Eastern and Irish dances.

- **Watching and Thinking**

1. At Beijing's Capital Museum.

2. On the seventh day of the seventh month on the Chinese lunar calendar.

3. Yuanyang birds, or mandarin ducks.

4. A love story between a goddess and a human.

- **Reading and Discussing**

1. By the time they are 3 years old.

2. The individual objects.

3. Because they hadn't developed a bias toward objects.

4. American adults can reason about relationships while Chinese adults can reason about objects.

Part 2   Learning in Class

Warm Up

1. On the one hand, with the help of technology, many interactive platforms and digital communities have been built to make the artifacts come to life and offer more fun to visitors. On the other hand, more and more young people have become fans of Chinese traditional culture.

2. The Disney blockbuster *Kung Fu Panda*, for example, explained quite well to the world about China's martial arts. Besides, the Confucius Institutes around the globe also play very important roles in teaching international people Chinese.

3. This is an open question. You may refer to some related websites like http://www.china.org.cn/e-news/news060525-3.htm.

4. This is an open question. You may refer to some related websites like https://wenku.baidu.com/view/eeb4ef8903d276a20029bd64783e0912a2167cde.html.

Text A

- **Multiple Choice**

1. B   2. C   3. A   4. A   5. D   6. B   7. D   8. C

- **Sentence Completion**

1. resources and capital   2. global governance system   3. sever the flows   4. a theory of survival

5. harmony of differences

Text B

- **True/False/Not Given**

1. True   2. False   3. True   4. NG   5. True   6. True   7. False   8. True   9. True   10. True

- **Summary**

1. psychologists   2. influenced   3. parenting   4. administering   5. individualist   6. pursuits

7. collectivist   8. indulgent   9. prioritize   10. disciplining

- **Short Answer Questions**

1. Unique behaviors and characteristics.

2. Adults from European cultures.

3. Individualism and collectivism.

4. Anxious, guilty and shameful.

5. When they are expected to pursue gratification.

Unit 3   Politics

Part 1   Learning Before Class

- **Listening**

1. They denied Prime Minister Boris Johnson's call for a general election on October 15.

2. On October 31.

3. They think that could create severe economic problems.
4. Some members of his own party have turned against him.

- **Watching and Thinking**

1. It refers to that America is slapping another round of tariffs (this time on 200 billion US dollars of Chinese goods).
2. First, the deficit number is overblown and secondly, deficit is not a bad thing for the US.
3. They will cause more casualties, and the world will be a place of confusion and pain.
4. Reforming itself and opening its arms to others.

- **Reading and Discussing**

1. Due to rapid industrialization and persistent poverty alleviation efforts by the Chinese government.
2. The Chinese government introduced ecological migration in 2000.
3. The approaches are production, migration, ecological conservation, education, minimal allowances, and mass public participation.
4. They tried ecological conservation to promote tourism and boost local revenue.

Part 2　Learning in Class

Warm Up

1. China is often singled out by the West for allegedly violating human rights, and China's human rights situation is often described by the West as deteriorating.
2. He believes most Chinese will agree that it's better than any other time in history.
3. They want to solve such human rights issues as food, jobs, the treatment of diseases and street safety.
4. It is the Iraq War launched by the United States.

Text A

- **Multiple Choice**

1. C　2. D　3. A　4. D　5. B　6. C　7. D　8. B

- **Matching**

1. A　2. C　3. D　4. F　5. G　6. J

- **Sentence Completion**

1. reputation; credibility　2. behaving irresponsibly　3. international agreements
4. strategic intentions　5. communicating intent

Text B

- **True/False/Not Given**

1. True　2. True　3. Not Given　4. True　5. False　6. False　7. False　8. False

- **Sentence Completion**

1. majority　2. adaptations　3. national challenges　4. respond coherently　5. propelling
6. accelerating

- **Matching**

1. D　2. G　3. H　4. I　5. M　6. N　7. O　8. P

Unit 4 Economy

Part 1 Learning Before Class

• **Listening**

1. The Greater Bay Area.
2. To link up its southern Pearl River Delta into a massive hub of technology, research finance and innovation.
3. To promote a high-level open market, to attract and drive investment and to tie together three different legal jurisdictions.

• **Watching and Thinking**

1. Equal treatment before investors, and protects intellectual property rights.
2. To enhance China's competition strength in the market of foreign investment.
3. The Law is part of China's reform and opening-up policy, and the further development of the latter necessarily leads to the birth of the former.

• **Reading and Discussing**

1. A global recession is not predicted conclusively, but may downward risks do exist. At the same time, that would be slower growth of global growth.
2. The recovery of 2019 world economy depends on a recovery in a number of developing economies, partially in the Eurozone. Besides, the US economy is likely to slow further.
3. Healthy regional economic cooperation can promote world economic development, and the stable growth of world economy, in turn, needs and benefits regional economic cooperation. They are interwoven with each other.

Part 2 Learning in Class

Warm Up

1. A tariff is a tax imposed by one country on the goods and services imported from another country.
2. A higher tariff can protect domestic industries but often at the expense of consumers, who may have to pay higher prices.
3. The answer to the question is open.

For more references:

A trade war happens when one country retaliates against another by raising import tariffs or placing other restrictions on the opposing country's imports. In a global economy, a trade war can become very damaging to the consumers and businesses of both nations, and the contagion can grow to affect many aspects of both economies.

Text A

• **Multiple Choice**

1. B 2. C 3. B 4. C 5. C 6. C

• **True or False**

1. True 2. True 3. False 4. True 5. False 6. False

- **Short Answer Questions**
1. Their shareholders.
2. Keeping wages down, fighting unions, reclassifying employees as independent contractors, and outsourcing anywhere around world where parts are the cheapest, shifting their profits around the world wherever taxes are the lowest, and paying their top CEOs ludicrous sums.
3. To improve the well-being of the Chinese people and become the world's largest and most powerful economy.
4. Dominance in American politics and their commitment to share prices.
5. Taxes, subsidies and regulations.

Text B
- **Multiple Choice**
1. D 2. C 3. A 4. A 5. B 6. D
- **Sentence Completion**
1. self-deception; ignorant 2. deal 3. attributed; registered 4. imaginary 5. soiling; overdrawing
- **Short Answer Questions**
1. If certain issues were not resolved to the US' satisfaction.
2. America would shoulder most of the cost of the tariff hike.
3. Criticism on the White House, which has squandered the chance to bolster US economic growth.
4. The US economy.
5. The America steel workers.

Unit 5   Science and Technology

Part 1   Learning Before class

- **Listening**
1. To try to detect whether the essay is composed by a ghostwriter at a paper mill.
2. A neural network trained and tested on 130,000 real essays from 10,000 Danish students.
3. To try to detect students who are at risk because their development in writing style isn't as you'd expect. And teachers could thus give extra help to kids who really need it, while sniffing out the cheaters too.
4. The answer to the question is open.

- **Watching and Thinking**
1. EMBERS is a computer-forecasting system that sifts through data that you post on social media every day. It mines big data for trends rather information on individuals.
2. While it can mine public data to forecast major social events before they happen, it can't predict spontaneous events like crowd stampedes or terrorists, an increasing concern in an overcrowded and unstable world.
3. Video surveillance, AI and complicated mathematical algorithm.
4. It is how much privacy we are willing to give up to be safe.

- **Reading and Discussing**
1. Object-detection software and satellite imagery can aid rescuers. Algorithms can help reduce poaching in

wildlife parks. Voice-recognition programs can be used in emergency calls to detect whether callers are experiencing cardiac arrest. "Reinforcement learning" can be used in simulated clinical trials involving patients with glioblastoma, the most aggressive form of brain cancer, to reduce chemotherapy doses. Moreover, AI can already detect early signs of diabetes from heart rate sensor data, help children with autism manage their emotions, and guide the visually impaired.

2. The obstacles are data accessibility and so-called last-mile implementation challenges. AI's tools and techniques can be misused intentionally or inadvertently. For example, biases can be embedded in AI algorithms or datasets, which in turn can amplify existing inequalities when the applications are used. Another obvious risk is misuse of AI by those intent on threatening individuals' physical, digital, financial and emotional security.

3. Stakeholders from the private and public sectors must work together to address these issues. To increase the availability of data, for example, public officials and private sectors should grant broader access to those seeking to use data for initiatives that serve the public good.

Part 2 Learning in Class

Warm Up

1. The heavy death toll in traffic accidents.
2. The differences between self-driving systems and driver assistance systems; how the car sees the world.

Text A

- **Multiple Choice**

1. A 2. C 3. B 4. D 5. C

- **Sentence Completion**

1. autonomous driving 2. the vulnerabilities 3. factory-to-junkyard monitoring 4. incentive
5. automotive-related cybersecurity incidents

- **Matching**

1. E 2. B 3. C 4. A 5. D

Text B

- **True/False/Not Given**

1. False 2. True 3. False 4. True 5. True

- **Matching**

1. C 2. G 3. B 4. E 5. J 6. H

- **Short Answer Questions**

1. Openness to experience, conscientiousness, extroversion, agreeableness and neuroticism.
2. Eye movements, how we speak / the way we speak, facial expressions.
3. An app that discerns mood by analyzing face-tracking data captured from the front camera of the iPhone X. It recognizes emotions such as happiness, sadness, anger and surprise in real time as someone looks at a news feed, and it delivers content based on the person's emotional state.
4. He says it is a warning, a call for increasing privacy.
5. Because machine-learning programs do not reveal the rules they apply in drawing conclusions.
6. Even if a company's computer algorithms were to finger terrorists correctly 99 percent of the time, the

false positives found 1 percent of the time could bring harm to thousands of innocent people in populous places where terrorists are rare, such as in Germany or the US.

Unit 6 Environment

Part 1 Learning Before Class

- **Listening**

1. An estimated 3.7 million premature deaths every year.
2. Nitrogen dioxide (NO_2) from car emissions as the leading cause of childhood asthma in many cities around the world.
3. Actually over 90% of annually pediatric asthma incidents occurred in areas that already met the World Health Organization guideline for annual average NO_2 pollution of 21 parts per billion.

- **Watching and Thinking**

1. Gases in the atmosphere such as carbon dioxide let the sun's light in, but keep some of the heat from escaping, like the glass walls of the green house. The more greenhouse gases in the atmosphere, the more heat gets trapped, increasing the earth's temperature.
2. Climate change has consequences for our oceans, our weather, our food sources, and our health. Rising sea levels caused by melting ice sheets flood the coastal regions; extreme weather conditions become more frequent; and pose new agricultural challenges; high levels of smog causes serious health problems.
3. Replace fossil fuels with renewable energy sources, like solar and wind, which don't produce greenhouse gas emissions, to prevent some of the worst effects of climate change.
4. The answer to the question is open.

- **Reading and Discussing**

1. The answer to the second question is open.

For more references:

The Paris Agreement is an agreement within the United Nations Framework Convention on Climate Change, dealing with greenhouse-gas-emissions mitigation, adaptation, and finance, signed in 2016. As of March 2019, 195 UNFCCC members have signed the agreement, and 186 have become party to it. The Paris Agreement's long-term goal is to keep the increase in global average temperature to well below 2℃ above pre-industrial levels; and to limit the increase to 1.5℃, since this would substantially reduce the risks and effects of climate change.

2. There always seem to be more pressing problems to deal with, so climate emergency cannot garner due attention and take precedence.
3. The answer to the question is open.

For more references:

(1) *The Most Important Thing You Can Do to Fight Climate Change: Talk about It* (Nov., 2018) by
    Katharine Hayhoe

https://www.ted.com/talks/katharine_hayhoe_the_most_important_thing_you_can_do_to_fight_climate_change_talk_about_it

(2) *What's Wrong with Our Food System* (Aug., 2010) by Birke Baehr

https://www.ted.com/talks/birke_baehr_what_s_wrong_with_our_food_system

(3) Pictures Change the World

https://video.nationalgeographic.com/tv/00000144-1108-db5f-af65-d7aa851e0000?source=searchvideo

(4) Saving Animals through Photography

https://video.nationalgeographic.com/video/ng-live/00000151-7e83-d1bf-ab51-ffd753240002?source=searchvideo

Part 2　Learning in Class

Warm Up

1. Both countries carry out ambitious tree-planting programs raising their green leaf areas and increase their food production through "multiple cropping" practices.

2. China aims to increase the forest coverage to 23.04% by 2020 and 26% by 2050 nationwide. To achieve this goal, China has taken a series of measures, such as reforesting hillsides and creating protected grassland and nature reserves.

3. The answer to the question is open.

Text A

- **Multiple Choice**

1. B　2. D　3. B　4. C　5. D　6. C

- **True/False/Not Given**

1. False　2. False　3. True　4. True　5. False　6. True　7. NG　8. True

- **Sentence Completion**

1. tax on carbon / carbon tax; promote innovations; a widespread adoption

2. the costs; the benefits; cost-benefit analysis

3. spread of renewables; rise in emissions

4. climate policy; average emissions cuts; the Paris targets

5. favorable market; technological conditions; retired; fall far faster

Text B

- **Matching**

1. F　2. H　3. I　4. G

- **Table Completion**

1. beyond petroleum　2. rise by 13%　3. the Paris Agreement　4. lobby against　5. renewables

6. monthballing　7. Texan shale　8. high-tech deep-water wells　9. curb emissions　10. expand

- **Short Answer Questions**

1. In America, extreme weather phenomenon takes place more frequently. Scientists, ordinary people, politicians and private companies are all responding to the change in their own ways.

2. The world needs to reduce its oil and gas production by about 20% by 2030 and by about 55% by 2050 respectively.

3. Because the energy firms and shareholders need to maximize profits, and the financial returns from oil are higher than those from renewables. Besides, world demand for oil is also growing.

4. According to the author, the key to win the support from centrist voters for emissions reduction is to show them that cutting emissions is practical and will not leave them much worse off.

5. The author holds that the best policy is to tax carbon emissions, and the policy should be designed to give the cash raised back to the public in the form of offsetting tax cuts to command popular support.

- **Summary**

1. rising   2. investments   3. financial   4. incentives   5. dwarfed   6. modest   7. congress
8. muscular   9. curb   10. tax

Unit 7   Social Security and Crime Prevention

Part 1   Learning Before class

- **Listening**

1. They are very helpful to our daily life.
2. We should tell those companies that we care about our privacy and they should stop doing that.
3. We had better turn on those systems when we need them and switch them off when we don't, and those companies should tell us what they are collecting.

- **Watching and Thinking**

1. Together with volunteers from China and their equipments, Niakomba finally spotted the elephant.
2. The first-ever resolution titled "Resolution on Tackling Illicit Trafficking in Wildlife".
3. Because we humans cannot isolate ourselves from the rest of Mother Nature.

- **Reading and Discussing**

1. They have to choose between life in prison without parole and the death penalty.
2. He was convicted of kidnapping and killing Zhang Yingying in 2017.
3. He premeditated the crime and tortured Zhang before "destroying" her body, and he disposed of her remains in a way in which they'll never be recovered.

Part 2   Learning in Class

Warm Up

1. Because the silly little story quickly spread through the school that the author got confused with pork chops and karate chops.
2. Because of a birthmark that takes up a little less than half her face.
3. Because there's something inside us that made us keep trying despite everyone who told us to quit.

Text A

- **Multiple Choice**

1. C   2. D   3. D   4. B   5. D

- **Sentence Completion**

1. test   2. post   3. incite   4. copyright   5. disruption

Text B

- **Multiple Choice**

1. D   2. C   3. D   4. C   5. D

- **True/False/Not Given**

1. NG   2. False   3. False   4. False   5. True

Unit 8　Health

Part 1　Learning Before Class

- **Listening**

1. Low-cost, packaged foods.
2. Highly processed foods.
3. They found people who ate more processed foods were more likely to have heart disease.
4. People with limited time and money.

- **Watching and Thinking**

1. How stress affects our heath.
2. When we are challenged or overwhelmed.
3. Because stress can change the composition and function of our gut bacteria.
4. We may have to curb our chronic stress.

- **Reading and Discussing**

1. It is largely attributed to China's medical reform.
2. From May 1, 2018, most of the imported drugs, particularly anticancer drugs, have become tariff-free in China. On October 10, 2018, the medical insurance began to cover 17 additional anticancer drugs. The newly negotiated drug prices are on average more than 50 percent lower.
3. Epidemic-prone diseases are prevented and controlled right from the start, and the overall medical expenses reduced.

Part 2　Learning in Class

Warm Up

1. He retained his incredible intellect.
2. After age 40.
3. Their ability to transfer messages.
4. Because there are so many elements involved.

Text A

- **Multiple Choice**

1. C　2. D　3. B　4. A　5. D　6. C　7. B　8. D

- **Matching**

1. C　2. F　3. I　4. K　5. O　6. R　7. S　8. T

- **Sentence Completion**

1. psychological distress　2. clinicians　3. substance abuse　4. a complicated undertaking
5. dedicated to　6. increased coverage　7. accessible　8. eliminate distortions

Text B

- **True/False/Not Given**

1. False　2. False　3. True　4. True　5. True　6. False　7. False　8. True

- **Matching**

1. B 2. A 3. D 4. C 5. E 6. B 7. E 8. B

- **Short Answer Questions**

1. They spoke with farm workers and their children who are battling cancer, as well as with local health care workers reaching out to the families.
2. More than 400,000 new cases.
3. It helps public health care experts assess the health of countries' populations and in turn develop strategies to treat patients.
4. Because few people have access to affordable health care and survival depends on luck.
5. The number of young patients diagnosed and treated is increased.

Unit 9　Arts and Youth

Part 1　Learning Before Class

- **Listening**

1. As a summer dance program, AileyCamp aims at providing students who have financial need or who have school, social or family difficulties with a free, six-week program.
2. It implies that she can control herself.
3. Because he received one of those scholarships and AileyCamp offered him a safe place and increased his confidence.

- **Watching and Thinking**

1. They are very abstract. They reflect her African identity in the new culture.
2. Yes, a lot of things that remind people of African print and African textiles, which will also remind us of things that are made in China.
3. Absolutely yes. When we were young, we painted lots of objects with our favorite colors to form a particular person or particular feeling.
4. Abstract art is an art form based on non-realistic portrayals, rather than visually accurate depictions of objects or scenes. Many abstract works are based on the concept that shape, color and texture have inherent value in their own rights, and can provoke a response even when used to create unidentifiable or non-realistic works.

- **Reading and Discussing**

1. In order to make the live-action remakes of cartoons the most lucrative innovations in cinema, Walt Disney Studios should focus on blockbusters and concentrate on developing original ideas and executing them well.
2. The animated backlist that generations of children might grow up on are probably *The Jungle Book*, *The Lion King*, *Cinderella*, the *Harry Potter* series and *Star Wars*.
3. The latest technology like digital art technology, like the latest motion-capture technology has been used. The precondition to transposes onto digital figures is that the actors have to move and extend their facial expressions.

Part 2　Learning in Class

Warm Up

1. His major at those universities was architecture. Pei's works around the world are built with stone, steel and glass.

2. The world-famous Louvre Museum in Paris, and other well-known Pei buildings include the John F. Kennedy Library in Dorchester, Massachusetts, the National Center for Atmospheric Research in Boulder, Colorado, the East Wing of the National Gallery of Art in Washington and the Dallas City Hall in Texas, the Museums in Luxembourg, Qatar and Suzhou Museum in his ancestral home.

3. Because his works were criticized and he argued that he had wanted to create a modern space that would not take away from the traditional part of the museum. He said the glass pyramids were based on the works of French landscape architect Le Notre. They honored French history.

Text A

- **Multiple Choice**

1. B　2. D　3. C　4. A　5. C

- **Matching**

1. B　2. C　3. E　4. D　5. A

- **Short Answer Questions**

1. Cutting-edge technology & Dazzling visual effects.

2. Break through limitations & Seek the unknown.

3. Reflection & Alert, before it's too late.

4. The permanent magnet technology, object network technology and instant communication make it possible that a more convenient future society are not that far away from us.

5. Human behaviors causing doomsday are quite common in sci-fi films. Sci-fi films have offered various possibilities that could trigger human reflection.

Text B

- **True/False/Not Given**

1. Not given　2. True　3. False　4. True　5. True　6. True　7. False　8. True

- **Short Answer Questions**

1. Yes, I do. For example, the researcher of Elpus's research has found that arts participation had a wide range of positive effects.

2. When young people get active interact with arts in variety of ways, they will acknowledge its social impact and do things with adults for meaning.

3. Creating poetry in one early age is one part of art education. By learning how to create, critique art, observe art, kids know how to engage with art.

4. Yes, I do. Arts participation for kids will have positive effects on their academic outcomes and behaviors.

5. Such countless art forms as dance, music, graffiti art, and more are the sample ways to make art in university.

Unit 10 Sports

Part 1 Learning Before Class

- **Listening**

1. You may worry that the feeling of skiing on the waste-mountain is not as good as you ski on the real snow. The long-term training on the waste may not effectively enhance the professional skiers' performance. And without the coldness of ice and snow, skiing might lose its charm of freezing and its power of strengthening athletes' willpower.
2. Yes. Because then the sport could be enormously developed for lower costs, less risks and more training opportunities in warmer areas.

   No. Since real snow will not be replaced by the waste-mountain in formal competitions.
3. The answer to the question is open.

- **Watching and Thinking**

1. For instance, you may talk about the Chinese F1 teams, sponsors, Shanghai International Circuit, and your personal experience of watching the race.
2. According to Chloe, a lot of talented females in F1 are working in various teams to serve for the production, promotion, operation and administration of the race.
3. Here is just an example for you: Chongqing. Because the mountainous city might offer more ups, downs and turns to inspire more exciting driving performance of the racers.

- **Reading and Discussing**

1. Yes. The inclusion is a huge step forward for breaking dancers and fans, and the sport will be recognized officially and internationally.

   No. Breaking might not be popular or even acceptable for many Olympic audiences.
2. It's easy to keep the life and beauty of breaking if dancers could preserve good breaking music and bring the Funk and the original style of the dance.
3. The answer to the question is open.

Part 2 Learning in class

Warm Up

1. Over the course of repeated contractions of muscles there may not be sufficient concentrations of potassium, sodium or calcium ions immediately available near the muscle cell membrane to reset the system properly.
2. The answer to the question is open.
3. If we pause and rest, muscle fatigue will subside as potassium, sodium or calcium ions replenish throughout the muscle.

Text A

- **True/False/Not Given**

1. False 2. True 3. False 4. True 5. False 6. True

- **Short Answer Questions**
1. Because people are frustrated by the cost, purpose and value of American colleges.
2. One place to start repairing is by fixing what ails one of its underappreciated elements: college sports.
3. College athletics—especially football and later basketball—worked as a central catalyst to promote the expansion of college enrollment in the history of American higher education.
4. The Report made recommendations focusing on college basketball—including NCAA governance changes, stricter penalties for violations, and greater freedom and flexibility for student-athletes to make decisions about pursuing professional opportunities.
5. American higher educational institutions might find decreasing support from public funds. Policy-makers will be increasingly adversarial and resources and institutional autonomy will be replaced by increased governmental intervention.

- **Summary**
1. devotes 2. critical 3. recruiting 4. democratized 5. created 6. question 7. supporting 8. victories 9. convincing 10. public

Text B
- **True/False/Not Given**
1. False 2. True 3. False 4. NG 5. NG 6. True

- **Sentence Completion**
1. deceased 2. degenerative 3. cognitive 4. concussions 5. spectacles

Appendix 5

Scripts

Unit 1　Education

Part 1　Learning Before Class

- **Listening**

College Success: Making Use of Academic Supports

July 7, 2019
VOA

When a student arrives at a college or university, they are likely to face many difficulties as they work towards earning their degree. Being far from their home, working a job in addition to the demands of their study programs and making friends are just a few of the issues they might deal with.

Yet what many students may not expect is just how hard it can be to meet the academic expectations of their professors.

Fuji Lozada says many students feel that simply gaining acceptance into a school is proof that they are ready for the requirements of their programs. But the truth is that almost every student, no matter the quality of their past educational experience, needs help, he says.

That is why almost every college and university in the United States offers some kind of service to help students succeed with their studies.

Lozada is the director of the John Crosland Jr. Center for Teaching and Learning at Davidson College in Davidson, North Carolina. The center is similar to offices at many schools around the country that provide services to help students.

The center has some full-time employees, but is mainly operated by students who are trained to assist others. These student assistants can gain a lot, too. By helping others in areas where they might have experience, students strengthen their own understanding of their field of study, Lozada says.

"When students first come to college, they still are in this mode of 'I'm here to learn by myself.' But academics is really a team sport," he told VOA.

He notes that one area students often struggle with is writing. Most American high schools teach students shorter forms of writing, often working in the five-paragraph essay form. College professors, however, expect students to be able to write about subjects at much greater length. They expect students to present complex arguments supported with lots of research.

While a student might be skilled in other areas, if they are not used to this kind of writing they can quickly find themselves falling behind their peers, says Lozada. International students can especially face difficulty writing at the level expected by American professors, even if their general English skills are strong. That is because U. S. schools have strong rules about how outside research is presented. And professors want students to be critical in their examination of all research.

Lozada notes that colleges and universities do not want their students to fail. The problem is that many students either do not know their school has offices, like the Crosland Center, that are designed to help them, or they are afraid to admit they may need help.

"When we check with students as to why they didn't come in for tutoring, they assume that nobody else is getting help. And so, actually, once they see … that many students are coming … meeting with other students for peer-tutoring, that usually gets them in the door," Lozada said.

The first step for any struggling college student is to recognize they are having some difficulties, he says. Then they should ask their professors for advice on the areas in which they need to improve and seek out their college's academic support services.

Lozada adds that one visit to such a center will not immediately solve the problem. Improving writing skills, for example, takes time. The same can be said about mathematics, computer science or any other subject.

He notes that about 40 percent of the Davidson students who seek academic support are first year students. But about 13 percent are students in the final year of their programs, still asking for help with high-level classwork and major projects. "Even … when I write a piece, I ask a peer or friend to read it and then they critique it," Lozada said. "That's the kind of academic experience we want to encourage."

I'm Pete Musto.

- **Watching and Thinking**

What Are the Most Educated Countries in the World?

December 6, 2018

https://www.msn.com

New job opportunities, higher wages, new perspectives, ideas and ways of life. These are just some of the benefits of having access to higher education. And most people agree that this can change the trajectory of your life.

With that in mind, let's find out which countries are the most educated in the world today. We'll be using data from 2017 compiled by the organization for economic cooperation and development, the OECD, which calculates the percentage of a given country's population between the age of 25 and 64 years old who have completed higher education programs, which includes 2-year and 4-year programs as well as vocational schools.

Let's jump straight into it.

No. 5 on our list of the most educated countries is the US. It has a population of over 328 million

Appendix 5

people. And nearly 46.4% of those between 25 and 64 have completed a higher education program. The US is home to some of the most prestigious universities in the world. At least 5 out of the top 10 are based in the states, according to some rankings. And while some of the great minds of the world flock to American institutions, they are considerably out of reach for the general population in the states. And while a significant number of Americans have completed a higher education program, many of them are left with an insurmountable amount of student loan debt. Collectively, Americans have an estimated 1.5 trillion dollars' worth of student loans.

Now onto No.4 on our list of the most education countries: South Korea. With a population of over 51 million people, 47.7% of South Koreans between 25 and 64 have completed a higher education program. That percentage is only slated to increase in the coming years. As the country tops the list of most educated young people, with an astounding 69.8% completing a higher education program who are between the ages of 25 and 34, the country has expected an incredible economic boom after rebounding from the Korean War in the 1950s that devastated the country. It has since become the 11th largest economy in the world and the 3rd largest in Asia.

According to the international Monetary Fund, this was the result of the South Korea government's shift in the 1980s toward industrialization. Despite the country's huge success in education more of its citizens, the societal pressure to get into the best colleges has had many psychological tolls on young people there. For school age children in South Korea, education is incredibly competitive with young kids working tirelessly to get into top universities when they are older. Many of them study at school and after school programs for 16 hours a day, 11 months out of the year. This intense level of stress, some studies say, has contributed to a growing mental health crisis in South Korea. It has the highest suicide rate in the world for adolescents between 10 and 19.

Next on our list coming in the No.3 is Israel, with a population of about 8.3 million people. 50.9% of Israelis between 25 and 64 have completed a higher education program. Most Jewish Israelis are required to serve in the military, following their primary education, with men having to serve 3 years, and a women roughly 2 years. That means, unlike most of the world, Israelis are entering college at a later age between 20 and 24, according to 2015 OECD calculations. That made Israelis on average the oldest undergraduate graduates in the world. Israel has the booming high-tech in start-up industry which has startlingly grown since 2012. These industries include cyber-security, automotives and artificial intelligence, which might be, while Bloomberg news recently rank Israel, the tenth most innovative country in the world.

Second on our list of the most educated countries in the world is Japan. With population of over 126 million people, 51.4% of Japanese between 25 and 64 have completed a higher education program. And things would only better for Japan as time goes on, with 60.4% of young people between 25 and 34 completing a higher education program. Japan has the third largest economy in the world, according to the IMF. This economic status is in part a result of the country's prioritization of education. Following the end of World War II, but that prioritization on education has created a stressful environment for school children. This pressure to be successful in school and the workplace, much like in South Korea, has contributed to a growing suicide crisis in Japan as well. Just last year, the country recorded its highest suicide rate among children and teens in 30 years. The Japanese government recently announced a plan to cut the country's suicide rate by 30% by 2026.

And now, onto the most educated place in the world, Canada. With a population of over 35 million people, 56.7% of Canadians between 25 and 64 have completed a higher education program. As time passes, that number is projected to increase since 60.9% of young people between 25 and 34 have completed a higher education program. Despite this, a growing number of young Canadians face a troubling trend. One were they're being over educated and under employed after graduating. There is no official calculation, but it's estimated that on average 1 in 3 college graduates between the age of 24 and 29 are underemployed. That basically means that someone may have a job, it is not paying them enough or making use of their full skill set. And while the financial aid for college is significant, a number of students are still unable to make by without loans. 60% of Canadians leave college with an average of 27 thousand dollars in debt.

Part 2　Learning in Class

Warm Up

Why You Should Read Books: 15 Benefits of Reading More

July 24, 2019

player.vimeo.com

People have been writing books for centuries. Someone's writing a book right now and books will be written for a long time to come. The question is, when was the last time you read a book?

While there's no doubt that reading is priceless activity, the habit of reading books has been on a decline. Most people claim they don't have the time to read, yet the average person watches TV for more than two hours a day. Reading is a workout for your mind and it's just as important as physical exercise, so here are 15 reasons why you should read more!

No. 1—acquire knowledge

This is the most obvious and important benefit of reading. Humans are the only species on earth that can transmit information and knowledge over a distance and over several generations. Written language separates us from all other species. It enables us to transfer knowledge rapidly, and allows us to develop faster. Everything you read fills your mind with new bits of information, and the more knowledge you have, the better equipped you are—and the more able you become to tackle challenges. Even if you were to lose everything you physically possess, no one can ever take away your knowledge.

No. 2—improve memory

Reading books offers the opportunity to stop and take a moment to rethink or reflect on the content.

When you read a book, you have to remember an assortment of characters, their backgrounds, ambitions, histories, and nuances as well as the various arcs and subplots that weave their way through the story. What's more, with every new memory you create, you create new pathways in your brain, and this strengthens the existing ones. Furthermore, staying mentally stimulated by reading regularly, can slow down the progress or possibly even prevent Alzheimer's or dementia.

No. 3—strengthen critical and analytical skills

Have you ever read an amazing mystery novel and solved the mystery yourself before finishing the book? If so, you were able to put your critical thinking skills to work, by taking note of all the details provided, and sorting them out. That same ability to analyze details comes in handy even in real life! In fact, critical thinking skills are essential. Being able to solve problems, given just certain elements, are a part of daily life from finishing a project for work to figuring out how to navigate difficult relationships.

No. 4—advance your career

The more you read, the more words you are exposed to. These words will inevitably make their way into your everyday vocabulary, and being articulate and well-spoken earns your bonus point in many professions. The ability to confidently communicate with your employers and peers, can be an enormous boost to your self-esteem, and it will also help you advance the career ladder. Studies have shown that those who are well-read, well-spoken and knowledgeable on a variety of topics, tend to get promotions more quickly and more often compared to those with smaller vocabularies and lack of awareness of literature, scientific breakthroughs and global events.

No. 5—improve writing skills

In addition to expanding your vocabulary, exposure to published, well-written work has a positive effect on your own writing as well. Many successful authors gained their expertise by reading the works of others. Observing the various styles of other authors, journalists, poets and writers will eventually be reflected in your own writing style. So, if you want to become a better writer, start by learning from previous masters!

No. 6—reduce stress and anxiety

Chronic escapism is by no means a healthy habit, but neither is dwelling on stressful life circumstances all the time. In short doses, allowing your mind to focus on things other than your challenges, can be highly beneficial, and even necessary. Reading offers a safe, healthy and productive replacement for negative thinking. It gives your mind a safe place to rest, until you regain the strength you need to overcome obstacles and challenges.

No. 7—improve focus and concentration

In our busty lifestyles, our attention is constantly drawn in different directions throughout the day. Studies have shown that in a single 5-minute span, the average person will divide their time between working on a task, checking an email, keeping an eye on social media, monitoring their smartphone, and chatting with a couple of people (either online or in person). Of course, this type of distracted behavior lowers productivity. When you read a book, all of your attention is focused on what you're reading, causing the rest of the world to fade away as you immerse yourself in the details. Reading at least 20 minutes a day will improve your concentration, and you'll be amazed at how much more focused you'll be.

No. 8—boost inspiration and motivation

Reading inspirational books can contribute to your growth and development. With the endless amount of perspectives and lives you can read about, books can give you an opportunity to have experiences that you haven't had the chance to, and still allow you to learn the life skills they entail. Essentially, reading is the seed to inspiration. The words plant the ideas in your brain, and those ideas flourish from there.

No. 9—learn at your own pace

Another benefit of reading a book is that you learn at your own pace. Since you have the book all the time, you can always go back to a section you feel you don't understand. You can read a chapter as many times as you wish, without worrying that you'll miss out a section. If it's a self-help book, you can tackle one issue at a time. Once you handle one problem, then you can move to the next issue whenever you feel you're ready. Everything is done at your own pace, and most importantly, your mind is free to interpret things the way you feel.

No. 10—stimulate imagination

You are limited only by what you can imagine. The worlds described in books, as well as other people's views and opinions, will help you expand your understanding of what is possible. By reading a written description of an event or a place, your mind is responsible for creating that image in your head instead of having the image placed in front of you when you watch TV. You connect all these creations and make changes while you keep reading all the while expanding your worldview. When you explore a new literary world, this opens doors for new ideas, subjects and situations that can get you thinking on trying new experiences.

No. 11—improve conversation skills

Because reading increases your vocabulary and your knowledge of how to correctly use new words, it helps you better articulate what you want to say. The knowledge you gain from reading also gives you more to talk about with others. You will be able to hold your own, and add to the conversation instead of having to make excuse and leave. You will be able to engage a wider variety of people, and in turn improve your knowledge and conversation skills. Ultimately, this will make you a much more interesting and refreshing person to be around.

No. 12—become more empathetic

According to studies, losing yourself in books, especially fiction, may increase your empathy. As you let go of the emotional and mental chatter found in the real world, you enjoy deep reading that allows you to feel what the characters in a story feel. And this in turn makes you more empathetic to people in real life. You become more aware and alert to the lives of others.

No. 13—sleep better

Poor sleep leads to low productivity. This is why so many experts recommend that you establish a regular destressing routine before you go to sleep. This will help clam your mind, and therefore help you sleep better. Reading a book is one of the best ways to calm yourself before going to bed. Even if it's just for ten minutes, reading can help you push whatever was keeping you awake out of your mind. So, while in bed, instead of watching TV or spending time on your smartphone, grab a book and read.

No. 14—source of companionship

During your life, you will experience numerous transitions. Changing schools, jobs or cities may require you to replace old relationships with new ones, and sometimes, these adjustments are harder or take longer than expected. Reading can help reduce feelings of alienation and loneliness. Whether it's through the comfort of a favorite book, or through an emotional connection to relatable characters, books provide a stable source of companionship, especially during times when you feel the only person you can count on is yourself.

No. 15—increase your lifespan

Researchers have found that adults who read at least three and a half hours a week, can expect to have a longer lifespan than those who do not read books. This is because reading can increase connectivity between brain cells, which can lower the risk of neurodegenerative (神经组织退化的) diseases that can shorten a lifespan. Developing a daily reading habit can be super beneficial for you; in fact, reading makes you more intelligent. Research shows that reading not only helps with fluid intelligence, but with reading comprehension and emotional intelligence as well; and as a result, you make smarter decisions about yourself and those around you.

Unit 2 Culture and Society

Part 1 Learning Before Class

- **Listening**

Asians Celebrate the Lunar New Year Around the World

By Hai Do

February 4, 2019

VOA

The traditional dragon and lion dances greeted several hundred Asian-Americans over the weekend at Fair Oaks Shopping Center in northern Virginia.

They had gathered to ring in the Year of the Pig.

Hank Chao is a Chinese-American and with the Hai Hau Community Center in Falls Church, Virginia. He said, "We used to call it the Chinese New Year. But we have a lot of Southeast Asians, like Korean, Japanese, Thai, Malaysian, Indonesian. Those people came to us and said, 'Hey, we celebrate, too.'"

Members of the community center have gathered to celebrate the Lunar New Year for the past 16 years. The holiday begins on the first new moon of the lunar calendar. Because the holiday is based on the moon, it falls somewhere between the end of January and the end of February. This year's holiday is on February 5. It marks the year 4717 of the lunar calendar.

Chao said each year people from many countries celebrate the Lunar New Year in northern Virginia. Some years, the celebration even includes Middle Eastern and Irish dances in addition to more traditional performances.

Many Asian cultures celebrate the Lunar New Year.

For many years, the holiday was not celebrated in North Korea. But in 1989, *The Korea Times* reports, then-leader Kim Jong-il brought back the holiday tradition.

In South Korea, family members play a popular game called *yutnori*. And they share traditional foods like *tteokguk*, a soup made of beef, vegetables, egg and rice cakes.

In Tibet, the first day of Losar acts as a sort of communal birthday. Everyone becomes one year older. And, at the end of the three-day celebration, Tibetans throw roasted barley flour, known as tsampa, to wish each other health and happiness.

It might be the Year of the Pig, but many in Hong Kong are not eating pork this year because of concerns over the African swine fever.

A woman named Liu told the *South China Morning Post*, "It does not really matter. Lunar New Year is more about live chickens anyway, pork is just the side dish and it will not affect our mood to celebrate."

In Vietnam, thousands filled Nguyen Hue Street in the southern city of Ho Chi Minh to watch a fireworks show on Monday. In Hanoi, the party chief and President Nguyen Phu Trong was seen handing out red envelopes to workers. The envelopes are filled with lucky money.

Many Vietnamese celebrate Tet with a traditional food called *banh chung*, a square-shaped cake of sticky rice filled with meat and beans, and then wrapped in green leaves.

I'm Ashley Thompson.

- **Watching and Thinking**

Couples Enjoy the Romantic Evening at Beijing's Capital Museum on the Qixi Festival

By Ding Siyue

August 8, 2019

CGTN

It's already evening, but things are still in full swing. Audiences at the Capital Museum are getting a chance to enjoy a special tour focusing on the topic of love.

Guides lead audiences through the exhibition hall's first floor, "Jade and Porcelain", and tell them the stories behind the objects' links to the theme of love and marriage.

"Here in the Capital Museum, we have many cultural relics related to Qixi and love and marriage. Through this tour, we can take a look at how our ancestors spent the Qixi Festival and what marriage was like in the past," said Wu Lingling, a volunteer guide at the museum.

The Qixi Festival is celebrated on the seventh day of the seventh month according to the Chinese lunar calendar. It has its origins in a 2,000-year-old love story of a weaver girl and a cowherd boy.

"As a cultural platform, we hope the audiences can feel the rich traditional culture of China at our museum. This year is the first time we've stayed open late for Qixi. We've especially looked for exhibits related to the festival to give the audiences a themed visit experience," said Yang Dandan, spokesperson for the museum.

In days gone by, the Qixi Festival was an occasion for girls to demonstrate their domestic skills necessary for marriage. These days it has become a romantic holiday like the Western Valentine's Day for couples that express their love for each other. One attraction for visitors to take part in was a sand-painting activity depicting one of the objects in the museum's collection—a jade box with yuanyang birds, or mandarin ducks, which symbolize love in traditional Chinese culture.

"We are very happy to attend this event and learn more about the traditions of the Qixi Festival. We've traveled to many countries, and the more we visit other countries, the more interested we are in our own culture. Because these are our roots. So we very much enjoy these kinds of activities at museums," said one visitor.

Meanwhile, a traditional opera *Tianxianpei* was played on the museum's upped stage. It tells a love story between a goddess and a human. It certainly makes the evening rich in romantic content and culture. (This is CGTN)

Unit 3 Politics

Part 1 Learning Before Class

- **Listening**

British Lawmakers Deal Another Blow to Johnson's EU Plan

By Susan Shand
September 4, 2019
VOA

British law-makers Wednesday denied Prime Minister Boris Johnson's call for a general election on October 15. They also approved a bill that could prevent Johnson from withdrawing the country from the European Union (EU) next month. Britain's House of Commons voted 329 to 300 to support the bill Wednesday. It now goes to parliament's upper house, the House of Lords, for consideration.

Both votes were a major defeat for the prime minister.

Johnson says his country must leave the EU on October 31, with or without an agreement between the two sides.

His promise to withdraw from the 28-member organization has Britain's parliament in an uproar. Many fear leaving the EU without a deal in place could create severe economic problems. The dispute is the worst political turmoil since Britain voted in 2016 to leave the European Union. Politicians and the media have been using the name Brexit for the proposed withdrawal.

The Labour Party and some rebel members of Johnson's own Conservative Party joined Wednesday to delay Brexit.

"To deliver Brexit like this is to create a poison pill which for 40 years will divide this country straight down the middle," former Conservative Party leadership candidate Rory Stewart told the BBC. "If you are going to deliver Brexit at all, try to do it legally, constitutionally and with consent."

On Wednesday, Johnson said the possible new law would destroy "any chance" his government would successfully negotiate a new deal with the EU by October 31.

However, the EU says Johnson's government has not given them any real new ideas about an agreement.

The British Parliament rejected the deal former Prime Minister Teresa May reached with the EU, forcing her to resign in June. It is unclear whether Johnson will have the votes to call an election later, after the bill is approved by the House of Lords. An election vote needs the approval of two-thirds of the 650 House of Commons law-makers.

The Labour Party had said it would not agree to an election until a law is in place to stop a no-deal Brexit. It also said it does not trust Johnson to deliver an election before the Brexit date.

Johnson needs the support of a few Labour members to get enough votes to hold an election because some members of his own party have turned against him.

- **Watching and Thinking**

Tariffs on China: Economics Out, Politics In

September 26, 2018
CGTN

America dropped bombs again. America is slapping another round of tariffs, this time on 200 billion US dollars of Chinese goods—that's half of what Americans buy from China in a year.

What is going on? To fully understand a situation, one must put themselves in the shoes of others. On the surface, this is about trade deficit. But even President Donald Trump's former chief economic adviser Gary Cohen admitted this is a non-issue. Almost all sane economists agree. First, the deficit number is overblown and secondly, deficit is not a bad thing for the US. It helps keep prices low and return the money to America as investment. Nothing is further from the truth than calling China a "piggy bank".

There is another story behind this: Reciprocity. The Chinese call it mutually benefits, but it does not mean measure-for-measure equality. America complains about limited market access to China. Yes, China should be more open—and it is opening up more. But zoom out a little bit and you'll see thousands of American businesses making money in China.

No one put a gun to their head. They come, they see and they win. If China is a thief's house or a robber's den, why is it then that Apple, GM, Starbucks, Tesla among many others are expanding their businesses here? Even Google and Facebook are knocking at the door, loud and clear.

But when you come in, you respect the rules of the house. You may have issues with the specifics, but don't even try to own the rules. As Tim Cook says, we believe in engaging with governments even when we disagree.

It can be worse! I got confused. I don't know what Mr. Trump wants and I am not sure he does either. But I know right now in America, anger sells and catharsis feels good. But America has become a political animal who refuses to think.

Trade war will open Pandora's box. Yes global trade has left many behind, and they are angry. But trade wars will cause more casualties, and the world will be a place of confusion and pain.

But let us not waste a good crisis. The world has seen the bad and it should be ready for the worse. One thousand years ago a Chinese poet who shared similar optimism with Cervantes said, "The brave are not frightened when confronted. The sane are not angered when challenged."

Today China is making its most ambitious social and economic experiment in history: Reforming itself and opening its arms to others. The world is a large place and China will be "in it to win it". It needs to be a better player and it will be. So, even when your partner loses their cool, it makes more sense that you don't.

Part 2　Learning in Class

Warm Up

The Politics of Human Rights

By Zhang Weiwei
March 9, 2019
CGTN

China is often singled out by the West for allegedly violation of human rights, and China's human rights situation is often described by the West as deteriorating. So we have to discuss human rights here openly and honestly.

To my mind, whether China's human rights are good or bad, one should first of all, ask the Chinese—not Washington, not Brussels, not Americans, not Europeans, but Chinese. You may ask any Chinese you meet, whether in China, in Europe, in America, or elsewhere, how is China's human rights situation today? I believe most Chinese will answer it's better than any other time in history. China now "exports" 130 million tourists a year, and 99.999 percent return to China. Why would they prefer to return to a country without human rights as alleged by the West? Obviously the opposite is true; China is a country where human rights progress is the greatest. It's so basic and it's a common sense assessment, at least, for most Chinese.

It's always mind-boggling for me that many in the West believe that they know China better than the Chinese, they know Africa better than Africans, they know Russia better than Russians. This is wrong, totally wrong. Take Africa as an example. I've travelled to Africa many times. The West always thinks that democratization should be Africa's top priority, but you should at least ask the Africans themselves how they think about it. I have traveled to many African countries, and I can say with certainty most Africans most local people want first of all to solve such human rights issues as food, jobs, disease treatment and street safety. But the West asks them to place democratization above everything else, and in the end, how many of these countries end up in chaos?

No country in the world can realize all human rights simultaneously, and there should be priorities in achieving human rights. China does not follow the Western preference and regards poverty eradication as its top priority in promoting human rights, and China has lifted over 700 million people out of poverty. This fact has changed China and the world forever. If China embraced only the Western approach and standards, then poverty eradication is not considered as human rights promotion—which is of course nonsense, but we have no time to wait for the West to wake up, we have done what we think is right.

Actually, the West should themselves reflect seriously on their human rights problems at home. For instance, most of the Western countries—if not all—have not yet practiced equal pay for equal work. This is wrong. This is violation of human rights. If you ask me what is the most serious and gross violation of human rights in the 21st century, I would tell you it's the Iraq War, launched by the United States against the will of the Iraqi people, against the will of the international community. How many innocent lives have been lost in this war? Hundreds of thousands. How many people have been made hopeless by this war? Millions upon millions.

With regard to the Western discourse on human rights as a whole, I also detect a few weaknesses in it. First, it has difficulty in keeping a balance between civil, political rights and economic social and cultural rights. For instance, the American concept of human rights does not include economic, social and cultural rights. If only the US could tackle the issue of nearly one in six Americans without medical insurance from a human rights perspective. This is social rights. It would be perhaps much better and much easier for the US to solve this problem.

In short, the protection of human rights is a noble cause for all nations, so please don't practice double standards.

Unit 4　Economy

Part 1　Learning Before Class

- **Listening**

China Launches Tech Hub Megalopolis to Rival Silicon Valley

By Bill Ide

March 4, 2019

VOA

China is stepping up its efforts, so announcing a long-awaited plan to link up its southern Pearl River Delta into a massive hub of technology, research finance and innovation.

The possibilities and challenges of the project are both equally challenging and promising, according to analysts. Some describe the plan as an attempt to create a megacity to rival Silicon Valley, the US technology powerhouse that is home to companies such as Google, Facebook, and Apple.

But while Silicon Valley has a population of 3.1 million, the Greater Bay Area will link up 9 cities together with Hong Kong and Macau with a total population of about 70 million, and the economic heft, state media argues, to drive the Chinese economy, let alone the world.

The plan was announced recently is expected to be a prominent topic during high-level political meetings going on this month in Beijing. It is not necessarily new. China's opening up to the world more than four decades ago began in the south and the Pearl River Delta has long been home to some of the country's leading companies from telecommunications—such as Huawei to Internet giant Tencent and host of other technology and manufacturing enterprises.

It also aims to drive investment to the area at a time when foreign funds flowing into the country are sagging. The plan will tie together three different legal jurisdictions and that makes the plan unique compared to the two other major mega-city projects in China—the Beijing, Hebei, Tianjin merger and the Yangtze River Delta integration plan near Shanghai.

China has long had deep pockets when it comes to making investments that push forward technological advances. China has already taken major strides to overcome some of the physical obstacles such as linking Hong Kong with Guangzhou and Shenzheng by high-speed rail and its recent opening of the 55-kilometer Hong Kong-Zhuhai-Macau Bridge.

- **Watching and Thinking**

Global Firms Welcome China's First Foreign Investment Law

March 18, 2019

Appendix 5

CGTN

China's new Foreign Investment Law addresses some long-time concerns from Western companies. Many choose Shanghai for their Chinese headquarters. Reporter Han Peng meets some high-profile investors to get their take on the new law. The highly-anticipated Foreign Investment Law has become a reality. Advanced, forced technological transfer vows equal treatment before investors, and protects intellectual property rights.

"By not forcing technology transfer, not even having the perception that there's a force technology transfer will lead to much greater openness, and once that's understood, and what's, once companies become more comfortable with that, it will really lead to a wave of investment."

Some say China rush the passing of the law, due to the pressure from the ongoing trade negotiations with the United States, but Beijing insists that is simply another chapter in China's opening up, lawmakers started drafts in the law years before US President Donald Trump took office. Last year Shanghai witnessed the opening of the first foreign car factory independently owned by a foreign investor.

"Gigantic factory Shanghai will be the first test gig factory outside of the United States."

In the past, China required foreign auto factories to enter the country by setting up a joint venture with the domestic car brand, causing suspicions, a forced attack transfer.

"The opening-up policies have been a steady movement towards opening, and we feel very optimistic about the long-term future."

Some foreign investors say the newly passed law makes Beijing's message clearer to investors around the world, but others say a few clauses of the law still lack specific details of how companies can utilize it to protect their rights.

"The law is written in a way which gives a lot of promises and hopes, and of course, many companies hope that the implementation is in a way they see it at the moment."

Tito's Band Guard has lived in the world's Shanghai for over 20 years; he witnessed the rides, the city skylines from literally nothing in the 1990s, with things moving so quickly, he says the Chinese government should not take all the blame, when foreign investors complain about having a difficult time in China.

"The happy times over in many industries, so in the past ... when foreign investors came to China, they ... they ... encountered certain industries where they were without competition, but today for many companies they face ... the domestic competition where you also have local players who are catching up."

The approval of the foreign investment law is a welcome move, but many foreign companies operating in China, some still have concerns, leaving more room for China to further open up.

Part 2　Learning in Class

Warm Up

US-China Tariff Dispute Threatens to Cause Economic Damage on All Sides

May 13, 2019

CBC News

China took steps today to retaliate against the US. It announced it will raise tariffs on sixty billion dollars' worth of American goods beginning June 1st. That's in response to the White House's decision last week to hike tariffs on two hundred billion dollars in Chinese products. Here's a reminder of how those tariffs work.

A tariff is essentially attacks. Governments implement them on goods coming in from another country. So let's say, an American company buys 100 washing machines from a Chinese company. Each has a price tag of $500, so the total cost is $50,000. At the border they face of 25% tariff. That means an additional $12,500 is owed.

But China doesn't pay that amount. The American importer does. Who collects the cash? US border agents! At 328 different ports of entry and the proceeds go to the US Treasury. The idea is to encourage domestic companies to buy local, or perhaps from another country often, though the company just passes on the cost to the consumer by raising the price of that washing machine. In fact, new research suggests President Trump's tariffs increase the cost of washing machines by 12% or about 86 to 92 dollars more per appliance.

The president is now threatening more tariffs after China announced his retaliation measures earlier. With neither side appearing willing to back down, global stocks are sinking over the potential impact on the world economy. Could this trade war trigger an economic slowdown?

Danu is an international trade lawyer with Dickinson right and he joins us via Face Time from Detroit. Brad House is deputy chief economist at Scotia Bank economics and he joins us from Toronto. Hi to both of you. Great to see you. Really appreciate your time …

Unit 5　Science and Technology

Part 1　Learning Before Class

- Listening

High School Cheaters Nabbed by Neural Network

By Christopher Intagliata

June 6, 2019

https://www.scientificamerican.com

The English-language version of Wikipedia has almost six million articles. And if you're a cheating student, that's six million essays already written for you, footnotes and all. Except plagiarism isn't really an effective tactic—just plug the text into a search engine and game over. But what about having a ghostwriter at a paper mill compose your final essay?

"Standard plagiarism software cannot detect this kind of cheating." Stephan Lorenzen is a data analyst at the University of Copenhagen. In Denmark, where he's based, ghostwriting is a growing problem at high schools. So Lorenzen and his colleagues created a program called Ghostwriter that can detect the cheats.

At its core is a neural network trained and tested on 130,000 real essays from 10,000 Danish students. After reading through tens of thousands of essays labeled as being written by the same author or not, the machine taught itself to tune into the characteristics that might tip off cheating. For example, did a student's essays share the same styles of punctuation? The same spelling mistakes? Were the abbreviations the same?

By scrutinizing inconsistencies like those, Ghostwriter was able to pinpoint a cheated essay nearly 90 percent of the time. The team presented the results at the European Symposium on Artificial Neural Networks, Computational Intelligence and Machine Learning. [Magnus Stavngaard et al., Detecting Ghostwriters in High Schools]

There's one more aspect here that could help students. Your high school essays presumably get better over time as you learn to write—and the machine can detect that. "The final idea is, of course, to try to detect students who are at risk because their development in writing style isn't as you'd expect." Teachers could thus give extra help to kids who really need it, while sniffing out the cheaters too.

- **Watching and Thinking**

  AI Is Monitoring Your Right Now and Here's How They're Using Your Data

April 4, 2018

https://www.onenewspage.com

Female dubber: We are living in an age of mass surveillance. And big data, mixed with the ever-increasing power of artificial intelligence, means all of our actions are being recorded and stored like never before. This information is being mined to identify social media trends for targeted advertising, but it's also being used to predict riots, election outcomes, disease epidemics, and that's not to mention the vast networks of surveillance cameras that could be used to track crowds and individuals in real time.

This is EMBERS, a computer-forecasting system that sift through the data that you post on social media every day. It mines platforms you'd expect like Twitter and Facebook and it tracks things that you might not expect like restaurant apps, traffic maps, currency rates and even food prices.

Naren Ramakrishnan: Data from tweets and social media is useful for predicting both disease outbreaks and events like civil unrest, domestic political crisis, elections and so on. And you can use these nontraditional data sources, like restaurant reservation information, hospital imagery and so on to predict the flu.

Female dubber: EMBERS mines big data for trends rather than information on individuals. For example, if EMBERS detects a mass cancellation of restaurant reservations and then hospital parking lots fill up, the system can predict that there is probably an outbreak of food poisoning or flu. And it's incredibly accurate. EMBERS correctly predicted Hantavirus outbreaks in Argentina and Chile in 2013 and political uprisings in Brazil and Venezuela in 2013 and 2014. In fact, EMBERS is correct in its predictions about 90% of the time.

But EMBERS does have its limits. While it can mine public data to forecast major social events before they happen, it can't predict spontaneous events, like crowd stampedes or terrorists, an increasing concern in an over-crowded and unstable world, which is what Dr. Mubarak Shah and his team are trying to do. They are using surveillance, AI and complicated mathematical algorithms to track and predict the movements of dense crowds and the individuals in those crowds.

Dr. Mubarak Shah: Crowd analysis is a very interesting area and very challenge when you have thousands of people. It becomes very, very complicated.

Female dubber: This is where AI comes in. It can help spot abnormal patterns in a crowd like bottlenecks. Take the Hajj pilgrimage in Saudi Arabia for example. In 2015, hundreds were crushed to death in a stampede. In the future, computers may be able to detect bottlenecks in real time and pilgrims can be diverted to uncrowded areas, thus avoiding stampedes and ultimately, saving lives.

Another application Shah's team is working on is to track individuals in crowds in real time.

Dr. Mubarak Shah: We want to be able to track that person, where the person enters, where he's going and where exact sitting and so on.

Female dubber: This kind of surveillance is done manually, but computers are beginning to be able to detect individuals acting suspiciously as they move through a crowd.

Dr. Mubarak Shah: We want to be able to analyze the video in each camera. We detect people, we track, we identify and so on.

Female dubber: Using video surveillance and the networks of cameras available in major cities, Shah's team is working on using AI to track individuals from place to place.

Dr. Mubarak Shah: The Boston bomber was seen in many different locations. The issue is you detect one person in one camera. Then it disappears because it was not visible. And after some time it reappear in another camera, maybe at a distance. So re-identification in a crowd is much, much harder because there are lots of people.

Female dubber: Camera networks data mined for suspicious behavior could stop future bombings. But it isn't easy and they aren't there yet. There is so much data that needs to be annotated so that machines can understand human behavior.

Dr. Mubarak Shah: It can help law enforcement so that they have eyes and it can make them more efficient and it can help solve crime.

Female dubber: But there is a downside to this. How much privacy are we willing to give up to be safe? The implications of these technologies are vast. Perhaps it depends on how much you trust the people who are mining your data.

Part 2 Learning in Class

Warm Up

How a Driverless Car Sees the Road

By Chris Urmson

So in 1885, Karl Benz invented the automobile. Later that year, he took it out for the first public test drive, and—true story—crashed into a wall. For the last 130 years, we've been working around that least reliable part of the car, the driver. We've made the car stronger. We've added seat belts, we've added air bags, and in the last decade, we've actually started trying to make the car smarter to fix that bug, the driver.

Now, today I'm going to talk to you a little bit about the difference between patching around the problem with driver assistance systems and actually having fully self-driving cars and what they can do for the world. I'm also going to talk to you a little bit about our car and allow you to see how it sees the world and how it reacts and what it does, but first I'm going to talk a little bit about the problem. And it's a big problem: 1.2 million people are killed on the world's roads every year. In America alone, 33,000 people are killed each year. To put that in perspective, that's the same as a 737 falling out of the sky every working day. It's kind of unbelievable. Cars are sold to us like this, but really, this is what driving's like. Right? It's not sunny, it's rainy, and you want to do anything other than drive. And the reason why is this: Traffic is getting worse. In America, between 1990 and 2010, the vehicle miles traveled increased by 38 percent. We grew by six percent of roads, so it's not in your brains. Traffic really is substantially worse than it was not very long ago.

And all of this has a very human cost. So if you take the average commute time in America, which is about 50 minutes, you multiply that by the 120 million workers we have, that turns out to be about six billion minutes wasted in commuting every day. Now, that's a big number, so let's put it in perspective. You take that six billion minutes and you divide it by the average life expectancy of a person that turns out to be 162 lifetimes spent every day, wasted, just getting from A to B. It's unbelievable. And then, there are those of us who don't have the privilege of sitting in traffic. So this is Steve. He's an incredibly capable guy, but he just happens to be blind, and that means instead of a 30-minute drive to work in the morning, it's a two-hour ordeal of piecing together bits of public transit or asking friends and family for a ride. He doesn't have that same freedom that you and I have to get around. We should do something about that.

Now, conventional wisdom would say that we'll just take these driver assistance systems and we'll kind of push them and incrementally improve them, and over time, they'll turn into self-driving cars. Well, I'm here to tell you that's like me saying that if I work really hard at jumping, one day I'll be able to fly. We actually need to do something a little different. And so I'm going to talk to you about three different ways that self-driving systems are different than driver assistance systems. And I'm going to start with some of our own experience.

So back in 2013, we had the first test of a self-driving car where we let regular people use it. Well, almost regular—they were 100 Googlers, but they weren't working on the project. And we gave them the car and we allowed them to use it in their daily lives. But unlike a real self-driving car, this one had a big asterisk with it: They had to pay attention, because this was an experimental vehicle. We tested it a lot, but it could still fail. And so we gave them two hours of training, we put them in the car, we let them use it, and what we heard back was something awesome, as someone trying to bring a product into the world. Every one of them told us they loved it. In fact, we had a Porsche driver who came in and told us on the first day, "This is completely stupid. What are we thinking?" But at the end of it, he said, "Not only should I have it, everyone else should have it, because people are terrible drivers." So this was music to our ears, but then we started to look at what the people inside the car were doing, and this was eye-opening. Now, my favorite story is this gentleman who looks down at his phone and realizes the battery is low, so he turns around like this in the car and digs around in his backpack, pulls out his laptop, puts it on the seat, goes in the back again, digs around, pulls out the charging cable for his phone, futzes around, puts it into the laptop, puts it on the phone. Sure enough, the phone is charging. All the time he's been doing 65 miles per hour down the freeway. Right? Unbelievable. So we thought about this and we said, it's kind of obvious, right? The better the technology gets, the less reliable the driver is going to get. So by just making the cars incrementally smarter, we're probably not going to see the wins we really need.

Let me talk about something a little technical for a moment here. So we're looking at this graph, and along the bottom is how often does the car apply the brakes when it shouldn't. You can ignore most of that axis, because if you're driving around town, and the car starts stopping randomly, you're never going to buy that car. And the vertical axis is how often the car is going to apply the brakes when it's supposed to to help you avoid an accident. Now, if we look at the bottom left corner here, this is your classic car. It doesn't apply the brakes for you, it doesn't do anything goofy, but it also doesn't get you out of an accident. Now, if we want to bring a driver assistance system into a car, say with collision mitigation braking, we're going to put some package of technology on there, and that's this curve, and it's going to have some operating properties, but it's never going to avoid all of the accidents, because it doesn't have that capability. But we'll pick some place along the curve here, and maybe it avoids half of accidents that the human driver misses, and that's amazing, right? We just reduced accidents on our roads by a factor of two. There are now 17,000 less people dying every year in America.

But if we want a self-driving car, we need a technology curve that looks like this. We're going to have to put more sensors in the vehicle, and we'll pick some operating point up here where it basically never gets into a crash. They'll happen, but very low frequency. Now you and I could look at this and we could argue about whether it's incremental, and I could say something like "80-20 rule," and it's really hard to move up to that new curve. But let's look at it from a different direction for a moment. So let's look at how often the technology has to do the right thing. And so this green dot up here is a driver assistance system. It turns out that human drivers make mistakes that lead to traffic accidents about once every 100,000 miles in America. In contrast, a self-driving system is probably making decisions about 10 times per second, so order of magnitude, that's about 1,000 times per mile. So if you compare the distance between these two, it's about 10 to the eighth, right? Eight orders of magnitude. That's like comparing how fast I run to the speed of light. It doesn't matter how hard I train. I'm never actually going to get there. So there's a pretty big gap there.

And then finally, there's how the system can handle uncertainty. So this pedestrian here might be stepping into the road, might not be. I can't tell, nor can any of our algorithms, but in the case of a driver assistance system, that means it can't take action, because again, if it presses the brakes unexpectedly, that's completely unacceptable. Whereas a self-driving system can look at that pedestrian and say, I don't know what they're about to do, slow down, take a better look, and then react appropriately after that.

So it can be much safer than a driver assistance system can ever be. So that's enough about the differences between the two. Let's spend some time talking about how the car sees the world.

So this is our vehicle. It starts by understanding where it is in the world, by taking a map and its sensor data and aligning the two, and then we layer on top of that what it sees in the moment. So here, all the purple boxes you can see are other vehicles on the road, and the red thing on the side over there is a cyclist, and up in the distance, if you look really closely, you can see some cones. Then we know where the car is in the moment, but we have to do better than that: we have to predict what's going to happen. So here the pickup truck in top right is about to make a left lane change because the road in front of it is closed, so it needs to get out of the way. Knowing that one pickup truck is great, but we really need to know what everybody's thinking, so it becomes quite a complicated problem. And then given that, we can figure out how the car should respond in the moment, so what trajectory it should follow, how quickly it should slow down or speed up. And then that all turns into just following a path:

Appendix 5

turning the steering wheel left or right, pressing the brake or gas. It's really just two numbers at the end of the day. So how hard can it really be?

Back when we started in 2009, this is what our system looked like. So you can see our car in the middle and the other boxes on the road, driving down the highway. The car needs to understand where it is and roughly where the other vehicles are. It's really a geometric understanding of the world. Once we started driving on neighborhood and city streets, the problem becomes a whole new level of difficulty. You see pedestrians crossing in front of us, cars crossing in front of us, going every which way, the traffic lights, crosswalks. It's an incredibly complicated problem by comparison. And then once you have that problem solved, the vehicle has to be able to deal with construction. So here are the cones on the left forcing it to drive to the right, but not just construction in isolation, of course. It has to deal with other people moving through that construction zone as well. And of course, if anyone's breaking the rules, the police are there and the car has to understand that that flashing light on the top of the car means that it's not just a car, it's actually a police officer. Similarly, the orange box on the side here, it's a school bus, and we have to treat that differently as well.

When we're out on the road, other people have expectations: So, when a cyclist puts up their arm, it means they're expecting the car to yield to them and make room for them to make a lane change. And when a police officer stood in the road, our vehicle should understand that this means stop, and when they signal to go, we should continue.

Now, the way we accomplish this is by sharing data between the vehicles. The first, most crude model of this is when one vehicle sees a construction zone, having another know about it so it can be in the correct lane to avoid some of the difficulty. But we actually have a much deeper understanding of this. We could take all of the data that the cars have seen over time, the hundreds of thousands of pedestrians, cyclists, and vehicles that have been out there and understand what they look like and use that to infer what other vehicles should look like and other pedestrians should look like. And then, even more importantly, we could take from that a model of how we expect them to move through the world. So here the yellow box is a pedestrian crossing in front of us. Here the blue box is a cyclist and we anticipate that they're going to nudge out and around the car to the right. Here there's a cyclist coming down the road and we know they're going to continue to drive down the shape of the road. Here somebody makes a right turn, and in a moment here, somebody's going to make a U-turn in front of us, and we can anticipate that behavior and respond safely.

Now, that's all well and good for things that we've seen, but of course, you encounter lots of things that you haven't seen in the world before. And so just a couple of months ago, our vehicles were driving through Mountain View, and this is what we encountered. This is a woman in an electric wheelchair chasing a duck in circles on the road. (Laughter) Now it turns out, there is nowhere in the DMV handbook that tells you how to deal with that, but our vehicles were able to encounter that, slow down, and drive safely. Now, we don't have to deal with just ducks. Watch this bird fly across in front of us. The car reacts to that. Here we're dealing with a cyclist that you would never expect to see anywhere other than Mountain View. And of course, we have to deal with drivers, even the very small ones. Watch to the right as someone jumps out of this truck at us. And now, watch the left as the car with the green box decides he needs to make a right turn at the last possible moment. Here, as we make a lane

change, the car to our left decides it wants to as well. And here, we watch a car blow through a red light and yield to it. And similarly, here, a cyclist blowing through that light as well. And of course, the vehicle responds safely. And of course, we have people who do I don't know what sometimes on the road, like this guy pulling out between two self-driving cars. You have to ask, "What are you thinking?"
(Laughter)

Now, I just fire-hosed you with a lot of stuff there, so I'm going to break one of these down pretty quickly. So what we're looking at is the scene with the cyclist again, and you might notice in the bottom, we can't actually see the cyclist yet, but the car can: it's that little blue box up there, and that comes from the laser data. And that's not actually really easy to understand, so what I'm going to do is I'm going to turn that laser data and look at it, and if you're really good at looking at laser data, you can see a few dots on the curve there, right there, and that blue box is that cyclist. Now as our light is red, the cyclist's light has turned yellow already, and if you squint, you can see that in the imagery. But the cyclist, we see, is going to proceed through the intersection. Our light has now turned green, his is solidly red, and we now anticipate that this bike is going to come all the way across. Unfortunately the other drivers next to us were not paying as much attention. They started to pull forward, and fortunately for everyone, this cyclists reacts, avoids, and makes it through the intersection. And off we go.

Now, as you can see, we've made some pretty exciting progress, and at this point we're pretty convinced this technology is going to come to market. We do three million miles of testing in our simulators every single day, so you can imagine the experience that our vehicles have. We are looking forward to having this technology on the road, and we think the right path is to go through the self-driving rather than driver assistance approach because the urgency is so large. In the time I have given this talk today, 34 people have died on America's roads.

How soon can we bring it out? Well, it's hard to say because it's a really complicated problem, but these are my two boys. My oldest son is 11, and that means in four and a half years, he's going to be able to get his driver's license. My team and I are committed to making sure that doesn't happen.

Thank you.

Chris Anderson: Chris, I've got a question for you.

Chris Urmson: Sure.

CA: So certainly, the mind of your cars is pretty mind-boggling. On this debate between driver-assisted and fully driverless—I mean, there's a real debate going on out there right now. So some of the companies, for example, Tesla, are going the driver-assisted route. What you're saying is that that's kind of going to be a dead end because you can't just keep improving that route and get to fully driverless at some point, and then a driver is going to say, "This feels safe", and climb into the back, and something ugly will happen.

CU: Right. No, that's exactly right, and it's not to say that the driver assistance systems aren't going to be incredibly valuable. They can save a lot of lives in the interim, but to see the transformative opportunity to help someone like Steve get around, to really get to the end case in safety, to have the opportunity to change our cities and move parking out and get rid of these urban craters we call parking lots, it's the only way to go.

CA: We will be tracking your progress with huge interest. Thanks so much, Chris.

Appendix 5

CU: Thank you.

Unit 6　Environment

Part 1　Learning Before Class

- **Listening**

Air Pollution Contributes to Childhood Asthma

May 15, 2019
VOA

We already know that traffic pollution is a big contributor to climate change, but new research suggests, it's also a huge driver of health problems around the world.

Recent estimates show that air pollution is actually the leading environmental health risk factor globally more than any other environmental cause of disease. According to the World Health Organization, air pollution causes an estimated 3.7 million premature deaths every year, but a new study from George Washington University in Washington DC points to a specific pollutant, nitrogen dioxide (NO_2), from car emissions as the leading cause of childhood asthma in many cities around the world.

NO_2 pollution has a really important impact on the number of children worldwide that are being diagnosed with asthma, and in fact the largest impacts were seen in cities where up to almost about 50% of new asthma cases among children, in some cities worldwide, were attributable to NO_2 pollution. And a really troubling element of the research, the cities where all this asthma is happening have levels of NO_2 that are within limits considered safe by the World Health Organization.

One of the most surprising findings for us was that actually over 90% of annually pediatric asthma incidents occurred in areas that already met the World Health Organization guideline for annual average NO_2 pollution of 21 parts per billion.

The solution these researchers say is to continue the fight against climate warming greenhouse gases because the 2 problems are so closely related. One of the things that we found in our study was that cities that had higher NO_2 levels also had higher greenhouse gases. And so one thing that can be done would be to avoid burning fossil fuels, and reduce it in any way we can.

The researchers say they hope to do more studies to understand which specific chemicals in NO_2 pollution trigger asthma, so they can help target those specific sources of emissions.

Kevin Enochs, VOA News.

- **Watching and Thinking**

Global Warming—Is It Real?

January 31, 2019
National Geographic

Human activities from pollution to over-population are driving up the earth temperature, and fundamentally changing the world around us. The main causes of the phenomenon are known as the greenhouse effect. Gases in the atmosphere such as water vapor, carbon dioxide, methane, nitrous oxide and chloro-fluorocarbons let the sun's light in, but keep some of the heat from escaping, like the glass walls of the green house. The more greenhouse gases in the atmosphere, the more heat gets trapped, strengthening the greenhouse effect and increasing the earth's temperature.

Human activities like the burning of fossil fuels have increased the amount of CO_2 in the atmosphere by more than 1/3 since the industrial revolution. The rapid increase in greenhouse gases in the atmosphere has warmed the planet at an alarming rate. While earth's climate has fluctuated in the past, atmospheric carbon dioxide has reached today's levels in hundreds of thousands of years.

Climate change has consequences for our oceans, our weather, our food sources, and our health. Ice sheets, such as Greenland and Antarctica, are melting. The extra water that was once held in glaciers causes sea levels to rise, and spills out of the oceans, flooding coastal regions. Warmer temperatures also make weather more extreme. This means not only more intense major storms, floods and heavy snowfall, but also longer and more frequent droughts. These changes of weather pose challenges. Growing crops becomes more difficult. The areas where plants and animals can live shift, and water supplies are diminished. In addition to creating new agricultural challenges, climate change can directly affect people's physical health. In urban areas, the warmer atmosphere creates an environment that traps and increases the amount of smog. This is because smog contains ozone particles which increase rapidly at higher temperatures. Exposure to higher levels of smog can cause health problems such as asthma, heart disease, and lung cancer.

While the rapid rate of climate change is caused by humans, humans are also the ones who can combat it. If we work to replace fossil fuels with renewable energy sources, like solar and wind, which don't produce greenhouse gas emissions, you might still be able to prevent some of the worst effects of climate change.

Unit 7 Social Security and Crime Prevention

Part 1 Learning Before Class

• **Listening**

Who Listens to Google Assistant Recordings?

July 21, 2019

VOA

American technology company Google says its contractors listens to recordings of what people say to artificial intelligence system Google Assistant.

The company admitted that people can review those recordings after some of its Dutch language audio clips were leaked to the public.

Google product manager David Monsees wrote about the leak in a recent blog post. He said the company is investigating their release.

Belgian broadcaster VRT NWS got hold of more than 1,000 Google Assistant recordings. It noted in a story that some recordings contained sensitive personal conversations, as well as information that identified the person speaking.

Google said the recordings do not identify user account information. It added that contractors who listen to the audio are told not to take notes of background conversations.

Google said its contract work force listens to recordings to better understand speech patterns and differences in regional accents. Google's user terms say the company may use the recordings. They state that Google Assistant "records your voice and audio on Google services to improve speech recognition".

Monsees wrote that Google works with contractors around the world to study the recordings.

Google's terms do not exactly say that people examine the recordings. But the user terms do say the company could study them as it improves services or creates new features.

Earlier this year, the Bloomberg financial service reported that Amazon's Alexa also uses contractors to listen to recordings. Amazon officials confirmed the report.

Google's recording feature can be disabled, but doing so means Assistant loses some of its technical abilities. Users who turn off the recording feature lose the ability for the Assistant to recognize individual voices and learn their speech patterns.

Google Assistant is available on more than 1 billion devices, including smartphones and smart speakers. It has become more popular in the smart speaker market, but still has fewer users than Amazon.

I'm John Russell.

- **Watching and Thinking**

Saving Them, Saving Us

By Chen Ran
August 12, 2019
CGTN

Ivory trade has been the leading cause of rampant elephant poaching in Africa. In Mana Pools National Park in northern Zimbabwe ①, a UNESCO ② World Natural Heritage site and one of the finest wildlife areas in Africa, a stray African elephant is in danger of being hunted at any time.

Zhang Guangrui (Chinese wildlife conservation volunteer): There are more than 30 elephants being poached across Africa every day. In Zimbabwe alone, as many as over 1,000 elephants are killed every year.

The elephant has been identified as the matriarch of a herd, and Niakomba, a senior wildlife conservation official in Mana Pools National Park, must find it before the poachers. He will put a satellite tag around the elephant's neck so he can track the herd's movement.

However, the park covers 2,196 square kilometers and boasts a wide range of animals, including rhinos, lions, over 350 bird species and aquatic life, which means spotting the elephant is not an easy job.

---

① Zimbabwe, officially the Republic of Zimbabwe, is a landlocked country located in southern Africa, between the Zambezi and Limpopo Rivers, bordered by South Africa, Botswana, Zambia and Mozambique. The capital and largest city is Harare and the second largest being Bulawayo. A country of roughly 16 million people, Zimbabwe has 16 official languages, with English, Shona, and Ndebele the most commonly used.

② UNESCO, or the United Nations Educational, Scientific and Cultural Organization, is a specialized agency of the United Nations based in Paris, France. Its declared purpose is to contribute to promoting international collaboration in education, sciences, and culture in order to increase universal respect for justice, the rule of law, and human rights along with fundamental freedom proclaimed in the United Nations Charter. It is the successor of the League of Nations' International Committee on Intellectual Cooperation.

Niakomba (Wildlife conservation official, Mana Pools National Park, Zimbabwe): The resources are very limited. We lack vehicles and boats.

Zhang and his teammates from the Beijing Peaceland Foundation, a non-governmental organization for wildlife conservation and emergency rescue, were the first participants in the joint anti-poaching program between China and Zimbabwe since 2015. This time, they brought an inflatable boat and a powered hang glider to assist Niakomba.

Zhang Guangrui: Local staff used to go patrol by walking or by driving a car. With our equipment, their mobility has been greatly improved. More importantly, a multi-dimensional patrol system had been set up.

Together with Zhang and his volunteer peers, Niakomba finally spotted the elephant some 20 kilometers away from the point of departure. Luckily, the elephant was safe and sound.

(Conservation staff put a satellite tracking tag on the elephant that is under general anesthesia.)

This rescue operation took place in May 2018, and by May 2019, the Sino-Zim Wildlife Foundation has initiated eight joint anti-poaching missions that involved 60 people since its establishment in 2015. The foundation echoed the Chinese government's position on wildlife protection and conservancy.

Zhang Guangrui: The wildlife belongs to the entire world. We are saving such a beautiful place for the global community.

Today, the world is coping with an unprecedented spike in the illegal wildlife trade. If no measures are taken, the African elephant, the largest land mammal on Earth that is the target of the illegal ivory trade, would be on the brink of functional extinction in the next 10 to 20 years.

On July 30, 2015, the United Nations adopted the first-ever resolution to fight smuggling of wild animals, titled "Resolution on Tackling Illicit Trafficking in Wildlife". All 193 UN member countries have committed to scaling up efforts to end the poaching and illegal trade on wildlife.

Two months later, both China and the US presidents promised to end their respective domestic ivory trades as part of the international contribution towards reducing the poaching crisis and saving elephants.

On December 30, 2016, China declared a complete stop to the domestic ivory trade within a year.

Since January 1, 2018, ivory trade has been banned nationwide.

Peter Knights (CEO of Wild Aid): So the African elephant is not in the clear yet, but certainly the [poaching] crisis is now on the decline, and in some countries, the populations are rebounding, and that is very positive.

Endangered species could become extinct 100 times faster than previously thought, scientists warned, adding that the Earth is likely to be amid the sixth mass extinction. Human activities, such as illegal poaching, habitat destruction and climate change, are all responsible for it. More importantly, halting biodiversity loss was inscribed on the list of UN 2030 Agenda for Sustainable Development.

Wang Ke (Founder of the Beijing Peaceland Foundation, Chinese wildlife conservation volunteer): Seeing wildlife in Africa including elephants made me feel this is how our planet should be, and how life should be. The beautiful creatures deserve to be protected at all costs.

Saving wildlife is saving ourselves. Sharing the Earth with other forms of life, we humans cannot isolate ourselves from the rest of Mother Nature. It is our urgent obligation and commitment to work together and save wildlife, including the elephant, from extinction.

Part 2　Learning in Class

Warm Up

To This Day

By Shane Koyczan

March 3, 2017

https://medium.com

　　When I was a kid, I used to think that pork chops and karate chops were the same thing. I thought they were both pork chops. And because my grandmother thought it was cute, and because they were my favorite, she let me keep doing it. Not really a big deal. One day, before I realized fat kids are not designed to climb trees, I fell out of a tree and bruised the right side of my body. I didn't want to tell my grandmother about it because I was scared I'd get in trouble for playing somewhere I shouldn't have been. A few days later, the gym teacher noticed the bruise, and I got sent to the principal's office. From there, I was sent to another small room with a really nice lady who asked me all kinds of questions about my life at home. I saw no reason to lie. As far as I was concerned, life was pretty good. I told her, whenever I'm sad, my grandmother gives me karate chops.

　　This led to a full-scale investigation, and I was removed from the house for three days, until they finally decided to ask how I got the bruises. News of this silly little story quickly spread through the school, and I earned my first nickname: Porkchop. To this day, I hate pork chops.

　　I'm not the only kid who grew up this way, surrounded by people who used to say that rhyme about sticks and stones, as if broken bones hurt more than the names we got called, and we got called them all. So we grew up believing no one would ever fall in love with us, that we'd be lonely forever, that we'd never meet someone to make us feel like the sun was something they built for us in their toolshed. So broken heartstrings bled the blues, and we tried to empty ourselves so we would feel nothing. Don't tell me that hurts less than a broken bone, that an ingrown life is something surgeons can cut away, that there's no way for it to metastasize; it does.

　　She was eight years old, our first day of grade three when she got called "Ugly". We both got moved to the back of class so we would stop getting bombarded by spitballs. But the school halls were a battleground. We found ourselves outnumbered day after wretched day. We used to stay inside for recess, because outside was worse. Outside, we'd have to rehearse running away, or learn to stay still like statues, giving no clues that we were there. In grade five, they taped a sign to the front of her desk that read, "Beware of dog."

　　To this day, despite a loving husband, she doesn't think she's beautiful, because of a birthmark that takes up a little less than half her face. Kids used to say, "She looks like a wrong answer that someone tried to erase, but couldn't quite get the job done." And they'll never understand that she's raising two kids whose definition of beauty begins with the word "Mom", because they see her heart before they see her skin, because she's only ever always been amazing.

　　He was a broken branch grafted onto a different family tree, adopted, not because his parents opted for a different destiny. He was three when he became a mixed drink of one part left alone and two parts tragedy, started therapy in eighth grade, had a personality made up of tests and pills, lived like the uphills were mountains and the downhills were cliffs, four-fifths suicidal, a tidal wave of antidepressants, and an adolescent being called "Popper", one part because of the pills, 99 parts because of the cruelty. He tried to kill himself in grade 10 when a kid who could still go home to Mom and Dad had the audacity to tell him, "Get over it." As if depression is something that could be remedied by any of the contents found in a first-aid kit.

To this day, he is a stick of TNT lit from both ends, could describe to you in detail the way the sky bends in the moment before it's about to fall, and despite an army of friends who all call him an inspiration, he remains a conversation piece between people who can't understand sometimes being drug-free has less to do with addiction and more to do with sanity.

We weren't the only kids who grew up this way. To this day, kids are still being called names. The classics were "Hey, stupid," "Hey, spaz." Seems like every school has an arsenal of names getting updated every year. And if a kid breaks in a school and no one around chooses to hear, do they make a sound? Are they just background noise from a soundtrack stuck on repeat, when people say things like, "Kids can be cruel." Every school was a big top circus tent, and the pecking order went from acrobats to lion tamers, from clowns to carnies, all of these miles ahead of who we were. We were freaks—lobster-claw boys and bearded ladies, oddities juggling depression and loneliness, playing solitaire, spin the bottle, trying to kiss the wounded parts of ourselves and heal, but at night, while the others slept, we kept walking the tightrope. It was practice, and yes, some of us fell.

But I want to tell them that all of this is just debris left over when we finally decide to smash all the things we thought we used to be, and if you can't see anything beautiful about yourself, get a better mirror, look a little closer, stare a little longer, because there's something inside you that made you keep trying despite everyone who told you to quit. You built a cast around your broken heart and signed it yourself, "They were wrong." Because maybe you didn't belong to a group or a clique. Maybe they decided to pick you last for basketball or everything. Maybe you used to bring bruises and broken teeth to show-and-tell, but never told, because how can you hold your ground if everyone around you wants to bury you beneath it? You have to believe that they were wrong. They have to be wrong. Why else would we still be here?

We grew up learning to cheer on the underdog because we see ourselves in them. We stem from a root planted in the belief that we are not what we were called. We are not abandoned cars stalled out and sitting empty on some highway, and if in some way we are, don't worry. We only got out to walk and get gas. We are graduating members from the class of "We Made It", not the faded echoes of voices crying out, "Names will never hurt me." Of course they did.

But our lives will only ever always continue to be a balancing act that has less to do with pain and more to do with beauty.

Unit 8　Health

Part 1　Learning Before Class

- **Listening**

What's So Bad About Processed Foods?

Jonathan Evans
June 25, 2019
VOA

Processed foods like chips, soda and frozen pizzas are full of salt, sugar and fat. Now, scientists are trying to understand if there is something else about such foods that may be bad for humans.

Scientists have already linked low-cost, packaged foods to rising obesity rates around the world. Obesity is a condition involving too much body fat. It increases the risk of many health problems.

Three recent studies offer more clues on how our increasingly industrialized food supply may be affecting our health.

What does processed mean?

The researchers created a system that places foods into four groups. The system says highly processed foods are made mostly of industrialized materials and additives. Sodas, packaged cookies, instant noodles and chicken nuggets are some examples of highly processed foods. But also included are products that can seem healthy, such as morning cereals, energy bars and some kinds of yogurt.

What's wrong with processed foods?

Researchers at the National Institutes of Health conducted a four-week study involving 20 people. They found that people eat about 500 more calories a day when fed mostly processed foods. That is compared to when the same people were given less processed foods. The researchers permitted the 20 participants to eat as much or as little as they wanted. They were taken to a medical center so their health and behavior could be observed.

In another study, researchers in France found people who ate more processed foods were more likely to have heart disease. A similar study in Spain linked eating more processed foods to a higher risk of death in general.

What is it about processed foods?

When fed less processed foods, people in the study produced more of a hormone that controls hunger, and less of a hormone that causes hunger. The reason for the reaction is not clear. The scientists also found that people ate processed foods more quickly.

Kevin Hall is one of the researchers who led the study. He told the AP that processed foods are usually "softer and easier to chew and swallow". Hall noted the source of nutrients might make a difference. For example, fibers from whole fruits and vegetables may be better for making people feel full than fiber added to packaged foods such as energy bars and yogurt.

What should you eat?

Avoiding processed foods can be hard, especially for people with limited time and money. Processed foods can also take many forms. In addition, companies continually re-engineer products to make them seem healthier. The newest studies may provide more reasons to avoid processed foods. But they also call attention to the difficulty of coming up with ways to do that.

I'm Jonathan Evans.

- **Watching and Thinking**

How Stress Affects Your Body

By Sharon Horesh Bergquist

https://www.ted.com

Cramming for a test? Trying to get more done than you have time to do?

Stress is a feeling we all experience when we are challenged or overwhelmed. But more than just an emotion, stress is a hardwired physical response that travels throughout your entire body. In the short term, stress can be advantageous, but when activated too often or too long, your primitive fight or flight stress response not only changes your brain but also damages many of the other organs and cells throughout your body.

When your brain senses stress, it activates your autonomic nervous system. Through this network of nerve connections, your big brain communicates stress to your enteric, or intestinal nervous system. Besides causing butterflies in your stomach, this brain-gut connection can disturb the natural rhythmic contractions that move food through your gut, leading to irritable bowel syndrome, and can increase your gut sensitivity to acid, making you more likely to feel heartburn.

Via the gut's nervous system, stress can also change the composition and function of your gut bacteria, which may affect your digestive and overall health. Speaking of digestion, does chronic stress affect your waistline? Well, yes. Cortisol can increase your appetite. It tells your body to replenish your energy stores with energy dense foods and carbs, causing you to crave comfort foods. High levels of cortisol can also cause you to put on those extra calories as visceral or deep belly fat. This type of fat doesn't just make it harder to button your pants. It is an organ that actively releases hormones and immune system chemicals called cytokines that can increase your risk of developing chronic diseases, such as heart disease and insulin resistance.

Meanwhile, stress hormones affect immune cells in a variety of ways. Initially, they help prepare to fight invaders and heal after injury, but chronic stress can dampen function of some immune cells, make you more susceptible to infections, and slow the rate you heal. Wanna to live a long life? You may have to curb your chronic stress.

Part 2　Learning in Class

Warm Up

Why Is It So Hard to Cure ALS?

By Sarah Brooks

May 10, 2019

http://kidpid.com

In 1963, a 21-year-old physicist named Stephen Hawking was diagnosed with a rare neuromuscular disorder called amyotrophic lateral sclerosis, or ALS. Gradually, he lost the ability to walk, use his hands, move his face, and even swallow.

But throughout it all, he retained his incredible intellect, and in the more than 50 years that followed, Hawking became one of history's most accomplished and famous physicists. However, his condition went uncured and he passed away in 2018, at the age of 76. Decades after his diagnosis, ALS still ranks as one of the most complex, mysterious, and devastating diseases to affect humankind.

Also called motor neuron disease and Lou Gehrig's Disease, ALS affects about two out of every 100,000 people worldwide. When a person has ALS, their motor neurons (运动神经元), the cells responsible for all voluntary muscle control in the body, lose function and die. No one knows exactly why or how these cells die and that's part of what makes ALS so hard to treat. In about 90% of cases, the disease arises suddenly, with no apparent cause. The remaining 10% of cases are hereditary, where a mother or father with ALS passes on a mutated gene to their child.

The symptoms typically first appear after age 40. But in some rare cases, like Hawking's, ALS starts earlier in life. Hawking's case was also a medical marvel because of how long he lived with ALS. After diagnosis, most people with the disease live between 2 to 5 years before ALS leads to respiratory problems that usually cause death. What wasn't unusual in Hawking's case was that his ability to learn, think, and perceive with his senses remained intact. Most people with ALS do not experience impaired cognition.

With so much at stake for the 120,000 people who are diagnosed with ALS annually, curing the disease has become one of our most important scientific and medical challenges. Despite the many unknowns, we do have some insight into how ALS impacts the neuromuscular system. ALS affects two types of nerve cells called the upper and lower motor neurons.

In a healthy body, the upper motor neurons, which sit in the brain's cortex, transmit messages from the brain to the lower motor neurons, situated in the spinal cord. Those neurons then transmit the message into muscle fibers, which contract or relax in response, resulting in motion. Every voluntary move we make occurs because of messages transmitted along this pathway.

But when motor neurons degenerate in ALS, their ability to transfer messages is disrupted, and that vital signaling system is thrown into chaos. Without their regular cues, the muscles waste away. Precisely what makes the motor neurons degenerate is the prevailing mystery of ALS. In hereditary cases, parents pass genetic mutations on to their children. Even then, ALS involves multiple genes with multiple possible impacts on motor neurons, making the precise triggers hard to pinpoint. When ALS arises sporadically, the list of possible causes grows: toxins, viruses, lifestyle, or other environmental factors may all play roles. And because there are so many elements involved, there is currently no single test that can determine whether someone has ALS.

Nevertheless, our hypotheses on the causes are developing. One prevailing idea is that certain proteins inside the motor neurons aren't folding correctly, and are instead forming clumps. The misfolded proteins and clumps may spread from cell to cell. This could be clogging up normal cellular processes, like energy and protein production, which keep cells alive. We're also learned that along with motor neuron and muscle fibers, ALS could involve other cell types. ALS patients typically have inflammation in their brains and spinal cords. Defective immune cells may also play a role in killing motor neurons. And ALS seems to change the behavior of specific cells that provide support for neurons. These factors highlight the disease's complexity, but they may also give us a fuller understanding of how it works, opening up new avenues for treatment.

And while that may be gradual, we're making progress all the time. We're currently developing new drugs, new stem cell therapies to repair damaged cells, and new gene therapies to slow the advancement of the disease. With our growing arsenal of knowledge, we look forward to discoveries that can change the future for people living with ALS.

Unit 9 Arts and Youth

Part 1 Learning Before Class

- **Listening**

Summer Camp Uses Dance to Teach Students Life Skills

By Ashley Thompson
28 July, 2019
VOA

American Anai Espinoza is in the eighth grade. This summer, she took part in a summer dance program called AileyCamp. Each morning, she and other campers would say several phrases together. Her favorite is this: "I am in control."

Espinoza said, "It makes me believe I have the power to choose the right thing." AileyCamp was created in 1989 in Kansas City, Missouri by world-famous dancer and director Alvin Ailey. About 1,000 students in 10 US states take part in AileyCamp every year. It is a free, six-week program aimed at young people in financial need or who have school, social or family difficulties.

In addition to dance, the camp introduces students to visual arts, creative writing and other communication skills. It also teaches them how to eat well, solve conflicts and become leaders, notes the camp's website.

Dianne Caroll Sales directs the Ailey Camp in Atlanta, Georgia. When the camp is over, the city's professional ballet company offers 10 students a full-tuition scholarship for a year of training. The scholarship can be renewed.

Kameron Davis received one of those scholarships when he was a young man. He trained with the Atlanta Ballet for three years. Then he became a dance teacher. Davis said he does not think his mother could have paid for dance classes without the scholarship.

Davis said children at school made fun of him when he began dancing. Ailey Camp, he said, offered him a safe place and increased his confidence. Today, he enjoys giving back to the program by helping new campers build their confidence, too.

"It's an open door to finding new things, doing new things," Davis said. "When I got to AileyCamp, it just reassured me that, 'Hey, it's okay. Everybody is different. You shouldn't be judged by what you do just because not a lot of people do it.'"

- **Watching and Thinking**

Art Explores African Americans' Past and Present

By Faiza Elmasry
March 8, 2019
The Associated Press

Since early childhood, the questions "Who am I?" and "Where did I come from?" puzzled artist James Turrell and his wife Zsudayka Nzinga Terrell. " The white kids were able to get up and talk about hundreds of years of their background and where they come from and who they are, and there was me and one other black kid in the class who could go back to a plantation of Virginia. "

That's the inspiration behind the exhibit. She talked about her family's history. "My people were brought here on the bottom of a ship. And they were sold and they were renamed. " This disconnected from their original identity over the years. Africans became African Americans with a new culture and her art reflects that.

"You'll see, a lot of things that remind people of like African print and African textiles, which will also see things that are reminiscent of American culture, and American printing textile". " Hope and Grace," showcases Nzinga Terrell's style, with linear patterns of fabric stitching and touches of realism. Nzinga Terrell's style reflected in Mami Wata, the first piece visitors see when they enter. The exhibit is more abstract. The black and white colors symbolize the era of slavery when Africans were brought to America in chains.

James Turrell said, "the lines are symbolized fact that people say that our race has been broken, but I say that we have been put back together, and we are stronger as a people. The different colors represent the fact that because of different backgrounds. We all come together and we are still together to form a particular person or particular feeling. "

That gives their work a universal message. "A lot of us in America you know, immigration is part of a lot of family history stories, so I do think it's a relevant theme it's a universal thing. I don't think it just relates to the African-American community. " "When I first walked in, the colors and the shapes were the first because I am a mathematician and I love those the geometry of the shapes and how they all fit together. "

"As I walked in the main door, I was just an 'ahh' experience. But when the light were turned to blue, it was a whole different experience. Everything popped. You saw colors that you don't even really recognize during the the actual natural lighting. "

The artists hope to take their exhibit on tour across America and around the world. For writer Faiza Elmasry in Manassas, Virginia. Faith Lapidus, VOA News.

Part 2　Learning in Class

Warm Up

Architect I. M. Pei Dies at 102

By Caty Weaver
May 17, 2019
The New York Times

I. M. Pei, one of the best-known architects of the 20th century, has died. He was 102. Born in China, Ieoh Ming Pei moved to the United States in 1935 to study architecture at the Massachusetts Institute of Technology and Harvard University.

Pei's works around the world include museums, government buildings, hotels, schools and other structures built with stone, steel and glass.

One of his best-known and most disputed works was built 30 years ago. Pei created a new entrance for the world-famous Louvre Museum in Paris. Pei first spent four months studying the museum and French history. He then drew plans for a 21-meter-tall steel and glass pyramid, with three smaller pyramids nearby. It was a very futuristic style of work for the 12th-century building.

A French newspaper denounced Pei's pyramids as "an annex to Disneyland". An environmental group said they belonged in a desert. Others accused Pei of ruining one of the world's greatest landmarks.

Pei said the Louvre was the most difficult job of his career. He argued that he had wanted to create a modern space that would not take away from the traditional part of the museum. He said the glass pyramids were based on the works of French landscape architect Le Notre. They honored French history.

The pyramids opened in the spring of 1989. Over the years that followed, the structure came to be loved by most, if not all, of its critics.

Other well-known Pei buildings include the John F. Kennedy Library in Dorchester, Massachusetts, the National Center for Atmospheric Research in Boulder, Colorado, the East Wing of the National Gallery of Art in Washington and the Dallas City Hall in Texas.

Pei officially retired in 1990. However, he continued to work on projects—including museums in Luxembourg, Qatar and his ancestral home of Suzhou.

Unit 10　Sports

Part 1　Learning Before Class

• Listening

Copenhagen Turns Mountain of Waste into Sport

February 19, 2019
VOA

What do you do with the mountain of waste that a major city produces? It is a continuing question. And, Copenhagen—the capital of Denmark—has come up with an answer. Ski on it!

The waste is inside Copenhill, a waste treatment factory 10 minutes from the center of the city. The main building is a futuristic-looking structure 85 meters high. It includes a long hill from the top of the building to the ground. The hill is covered in a material called "neveplast" creating a snowless ski slope.

"I think everybody is surprised to start with when they look at it and it's not snow," said Christian Ingels, the director at Copenhill. He said that, after one or two tries on the neveplast hill, "you feel exactly like skiing."

Danish designer Bjarke Ingels designed the place—an important step in Copenhagen's aim of becoming the world's first carbon-neutral capital. He wanted to build a waste treatment factory that local people are happy to see in their neighborhood. It seems to be working.

Visiting skier Pelle Hansen said being able to ski in the middle of a city is a wonderful experience. Instead of "having to go six, seven, eight or ten hours" to a ski area, "you can be here in ten minutes," he said.

The factory will also burn waste from about 600,000 homes and 68,000 businesses to produce electricity. Some of the other waste will be recycled. The company began in 2017 and the sports area will open permanently this spring. The ski slopes will stay open throughout the year.

"It's fantastic that one can ski without snow," said visitor Tommy Christensen. "It's a ... different experience than skiing in real snow, but it's my second run and I'll try it again. It looks promising."

- **Watching and Thinking**

The Woman Leading the Global Promotion of F1

August 29, 2018

CNN

A decade ago, Chloe Targett-Adams joined the Formula One team as an in-house lawyer. Today, she's climbed the ranks and is the global director for commercial relations.

Host: One of your jobs is promoting Formula One around the world. How important is it for the sport to be seen to be embracing women?

Chloe: We're in 21 markets currently, we have 21 races, and we broadcast in over 200 countries. So we're a global sport. And to really engage with those markets successfully, we need to appeal to both men and women. You know, we have 503 million fans globally, 38% of which are women. We need to represent the diverse kind of fan base that we have. And so when we look at new race opportunities and we take a very strategic look at what are they really going to engage with Formula One. You know the excitement on track. What about the excitement off track? You know what about the new lifestyle initiatives, the hospitality the F1 experiences, the travel the tourism expects? There is the F1.

H: Has enough been done to promote the number of women across the board doing all the different jobs that they do in F1? A lot of people see the drivers on the grid, and the team principals, and that's it, really.

C: There are a lot of talented women in F1 currently across many different functions within the teams from the engineering side to, you know, our business, from the TV side, the production, the commercial, the business administrator, the legal, the finance. And I think it's actually about how collectively these women and also with men, you need strong male advocates obviously, to push everyone forward, if you're talented. You know, we want equal representation within sport, because that's really how society functions, and that will make sport more successful and business more successful in the long term.

H: What's the most important fact for reaching gender equality in F1 community moving forward?

C: I think it's about open-mindedness and actually, the need to create more opportunity within that pipeline at that earliest stage.

Part 2 Learning in Class

Warm Up

The Surprising Reason Our Muscles Get Tired

By Christian Moro

April, 2019

https://www.ted.com

You're lifting weights. The first time feels easy, but each lift takes more and more effort until you can't continue. Inside your arms, the muscles responsible for the lifting have become unable to contract.

Why do our muscles get fatigued? We often blame lactic acid (乳酸) or running out of energy, but these factors alone don't account for muscle fatigue. There's another major contributor: the muscle's ability to respond to signals from the brain.

To understand the roots of muscle fatigue, it helps to know how a muscle contracts in response to a signal from a nerve. These signals travel from the brain to the muscles in a fraction of a second via long, thin cells called motor neurons (运动神经元). The motor neuron and the muscle cell are separated by a tiny gap, and the exchange of particles across this gap enables the contraction.

On one side of the gap, the motor neuron contains a neurotransmitter called acetylcholine (乙酰胆碱). On the other side, charged particles, or ions, line the muscle cell's membrane: potassium (钾离子) on the inside, and sodium (钠离子) on the outside.

In response to a signal from the brain, the motor neuron releases acetylcholine, which triggers pores on the muscle cell membrane to open. Sodium flows in, and potassium flows out. The flux of these charged particles is a crucial step for muscle contraction: the change in charge creates an electrical signal called an action potential that spreads through the muscle cell, stimulating the release of calcium (钙) that's stored inside it. This flood of calcium causes the muscle to contract by enabling proteins buried in the muscle fibers to lock together and ratchet towards each other, pulling the muscle tight. The energy used to power the contraction comes from a molecule called ATP (三磷酸腺苷). ATP also helps pump the ions back across the membrane afterward, resetting the balance of sodium and potassium on either side.

This whole process repeats every time a muscle contracts. With each contraction, energy in the form of ATP gets used up, waste products like lactic acid are generated, and some ions drift away from the muscle's cell membrane, leaving a smaller and smaller group behind.

Though muscle cells use up ATP as they contract repeatedly, they are always making more, so most of the time even heavily fatigued muscles still have not depleted this energy source. And though many waste products are acidic, fatigued muscles still maintain pH within normal limits, indicating that the tissue is effectively clearing these wastes. But eventually, over the course of repeated contractions there may not be sufficient concentrations of potassium, sodium or calcium ions immediately available near the muscle cell membrane to reset the system properly. So even if the brain sends a signal, the muscle cell can't generate the action potential necessary to contract.

Even when ions like sodium, potassium or calcium are depleted in or around the muscle cell, these ions are plentiful elsewhere in the body. With a little time, they will flow back to the areas where they're needed, sometimes with the help of active sodium and potassium pumps. So if you pause and rest, muscle fatigue will subside as these ions replenish throughout the muscle.

The more regularly you exercise, the longer it takes for muscle fatigue to set in each time. That's because the stronger you are, the fewer times this cycle of nerve signal from the brain to contraction in the muscle has to be repeated to lift a certain amount of weight. Fewer cycles means slower ion depletion, so as your physical fitness improves, you can exercise for longer at the same intensity. Many muscles grow with exercise, and larger muscles also have bigger stores of ATP and a higher capacity to clear waste, pushing fatigue even farther into the future.